The Languages of East and Southeast Asia

The Languages of East and Southeast Asia

An Introduction

Cliff Goddard

OXFORD
UNIVERSITY PRESS

OXFORD
UNIVERSITY PRESS

Great Clarendon Street, Oxford OX2 6DP

Oxford University Press is a department of the University of Oxford.
It furthers the University's objective of excellence in research, scholarship,
and education by publishing worldwide in

Oxford New York

Auckland Cape Town Dar es Salaam Hong Kong Karachi
Kuala Lumpur Madrid Melbourne Mexico City Nairobi
New Delhi Shanghai Taipei Toronto

With offices in

Argentina Austria Brazil Chile Czech Republic France Greece
Guatemala Hungary Italy Japan Poland Portugal Singapore
South Korea Switzerland Thailand Turkey Ukraine Vietnam

Oxford is a registered trade mark of Oxford University Press
in the UK and in certain other countries

Published in the United States
by Oxford University Press Inc., New York

British Library Cataloguing in Publication Data

Data available

Library of Congress Cataloging-in-Publication Data
Goddard, Cliff.
   The languages of East and Southeast Asia: an introduction / Cliff Goddard.
      p. cm.
   Includes bibliographical references and index.
   ISBN 0-19-927311-1 (alk. paper) — ISBN 0-19-924860-5 (pbk. : alk. paper)
   1. East Asia—Languages. 2. Linguistics—East Asia. I. Title.
   PL493.G63 2005
   495—dc22

                                                            2004024004

Typeset by Newgen Imaging Systems (P) Ltd., Chennai, India
Printed in Great Britain on acid-free paper by Biddles Ltd., www.biddles.co.uk

ISBN 0-19-927311-1 (hbk.)
ISBN 0-19-924860-5 (pbk.)

Contents

Preface

This book surveys the languages of East and Southeast Asia from the perspective of general descriptive linguistics, and explores the ways in which language, culture and history are intertwined. My goal is to provide an accessible resource for students and teachers of linguistics, language studies, and Asian Studies. I have tried to use plenty of concrete examples throughout, drawing on little-known minority languages as well as the major national languages of a dozen countries. To help linguistics students consolidate their knowledge and skills, there are exercises with solutions for each chapter. Though readers who are not studying linguistics may wish to skip lightly over sections of certain chapters, most of the book should make sense and be interesting reading for those with a minimal background in linguistics, and little or no personal knowledge of any East or Southeast Asian language.

Obviously, no one person can be a specialist on the number of languages and language families found in East and Southeast Asia, so I have had to rely on the works of a great number of dedicated linguistic scholars. My task has been to locate and select a range of comparable material, and then to digest, explain, and contextualize it so as to fashion it into a coherent, clear, and above all interesting story. Researching and writing this book has been a journey of discovery for me, often challenging, mostly enjoyable, and in the end immensely rewarding. I can only hope that some of my own pleasure and excitement comes across to readers.

For reasons of space, there are certain topics which have not received much treatment. For example, though grammaticalization is mentioned at several points there is no systematic overview, and though language contact is another of my themes I have not dealt with code-switching. The various "Englishes" of East and Southeast Asia have not been touched upon either. Ultimately, however, any book of this kind is necessarily selective. Despite my best efforts, there are bound to be sundry small errors of fact and interpretation scattered throughout the text. I would be most grateful to anyone who can bring these to my attention.

I hope you enjoy your studies of the languages of East and Southeast Asia.

C.G.

University of New England

Acknowledgements

I have drawn liberally on some texts, especially for the better described languages: Li and Thompson (1981) and Ramsey (1987) on Chinese, Matthews and Yip (1994) on Cantonese, Lee and Ramsey (2000) on Korean, Shibatani (1990) on Japanese, Sneddon (1996, 2003) on Indonesian, Smalley (1994) on Thai, Nguyễn (1997) for Vietnamese. The scholarship of James Matisoff will be evident in many places. I am grateful to the following people for generously contributing their personal knowledge of individual languages: Zhengdao Ye, Hilary Chappell, Cuncun Wu, Meili Yeh (for Chinese), Yuki Sato, Yoshika Yamaguchi, Sato van Aacken (Japanese), Kyung-Joo Yoon, Seung-Woo Han (Korean), N. J. (Nick) Enfield (Lao), Tony Diller, Ingrid Wijeyewardene, Chintana Sandilands, Narunard (Jang) Sarapaivanich, Jaew Davies (for Thai), Giao Quynh Tran (for Vietnamese).

Nick Enfield contributed valuable linguistic advice and language information on many fronts. A number of people who read and commented on the entire manuscript at various stages also deserve special thanks: Masayoshi Shibatani, Zhengdao Ye, Mee Wun Lee, and Harold Schiffman. Julia Read, Nick Reid, Anna Wierzbicka, and Helen Fraser contributed useful information and ideas on specific topics. Thanks to Cuncun Wu for the Chinese character illustrations, and to Yuki Sato for the Japanese handwriting material in Chapter 6, and to Lachana (Toom) Inchaiwong for the Thai illustration in Chapter 7. Thanks to Michael Roach for preparing the languages distribution maps in Chapter 2. Thanks also to Paul Sidwell for advice on the distribution of Chamic languages.

I am indebted to Harold Schiffman, who devised a number of the exercises. Several cohorts of students studying LING 380 'The Languages of Asia' at the University of New England have made a great impression on the content and tone of this book, by way of their reactions to earlier versions.

I owe a deep debt of gratitude to my research assistant, Vicki Knox, who managed a complex manuscript through multiple versions with unfailing professionalism, as well as making numerous helpful suggestions about content.

Last but not least, a special thank-you to two very special people, Mee Wun and Kwan.

List of maps and figures

Maps

Figures

List of tables

Conventions and symbols

Italics are used for citing linguistic forms (words, sentences, or phrases) in any language, including English.

'Single inverted commas' are used for glosses, and translations, and for citing meanings.

"Double inverted commas" are used for quotations, and to draw attention to a term, either because it is new or because there is something peculiar or figurative about it.

An asterisk (*) before a phrase or sentence means it is ungrammatical.

The term Mandarin Chinese (or Mandarin) is used as a cover term for the national language of China (Putonghua 'common language') and Taiwan (Guoyu 'national language'). It is also sometimes referred to as Modern Standard Chinese. The term Chinese is used to refer even more broadly, for example, when speaking of historically earlier forms of the Chinese language. The term Malay is used as a cover term for the national languages of Indonesia (Bahasa Indonesia) and Malaysia (Bahasa Melayu, previously known as Bahasa Malaysia).

Many of the languages treated in this book have their own scripts, but generally speaking all language material is presented in a romanized form. The following systems are used: for Mandarin Chinese (Modern Standard Chinese), the pinyin system, without marking for tone sandhi; for Korean, the government-sponsored New Romanization of Korean; for Japanese, the Hepburn system; for Cantonese, the Yale system with minor modifications as per Matthews and Yip (1994); for Hmong, the Popular Romanized Alphabet. There is no commonly used system of romanization for Thai. In this book we use one of the two main transcriptions widely used by linguists, even though it makes use of several symbols from the International Phonetic Alphabet in addition to English letters. There is even less consensus about romanizations for Lao and for Burmese. For these languages I have used the preferred system of the main linguistic authorities on whom I am relying: N. J. Enfield (Lao) and Julian Wheatley (Burmese). In the interests of a consistent romanization, it has sometimes been necessary to convert the romanization used by the original author into one of the systems just listed. Most other languages are presented in the orthography favoured by the source linguist, even if this involves symbols from the International Phonetic Alphabet.

The following symbols and abbreviations are used at various places in the text:

C	consonant
N	(i) nasal sound (ii) an underspecified nasal phoneme or archiphoneme
NP	noun phrase
O	object
PP	prepositional or postpositional phrase
S	subject
V	(i) verb (ii) any vowel sound
VP	verb phrase
ø	zero-morpheme

Interlinear glosses are as follows:

I	first person
2	second person
3	third person
ACC	accusative
ACT	actor
ANIM	animate
ART	article
ASP	aspect marker
AT	agent trigger
BENEF	benefactive
CAUS	causative
CL	classifier
CONT	continuous
COP	copula
CRS	currently relevant state
CSC	complex stative construction
DAT	dative
DECL	declarative
DEF	definite
DIM	diminutive
DIR	directional marker
EMPH	emphatic
ERG	ergative
EXCL	exclusive
EXP	experiential

FOC	focus
GEN	genitive
GER	gerund
HAB	habitual
HON	honorific
HUM	humbling
INV	inverse
LOC	locative
LP	linking particle
NEG	negative
NOM	nominative
NONPAST	nonpast tense
O	object
OBJ	object marker
OBL	oblique
PASS	passive
PAST	past tense
PAT	patient
PERF	perfective
PL	plural
POL	polite
POSS	possessive
POT	potential
PRES	present tense
PROG	progressive
PRT	particle
PT	patient trigger
QUES	question particle
REFL	reflexive
RESP	respect
S	subject
SG	singular
SUBJ	subject marker
TENSE	tense
TENT	tentative
TOP	topic
TRIG	trigger

CHAPTER 1

The languages of East and Southeast Asia: a first look

1.1 Introductory remarks

This book is all about the similarities and differences among the languages and "language cultures" of East and Southeast Asia. Moving from south to north, the countries we will cover can be grouped as follows: (a) Indonesia, East Timor, Malaysia, Singapore, Brunei, and the Philippines, (b) Myanmar (Burma), Thailand, Cambodia, Laos, Vietnam, (c) China, (d) Korea and Japan.

How many languages are there in this broad area? Many people would probably answer: about a dozen or so, to match the number of countries involved. This would be roughly correct if we were only talking about national languages, i.e. languages which are the official medium of government, education, and media—Indonesian (Bahasa Indonesia) and Malaysian (Bahasa Melayu), Tetum and Portugese (in East Timor), Pilipino (Tagalog), Burmese, Thai, Lao, Khmer, Vietnamese, Chinese (Modern Standard Chinese), Korean, and Japanese. But if we are talking about all the languages of the area, including the hundreds of minority languages spoken in the hills and jungles, then the total number is vastly greater. There are hundreds of languages in countries such as China, the Philippines, and Indonesia, and dozens in most other countries of the region.

Languages can be grouped in various ways. One way is by their family trees, i.e. by their historical origins. For example, many people would know that the so-called Romance languages (e.g. French, Spanish, Italian) all descend from a common ancestor language (Latin). They form a small "language family", or more accurately a branch of a larger family which, once all the branches of the family tree (e.g. the Germanic branch, the Slavonic branch) are taken into account, embraces most of the languages of Europe. We say that all these languages are genetically related. How many language families, then, are there in East and Southeast Asia? Setting aside various complications which we will look into later, the short answer is that there are six main families (Austronesian, Mon-Khmer, Tai-Kadai, Tibeto-Burman, Sinitic, and Hmong-Mien), plus several major languages (Japanese, Korean) whose ancestry is unclear. From a genetic point of view, the languages of East and Southeast Asia are much more varied than those of Europe.

The family tree is not the only way of grouping languages. Another approach is to group them according to their similarities to one another—in pronunciation, grammar, and vocabulary. This is called a "typological" approach to grouping. If we do this, then the language situation comes out a bit differently. The reason is that many languages of different families have been in contact with one another—living together, so to speak—for many, many years and have mutually influenced each other in various ways. The result is that languages which are not genetically related nevertheless share many features of language structure. In fact, we can say that most of the languages of mainland Southeast Asia fall into a single "linguistic area", on the basis of pervasive similarities which cross-cut the genetic classification. There are also important cultural similarities across regions of East and Southeast Asia—similarities which have their reflections in vocabulary and semantics, in social aspects of language use, and sometimes even in aspects of language structure. For example, many East and Southeast Asian languages have special forms of respectful or deferential language to be used when talking with or about people who are older or socially higher than oneself.

In this chapter, we are going to survey some of the similarities and differences among languages of East and Southeast Asia, especially the kind of features which are different from English. This will also help us establish some descriptive terminology which we will use throughout the book. For the purposes of illustration, we will stick mainly to major national languages. Then in Chapter 2 we will survey the language families, linguistic areas and language situations of the region to get a truer picture of the language diversity of the region. These first two chapters form an introductory package. After that, the remainder of the book consists of closer examinations of various topics, both sociocultural and structural.

1.2 Lack of inflection

One feature of many—not all—languages of East and Southeast Asia which is very different from English and other European languages is what linguists call "lack of inflection". In simple terms, inflection occurs when the form of a word changes to indicate an added aspect of meaning which is relevant in a particular grammatical context. In English, for example, nouns have a special form (plural) which indicates that we are referring to more than one of the items in question (*dog, dogs*). We say that English nouns inflect for number, i.e. they have various forms indicating the "number" category (singular vs. plural). Similarly, we say that English verbs inflect for tense, meaning that they have different forms (e.g. *kills, see*, present tense; *killed, saw*, past tense) to indicate whether the event is happening now or happened previously. Notice that in English tense inflection is sometimes done by suffixes (endings), and sometimes by modifying the vowel.

If you look at the following example sentences from Thai, you will see that in this language the verbs do not inflect for tense. That is, the verb for 'read' (*àan*) remains the same regardless of whether we are talking about the present, the past, or the future.

(1) a. *Khǎw àan nǎngsɨ̌ɨ dǐawnii.*
   he/she read book now.

 b. *Khǎw dây àan nǎngsɨ̌ɨ.*
   he/she PAST read book.

 c. *Khǎw cà àan nǎngsɨ̌ɨ.*
   he/she will read book.

In (1a) the adverb *dǐawnii* 'now' makes it clear that we are talking about the present time. In (1b) and (1c) the fact that the action is in the past or the future is indicated by separate grammatical words—*dây* and *cà*, respectively. However, sentences in Thai can refer to the present or to the past without this being overtly marked in any way. Example (2), for instance, could be translated into English as either 'He/she sat down' or as 'He/she is sitting down', depending on the context.

(2) *Khǎw nâng long.*
   he/she sit down.

Again unlike English, Thai nouns do not inflect for number. That is, although the word *nǎngsɨ̌ɨ* in examples (1a)–(1c) has been glossed as 'book', it could in fact be referring not to a single book, but to some particular books, or to books in general. Of course, if the Thai speaker wants to specify the number of books, that is perfectly possible by using a number word or other quantifying word.

You can also notice from examples (1a)–(1c) that Thai doesn't have any words which correspond exactly to *the* and *a*—the so-called "definite article" and "indefinite article" of English. This is also a widespread feature of the languages of East and Southeast Asia, though often these languages use demonstrative words, i.e. words for 'this' and 'that', in "article-like" ways. Another notable feature is that there is no gender distinction in the third person pronouns; that is, the word *khǎw* is used regardless of whether the person is male or female.

If we look at other languages of mainland Southeast Asia, we find that most of them are like Thai in lacking inflection for tense and number. As well, these languages do not show any inflection according to the grammatical role, such as subject or object, that a word or phrase has in a sentence. Consider the following question–answer pair from Malaysian (Bahasa Melayu), which is Thai's southern neighbour but belongs to a completely different language family.

(3) a. *Awak marah pada saya ke?*
      you   angry at   I   QUES
      'Are you angry at me?'

   b. *Ye, memang saya marah pada awak.*
      yes certainly I   angry at   you
      'Yes, I certainly am angry at you.'

In English the first person singular pronoun changes its form depending on its position in the sentence, which is linked with its grammatical role. If it comes before the verb (i.e. in subject position), it is *I*, but if it comes after the verb it takes the form *me*. Most English pronouns have two forms (e.g. *he/ him*, *she/her*, *we/us*, *they/them*). The English second person pronoun is unusual in retaining the same form (i.e. *you/you*); in older English it was *thou/thee*. All other European languages have several different pronoun forms for different grammatical "cases" (nominative, accusative, dative, etc.). Anyhow, the main thing we can see from examples (3a) and (3b) above is that in Malaysian (Bahasa Melayu), the pronouns stay the same regardless of their position or grammatical role. That is, *saya* is used, whereas in English we would have to switch between *I* and *me*.

The story is the same in Mandarin Chinese (Modern Standard Chinese). The first person pronoun *wǒ* is used in both subject and object roles, without changing its form.

(4) a. *Wǒ xǐhuān Susan.*
      I   like   Susan.
      'I like Susan.'

   b. *Susan xǐhuān wǒ.*
      Susan like   me.
      'Susan likes me.'

To summarize: in most languages of mainland Southeast Asia and East Asia, words do not inflect for tense, number, gender, or grammatical role (case). It is important to point out, however, that this generalization does not apply to all languages in this region. Especially in the northern area there are languages such as Japanese and Korean which have plenty of inflection in their verbal systems. Looking at (5a) and (5b) below, we can see that Japanese verbs have suffixes indicating tense. Suffixes -*ru* or -*u* indicate present (or, non-past) tense, while -*ta* or -*da* indicate past tense.

(5) a. *Akiko ga oki-ru.* 'Akiko is getting up.'
    Akiko ga oki-ta. 'Akiko got up.'
  b. *Akiko ga shin-u.* 'Akiko is dying.'
    Akiko ga shin-da. 'Akiko died.'

These examples also show another feature of Japanese which differs from the other languages we have seen so far. The word *ga* which follows the noun phrase *Akiko* is a grammatical word whose function is to mark the subject of the sentence (more on this in Chapter 4). Since *ga* is a separate word rather than a suffix, this does not qualify as inflection, but it is still a way of explicitly marking grammatical function. In Thai, Malay, and Chinese, in contrast, there is no explicit marking of grammatical function.

Table 1.1 lists some inflected forms of Japanese verbs. Comparing the columns, we can see that the form of a suffix is determined by whether the verb stem ends in a consonant or in a vowel. The Japanese verb system is actually a good deal more complicated than this, but this is enough for our purposes. The main point is that although the majority of East and Southeast Asian languages lack inflection, this generalization does not apply to Japanese or Korean, or to some of the minority languages of the region.

A technical term often used to describe languages like Thai, Chinese, and Vietnamese is "isolating". Essentially the term refers to a language in which

Table 1.1. Some Japanese verb forms

	C-final stem	**V-final stem**
	kir- 'to cut'	*ki-* 'to wear (clothes)'
imperative	*kir-e*	*ki-ro*
present	*kir-u*	*ki-ru*
past	*kit-ta*	*ki-ta*
participial	*kit-te*	*ki-te*
provisional	*kir-eba*	*ki-reba*
tentative	*kir-oo*	*ki-yoo*

words have a single, fixed shape; that is, words do not change their shape as a result of affixation or other morphological processes. In European languages, nouns and verbs do change their forms as they inflect for categories such as case, tense, number, and gender, and so these languages are not isolating. In effect, isolating implies non-inflecting.

Since Korean and Japanese do have inflection, they are similar to European languages in this respect, but there is still a significant difference. In European languages it is common for a particular suffix to combine several different inflectional meanings; for example, the English verb suffix -*s* indicates 'third person singular subject, present tense'. In Japanese and Korean, however, it is more usual for each inflectional suffix to represent a single category. If it is appropriate to mark several inflectional categories at the same time, then several different suffixes are used, one after another. Languages whose inflectional morphology bundles several meanings into a single form (like French and German) are known as fusional. Languages which allot one morpheme per inflectional meaning (like Japanese and Korean) are known as agglutinating.

It's important to point out that a language can be isolating and still have complex word forms. Being an isolating language is not a matter of the internal complexity of words, but rather of how words behave when they occur in different grammatical contexts. Some of the classic isolating languages of Asia, such as Mandarin Chinese and Vietnamese, have a high proportion of complex words formed by compounding or by reduplication.

1.3 Word order (constituent order)

Linguists often use the term "word order" in a rather loose way to refer, not to the order of words in a strict sense, but to the order of the major constituents of a simple clause, i.e. the subject (S), the object (O), and the verb (V). The most common order of these constituents in a simple, ordinary clause is often called the "basic word order" of a language. Various permutations are found in the world's languages. For example, the verb (V) can come in the middle (medial position), as in English; it can come at the beginning of the sentence (initial position); or it can come at the end of the sentence (final position). Regardless of the position of the verb, however, most of the world's languages place the subject before the object. This means that the most common constituent orders are SVO (as in English), SOV, and VSO. All three of these are found in languages of East and Southeast Asia, though VSO order is much rarer than the others. In Chapter 4, we will expand this discussion by distinguishing between the notions of subject and topic, and even questioning whether "subject" is a valid grammatical category in some languages of the region, but we can ignore these complications for now.

1.3.1 Verb-medial, verb-final, and verb-initial languages

Most of the mainland Southeast Asian and East Asian languages have SVO order, including Thai, Malay, Vietnamese, Khmer, and all the Sinitic (Chinese) languages (Clark 1989). A few more examples of SVO order follow. In (7) and (8) I use square brackets to indicate multi-word noun phrases.

Vietnamese

(6) *Tám yêu Hiến.*
     Tam love Hien
     'Tam loves Hien.'

Cantonese

(7) *Ngóh jìdou [go daapon].*
     I   know   CL answer
     'I know the answer.'

Hmong

(8) *[Tus dev] tom [tus npua].*
       CL dog bite CL pig
     'The dog bit the pig.'

Most Tibeto-Burman languages have the verb at the end of the clause in SOV order (Okell 1994), and so do the North Asian languages, Korean and Japanese. Notice that Korean marks the grammatical role of noun phrases by means of special little grammatical words (particles), as does Japanese.

Burmese

(9) *Ko thè hlain-gá   əko-shi-go   mɛʔgəzìn-de hmanhman*
     name-SUBJ   brother-place-to magazine-PL regularly
     pó-pè-ba-dɛ.
     send-give-POL-TENSE
     'Ko Htay Hlaing sent magazines regularly to his brother.'

Korean

(10) *[John i]   [Mary ege] [chaek eul] ju-ess-da.*
       John SUBJ Mary DAT   book OBJ   give-EXP-PAST
     'John gave Mary the book.'

As for the rarer verb-initial order, this is found in Pilipino (also known as Tagalog), the national language of the Philippines (Schachter 1987). Don't worry about the unfamiliar glosses. The main thing is that the verbs *magaalis* 'will take out' and *nakita* 'saw' come first in the sentences.

(11) *Magaalis*   *[ang bata] [ng laruan] [sa kahon].*
AT:will.take.out   TRIG child   PAT toy   DIR box
'The child will take the toy from the box.'

(12) *Nakita*   *[ng Juan] [si   Maria] kahpon.*
PT:PERF:see   ACT Juan   TRIG Maria   yesterday
'Juan saw Maria yesterday.'

After this brief look at the main constituent order variations, I should point out that we have only been talking about the most common or neutral order in each language. As a matter of fact, almost all languages of East and Southeast Asia allow some variation in the constituent order of a simple sentence. It is often possible to swap around the order of the subject and object: that is, to put the object first in order to focus some extra attention on it (in some languages, this kind of switch-around is accompanied by some other grammatical changes as well). Generally speaking, the languages of East and Southeast Asia tend to have a more flexible and "expressive" word order than English.

1.3.2 Prepositions or postpositions?

There is often a correlation between the basic constituent order of a clause and the order in which other kinds of elements occur (which is one of the reasons linguists are interested in constituent order). The most relevant factor is generally the position of the verb. Verb-final languages tend to have "postpositions" instead of prepositions. Postpositions are simply words which are functionally equivalent to prepositions but which come after the noun phrases they relate to.

Since Japanese and Korean are verb-final languages, we would expect them to show this property—and they do. For example, in the Japanese sentences in (13a)–(13c) below, the postposition *e* indicates motional 'to'; postposition *ni* indicates location 'at' a place; and postposition *de* indicates 'by (means of)'.

(13) a. *Taroo ga   gakkoo e ikimasu.*
Taroo SUBJ school to goes
'Taroo goes to school.'

b. *Masumi ga   gakkoo ni imasu.*
Masumi SUBJ school at is
'Masumi is at school.'

c. *Kazuko ga   basu de kimasu.*
Kazuko SUBJ bus by comes
'Kazuko comes by bus.'

As we've already seen, both Japanese and Korean make use of particles (such as *ga*) to indicate grammatical function, e.g. subject or object. These particles too come after the phrases they mark.

1.3.3 Word order in questions

In English, and most other European languages, questions have a different word order from affirmative sentences. For example, in questions containing an interrogative pronoun such as 'who', 'what', and 'where' (information questions or "wh-questions"), the interrogative pronoun generally comes at the beginning of the sentence. The special word order is one of the grammatical indications that a question is being asked. Many languages, however, do not use any special word order in questions. In Thai, for example, the order of constituents in a question is the same as in a statement.

(14) *Khăw àan àray dĭawníi?*
he/she read what now
'What is he reading now?'

Another kind of question is known as a "polar question" ("yes/no question"). In English, this kind of question is formed by means of "subject–auxiliary inversion", i.e. instead of the normal English word order in which the subject comes first, an auxiliary verb (such as *will* or *do*) comes first. In Thai, polar questions are formed simply by adding a question-particle to the end of the sentence. There are two main question-particles: *máy* and *rɨɨ*. Particle *máy* creates a more or less neutral question, whereas *rɨɨ* indicates that the speaker expects that the answer will be positive.

(15) a. *Khun cà   pay hăa phɨan máy?*
you   will go see friend QUES
'Will you go and see a friend?'

   b. *Khun cà   pay   hăa   phɨan   rɨɨ?*
you   will go   see   friend QUES
'So you're going to see a friend, are you?'

Similar examples could be given from Chinese, Japanese, or Korean. On the other hand, there are also languages (e.g. Malay) which do have a special word order for questions, or at least, for wh-questions. This is another reminder that whatever generalizations we make about the languages of East and Southeast Asia, there are almost certainly going to be exceptions somewhere.

1.4 Sounds and writing

From a pronunciation point of view, the most famous aspect of the languages of East and Southeast Asia is, no doubt, the existence of "tone" in languages such as Chinese, Vietnamese, and Thai. This means, roughly speaking, that words in these languages each have a distinctive intonation pattern and have to be pronounced with the correct intonation in order to be recognizable. We will look at tone in the next section. Meanwhile, however, what about the consonants and vowels?

As far as consonants are concerned, few of the major national languages present very severe pronunciation problems for an English speaker—at least, not compared with languages from various other parts of the world, e.g. central America, southern Africa, the Caucasus, which have a great number of difficult or "exotic" sounds to contend with. The most straightforward are languages like Malay and Tagalog, in the south of Southeast Asia, and Japanese toward the top of North Asia. These languages have fairly small numbers of consonants, which are distinguished from one another in ways which are fairly familiar to speakers of English. For example, they have distinctive "voicing" of stops; e.g. contrasts between /p/ and /b/, between /t/ and /d/, and between /k/ and /g/.

In the languages of mainland Southeast Asia and China, voicing is usually not distinctive. Instead, one commonly finds contrasts between "aspirated" and "unaspirated" stops; e.g. contrasts between /p/ and /p^h/, between /t/ and /t^h/, between /k/ and /k^h/. Some of these languages also have consonants which are pronounced at different places of articulation to those of English. There can also be unfamiliar manners of articulation, as with stops in Korean or Khmer. Generally speaking, however, the overall size of the consonant inventories in the languages of mainland Southeast Asia and China is not very large, if we stick to national languages.

Still on the subject of consonants, most languages of East and Southeast Asia have more restricted possibilities for consonant clusters than does English, which has many two-consonant clusters, e.g. in words like *snake*, *tree*, and *clean*, and even some three-consonant clusters, e.g. in words like *strike*. It is quite typical for these languages to allow no more than a single consonant at the beginning of a word. Usually, just about any consonant is acceptable word-initially, but at the end of a word, the possibilities are usually more restricted. In most languages only a handful of consonants can occur word-finally, in some languages none at all.

When it comes to vowels, the situation is rather different. It is true that Japanese and some of the languages of insular Southeast Asia have fairly small and simple vowel systems, but most other languages of the region have fairly complex vowel systems. Even when the number of vowel phonemes is smallish (say, five or six as in Chinese), they can often occur in diphthongs (two-vowel combinations) and even triphthongs (three-vowel combinations)—thus multiplying the overall number of vowel sounds in the language. In fact, Southeast Asia is home to languages (such as Khmer) which can lay claim to having the greatest number of vowel sounds in the world.

We can make two generalizations about the sound systems of this broad region. First, the languages in the centre of the area (mainland Southeast Asia and China) tend to be more phonologically complex than those on the periphery. Second, phonological complexity tends to be concentrated in the realm of vowel sounds. However, as before, we have to qualify such generalizations with the acknowledgement that there are exceptions, sometimes striking ones, as one would expect of an assemblage of languages as numerous and as diverse as those in East and Southeast Asia.

Most people know that important national languages such as Chinese Japanese, Korean, and Thai are not usually written using roman letters, i.e. the familiar ABC letters used for English and other languages of Western Europe. In their own countries these languages are usually written in entirely different scripts, like those illustrated below. For outsiders such scripts are completely unintelligible. We can't even tell where one word ends and another begins, let alone figure out any of the pronunciation.

คำภาษาไทย
'words in the Thai language'   Thai

中 國 文 字 最 為 美
'Chinese characters are the most beautiful'   Chinese

お習字　で　習った　字
'the characters that we learned in calligraphy' Japanese

우리 나라의 말은
'our country's language'   Korean

For anyone learning one of these languages, learning how to read and write in the national scripts is indispensable. In some cases, as with Chinese and Japanese, it is a task which requires a great deal of time and study. Fortunately, for the purposes of this book we do not need to learn any new writing systems. We will use roman letters to represent the words of all the languages we will discuss.

Although writing systems are the topic of a chapter of their own (Chapter 6), it is worth quickly mentioning a couple of points here to dispel some common misconceptions. You may have heard it said that Chinese characters stand not for sounds (in the way that roman letters do, however imperfectly) but for ideas or meanings. You may even have heard that Chinese characters are like pictures—albeit cryptic ones—of the meanings they stand for. Though there is a grain of truth in these ideas, they are essentially mistaken. First, the pictorial basis for Chinese characters is very slight. Second, 90 per cent of commonly used characters do not represent meanings alone: they have both phonetic (i.e. sound-based) and semantic (i.e. meaning-based) components.

A second misconception about the non-roman writing systems of East and Southeast Asia is that they are all like Chinese in being based on "characters". This belief is partly true in relation to Japanese, but it is completely false in relation to Burmese, Thai, and Korean. The writing systems used for these languages are essentially alphabetic systems, just like the roman letter system we use for English—the main difference is simply that the letters in Burmese, Thai, and Korean writing are different. Of course, we should not forget that many languages of the region, such as Indonesian, Pilipino (Tagalog), and Vietnamese, are normally written using ordinary roman letters.

1.5 Lexical tone

One of the most famous aspects of many languages of East and Southeast Asia is generally known as "tone". Most people probably know that in Chinese, for example, the same sequence of sounds can have several different meanings depending on the tone in which it is pronounced. Using a more precise terminology we call this phenomenon "lexical tone", to make it clear that tone is part of the lexical identity of words in Chinese. That is, it is an integral part of the pronunciation of the word, and it serves to distinguish one word from another. For speakers of a tonal language, the tones are not extra features added to the segmental shape of a word. Speakers often have no auditory image of the word at all independent of tone, and a mispronunciation of tone can make the word completely unrecognizable.

But what is this thing called tone? Basically, to pronounce words with tones means to use the pitch and quality of your voice in various ways, not just to convey emphasis or to convey attitudes or feelings as we do in English, but on a word-by-word basis. Some tones are "level", meaning that they do not change very much in pitch. In Mandarin Chinese, for example, one of the four tones is called the "high-level" tone. It is found in the word ma^{55} 'mother'. The superscript numerals refer to a set of five pitch levels in your voice, with 5 as the highest and 1 as the lowest level. The first digit indicates the starting pitch level and the second digit indicates the final pitch level. So a tone notated as 55 means using a consistently high pitch. Of course, the actual pitch level varies according to every individual's voice. A 55 tone spoken by someone with a very low voice (e.g. an old man) would be much lower, in absolute terms, than a 55 tone spoken by someone whose voice is generally higher (e.g. a young girl). It is not the absolute pitch that matters but how it sits relative to each individual's voice.

Aside from "level" tones (technically called register tones), there are also "moving" tones (technically called contour tones), which change pitch as the word is being pronounced. Mandarin Chinese has three moving tones. The word ma^{35} means 'hemp', for example, and ma^{51} means 'to scold'. So a 35 tone starts somewhere in the middle of a person's pitch range, and moves up towards the top of the range. This tone is usually called "high rising" (though "rising to high" would be a more accurate description). The 51 tone starts at the top of the range and falls steeply. It is often labelled as "high falling" (though "falling from high" would be a better description). With both the 35 tone and the 51 tone, the pitch change moves in only one direction (rising or falling, respectively). Another type of moving tone involves a fall followed by a rise, or a rise followed by a fall. The final Mandarin tone is of this type. For example, the word ma^{214} means 'horse'. It starts a little low, dips even lower, then moves up (hence the label "falling-rising").

The four tones of Mandarin are sometimes notated as shown in the second column of Table 1.2. These are simplified graphs of the pitch over time. The vertical line at the right of each one just serves as a reference for the possible pitch range.

Tones can be a problem for writing systems. It isn't very economical to use two superscript numbers. So for practical purposes various other systems are usually used. The first is just to assign each tone a single identifying number: for example, we could call the 55 tone "tone 1", the 35 tone "tone 2", the 214 tone "tone 3", and the 51 tone "tone 4". Thus we could write the four words in Table 1.2 as ma^1, ma^2, ma^3, and ma^4. In this kind of system the numbers do not indicate the pitch level: they are just identifying numbers.

Another approach is not to use numbers at all. After all, they look messy and take up extra space. Instead we can use diacritics (i.e. extra marks) above the vowels of each syllable. This is what is done in the official Pinyin system for writing Mandarin Chinese using roman letters, as shown in the third column of Table 1.2. As you can see, the diacritics correspond to the pitch graphs. I can't resist illustrating here with one of the many "tongue twisters" which have been devised based on tone contrasts: *Māma qí mǎ. Mǎ màn. Māma mà mǎ.* 'Mother rides horse. Horse slow. Mother scolds horse' (Crystal 1987: 172). Strictly speaking, tongue twister is not really an accurate description, however, because it is the larynx or voice-box which is involved

Table 1.2. Four [ma] words in Mandarin Chinese, Beijing dialect

[ma]^{55}	⌐	mā	'mother'
[ma]^{35}	⟋	má	'hemp'
[ma]^{51}	⟍	mà	'to scold'
[ma]^{214}	⟍⟋	mǎ	'horse'

in tone production, not the tongue (see chapter 5). Other sets of four-way tone contrasts are: *fān* 'turn over', *fán* 'annoying', *fǎn* 'opposite', *fàn* 'meal'; and *tāng* 'soup', *táng* 'sugar', *tǎng* 'lie', *tàng* 'hot'.

Tone diacritics work fine for Mandarin Chinese, but they don't work so well for languages with more than four tones, such as Cantonese or Thai, because the number of diacritics gets confusing and difficult to read. Another option is to coopt some letters of the alphabet to indicate tones, either by themselves or in combination with diacritics. For example, the Romanized Popular Alphabet for Hmong (which has eight tones) uses final consonant symbols to indicate tones: *-b* for 'high level', *-j* for 'high falling', *-v* for 'mid rising', *-g* for 'low falling breathy', and so on. This is made possible by the fact that all words in Hmong end with a vowel or with /ŋ/. A limited use of letters to indicate tone is found in Matthews and Yip's (1994) system for writing Cantonese. They use a syllable-final letter *h* to signal that the tone is one of the low tones, with diacritics to add further specification. For example, *ah* stands for the vowel /a/ with a 'low level' tone, *áh* stands for the same vowel with 'low rising' tone, and *àh* for 'low falling' tone. It is feasible to use the letter *h* in this way because the phoneme /h/ is never found at the end of a syllable in Cantonese.

Languages with lexical tone can differ substantially from one another in the nature of the tonal system. Not only can there be different numbers of tones, but the quality of tones differs from language to language. For example, Cantonese has six contrastively different tones, including three "level" tones as shown below (Matthews and Yip 1994: 21). The mid level and low level tones have no counterparts in Mandarin Chinese. Vietnamese also has six tones (Thompson 1987), but they do not match those of Cantonese.

Hong Kong Cantonese

high level	55 *yau* 'worry'	high rising 35/25 *yau* 'paint'	
mid level	33 *yau* 'thin'	low rising 23/13 *yau* 'to have'	
low level	22 *yau* 'again'	low falling 21/11 *yau* 'oil'	

Some languages have been reported to have even more tones. As just mentioned, Hmong has eight tones and so does Chaozhou (a Sinitic language). In many languages, tones can combine and influence one another in speech. The rules governing this (called "tone sandhi" rules) also differ from language to language. Although I have been concentrating on pitch contour, it has to be stressed that in many languages other aspects of "voice quality" work together with pitch in constituting the distinctiveness of tones. For example, Burmese is said to have four tones, but one of the high-pitched tones is distinguished by "creaky" pronunciation (the syllable is pronounced with tension or constriction in the throat) and another by a final glottal stop, which shortens the duration of the vowel. Several of the

Vietnamese tones are also distinguished by strong glottalization. We will return to tones in more detail in Chapter 5.

Finally, remember that although many East and Southeast Asian languages have lexical tone, many others are not tonal. In the south, the national languages Malaysian (Bahasa Melayu), Indonesian (Bahasa Indonesia), and Pilipino have no traces of lexical tone whatsoever. To the far north, Japanese and Korean are not tonal. Most of the minority languages of mainland and insular Southeast Asia are not tonal either.

1.6 Classifier constructions

Another celebrated feature of the languages of East and Southeast Asia is the existence of classifier constructions. We say that a language has classifier constructions when it has grammatical devices which, in certain contexts, oblige speakers somehow to categorize the person or thing they are speaking about (the referent) in terms of certain semantic dimensions. For living things, these dimensions may include whether or not the referent is human, and if not, what kind of life form (e.g. animal, fish, plant) or functional category (e.g. edible, dangerous) it belongs to. For inanimate things, semantic dimensions may include physical properties (e.g. shape, size, material) and functions (e.g. vehicle, tool).

Many different types of classifier construction are found in the world's languages (Aikhenvald 2000), but in East and Southeast Asian languages the most common type is the numeral classifier construction. Numeral classifiers are found within certain kinds of noun phrase, appearing next to numerals and other quantifying expressions, and sometimes also with demonstratives. The classifier may be a word or, less commonly, an affix. To get a quick idea of how classifiers work, look over the following extract from a Japanese shopping list. In Japanese, classifiers are suffixes which attach to the numerals.

nasu [eggplant]   *nana* [seven] -*ko* [CL: smallish, solid thing] 'seven eggplants'
kyuuri [cucumber] *hachi* [eight] -*hon* [CL: long cylindrical thing] 'eight cucumbers'
hamu [ham]   *juu* [ten] -*mai*   [CL: flat thing]   'ten slices of ham'

The examples below show classifier constructions in Malaysian (Bahasa Melayu), Thai, and Cantonese, languages which are more typical of East and Southeast Asia in having classifiers which are separate words. By the way, as you can see from the Cantonese example in (18), the term "numeral classifier" is a slight misnomer, because classifiers are found with quantifying expressions of all kinds, including words like 'many' and 'several', as well as numerals in the strict sense.

Malaysian (Bahasa Melayu)

(**16**) *empat ekor   kucing*
    four   CL:ANIMAL cat
    'four cats'

Thai

(**17**) *burìi   sɔ̌ɔng múan*
    cigarette two   CL:STICK-LIKE
    'two cigarettes'

Cantonese

(**18**) *géi   gāan   ngūk*
    several CL:BUILDING house
    'several buildings'

Classifier constructions have a structure similar to English expressions like *two sheets of paper*, *two drops of water*, *two articles of furniture*, and *two members of the family*. English words like *sheet*, *drop*, *article*, and *member* are not true classifiers, however, because they do not categorize the things being spoken about. They are better termed either "measure words" or "unit counters". We call a word a "measure word" when it specifies the form in which an amount of a mass substance is found; for example, in phrases like *two sheets of paper* or *three drops of water*. The term "measure word" is also applied to units of measurement and "containerfuls", for example, in phrases like *two litres of milk* and *three cups of sugar*. The term "unit counter" is used for words which single out a number of individuals from a collective; for example, in phrases like *two articles of furniture* and *three members of the family*. The languages of East and Southeast Asia also have various measure words and unit counters, in addition to classifiers. Unfortunately, some descriptions of these languages describe measure words and unit counters as subcategories of classifiers. This is confusing, because it gives the impression that these languages have scores or hundreds of classifiers, which is not true.

Numeral classifiers originate historically from ordinary nouns with concrete meanings. In some languages, classifiers are still identical in form with ordinary nouns. In Malaysian (Bahasa Melayu) the classifier *ekor*, for example, is identical with the ordinary noun meaning 'tail'. On the other hand, in many other languages the classifiers are completely unrelated to ordinary nouns.

It might head off potential misunderstandings to point out the main difference between a numeral classifier system and a system of gender (noun class), such as we find in German, French, and many other European languages. A gender system is essentially a classification of nouns, i.e. of words. Though there is always a semantic basis for parts of a gender system (e.g. for words referring to humans), for the most part the system is not semantically based. Gender is also intimately connected with the grammatical process of

A first look   17

"agreement"; that is, the phenomenon whereby other words in the clause adopt different forms to "agree with" the gender of a noun. The number of genders is usually fairly small and quite fixed, e.g. in European languages: masculine, feminine, and (sometimes) neuter.

Numeral classifiers do not classify nouns but the referents of nouns—the actual things in the world which the speaker "picks out" to say something about on a particular occasion. The basis for the system is always predominantly, if not exclusively, semantic. Because of this, it is usual in some circumstances to have a choice of classifiers, depending on how one is viewing the referent in question. To illustrate this from Cantonese (Matthews and Yip 1994): *chēung* 'gun' could be classified as *jī* (by its cylindrical shape) or as *bá* (by its function); and *syùhn* 'sailing vessel' could be classified as *ga* (large vehicle) or as *jek* (small object), yielding the meanings 'ship' vs. 'boat', respectively. Unlike genders, numeral classifiers are not normally involved in grammatical agreement processes. They are often found in sizable numbers, and sometimes form a "semi-open" class, lacking clear boundaries.

Classifier systems may differ according to: (a) the kinds of semantic parameters involved, (b) whether the system is exhaustive or partial, i.e. do all nouns receive classifiers, or only some, (c) whether the use of classifiers is obligatory or not. We will return to classifiers in greater detail in Chapter 4.

1.7 Serial verb constructions

A serial verb construction involves two or more verbs, all of them sharing a single grammatical subject, packed into a single clause without any intervening conjunctions. They are widespead in the languages of East and Southeast Asia, especially in those of the isolating type. As we will see later (in Chapter 4) there are several different kinds of serial verb constructions and they can serve various grammatical purposes. Just to get the general idea, however, take a look at these examples from three genetically unrelated languages—Mandarin Chinese, Khmer, and Hmong. They are typical of serial constructions in that they involve at least one verb which is a verb of motion or posture.

Mandarin Chinese

(19) *Tā gùi-xialai   qíu Zhāng-sān.*
    3SG kneel.down beg Zhang-san
    'He knelt down begging (or: knelt down and begged) Zhang-san.'

Khmer

(20) *Viə deek luək.*
    3SG lie   sleep
    'He lay sleeping (or: lay down and slept).'

Hmong

(**21**) *Nws khiav rov   qab   mus tsev.*
     3SG run   return back go   home
     'He ran back home.'

In each case, you can see that the sentence contains more than one verb—
'kneel down' and 'beg' in (19), 'lie' and 'sleep' in (20), 'run', 'return' and
'go' in (21)—inside a single clause. Notice that there are no conjunctions
(i.e. words like English 'and') separating the verbs.

You may be able to tell from the translations that in each case there is a
very close semantic connection between the verbs. In a sense, each of these
sentences depicts a single event, even though this event can be seen as
consisting or two or more closely related "sub-events". For example, sentence (19) can be understood as depicting either a single event of "kneeling
down begging" (both actions happening at the same time) or a single event
of "kneeling down, then begging" (one action following the other but both
seen as part of a single two-part event).

In cases where the events are understood as happening simultaneously,
English has a somewhat similar grammatical option involving the so-called
"gerund" form of the verb, i.e. the *ing*-form; as in *He knelt down begging* or
He lay sleeping. The difference between this kind of English sentence and a
genuine serial construction are: (a) the *ing*-form is a marked verbal form,
whereas in the Chinese, Khmer and Hmong examples above all the verbs
appear in their normal, unmarked forms; (b) the *ing*-form can only be used
where simultaneous actions are involved, whereas serial constructions can
indicate sequences of closely related actions; (c) in many cases, it is possible
to combine three or more verbs in a serial construction.

Be careful not to assume that any old sequence of verbs is a serial verb
construction. In most East and Southeast Asian languages, it is possible to
get sequences of verbs which do not fit the definition of serialization either
because they are not all in a single clause or because they do not all share the
same subject. We will only look at some examples of the first kind, from Lao
(Enfield 1994: 26; 1998 p.c.).

(**22**) *Khòòj⁵ jaak⁵ lin⁵ phaj⁴.*
     I   want play cards
     'I want (to) play cards.'

(**23**) *Laaw² sùù⁴ khaw⁵-niaw³ kin³.*
     3SG   buy rice-sticky   eat
     'She bought some sticky rice (to) eat.'

In (22) the phrase *lin⁵ phaj⁴* 'play cards' is a complement of the verb *jaak⁵*
'want', but because there is no explicit marking of the fact, it looks like a
serial construction. In (23) the word *kin³* 'eat' is a purposive clause even

though it is not marked as such (in fact, the purposive marker *phùa¹* 'in order to, so that' can be inserted in front of *kin³* 'eat' with no change of meaning).

1.8 Multiple pronouns and other systems of address

One of the most interesting features of many of the languages of East and Southeast Asia is that aspects of the language structure seem to be specially adapted to allow people to express "social messages", especially messages to do with differences in social standing, respect, deference, and the like. From the perspective of speakers of these languages, the pronouns of modern-day English are particularly insensitive to social distinctions. There is only one form each for 'I' and for 'you', and English speakers feel free to use these words even with social superiors, such as respected older relatives, one's boss, or teachers. At least in other European languages there are two different ways of saying 'you', e.g. French *tu* and *vous*, German *du* and *Sie*, one of which expresses greater social distance than the other. Many East and Southeast Asian languages go far beyond European languages in having a whole range of alternative pronominal and quasi-pronominal forms (such as kin terms).

Table 1.3 shows some address forms in Thai, a language with a particularly wide range of choices. The choice depends on the speaker's attitude towards the addressee, which is normally conditioned by the nature of the social relationship and by factors such as age and sex. You will see that there are some gaps in Table 1.3. This reflects the fact that in some situations one would not feel comfortable using pronouns at all (preferring to use names, or to avoid direct reference altogether). Also, there are additional pronouns *kuu* 'I' and *miŋ* 'you', which are plainer and "lower" than any shown in Table 1.3. For third persons, the choices are fewer. *Khǎw* is the general polite form, and *thân* expresses special respect for social superiors. There is a third form, *man*, which is used for social inferiors, for non-humans, and when expressing anger. Additional, special forms are used with royalty and clergy.

A more typical-sized system is found in Malay, which offers its speakers essentially two choices each for first and second person pronouns. As in Thai, the choice ultimately depends on one's attitude to the person one is speaking to, but this is strongly conditioned by factors such as social standing and relative age. One would not normally use the plain forms *aku* 'I' and *kau* 'you' unless one is on rather casual or intimate terms with the addressee. The plain forms are used in "unguarded" situations, for example, in thinking aloud to oneself, among intimates and familiars in informal situations, and (sometimes) from senior family members to junior family members. A good description of pronominal variants and usages can be found in Koh (1990: 104–46). She describes *aku* 'I' and *kau* 'you' as

Table 1.3. Some Thai forms of address (after Hudak 1987: 41; adapted with input from Nick Enfield)

Situation	First person 'I'	Second person 'you'
Polite conversation with strangers and acquaintances	phŏm (used by males)[a]	khun
Speaking to a superior, showing deference	phŏm (used by males)[a]	thân
'Plain' forms: for informal conversation with close friends/family	chăn	thəə
Between intimates of same sex	kan	kɛɛ
Adult to child	chăn, or kin-term	nǔu (lit. 'mouse') or kin-term
Child to adult, e.g. teacher	nǔu (lit. 'mouse')	kin-term
Child to older sibling	nǔu (lit. 'mouse')	(phǐi 'elder sibling')

[a] According to standard descriptions of Thai, dìchăn can be used by females, but it is very formal and extremely rare in face-to-face conversation.

Table 1.4. First and second person pronouns in Malay and Japanese

		First person 'I'	Second person 'you'
Malay	Plain	aku	kau (or: engkau)
	polite or formal	saya	awak, kamu, anda
Japanese	plain ('rough')	ore	omae
	casual	boku	kimi
	normal ('polite')	watashi	anata
	formal	watakushi	—

"non-polite" rather than as "impolite", saying: "these forms do not indicate impoliteness when used correctly. They merely do not express extra politeness" (1990: 111). Because Malay society is extremely conscious of verbal politeness, however, the more formal pronouns (such as *saya* 'I', *awak/kamu* 'you') are required in a wide range of social situations.

Japanese also has linguistic devices for expressing social messages (see the section on "honorifics" below). When it comes to pronouns, there are several options depending on the "social tone" which the speaker wants to convey. Using the very "plainest" pronouns *ore* 'I' and *omae* 'you' often conveys a "rough" tone. The alternatives *boku* 'I' and *kimi* 'you' convey a "casual" tone. In traditional society, both these sets of pronouns tended to be confined to men and boys. It was seen as socially inappropriate for woman and girls to use them. The normal pronoun choices in polite inter-action are *watashi* 'I' and *anata* 'you'. In addition, there is a specially formal variant for 'I', namely *watakushi*.

Notice that the three examples we have looked at here come from Southeast Asia and from North Asia. It is an interesting fact that the languages which are geographically in-between these regions, i.e. the Sinitic (Chinese) languages, do not have elaborate pronoun forms (though they use various other means of expressing respect and deference in speech).

Despite the range of pronoun choices, there are many situations in which it may feel better not to use pronouns at all. Alternative strategies include using some other way of referring, such as personal names, kinship designa-tions, or words for a person's occupation or role, or avoiding explicit references altogether. In Malaysia, it is normal in everyday interaction to refer to oneself and one's interlocutors not by any of the pronouns, but by using a person's name or "kinship" designation, such as *abang* 'big brother', *kakak* (or *kak* for short) 'big sister', and *adik* 'younger brother or sister'. The inverted commas around the term "kinship" are necessary because terms like *abang*, *kakak*, and *adik* are used not only between real family members but in a range of other situations where there is a small or moderate age difference between the people involved. Similarly, in conversation with someone much older, it is normal to address the older person as *pakcik* 'uncle' or *makcik* 'auntie', and for that person to refer to him or herself in the same way.

The cartoon in Fig. 1.1 shows names and kinship designations being used in place of pronouns. Shamsul Azhar is telephoning his close friend Siti to apologize about a misunderstanding. Throughout the exchange both participants refer to him as *abang*, literally, 'big brother', and to her as *Ti* (a shortened form of *Siti*). No pronouns are used at all.

Our Malaysian example concerned a friendly social situation, between people who knew each other well and were more or less equal in social status. In asymmetrical social situations, i.e. when the people involved are of different social level or status, it is even more common to find that pronouns are avoided. For example, in Japanese one would not use the polite *anata* 'you' when speaking to a higher-status person. As Inoue (1979: 284) puts it: "Should one dare to use *anata* in speaking to a person of higher status, it would convey a special message—either of a sense of camaraderie or of indignation or rebellion."

In Korean, a respected person would be addressed in many situations using a job title or role term, or a kinship word, often in combination with the honorific suffix *-nim* (Lee and Ramsey 2000: 225–38). For example, *seonsaeng-nim* 'respected teacher', *sojang-nim* 'respected director', *gisa-nim* 'respected engineer, technician', *son-nim* 'respected guest', *ajwumeni* 'Auntie'. Calling someone by their bare personal name in Korea is a highly

Fig. 1.1. Kinship designations and names used instead of pronouns in Malaysian.

"Hello *Ti!.. Abang* here. Forgive *abang* for once again disturbing *Ti's* peace and quiet in the morning."

Shamsul Azhar decides to contact Siti in the office early in the morning.

"Hah! What's up that *abang* suddenly telephones *Ti* at this time?"

"Especially since before this *abang* never got in touch except once... Hadn't *abang* misplaced the number?"

sensitive matter. To address anyone by name who is more than five or six years older than oneself would be unusual, no matter how close one feels towards them, and even the closest friends start to feel uncomfortable using each other's names once they reach 30 or 40 years of age. Within the family the only people one can address by name are one's children or younger siblings.

A widespread strategy for avoiding pronouns is simply to avoid explicit references to oneself or one's interlocutor altogether. In English this is rather difficult, but it is easier if the grammatical structure of a language allows "incomplete" sentences, i.e. sentences in which the subject or object is not stated explicitly. This phenomenon (known as ellipsis) is extremely common in Japanese, Korean, Sinitic languages, and in mainland Southeast Asian languages. Accordingly, in these languages the solution to the problem of how to refer to someone is often not to refer them at all.

1.9 Honorific forms

Some languages of East and Southeast Asia—the best-known in this respect being Japanese, Korean, and Javanese—have morphological and lexical means of adding "respect" messages for either (a) the person being spoken to, i.e. addressee, or (b) the person or people being spoken about, i.e. the referent. We can illustrate quickly from Japanese: the verbal suffix *-masu*

Box 1.1. Thai nicknames (*chîi lên* 'play name')

Given names in Thai often have two, three, or more syllables and generally express elegant or "high-sounding" meanings; for example, Chalermwan 'celebrated beauty' or Kittichai 'famous victory'. Except in formal contexts and with people one doesn't know well, however, one often goes by a monosyllablic "nickname". It is usually chosen by parents or other family members soon after the baby is born—before the formal name is chosen, in fact—on the basis of some appealing or distinctive characteristic of the baby. Here are some common ones grouped by meaning type. The names are given in approximate English spellings, rather than in the phonemic spelling used elsewhere in this book. Actually there is a lot of variation, so you may see variants on all or most of these spellings, e.g. Nueng for Neung, Noy for Noi, Choy for Joy, Gop for Kop, Khao for Khaw, Moo for Mu.

Birth order and/or size	Animal	Fruit and flowers	Appearance and character	Colour
Neung, Ek (one)	Maew (cat)	Som (orange)	Ke (smart-looking)	Daeng (red)
Song (two)	Pla (fish)	Ple (apple)	Uan (fat)	Leuang (yellow)
Nong (young)	Nok (bird)	Kluay (banana)	Neng (bald)	Faa (blue)
Tow (big)	Mu (pig)	Ngo (rambutan)	Geng (clever)	Kheow (green)
Yai (big)	Kai (chicken)		Gaen (naughty)	Dum (black)
Lek (little)	Chang (elephant)		Jaew (bright-eyed)	Khaw (white)
Noi (little)	Kop (frog)		Tui (chubby)	

Nicknames can also be a shortened form of one's true name, e.g. Bat from Sombat, Pat for Patcharee, Da from Ladda, or a blend of syllables from the parents' names, or come from another language such as English, e.g. Baby, Pepsi, May, A, B, Rose. The well-known Thai tennis player Paradorn Srichaphan comes from a dedicated tennis family who gave him the nickname Ball. During the World Cup soccer, a number of Thai babies also got the name Ball, after the soccer ball.

expresses respect for the addressee, whereas the nominal prefix *o-* expresses respect for the person being spoken about.

Some scholars draw a terminological distinction on this basis. They point out that linguistic devices which code respect for the addressee can be seen as belonging under the broad rubric of "politeness". Linguistic devices for expressing respect for a referent, on the other hand, seem to be rather different in nature, and deserving of a special term. For this reason, some scholars reserve the term "honorific" (or "honorification") for referent-related phenomena. This seems like a good idea—or it would be, except for the fact that other scholars use the terms "honorific" (or "honorification") indifferently for both addressee-related and referent-related phenomena.

In Chapter 7 we will look closely at the Japanese honorific system, but here let us look briefly at Korean. Various Korean nouns have not only their

Table 1.5. Some Korean honorific nouns and verbs

	Honorific noun	Plain noun
'father'	*abeonim*	*abeoji*
'grandmother'	*halmeonim*	*halmeoni*
'food, meal'	*jinji*	*bap*
'name'	*seongham*	*ireum*
'body'	*okche*	*mom*
'word, speech'	*malsseum*	*mal*
	Honorific verb	**Plain verb**
'to eat'	*japsusi-*	*meok-*
'to sleep'	*jumusi-*	*ja-*
'to be, to exist'	*gyesi-*	*iss-*

ordinary forms but also a special honorific form. Honorific nouns express special respect for the person referred to by such a noun (or, in the case of objects, for the person associated with the object). Honorific verbs are formed by means of the honorific suffix -*si*/-*eusi*. In addition, there are a few plain verbs which bear no obvious relationship to their honorific counterparts. Examples of pairs of plain nouns and honorific nouns are given in Table 1.5 (Lee 1989: 57–8).

Honorific nouns and verbs tend to occur together. Plain nouns which lack honorific counterparts can also occur in sentences with honorific verbs. A couple of examples (Lee 1989: 59, 87; cf. 104):

Korean

(**24**) *Abeonim   i   jumusi-n-da.*
father(HON) SUBJ sleep:HON-PRES-DECL
'My father is sleeping.'

(**25**) *Gunin   i   bange   gyesi-eo-yo.*
soldier SUBJ in.room is:HON-DECL-PCT
'A soldier is in the room.'

1.10 Other common features

Other linguistic features are widespread among East and Southeast Asian languages, at least in some regions. We will come to these later in the book. They include: (a) sentence-final particles, i.e. invariable little words which express nuances of the speaker's attitudes and feelings, usually appearing at the end of a sentence (see Chapter 4); (b) widespead ellipsis, also known as zero anaphora, i.e. the phenomenon whereby noun phrases are simply omitted if the identity of the referent can be understood from context; (c) topic prominence, i.e. when the organization of a sentence is heavily influenced by factors such as where the speaker's focus of interest and attention is, what the speaker and listener are taking for granted, and other so-called "discourse" factors (see Chapter 4).

Key technical terms

agglutinating	lexical tone
constituent order	measure word
contour tone	minority language
diacritic	national language
honorific	numeral classifier
inflection	postposition
isolating	register tone
language family	

CHAPTER 2

Language families, linguistic areas and language situations

In this chapter we survey the diversity of languages in East and Southeast Asia, both in terms of their sheer numbers and in terms of their genetic ("family tree") groupings. We will expand on the fact that mainland Southeast Asia is a linguistic area where languages share many features, despite belonging to six different language families. Then we will run through the language situations in East and Southeast Asia country by country.

2.1 What is a language family?

Languages change over time. Even without external influences small changes in vocabulary, pronunciation, and grammar gradually accrue so that, after hundreds of years, an ancestor language and a descendant language would no longer be mutually intelligible (if anyone were alive to compare them). We can see this by looking at a sentence from Old English (Allen 1995: 60).

(26) *þa gelamp hit þæt æt ðam gyftum . . .*
    'Then it happened that at the wedding . . .'

Eventually the descendant language can become so different from the ancestor language that very close study would be needed to discover the relationship.

In the preceding paragraph I spoke of "an ancestor language" and "a descendant language", but languages (like people) often have more than a single descendant. There may be a whole family of languages which all descend from a common ancestor. This comes about when over a particular period of time a community of speakers is divided in some way, for instance because of a geographical barrier such as a mountain range or river, or because one part of the group migrates to another locale. Once the speech communities are separated, the natural process of language change leads them to diverge from one another, eventually becoming different languages. Over thousands of years there are many ways in which the descendants of a single ancestor language can split and diverge, then split and diverge again. The family trees of languages can therefore be very complex, with many branches and sub-branches.

Given reliable information about a set of present-day languages, linguists can sometimes figure out which ones are related through descent from a common ancestor, i.e. which are genetically related. If there are written records which have survived from ancient times this is a great help, but it is not essential. A procedure known as the "comparative method" can enable linguists to work out genetic relationships—and even to reconstruct aspects of the ancestor languages—by painstakingly sifting through and comparing words in present-day languages.

We cannot go into the comparative method in any detail here, except to say that it relies to a large extent on being able to distinguish between words (known as "cognates") which have descended from a common ancestor, and words which have been borrowed from language to language as a result of cultural contact. This is no easy task, especially in a region such as mainland Southeast Asia, where the language stocks have been in touch with one another for over a thousand years. In this kind of situation, all sorts of linguistic features (lexical, phonological, grammatical) diffuse from language to language, regardless of the genetic affiliation of the languages involved. This makes the family trees difficult, or even impossible, to reconstruct with any certainty. Consequently there have been many changing theories about the family trees of East and Southeast Asian languages, especially at the higher levels of the trees, i.e. in relation to very ancient time depths. For example, for a long time there was controversy about whether Vietnamese belonged to the Mon-Khmer family or to the Tai-Kadai family (consensus now favours Mon-Khmer); and similarly, about whether or not the Hmong-Mien group of languages belong to the Sinitic family (the jury is still out). Matisoff (1992: 45) says about the higher-level groupings that "almost every possible grouping has been proposed". We will try to minimize these inconsistencies by sticking to lower-level groupings, but even so, some controversial points remain. Aside from disputes about where particular languages belong, there are a few languages which on current evidence cannot be plausibly assigned to any language family. Languages with this status are known as "language isolates".

Another kind of difficulty concerns deciding how many languages are out there. In principle, linguists usually say that two ways of speaking, say, A and B, deserve to be called separate "languages" if they are mutually unintelligible. Otherwise A and B are "dialects" of a single language (which may be named after one or other of the dialects or be given a distinct name of its own). In practice, however, it is often difficult to decide from the available information whether two particular speech varieties are mutually unintelligible or not. In addition, speakers of languages themselves do not usually work according to linguists' definitions. Very often a set of dialects will each have a distinct name, and speakers, if asked, will say their dialect is a different language from all the others. Political, social, and cultural factors heavily influence whether or not one set of people see themselves as speaking the same language as another set of people. For example, many linguists would say that Danish, Swedish, and Norwegian are dialects of a single language, since they are mutually intelligible; but the Danes, Swedes, and Norwegians see themselves as having different languages, just as they have different nationalities. A similar situation applies in relation to Indonesian and Malaysian. Conversely, on account of a strong sense of national and cultural unity, speakers of different languages (on linguistic criteria) may see themselves as all speaking versions of a single overarching language. This happens in China and in Thailand.

Another problem is that a single dialect or language is likely to be known by multiple names, by its autonym (what the people call themselves), and perhaps by several exonyms (what other groups call them), some of which are based on place names, cf. Matisoff (1986a). Since most languages are spoken in inaccessible areas by small populations of indigenous peoples, in many cases there just isn't enough reliable information to go on. For example, on the island of Borneo up to seventy "language names" have been recorded but it is not known exactly how many distinct languages or dialects these refer to (the term "Dayak" is often used as a cover term). For reasons of this kind, you will see widely differing estimates of how many languages there are in a particular area or in a particular language family.

2.2 The major language families of East and Southeast Asia

In this section we go through the major language families which are generally recognized for Southeast Asia and East Asia. Moving from south to north these are: Austronesian (its western division), Mon-Khmer (a subfamily of Austroasiatic), Tibeto-Burman (a sub-family of Sino-Tibetan), Tai-Kadai, Hmong-Mien, and Sinitic (a sub-family of Sino-Tibetan). Every one of these families has numerous members, including (except for Hmong-Mien) one or more major national languages along with sundry minority languages. Some of the minority languages are endangered, with very small numbers of speakers. Others have hundreds of thousands, or even millions, of speakers (as in the case of Zhuang, a northern Tai language with about 20 million speakers). For convenience, we will illustrate the typical characteristics of these families from the major national languages. In the North Asia region, the affiliations of Korean, Japanese, and Ainu are still not settled.

I should point out that our coverage is not completely even for several reasons. First, it tends to under-represent the many small Tibeto-Burman languages in the interior of Southeast Asia, mainly on account of the difficulty in getting reliable information. Second, we are not covering any of the languages of Papua (formerly Irian Jaya), the easternmost province of Indonesia. Third, we are not covering the non-Sinitic languages in the far reaches of North Asia, such as Uighur and Mongolian.

2.2.1 Austronesian

The Austronesian language family is the largest and most widespread in the world, with somewhere around 700 (maybe as many as 1,200) languages altogether and 300 million native speakers. Aside from Southeast Asia, Austronesian languages are found on numerous islands in the eastern and central Pacific Ocean all the way to Easter Island. There is also a western outpost language (Malagasy), spoken on the island of Madagascar.

In Southeast Asia the major languages in this family are Indonesian (Bahasa Indonesia) and Malaysian (Bahasa Melayu), collectively referred to as Malay (200 million speakers, about 40 million as a first language), Javanese (75 million speakers), Sundanese (30 million), and Pilipino (Tagalog) (50 million, 17 million as a first language). There are hundreds of other, closely related languages in Malaysia, Indonesia, and the Philippines. All the native languages of these countries are Austronesian except for the Aslian languages of interior Malaysia. There are also some Austronesian pockets in southern Vietnam and Cambodia, such as the Chamic languages (Thomas 1998; Grant and Sidwell Forthcoming). Estimates of the number of Austronesian languages vary a lot, mainly because of difficulties in drawing the "language/dialect" distinction.

The Austronesian languages of insular and peninsular Southeast Asia all belong to the western division of Austronesian. This is usually regarded as consisting of two further groups, the Central Malayo-Polynesian branch (in the Moluccas and Lesser Sunda islands, about 100–150 languages) and the much larger Western Malayo-Polynesian branch (which includes Malay and the Philippine languages). Another group of about ten Austronesian languages, in a distantly related subgroup, is located on the island of Formosa (Taiwan). These languages have about 400,000 speakers.

Austronesian languages tend to have phoneme inventories which are medium to small in size (see section 5.1). They have abundant morphology,

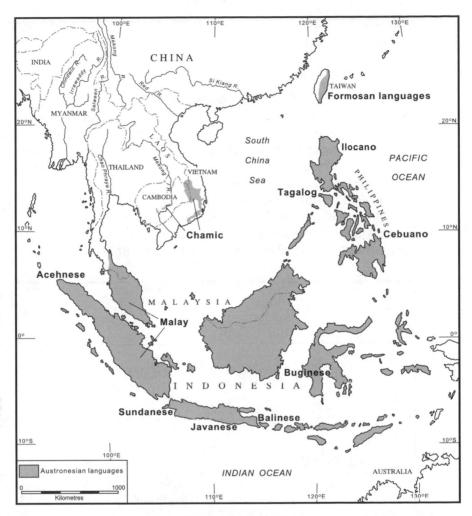

Map 2.1. Approximate distribution of Austronesian languages in Southeast Asia (after Comrie, Matthews, and Polinsky 2003).

using affixes of all kinds (prefixes, suffixes, infixes, circumfixes) and reduplication to build up complex words from simpler ones (see section 3.2.5). All of these languages have an inclusive/exclusive distinction in plural pronouns, i.e. there are two words for 'we'—one including the addressee and one excluding the addressee. This is a feature shared by no other language family in Southeast Asia or East Asia. On the western side of insular Southeast Asia most Austronesian languages have intricate systems of voice or focus marking (see section 4.4), and many are verb-initial, including Toba Batak, Tagalog, Chamorro, and the Formosan languages. In the centre and eastern side of the region, closer to Papua, voice systems are either much more restricted or lacking altogether, verb-medial constituent order is common, and subjects and objects are often expressed by pronominal clitics (Klamer 2000; Grimes 2000).

2.2.2 Mon-Khmer

This family has well over a hundred languages. It is one branch of Austroasiatic, the other main branch being the Munda languages of East India. Mon-Khmer is probably the most archaic family in Southeast Asia, i.e. the family which has been in the region for the longest time. Most Mon-Khmer languages are spoken by so-called "hill tribes" in remote mountainous areas, surrounded by languages belonging to other families.

The best known Mon-Khmer languages are Khmer (Cambodian, about 13 million speakers) and Vietnamese (nearly 70 million), though Vietnamese is not typical of the family. There are dozens of other related languages in Cambodia, Laos, Thailand, and Vietnam. Among the better known of the

Map 2.2. Approximate distribution of Mon-Khmer languages (after Comrie, Matthews, and Polinsky 2003).

minority Mon-Khmer languages are Mon in Myanmar (Burma) and central Thailand, Paluang and Wa in central Myanmar, Khmu in northern and central Laos, Bahnar and Katu in central Vietnam and southern Laos, and the so-called Muong languages of northern Vietnam. Another branch of Mon-Khmer are the sixteen or so Aslian languages found in the mountainous spine of the Malay peninsula (Matisoff 2003). The best known are Semai and Temiar, and the northern "Semang" languages.

Mon-Khmer languages have a number of distinctive phonological characteristics. They are famed for their large vowel inventories, with twenty or more units being not unusual. Systems with four degrees of vowel height are common, and there are often several series of vowels differing according to "voice register" or phonation type, e.g. breathy vs. clear. Mon-Khmer languages commonly have a complete set of stops and nasals in labial, alveolar, palatal, and velar positions, but few fricatives—mainly /s/ and /h/ (see section 5.2). Unlike Tai-Kadai and Sinitic languages, they typically allow a reasonable range of consonant clusters in initial position, especially of the form stop + sonorant. Many languages have a so-called sesquisyllabic pattern, with a minor "half-syllable" preceeding a full syllable. Tones are not common. Vietnamese is atypical in having tones and disallowing initial consonant clusters.

Morphologically the Mon-Khmer languages have a large number of infixes (usually a nasal, a liquid, or a vowel), which are inserted after the first consonant (again, Vietnamese is atypical in this respect). There is little or no inflection. Syntactically, Mon-Khmer languages have SVO constituent order. Possessors generally precede possessed nouns; but adjectives and demonstratives follow the nouns they modify. However, these latter characteristics are widely shared among Southeast Asian languages, regardless of family. Some Mon-Khmer languages are reported to be verb-initial in intransitive sentences.

2.2.3 Tibeto-Burman

Tibeto-Burman is a sister family of Sinitic, the two branches together constituting Sino-Tibetan. Most of the 300 or more Tibeto-Burman languages are found to the west of the area covered by this book, in Tibet, Nepal, Bhutan, northern and northeastern India, and Pakistan. As the name of the family suggests, however, there are many Tibeto-Burman languages in Myanmar (Burma), about seventy-five, including notably Burmese, Lahu, and the Karen languages (spoken in the Thai–Burma borderlands). A sizeable number are spoken in southern China, and pockets extend into Thailand, Laos, and northwestern Vietnam.

Within the area covered by this book, Tibeto-Burman languages are mostly minority "hill tribe" languages, with speakers numbering in the thousands and tens of thousands. The big exception is Burmese, a national

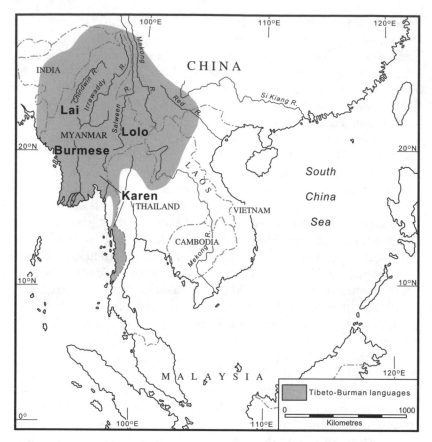

Map 2.3. Approximate distribution of Tibeto-Burman languages in Southeast
Asia (after DeLancey 1992, Comrie, Matthews, and Polinsky 2003).

language with 30 million speakers and a long literary tradition. The Karen
subgroup in Myanmar (Burma) number about 4 million combined (S'gaw is
the largest, at about 2 million). Two other relatively large Tibeto-Burman
languages are found in southern China: Lolo (Yi), with around 3 million
speakers, and Bai, with well over a million speakers. A whole "new" branch
of Tibeto-Burman came to scholarly attention in the 1970s, with the discovery of the nine or ten Qiangic languages in Sichuan province.

Although Tibeto-Burman is a sister family to Sinitic, taken as a whole
Tibeto-Burman languages are quite different in their morphology and
syntax from Sinitic languages, being agglutinating and verb-final. In
Southeast Asia, however, this observation does not really apply, because
many Tibeto-Burman languages in this region share areal features such as
the tendency towards monosyllabic words, few initial clusters or final consonants, complex tone systems, classifiers, and serial verb constructions.
With the exception of the Karen subgroup, however, they have retained
SOV word order, and they usually have postpositions rather than prepositions. Generally speaking, Tibeto-Burman languages are less thoroughly

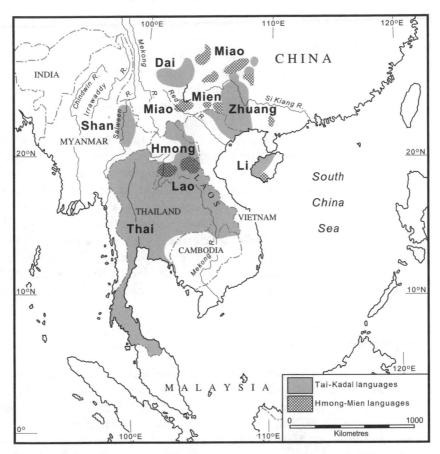

Map 2.4. Approximate distribution of Tai-Kadai and Hmong-Mien languages (after Comrie, Matthews, and Polinsky 2003).

isolating than neighbouring families in Southeast Asia. Some, such as the Kuki-Chin subgroup of western Myanmar (Burma) and adjacent areas, have developed person-marking prefixes on the verb.

2.2.4 Tai-Kadai

The largest language in the Tai-Kadai family (sometimes called simply Tai) is Thai, the national language of Thailand. Thai has about 60 million speakers, and Lao, the next most populous language, has over 4 million. These statements are an oversimplification, however, because of the existence of several divergent Thai dialects, some of which could be considered as languages in their own right and some as dialects of Lao. Nevertheless, the considerable variation in Thai is overshadowed by the existence of more than 50 other Tai-Kadai languages. They are centred on Thailand and Laos, though some are found in southern China and in eastern Myanmar (Burma), notably Zhuang and Shan respectively.

The main subgroups in the family are the Tai group, which contains by far the most languages, the Kam-Sui group, a small number of languages in mainland southern China, and the Kadai group, including Li and Be on Hainan Island. The total number of speakers of Tai-Kadai languages is probably somewhere up to 100 million.

Tai-Kadai languages tend to have a sizeable number of tones. Standard Thai has five. The Kam-Sui languages are reported to have as many as fifteen, but this figure may include allotones (non-contrastive tone variants: see section 5.3). Phoneme inventories are typically moderate in size. There is little or no inflection. Compounding and reduplication are the most common types of derivational processes. Almost all Tai-Kadai languages have SVO word order. Serial verb constructions are common. These languages all make heavy use of classifier constructions. In Thai and other languages of the west and south, the order is noun–numeral–classifier, but in the Tai-Kadai languages of Vietnam and southern China the order is usually numeral–classifier–noun, probably due to the influence of Sinitic languages. Aside from this, noun modifiers tend to follow the nouns they modify.

2.2.5 Hmong-Mien

This is a group of some thirty-five languages spoken mainly in southwestern China, with several spoken in adjacent parts of Southeast Asia. The main languages are Hmong (also known as Miao), which has perhaps close to 5 million speakers, and Mien (also known as Man and as Yao), which has nearly 2 million. Most of the linguistic documentation of Hmong-Mien languages has been conducted by Chinese scholars, and the family is still relatively little known in the West. The Vietnam war in the mid-1970s forced thousands of speakers of Hmong-Mien languages from Laos to resettle in Australia, the USA, and France, which allowed Western linguists easier access, especially to the language known as White Hmong.

The higher-level affiliation of the Hmong-Mien family is disputed. The languages share many of the areal features of Southeast Asia, such as lack of inflection, presence of numeral classifiers, widespread ellipsis, serial verb constructions, and an abundance of sentence particles. Within the noun phrase, possessors and classifiers generally precede nouns, while adjectives follow. All Hmong-Mien languages are tone languages, some of world-record complexity. Shidongkou Hmu (also known as Black Miao) has been reported to have five level tones, and Longmo and Zongdi Hmong each have twelve tonal contrasts. Hmongic languages have very large consonant inventories, including retroflex and uvular places of articulation, pre-nasalized, aspirated, and glottalized stops, and voiceless sonorants, but a very restricted range of syllable types (see section 5.1.2). Mienic languages have fewer consonants but more variety in syllable types.

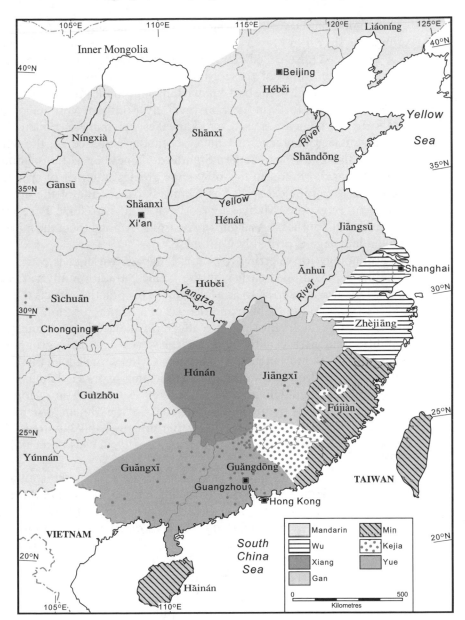

Map 2.5. Approximate distribution of Sinitic languages (dialects) in China (after Li 1992).

2.2.6 Sinitic

Sinitic languages are spoken by a huge number of people (over 1,000 million) in mainland China, and Taiwan, and in Southeast Asia (see Norman 1988; Ramsey 1987; Li 1992; Chappell 2001). There are numerous mutually unintelligible Sinitic varieties, which are usually classified into seven different groups, as shown in Map 2.5. Running roughly from south to north, these are: Yue, Kejia (also called Hakka), Min, Xiang (Hsiang), Wu, Gan (Kan), and Mandarin. Some of these groups are often referred to, more or less loosely, by reference to the best-known language in the group, e.g. Cantonese for Yue, Hokkien for Min (or more precisely, Southern Min). Geographical terms are also sometimes used, e.g. Taiwanese, Hainanese, Fujian.

The standard language of China is Mandarin (based on the dialect of Beijing), also known as Modern Standard Chinese or as Putonghua 'common language'. Mandarin has by far the greatest number of speakers and the widest geographical spread in China. It is also one of the official languages of Singapore. Many Chinese from southern China have migrated and settled in Southeast Asia and in Australia. Among them the most widely spoken language is probably Cantonese.

Terminology for referring to Sinitic language varieties is confusing and variable. As mentioned earlier, in the Chinese tradition any variety other than Mandarin is referred to as a "dialect". This practice reflects the cultural and historical unity of China and the use of a common script, but it is confusing because in linguistic usage the term dialect implies mutual intelligibility. Linguists usually refer to the seven language groupings just mentioned as "Sinitic languages", and that is what we will do in this book too; but it is not entirely satisfactory, because some of these "languages" have many mutually unintelligible varieties. For example, Min is reported to have nine mutually unintelligible varieties in the Fujian province alone (Li 1992). On strictly linguistic criteria there are probably hundreds of Sinitic languages in China (which is not surprising, really, in view of the population size).

Sinitic languages all have tones and classifiers, with the southern languages (Yue, Min, Kejia) generally having more of both than the northern languages. They have little or no inflection. They are generally described as SVO in word order; but things are a little more complex than this, because the position of a noun phrase can vary depending on whether it is definite or indefinite (indefinite noun phrases tend to follow the verb). Inside the noun phrase, modifiers such as demonstratives, possessives, and adjectives usually precede the noun, as do classifiers, except that in the southern languages the modifiers follow in some structures. Sinitic languages have both prepositions and postpositions. As you can gather even from this brief description, the main linguistic division among Sinitic languages is between southern languages and northern languages, as delineated roughly by the Yangtze (Yangze) River. The southern group has been influenced by long-term contact with Tai-Kadai and Hmong-Mien languages, while in the north the influence has been from Altaic languages (not considered in this book). For information about Sinitic languages other than Mandarin, see Ramsey (1987: ch. 6) and Chappell (2001).

2.2.7 Japanese, Korean, and Ainu

Japanese has about 125 million speakers, almost all of them in Japan. It is the eighth most populous language, in terms of native speakers, in the world, and has many divergent dialects on islands and in mountainous regions. Ryukyuan, a dialect group spoken on islands to the southeast of Japan, is a separate language on linguistic criteria, but is often regarded as a dialect of Japanese. Korean is spoken by more than 70 million people, mainly in Korea and adjacent areas of northeast China and Russia. The two languages have significant similarities in their general structure (e.g. both are agglutinating and have SOV word order), especially when compared with the isolating SVO Sinitic languages. They also share many related words, because both have borrowed massively from Chinese.

Though theories abound, it is not known for certain whether Japanese and Korean are genetically related. If there is a genetic relationship, it must be in the fairly distant past. Some linguists regard one or both languages as belonging to the Altaic family, which also contains Uighur and Mongolian and (more distantly) Turkish. Others advocate an ancient link with Austronesian. You will sometimes see one or other of these theories, or a combination of the two, presented as established fact, but the truth is that the experts still disagree.

Ainu is an indigenous language of Japan which is (or rather, used to be) spoken on the northern island of Hokkaidō. No plausible genetic link has been established with any other language or language family, so it too is a language isolate.

2.3 Mainland Southeast Asia as a linguistic area

As mentioned earlier, if languages of different families "live together" for long enough, they often tend to converge in their phonology, lexicon, and grammar. Recognizing this fact, the term "linguistic area" (or *Sprachbund*) refers to a geographical area in which genetically unrelated languages have come to share many linguistic features as a result of long mutual influence (Emeneau 1956). One of the classic examples of a linguistic area is South Asia, where Indo-Ayran, Dravidian, and Munda languages have been co-located for 3,000 years. Languages of all three families now share many features—in vocabulary, phonology, and grammar. Similarly, mainland Southeast Asia (including southern China) is a linguistic area because there are many shared features across the main language families of the region (Matisoff 1992; Enfield 2003: ch. 2). Among these features we have already seen the limited range of syllable structures and presence of lexical tone (phonological features), and the lack of inflection and existence of classifier constructions (morphological and syntactic features). In the next chapter we will encounter some shared lexical features as well. I am not talking purely about shared vocabulary items, in the sense of words which have been borrowed from one language into another. That is common enough, but even more interesting is the phenomenon which James Matisoff has dubbed the "areal lexicon" of shared cultural vocabulary. He is referring not to the forms of words, but to the content and structure of the vocabulary as a whole. "Due to long cultural contact, [they]... have come to share a certain worldview, similar conceptual frameworks about people and nature, a sort of consensus as to what is worth talking and thinking about" (Matisoff 1991b: 484–5).

In Chapter 4 we will treat some widespread syntactic features in detail. These include the prevalence of serial verb constructions (introduced in section 1.7) and so-called "topic prominence". This is a way of describing languages in which the order of words and phrases in normal spoken conversation is not rigidly determined by grammatical rules but depends on discourse considerations, such as what the topic of interest is in a particular utterance, what is being taken for granted by the speaker and listener, and so on. Linked with this is the phenomenon known as ellipsis, which refers to the leaving out of phrases which refer to participants whose identity is obvious in context. Topic prominence and ellipsis are part of a broader tendency to leave a lot of the interpretation of an utterance to context. We will also see in Chapter 4 the remarkable importance and abundance of "sentence-final particles" in the languages of mainland Southeast Asia. This term refers to small expressive words frequently put at the end of sentences to indicate the speaker's attitude or feeling towards what he or she is saying.

Table 2.1 summarizes some of the mainland Southeast Asian areal features (Enfield 2003), ignoring some exceptions within individual families. As you can see from the presence of the ± sign in some cells of the table, there are some features which vary within certain families. For example, as mentioned earlier, many Mon-Khmer languages lack tones, and except

Table 2.1. Some areal features of mainland Southeast Asia

	Mon-Khmer	Tai-Kadai	Hmong-Mien	Sinitic	Tibeto-Burman
lexical tone	±	+	+	+	+
case-marking	−	−	−	−	−
classifiers	+	+	+	+	+
serial verbs	+	+	+	+	+
verb-final	+	+	+	+	±
prepositions	+	+	+	±	−
noun–adjective order	+	+	+	−	±

for the Karen languages, Tibeto-Burman languages are generally verb-final. Most of the language families have prepositions, but Tibeto-Burman languages generally have postpositions, and Sinitic languages generally have both. In most of the families, adjectives follow nouns, but the opposite order is often found in Tibeto-Burman languages, and is uniformly present in Sinitic languages.

How did so many language families come to be crammed into one geographical region? With inevitable oversimplifications, here is a thumbnail sketch of the language geography and history (cf. SarDesai 1997). The basic ground plan of mainland Southeast Asia is determined by its rivers and mountain ranges (see Map 2.5). From the mountainous core in Tibet to the northeast, long mountain ranges snake down between Myanmar (Burma) and Thailand, and between Laos and Vietnam. Between these great dividing ranges the major rivers descend into the valleys and broad river basins of the south. In Myanmar there is the Irrawaddy, in Thailand the Chao Phraya, and in northern Vietnam the Red River (Song Koi). The Mekong River runs down between Laos and Thailand, through the plains of central and western Cambodia, to meet the sea in southern Vietnam. Each of these rivers has a fertile delta separated from one another by rugged mountain ranges. From a linguistic (but not geographical) point of view, southern and southwestern China belong with mainland Southeast Asia, in the sense that they are part of the same linguistic area. As we have seen, many languages of the Tai-Kadai, Hmong-Mien, and Tibeto-Burman families are located in the mountains and highlands of Yunnan, Guizhou, and Guanxi provinces, and in parts of Sichuan.

Speaking of greater Southeast Asia, James Matisoff points out how geography has helped shape the lifestyles and destinies of peoples:

In this area of precipitous mountains cut into innumerable valleys of all widths by ranging [sic] rivers, which eventually reach the sea in calmer flow in huge fertile deltas, the primary sociolinguistic dichotomy is not horizontal, but vertical: the uplands versus the lowlands. (1991c: 191)

On the lowlands, paddy rice farming (wet rice cultivation) can support relatively large populations. The peoples who have adopted this method of agriculture, which demands year-long discipline and a high level of collective work, include the populous Vietnamese, Khmer, Burmese, and Thai. In the high rugged mountainous areas, on the other hand, shifting, slash-and-burn type cultivation supports hundreds of much smaller groups. In between there is a mixture of different agricultural methods depending on the terrain and on preferred crops, including dry rice cultivation (Burling 1965). Different "hill tribes" tend to have their villages at different elevations. Hmong peoples, for example, usually live at very high elevations, from 1,000 to 1,500 metres. Mon-Khmer peoples tend to live at somewhat lower altitudes, and Tai peoples live in the valleys and plains.

Historically, it is believed that speakers of Mon-Khmer languages inhabited the favourable inland areas as far back as 4,000 years ago. Around 2,000 years ago, the ancestors of the Tai-speaking peoples began to separate and disperse from present-day southern China, probably under pressure from the northern Han Chinese, who were extending southwards over the same period. The expansion of the Tai people initially followed the river valleys, establishing a pattern of lowland settlement which persists to this day. Around 1,000 years ago, a snapshot of the region would have shown rural Tai peoples surrounded by several great empires of the Mon-Khmer stock, including the Mon kingdom of Burma, the Khmer empire of Angkor (centred on present-day Cambodia), and a Vietnamese state (centred on present-day northern Vietnam), which was under heavy influence from China. In southern Vietnam there was the once powerful Cham empire, whose people spoke Austronesian languages.

Over the next few centuries, the Tai-speaking population swelled greatly, due to mass migration in the wake of the Mongol invasion of southern China; and this lead to a shift in the overall ethnic composition of Southeast Asia. The Khmer empire of Angkor declined, and the river plains of present-day Laos and Thailand saw the growth of several Tai kingdoms, heavily influenced by the culture and society of their Khmer precursors. Many Mon-Khmer groups apparently underwent language shift and adopted Tai languages. In the mid-fourteenth century, the great Tai kingdom of Ayutthaya (Ayudhya) was founded in central Thailand, which was to hold sway for the next four centuries. To the west, in present-day Myanmar (Burma), the Mon-Khmer ascendancy, which had peaked with the Mon empire, was brought to an end by Tibeto-Burman peoples moving down the river valleys. First came the Pyu, who in turn were supplanted by the Burmans. The Pyu language is now extinct, and Mon survives in a small pocket in eastern Burma. In this millennium-long saga of the rise and fall of kingdoms, and power struggles between states large and small, warfare played a great part. The recurrent wars between the Thai and the Burmese, or between the Thai and the Vietnamese, were waged with large conscripted armies and elephant corps. The name of the old central Lao kingdom, Lãn Xãng, literally 'million elephants', was itself a claim to military power (Stuart-Fox 1997: 11).

As for the Hmong-Mien peoples, until about 150 years ago they were located solely in what is now southwestern China. Their recent history is not well known, but they were always minority peoples, under the domination of the more numerous and more powerful Han Chinese.

Western powers intruded into Southeast Asia militarily in the nineteenth century. By the beginning of the First World War most of the region was under Western colonial rule. Myanmar and Malaya were under British control while France ruled over the rest of mainland Southeast Asia, except for Thailand, which alone remained independent. Even Thailand lost some of its territories, notably present-day Laos, which became part of French Indochina. In insular Southeast Asia, the East Indies (present-day Indonesia) was ruled by the Dutch, the Philippines by the United States (which had replaced Spain), and East Timor by Portugal. The modern-day map of Southeast Asia, with its nation states and borders, was not drawn up until after the Second World War.

2.4 Language situations

This section gives a general overview of the language situations in the countries covered in this book. It is broken into four regions—insular Southeast Asia, mainland Southeast Asia, China, and Japan and Korea. It is impossible to give a full overview of sociolinguistic and language policy situations, which vary greatly from country to country. Summary information is given in Tables 2.2–2.5, using language data from the Ethnologue website and population data from the United Nations population website. Except where otherwise indicated, most of the other information is drawn from *The Encyclopedia of Languages and Linguistics* (Asher and Simpson 1994).

2.4.1 Insular Southeast Asia

Indonesia. With its vast swathe of islands, Indonesia has a huge number of regional vernacular languages. The national language is Bahasa Indonesia. Indonesia was formerly a Dutch colony, gaining independence (after armed struggle) in 1945 in the wake of the Second World War. Since the borders of the new nation were effectively those of the old colonial regime, the new nation brought together numerous different societies which had not previously been part of any single political unit.

By far the largest regional language in Indonesia is Javanese (75 million speakers), but the nationalist movement deliberately chose not to impose this or any other ethnic language as the national language (Sneddon 2003). Instead they installed a modified version of Malay, which had long functioned as a trade lingua franca across the archipelago. At the time of independence, Bahasa Indonesia was the mother tongue of only a small fraction of the population, but since then it has been successfully established as a genuine national language in a linguistically pluralist society. The Indonesian constitution recognizes the place of "regional languages", and early primary school education can be carried out in a local vernacular, so long as Bahasa Indonesia is taught simultaneously. There is widespread diglossia, i.e. stable bilingualism with different languages being used for different purposes.

There are significant differences between the big island populations and languages of the western side of the country, e.g. Javanese, Sundanese (30 million), Madurese (13.5 million), Minangkabau (8.5 million), and the

Table 2.2. Languages of insular Southeast Asia

Country	National or official languages	No. of languages	Other major languages spoken[a] or languages of business/ education	Sample of indigenous and/or minority languages
Brunei 358,000	Bahasa Melayu, English	17	Chinese: Mandarin, Min Nan, Min Dong, Yue, Hakka; Brunei Malay, English	Dusun, Tutung, Belait, Bisaya, Murut
East Timor 997,853[b]	Tetum (Tetun), Portuguese	19	Mambae, Makasae, Bahasa Indonesia	Bunak, Kemak, Galoli, Tukudede
Indonesia[c] 219,883,000	Bahasa Indonesia	463[c]	Javanese, Sundanese, Madurese, Minangkabau, Balinese, Buginese, Acehnese	Banjarese, Betawi, Toba Batak, Sasak, Macassarese
Malaysia 24,425,000	Bahasa Melayu	136	Chinese Min Nan, Tamil, Chinese: Hakka, Yue, Mandarin; English	Banjar, Iban, Temiar, Semai
Philippines 79,999,000	Pilipino, English	168	Tagalog, Cebuano, Ilocano, Hiligaynon	Bikol, Waray-Waray, Pampangan, Pangasinan, Magindanaon
Singapore 4,253,000	Bahasa Melayu, Chinese Mandarin (Huayu), Tamil, English	20	Chinese: Min Nan, Yue	

[a] With speakers numbering over 3m. or representing over 5% of the population.
[b] July 2003 est. from *The World Factbook*; other estimates range as low as 800,000.
[c] For the purposes of this table, Papua has not been included in the statistics for Indonesia.

myriad small languages of the eastern side, many of which have only a few thousand, or even a few hundred, speakers. There are several hundred languages in Indonesia's westernmost province of Papua (formerly known as Irian Jaya). Many of them are non-Austronesian, in which case they are referred to generically as "Papuan" (a misleading term, because they belong to multiple different language families). This region is outside the coverage of this book. Some non-Austronesian "Papuan" languages are also found in the Moluccas and in West Timor.

There are some 2 million Chinese Indonesians scattered over the islands, many of whom speak various Sinitic languages, but this number doesn't show up in Table 2.2 in view of the huge overall population.

East Timor. The newest and smallest nation in Southeast Asia, East Timor has a dozen Austronesian languages and a smaller number of "Papuan" languages. For over two hundred years East Timor was under the colonial rule of Portugal, then from 1975 it was under the control of Indonesia, until independence was achieved in 1999. The official languages are Tetum (sometimes spelt Tetun) and Portuguese—though at present, the latter is known mainly by educated people. Indonesian is widely known and still used in the media, but it is being phased out as the medium of instruction in schools. Tetum exists in two varieties: Tetun Dili, which is spoken as a first language in the capital Dili and which shows heavy influence of Portuguese, and a more conservative rural dialect Tetun Terik. Language policy, including the ongoing standardization of Tetum, is discussed in Hajek (2000).

Malaysia. The modern state of Malaysia achieved independence (initially as the Federation of Malaya) in 1957 by agreement with the departing British colonialists. Present-day Malaysia consists of peninsula Malaysia on the western side, and East Malaysian states of Sarawak and Sabah on the island of Borneo. The two sides of the country are very different. The national language is now known as Bahasa Melayu, though for most of the time since independence it was called Bahasa Malaysia to emphasize its national scope. This was deemed necessary on account of the existence of large non-Malay populations (ethnic Chinese and Indians) whose forebears were brought into the country over the colonial period. There is a lot of dialect variation in spoken Malay. On purely linguistic criteria the most divergent dialect, spoken in Kelantan state, could qualify as a separate language.

Mandarin and Tamil are permitted as languages of instruction in certain schools. There are also some Arabic-medium schools. Malaysian TV airs programmes in Malay, Mandarin, Tamil, and English. English also has a major presence in the professions, business, and academic life, and functions to some extent as an alternative language of national solidarity. A high-profile national language-planning institute endeavours to ensure that Malay remains the high-status language.

In the mountainous interior of peninsular Malaysia, a dozen or so indigenous Aslian languages of Mon-Khmer stock are spoken. There are numerous small Austronesian languages in East Malaysia (Asmah 1983), the most prominent being Iban.

Brunei Darussalam. This tiny sultanate, located in Borneo in between the Malaysian states of Sarah and Sarawak, is like a mini-Malaysia in language terms (see Table 2.2).

Singapore. The quintessential modern city state, the population of Singapore is predominantly ethnic Chinese, but with a substantial Malay minority and a smaller Indian minority. Singapore was part of the Federation of Malaya for some years before seceding in 1965. For symbolic reasons, Malay is the national language of Singapore, but English (including Singapore English or Singlish) and Mandarin are the most important official languages. Tamil is also recognized as an official language, making four official languages in all. The main medium of instruction in schools is English, with a second official language being used for some subjects.

Philippines. The standardized national language (proclaimed in 1937) is Pilipino (also spelt Filipino). It is based on Tagalog, which is native to the southern part of the island of Luzon. English is also an official language, with a range of functions in the media, science and technology, government and business. The vocabulary of Manila Tagalog has many loans from Spanish and English, reflecting 300 years of colonial rule by Spain, followed by fifty years of American occupation prior to independence in 1946. There are eight major regional languages with a million or more speakers (the largest Cebuano and Ilocano, with 19 million and 8.5 million speakers, respectively), and more than 150 smaller local vernaculars. The sheer number of languages is impressive, and surprisingly enough, most of them are not under immediate threat. This is not due to direct government support, but rather to widespread bilingualism (or trilingualism) coupled with a strong sense of local ethnic pride, i.e. diglossia (Quakenbush 1998: 8). Code-switching (colloquially *halo-halo* 'mix-mix') is common.

2.4.2 Mainland Southeast Asia

Myanmar (Burma). Burmese is the national language of Myanmar (Burma). Traditionally, the ethnic Burmese lived mostly in the large central plain drained by the Irrawaddy River. Presumably because of the ease of communication in this environment, the language of this region is fairly uniform. Divergent dialects (sometimes regarded as separate languages) are found in peripheral areas, such as Arakan to the west. There are significant ethnic minorities speaking Karen, Shan, Mon, and Kachin, and a large number of smaller minority languages, all mostly found in the hills and mountains. Prior to independence in 1948, Britain was the colonial power. English still has a significant role in university education and aspects of public life. Minority languages have an ambivalent status in Myanmar (Burma) on account of the fact that many minority groups are involved in resistance or insurgency against the military regime, which seized power in 1988.

Thailand. Thai people generally pride themselves on being the only country in Southeast Asia which has not been under the domination of a colonial power. They have a strong sense of national unity under the king, and the Buddhist religion. Thailand has an unusual sociolinguistic situation

Table 2.3. Languages of mainland Southeast Asia

Country	National or official languages	No. of languages	Other major languages spoken[a] or languages of business/education	Sample of indigenous and/or minority languages
Cambodia 14,144,000	Central Khmer	19	Vietnamese, Chinese Mandarin, English	Western Cham, Jarai, Tampuan, Central Mnong, Kuy
Laos 5,657,000	Lao	82	Mon Khmer: Khmu, Sô	Phu Thai, Hmong Njua, Bru, Lü, Phuan, Kataang
Myanmar (Burma) 49,485,000	Burmese	107	Shan, Karen: S'gaw, Eastern Pwo, Pa'o, English	Arakanese, Yangbye, Jingpho, Mon, Chin, Vo, Akha
Thailand 62,833,000	Thai 50 minority languages	72	Isan (Northeastern Thai), Lanna (Northern Thai), Pak Tai (Southern Thai), Pattani Malay, Chinese Min Nan, English	Shan, Karen languages, Hmong, Lahu, Akha, Mien, Lisu, Khmu
Vietnam 81,377,000	Vietnamese 54 official ethnic minorities	93	Tày, Thai	Muong, Central Khmer, Nung, Hmong Daw, Tai Dam, Mien

[a] With speakers numbering over 3m. or representing over 5% of the population.

(Smalley 1994). On linguistic criteria, there are four major regional languages, but Thais themselves downplay the differences and regard them all as "varieties of Thai". Only about 25 per cent of the population natively speaks "Standard Thai", which is based on the central dialect. The northeastern dialect is actually the same language as spoken in Laos. There are speakers of Malay (Pattani Malay) in the south, who also follow the Islamic religion. Though English has virtually no native speakers, it plays a major role as a language of external communication and in higher education. There is a form of Thai English with pronunciation and grammar heavily influenced by Thai.

There are many so-called "hill tribes" languages in Thailand (Hmong-Mien, Tibeto-Burman, and Tai-Kadai families), but this label conceals the diversity of situations. Some of these populations, such as the Hmong, Mien, Lahu, and Akha, are immigrants from the past hundred or so years, and others, such as the S'gaw and the Phlong, are displaced people from neighbouring Myanmar (Burma).

Cambodia. The national language of Cambodia is Khmer, and it is the native language of about 90 per cent of the population. Of the indigenous minorities, the largest are the Cham, whose numbers have been estimated to up to 200,000. Smaller minorities mostly speak Mon-Khmer languages. There are substantial Chinese and Vietnamese immigrant communities, numbering altogether more than 1.7 million. Cambodian society was devastated by the Khmer Rouge regime (1975–9), and in many ways is still recovering. The main foreign languages today are English and Thai, reflecting contact and influence with the wider world and with the country's most prosperous neighbour, respectively.

Laos. A landlocked country, Laos is the smallest nation in mainland Southeast Asia. The national language, Lao, is essentially unstandardized (Enfield 2000*a*), though the pronunciation of the capital Vientiane is widely understood and used in the national level media. Paradoxically, the majority of the Lao-speaking population is located in northeast Thailand, the legacy of a treaty between the former colonial power France and Thailand, signed in 1893. Most Laos can understand spoken Thai (Central Thai) which they receive in popular radio and TV shows.

There are numerous ethnic minorities in Lao, many speaking small Mon-Khmer languages, which are said to number about fifty. This makes Laos, despite its small size, the country which hosts more Mon-Khmer languages than any other. Tai languages and Hmong-Mien languages are also amply represented.

Vietnam. Like neighbouring countries, Vietnam has a great diversity of languages, but the national language, Vietnamese, is spoken by the great majority of the population and is clearly dominant. Sociolinguistically, one can say that Vietnam is more homogeneous than most Southeast Asian countries. Minority ethnic groups are recognized by the constitution, including the right to mother tongue education, but the potentially positive effects of this policy are outweighed by government programmes to move and resettle indigenous minorities away from the highlands. French, the language of colonial power prior to the Second World War, still has a certain profile in the country, but the foreign language in greatest demand today is English. A large number of Vietnamese, upwards of 1.5 million, left their country after the fall of South Vietnam in 1975 and resettled in North America, Australia, Europe, and other countries.

2.4.3 China

China. The national language of China is Putonghua (Modern Standard Chinese), a standardized version of the Beijing dialect of Mandarin

Table 2.4. Languages of China

Country	National or official languages	No. of languages	Other major languages spoken[a] or languages of business/education	Sample of indigenous and/or minority languages
China (Mainland) 1,311,709,000	Modern Standard Chinese (Mandarin, Putonghua)	200	Chinese: Wu, Yue, Jinyu, Xiang, Min Nan, Hakka, Gan, Min Bei; Zhuang, Uighur, Yi, Mongolian	Tibetan, Li, Be
Taiwan	Chinese Mandarin (Guoyu)	21	Chinese: Min Nan, Hakka	Kaoshan languages, e.g. Amis, Atayal, Paiwan, Bunun, Taroko

[a] With speakers numbering over 3m. or representing over 5% of the population.

Chinese. As described earlier, there are hundreds of other regional languages spoken in China, normally referred to as dialects or dialect groups. Since the founding of the People's Republic of China in 1949, knowledge and use of Putonghua has been successfully promoted across the country by a range of government measures, especially in education. Most of the population are able to speak the language, and an even greater percentage, perhaps as many as 90 per cent, can understand it (Chen 1999: 27–30).

There are more than fifty-five officially recognized minority nationalities, speaking scores of languages of the Tibeto-Burman, Tai, and Hmong-Mien families in the south, and the Altaic family in the north (Ramsey 1987: chs. 10 and 11; Blum 2002). In geographical terms the most widespread are Uighur/Uyghur, Mongolian, and Tibetan, but these lie outside the geographical area covered by this book. The greatest degree of linguistic diversity is in the south and southwest in the provinces of Guangxi, Guizhou, and Yunnan. Population-wise, the largest non-Sinitic language is Zhuang (Tai), mainly in Guangxi province, where it has some official functions. Rather confusingly, there is no one-to-one match between ethnic nationality names and language names; for example, the nationality identified as Yi contains speakers of several distinct languages (including, notably, Lolo). Under the Chinese constitution the national minorities all have "the freedom to use and develop their own spoken and written languages", but in practice official support mostly goes to the larger minorities.

Taiwan has two major Sinitic languages: the national language, Modern Standard Chinese (termed Guoyu in Taiwan), and a form of Southern Min, sometimes called Taiwanese. The latter enjoys minimal official support but is the mother tongue of two-thirds of the population. Hakka (Kejia) is spoken by about 10 per cent of the population. Taiwan retains an older form of Chinese script, having not adopted the character simplifications of the People's Republic of China (see section 6.3.4).

In the mountainous central and eastern parts of the island (Formosa), there are a dozen or so indigenous Austronesian languages, usually termed Kaoshan or simply Formosan languages.

2.4.4 Korea and Japan

Korea. Historically the Korean peninsula was a united political entity for many hundreds of years, but after the Second World War it was divided into two countries. Relationships between the North (People's Democratic Republic) and the South (Republic of Korea) have always been tense and hostile, peaking in the terrible Korean War, which ended in 1953 (technically by a ceasefire rather than a peace settlement). Both countries are relatively linguistically homogeneous, with no linguistic minorities of significant size. The two governments have different language policies, with the North taking an ambitious and intrusive "purification" policy intolerant of Chinese and other non-native words.

Japan. There is a great deal of dialect variation in mountainous mainland Japan, with the main division being between western and eastern groups

Table 2.5. Languages of Japan and Korea

Country	National or official languages	No. of languages	Other major languages spoken[a] or languages of business/education	Sample of indigenous and/or minority languages
Japan 127,654,000	Japanese (Nihongo)	14	English	Ainu, Ryukyuan languages, e.g. Okinawan; Chinese Mandarin, Korean
Korea, North 26,000,000	Korean	1		
Korea, South 47,700,000	Korean	1	English (education)	

[a] With speakers numbering over 3m. or representing over 5% of the population.

centred on Kyoto (the ancient capital) and Tokyo (the modern capital). A sense of linguistic unification is provided by the common and standard language (*kokugo* 'national language', *hyoojungo* 'standard language'), used in the media and in tertiary education. Ethnic Koreans are a notable linguistic minority, and varieties of Chinese (principally Mandarin Chinese) are spoken by significant numbers. English is widely studied in secondary and tertiary education. English has a continuing influence on modern Japanese (cf. Loveday 1996).

The Ainu language was once widely spoken on the northern island of Hokkaidō and the northern part of Honshu. It is no longer in daily use, though it still has various community-level and cultural functions.

Ryukyuan dialects are spoken along the island chain extending from the south of "mainland" Japan southwest almost down to Taiwan. The best-known is the language of Okinawa, sometimes called Shuri. On linguistic criteria, it is a distinct language from Japanese. Over a million people live on Okinawa and nearby islands, which are still heavily influenced by the ongoing American military presence.

Key technical terms

Austronesian	linguistic area
genetic relationship	Mon-Khmer
Hmong-Mien	Sinitic
language family	Tai-Kadai
language isolate	Tibeto-Burman

CHAPTER 3

Words: origins, structures, meanings

In this chapter we look at the vocabulary of East and Southeast Asian languages. First we see how the lexicon reflects the cultural history of speech communities, through its stock of words borrowed over the centuries from other languages. Then we will turn to the internal structure of words, i.e. to the area of study linguists call morphology. In the second part of the chapter we look at words from a different angle—as the bearers of meanings which may be language-specific and culture-specific. We survey some of the distinctive meanings and meaning patterns in East and Southeast Asian languages, then examine some of the cultural key words of Malay, Chinese, and Japanese.

3.1 Loans as indicators of cultural history

One interesting aspect of the vocabulary of any language emerges when we ask the question: Where have the words come from? Most languages have not only "native" or indigenous words, i.e. words which have been inherited from ancestral forms of the language, but also many so-called loan words, i.e. words which have entered the language from other languages. Loan words are linguistic echos of past cultural contact, and the nature of the loan words can tell us much about the nature of that contact. To get an idea of the kind of factors which can be involved it is helpful briefly to review the English language from this point of view.

3.1.1 A short history of English loan words

As much as three-fifths of the English lexicon consists of words originally borrowed from other languages. Some of the oldest go back to the ninth and tenth centuries when Scandinavian settlers lived in parts of Britain. Their way of life was similar to that of the Anglo-Saxons, and their language, Old Norse, was similar to that of the Anglo-Saxons. Many words for ordinary objects and actions entered English over this period—words like *gift, root, skin, low, happy, die, get, hit, take*, and *want*. They have been so thoroughly indigenized, i.e. adapted to the pronunciation and usage patterns of the native language, that modern-day speakers have no idea of their origin.

A larger swag of loans entered the English language after England was conquered by a French king in 1066 (the Norman Conquest). For three centuries the Normans ruled England, and French was the language of the court and the upper classes. Ordinary people continued to speak varieties of English in the home, but government and commerce, higher learning, and the law were all conducted in French. Not surprisingly, many loans from this period concern government, including *country, crown, nation, parliament, people, prince, royal, state*, and of course, *government* itself. Others concern legal and military matters, e.g. *court, crime, judge, jury, army, navy, war*. Long after French speakers lost their socially dominant position in England, the prestige of French endured, encouraging later writers to exploit the scholarly vocabulary of French. This trend intensified after the introduction of the printing press in England in the late 1400s. Many learned words borrowed from French had Latin or Greek origins (so we say that they were borrowed into English from Latin and Greek indirectly, via French). Latin had, of course, been the common language of learning and scholarship across the whole of Europe in the Middle Ages. As well as numerous Latin loan words (e.g. *bonus, describe, exit, scientific*), the English language acquired some productive prefixes and suffixes, such as the prefix *ex-* (as in *ex-wife*) and the suffix *-able/-ible* (as in *legible, movable, answerable*).

In recent centuries as the British expanded across the globe, sundry loans for exotic items joined the English language: *pony, potato, tobacco*, and *tomato* from American Indian languages, *coffee* from Arabic (via Turkish), *sushi* from Japanese, and so on. But generally speaking, as the English-speaking peoples have grown in power, the rate of borrowing into English has slowed. These days words are more often borrowed from English, than into English.

It's clear, isn't it, that loan words can tell a story about cultural history? Another point about borrowing which can also be illustrated from English is that despite the tendency to phonological adaptation, loan words occasionally keep some of the phonological baggage they bring with them, and so change the phonology of the borrowing language. English gained the phoneme /v/ as a result of French loans in the Norman period. In Old English the sound [v] had been a pronunciation variant (an allophone) of the phoneme /f/ (pairs like *leaf–leaves* and *wife–wives* linger on to this day). When French words with [v] in initial position, like *veal*, entered the language, it brought about a direct contrast between the f-sound and the v-sound, which caused /v/ to become an independent phoneme. Sometimes a whole set of loans survives as a distinct layer or lexical stratum in the vocabulary—a kind of lexical "suburb" inside which certain rules and processes apply (or don't apply), unlike in the rest of the lexicon. This is the case in the Latinate vocabulary of English, i.e. words which have been borrowed, directly or indirectly, from Latin. We will come back to these phonological topics in Chapter 5.

In the remainder of this section we will survey the loan vocabulary of the major national languages of Southeast Asia and East Asia from a cultural and historical point of view.

3.1.2 Malay: Malaysian and Indonesian

The geographical region which is present-day Indonesia and Malaysia occupies a strategic crossroads between South Asia (India) and East Asia (China). The straits separating Sumatra from the Malay Peninsula have been an important maritime trade route for thousands of years, and Malay has been a trade lingua franca for many centuries. The oldest loans into Malay date from the period of Indic influence, which lasted from about the second century BC till about the ninth century AD. Over this period many cultural traditions from India (such as the concept of kingship) were incorporated into the local cultures. Some parts of Southeast Asia, such as the island of Bali, remain strongly influenced by Hinduism to this day. But although an echo of early Indian influence remains in most of the cultures of Indonesia and Malaysia, the dominant religion is Islam, which was introduced in the 1400s by Arab traders and scholars. Not surprisingly, therefore, the main source of loans in Malay and related languages are Sanskrit (the high language of classical Indian culture) and Arabic (the language of the Koran/Qur'ān). Many of the oldest loans are so thoroughly indigenized that speakers are unaware of their origins (unless they learn about it in formal education). They include many common basic words, such as *rasa* 'feel, taste', *malas* 'lazy, disinclined', *guru* 'teacher', and *nama* 'name, reputation' (from Sanskrit), and *fikir* 'think' and *lihat* 'see' (from Arabic).

Some other examples of loan words in Malay are listed in Table 3.1 (cf. Sneddon 2003: 46–8, 75–6). One can discern a tendency for words to do with government and administration to originate in Sanskrit, and an even clearer tendency for religious and legal terms to come from Arabic; but there are counter-examples in both directions, and there is a miscellany of terms

Table 3.1. Sanskrit and Arabic loan words in Malay

Sanskrit origin		Arabic origin	
raja	'ruler, king'	*adat*	'customs, rules for living'
cuaca	'weather'	*nikah*	'marriage ceremony'
ketika	'period of time'	*haram*	'forbidden'
dara	'maiden'	*rezeki*	'livelihood, good fortune'
denda	'fine'	*khalwat*	'illicit sexual liaison'
dosa	'sin'	*khemah*	'tent'
gua	'cave'	*daftar*	'list, register'
mula	'begin'	*doa*	'prayer'
penjara	'prison'	*jawab*	'answer'
rugi	'loss'	*sabun*	'soap'
rupa	'looks, appearance'	*musim*	'season'

for concrete objects from both languages. It is noticeable that the Sanskrit loans (being older) are usually more thoroughly indigenized than the Arabic ones. Many Arabic loans still betray their origins in their phonology (e.g. presence of fricatives) or spelling (especially the digraph *kh*, intended to designate the Arabic phoneme /x/, which has no counterpart in Malay).

European influence in the Malay world intensified after the fall of Malacca to the Portuguese in 1511. Loans from Portuguese include *gereja* 'church', *garpu* 'fork', *almari* 'cupboard', *meja* 'table', and *kemeja* 'shirt'. There are also a smattering of loans from Dutch, e.g. *senapang* 'gun' and *pelakat* 'gum'. Non-European languages such as Tamil and Chinese have contributed some words; for example, *percuma* 'free of charge', *kedai* 'shop', *mangga* 'mango', and *katil* 'bed' from Tamil, and *teh* 'tea' and *mi* 'noodles' from Chinese (Asmah 1975: 37–8). Some have been indirect, coming via the Indian English of the colonial period; for example, *kari* 'curry' from Tamil and *dobi* 'laundry' from Hindustani (Hogue 2001). We should not forget either that many words in present-day Indonesian and Malaysian have come from closely related languages such as Javanese, and are now indistinguishable from ancestral Malay words.

The loan vocabularies of Indonesian (Bahasa Indonesia) and Malaysian (Bahasa Melayu) bear the stamp of recent history. Before they gained independence (in 1945 and 1957, respectively), Indonesia was a Dutch colony and Malaysia a British colony. So Indonesian has many loans from Dutch, whereas Malaysian has many loans from English. Sometimes Indonesian and Malaysian have borrowed words for the very same items from their respective donor languages. Some examples are given in Table 3.2 (cf. Sneddon 2003: 12).

Many loans from the colonial period are for tools, machinery, and bureaucratic items. More recently, both languages have seen thousands of

Table 3.2. Parallel loans from Dutch and English in Indonesian and Malaysian

Dutch loans in Indonesian		English loans in Malaysian	
sepeda	'bicycle' (<*velocipede*)	*basikal*	'bicycle'
mesin	'engine' (in Malaysian 'machine')	*injin*	'engine'
rem	'brake' (<*remmer*)	*brek*	'brake'
ban	'tyre' (<*band*)	*tayar*	'tyre'
dongkerak	'jack'	*jek*	'jack'
fototustel	'camera'(<*fototoestel*)	*kamera*	'camera'
kantor	'office'	*ofis*	'office' (also *pejabat*)
ketik	'type' (<*tikken*)	*taip*	'type' (i.e. on a typewriter)
karcis	'ticket' (<*kaartjes* (pl.))	*tiket*	'ticket'
rok	'skirt'		

new loans from English, in two main categories. In the first category are scientific, technical, and sophisticated "modern" terms. Examples (from Malaysian) include: *prinsip* 'principle', *inflasi* 'inflation', *demokrasi* 'democracy', *sistem* 'system', and *fungsi* 'function'. Often the adoption of words of this type is regulated or facilitated by official language planning bodies. In the second category are colloquial words absorbed through the Western media and "youth culture". For example: *imej* 'image', *filem* 'film', *frus* 'fed-up' (from 'frustrated'), *member* 'friend'. Aside from the impressive numbers of loans, the influence of English is also found (less obviously) in the existence of calques (i.e. literal translations of foreign expressions) and semantic extensions of Malay terms under English influence (Heah 1989).

3.1.3 Mainland Southeast Asia

Most of mainland Southeast Asia can be seen as belonging to a particular kind of Buddhist civilization (Theravada Buddhism) which has developed from a blend of local cultures under long-standing influence from India (which included Hinduism as well as Buddhism). This generalization applies to Myanmar (Burma), Thailand, Laos, and Cambodia. One reflex of this influence is the fact that the national scripts for all these languages are based, one way or another, on ancient Indic scripts (see Chapter 6). With all these cultural influences came many hundreds of loan words. The learned vocabulary of Burmese, Thai, Lao, and Khmer consists substantially of words from the ancient Indian languages Sanskrit and Pali (which, along with other ancient Indian sources, are referred to collectively as "Indic"). When there are both Indic and indigenous words with the same, or similar, meanings, the Indic words have a more formal or literary flavour. They

Table 3.3. Parallel Indic and native Thai words

Indic	Native Thai	
sĭisà'	*hŭa*	'head'
sawš̌əy	*kin*	'eat'
banthaw	*lút*	'alleviate'
patibàt	*tham*	'do'
sunák	*mǎa*	'dog'
sadèt	*pay*	'go'
sukɔɔn	*mǔu*	'pig'
phranêet	*taa*	'eye'

constitute a distinct lexical stratum. Some examples from Thai are listed in Table 3.3. Notice that the Indic borrowings are disyllabic while the native Thai words are monosyllabic.

Recently, new words have been coined from Indic vocabulary elements to meet the need for modern technical terminology. Many are calques patterned on Western prototypes. For example, *thoola²* is Indic for 'far'. In Lao, it is found in *thoola²that¹* 'television', *thoola²sap²* 'telephone', and *thoola²saan³* 'telex'. The parallel with English *tele-* (from Greek *tēle* 'far off') is striking. The second element in *thoola²that¹* 'television' is Indic *that¹* 'vision, sight', found also in *culathat¹* 'microscope'. Other examples of Lao neologisms are *qeeka⁵laat⁴* 'independence, sovereignty' and *qeeka⁵phaap⁴*. The first element *qeeka⁵* is Indic for 'one'; *laat⁴* (from *raja*) is Indic for 'kingdom' and *phaap⁴* for 'state, condition'. If we take both kinds of Indic terminology together, up to half the entries in a standard Thai dictionary could be regarded as Indic.

In the heartland of Southeast Asia, where numerous Mon-Khmer languages and Tai-Kadai languages have been in close contact for hundreds of years (cf. section 2.3), there has been extensive borrowing, in multiple directions, across all areas of the lexicon—so much so that it can be difficult to distinguish between native and borrowed words. For example, Stieng, a minority Mon-Khmer language of southern Vietnam and eastern Cambodia, includes the following loans from Khmer (Sidwell 2000: 9–10): *hɔɯ* 'already' (from Khmer *haəj*), *dɯɔi* 'also' (from Khmer *daə*), *lɯɔk* 'to lift' (from Khmer *lə:k*), *sɔ-ɔt* 'sticky' (from Khmer *sʔət*). Many of the (non-Indic) disyllabic words of Thai are old indigenized loans from Khmer and Mon.

Although we began this section by saying that the Indian-influenced Buddhist civilization was a dominant influence across most of mainland Southeast Asia, this is not the whole story. The other main source of external influence was from the north—from China. Many Chinese loans into Thai, Lao, and Vietnamese date back a thousand years. They are now so well assimilated that some of the identifications are controversial. (Loan influence may also have operated in the opposite direction, so that the Sinitic languages in the south of China have a Tai substrate.) Examples include number terms, classifiers, several hundred basic nouns and verbs, and a few common adverbs. For example, the following are Lao loans from Chinese: kaw^4 'nine', sip^2 'ten', cia^4 'paper', $ñin^4$ 'hear', *qaan* 'saddle, seat (of bike)', toq^2 'table', $ngen^2$ 'money, silver', $kham^2$ 'gold', $bòò^1$ 'not'. Chinese influence is even more pronounced on Vietnamese (see below).

Generally speaking, loan words from European languages are more recent and less common in mainland Southeast Asia than in Indonesia and Malaysia. In the case of Thailand, one could be tempted to put this down to the fact that the country is the only one in the region which has never been ruled by a colonial power; but Lao and Vietnamese also have relatively few European loans, even though both countries were formerly ruled by the French. Perhaps a certain linguistic traditionalism can be regarded as part of the "language culture" of mainland Southeast Asia. Among recent loans from English we can number Thai words like: *fέεk* 'fax', *mɔɔtəəsay* 'motorcycle', *séksii* 'sexy', *'èppên* 'apple', *'oovôə* 'excessive' (< 'over'), *kee* 'gay', *thiiwii* 'TV', and *sɔɔphraay* 'surprise'. Words like these are often avoided in formal speech and writing, but they are common in commerce, journalism, and entertainment, and in colloquial urban speech.

3.1.4 The influence of China

As one would expect, the language of the Chinese empire has had a massive and enduring influence on the other Sinitic languages, the so-called "dialects". It is an influence which goes beyond the huge numbers of loan words, extending also into grammar and phonology. To the south of China, the language most heavily influenced by Chinese is probably Vietnamese. The Vietnam region was under direct Chinese administration for 1,000 years, from 111 BC to 939 AD. Modern Vietnamese has many thousands of old Chinese loans.

Chinese influence on Korean and Japanese is ancient and pervasive. Chinese civilization was already influential in the first millennium. One historic date is 552 AD, in which Buddhism was officially adopted by the Yamato court of central Japan. Over the succeeding centuries, Japanese borrowed not only religious terminology but also terms in the areas of government, the arts, architecture, music, medicine, animals and plants, clothing, and food. There were renewed waves of Chinese influence at different periods of Japanese history. Some examples are given in Table 3.4. As much as one-half of Japanese vocabulary originates with Chinese, chiefly from the dialect of present-day Xian (the old capital of the Tang Dynasty) and from the Wu dialect in the south.

Table 3.4. Japanese loan words from Old Chinese (from Inoue 1979: 244)

Meaning	Japanese	Old Chinese
'grave'	haka	hak
'silk'	kinu	kin
'horse'	uma	ma
'wheat'	mugi	muk
'cedar tree'	sugi	sung
'to sharpen'	togu	tak
'picture'	e	we
'nun'	ama	amba (orig. from Sanskrit)
'Buddha'	Shaka	sâkya (orig. from Sanskrit)
'bowl'	hachi	pâtra (orig. from Sanskrit)
'temple'	tera	thera (orig. from Pali)

Many of the Chinese loan words are so thoroughly indigenized that they are indistinguishable from genetically Japanese words, but many others constitute a distinct stratum. Most of the Sino-Japanese (S-J) stratum consists of bound forms, which appear compounded with other S-J forms, in a great number of technical and learned terms (see section 3.2). A further stratum in Japanese are the so-called Foreign (i.e. non-Chinese) loans. These have come from many sources. In the mid-1500s Portuguese traders and missionaries established a base in Japan. Sakai (modern Osaka) became a commercial and industrial centre, and the Christian religion gained a foothold. Over the sixteenth and seventeenth centuries Japanese borrowed words from Portuguese. In the eighteenth century, various Dutch loan words entered Japan, mainly through technical books on the Western sciences. In the nineteenth century, Western influence intensified as Japan modernized itself under the Meiji Restoration, and this influence continued in the twentieth century, especially in the period after the Second World War, which saw Japan become one of the world's leading industrial and technological nations. Table 3.5 gives some loan words from English and other European languages.

Loan words are flooding into contemporary Japanese, particularly in areas of life such as fashion, cosmetics, food, audio technology, sport, housing, music, art, business management, computers, and engineering. Aside from "straight" loans (with a greater or lesser degree of phonological adaption), one also finds hybrids of European and Japanese (usually Sino-Japanese) bases, e.g. *ichigo-ēdo* Japanese 'strawberry' + English *-ade*. There are also novel compounds using European elements, such as *sukinshippu* (<*skin* + *ship*) denoting 'intimate, physical closeness', and *wan-man-kaa* (<*one* + *man* + *car*) 'bus without a conductor'. For a fascinating book-length treatment, with an emphasis on sociolinguistic and cultural aspects, see Loveday (1996).

Table 3.5. Foreign (non-Chinese) loans in Japanese

Meaning	Japanese	Source	
'a deep-fried dish'	*tempura*	Portugese	*tempero*
'glass'	*garasu*	Dutch	*glas*
'cook'	*kokku*	Dutch	*kok*
'paint'	*penki*	Dutch	*pek*
'artist's studio'	*atorie*	French	*atelier*
'rope'	*zairu*	German	*seil*
'meter'	*meetoru*	French	*mètre*
'gasoline'	*gasorin*	English	*gasoline*
'salary'	*sararii*	English	*salary*
'typewriter'	*taipuraitaa*	English	*typewriter*
'television'	*terebi*	English	*TV*
'supermarket'	*suupaa*	English	*supermarket*
'hunger strike'	*han-suto*	English (with truncation)	*hunger strike*

Foreign loans often exist for items or concepts which apparently already have native Japanese words, but closer inspection shows that the meaning of the loan word designates a more "modern" or Western perspective. For example, *raisu* 'rice' is cooked rice served on a flat, Western-style dinner plate rather than in a bowl; *uedingu* 'wedding' does not refer to the traditional Shinto wedding but to the Western-style reception afterwards, complete with white wedding dress and wedding cake; and *beddo* 'bed' refers to a Western-style bed as opposed to the quilted bedding futon. Even a word like *rabu* (<love) differs in meaning from its nearest native Japanese counterparts *ai* 'love' and *koi* 'passion'. *Rabu* is used only in compounds which refer to physical intimacy, so that in effect it is a euphemism for sex; for example, *rabu hoteru* (<love hotel) 'rooms rented to couples', and *rabu shiin* 'love scene'.

This completes our treatment of loan words in the languages of East and Southeast Asia. Later in the chapter we will spend some time looking into another way in which the lexicon can reflect aspects of culture, namely, the area of meaning differences between languages. Before that, however, let us inquire into the various ways in which words can be structured in East and Southeast Asian languages.

3.2 Word structure: derivational morphology

Morphology refers to the study of word structure. Early in the book, we saw that many East and Southeast Asian languages differ from European languages in lacking inflection. That is, in these languages nouns and verbs do not change their forms according to number, tense, or grammatical function. Inflection is one of the two main divisions of morphology. The other division is known as "derivation". The basic idea is that whereas inflection concerns different forms being assumed by the same word, derivation concerns the creation of new words.

Some of the common derivational processes—affixation, compounding, reduplication—can be illustrated from English. Consider words like *unreliable, rewritten*, and *prehistory*. They are derived from the words *reliable, written*, and *history* by the addition of the prefixes *un-, re-*, and *pre-*. Suffixes also play a part in English derivational morphology, as we can see from the fact that *reliable* and *written* are in turn derived from *rely* and *write* by the addition of the suffixes *-able* and *-en*. Other common derivational suffixes are found in the words *sadness, conversion, denial*, which are derived from *sad, convert, and deny*, respectively, by the suffixes *-ness, -ion*, and *-al*. English affixes like *un-* and *-ness* are quite productive, meaning both that they are found in a great number of words and that they can be applied to new words (of the appropriate kind) which enter the English language. Productivity is of course a matter of degree.

Compounding refers to the joining together of existing words without the aid of any affixes. Compounding is a productive derivational process in English, as we can see from words like *bookshop, underground, blackboard, blue-green*, and *jetlag*. Reduplication is also found in English, but it isn't so productive. It tends to give rise to childish or emotive effects, as in words like *choo-choo, no-no*, and *so-so*. There is a special kind of reduplication (sometimes called rhyming or chiming reduplication) where the vowels in the two forms are different, but this too is fairly restricted in English, e.g. *zig-zag, shimmy-shammy*. Reduplication can also be partial, meaning that only part of the item (e.g. the first syllable) is repeated, but this isn't found in English at all. With this by way of introduction, we will now survey the main derivational processes found in East and Southeast Asian languages.

3.2.1 Compounding

The Sinitic languages, and most of the languages of mainland Southeast Asia, do not use much affixation for derivational purposes but they use compounding a great deal. Many of these languages have a preference for two-element compounds. Table 3.6 gives some examples of Vietnamese (cf. also Nguyễn 1996: 146–9) and Cantonese. Notice that the derived words may be nouns, adjectives, or verbs. As usual with compounds around the world, the meaning of the compound word is often not completely predictable from the base words involved.

Now let's take a closer look at some of the compounding processes in Mandarin Chinese and in Japanese, two languages in which compounding

Table 3.6. Compounds in Vietnamese (Nguyễn 1987: 65) and Cantonese (Matthews and Yip 1994: 49ff.)

Vietnamese		Cantonese	
bàn ghế	[table chair] 'furniture'	*jáu-dim*	[wine-shop] 'hotel'
nhà cửa	[house door] 'home'	*hēung-pín*	[fragrant-leaf] 'jasmine (tea)'
nước mắt	[water eye] 'tears'	*chī-sām*	[crazy-heart] 'infatuated'
bánh ngọt	[pastry sweet] 'cake'	*jih-daaih*	[self-big] 'arrogant'
buồn ngủ	[want sleep] 'sleepy'	*tái-syū*	[look-book] 'read'
qua đời	[pass life] 'pass away'	*hōi-dōu*	[open-knife] 'carry out an operation'

has received close linguistic study. For a comparable treatment of Vietnamese, see Nguyễn (1997: 66–80). Though it is sometimes said that Mandarin Chinese is a "monosyllabic language", this is one of the myths about Chinese (DeFrancis 1984). A high proportion of Mandarin Chinese words are disyllabic, and many of these are compounds. Numerous compounds are fully lexicalized—i.e. fixed combinations whose meanings are not fully predictable from their component parts, and which speakers must learn one by one, as individual lexical items. Our description of Mandarin Chinese follows Li and Thompson (1981: ch. 3). In general, the types of fixed compound nouns and compound verbs are similar to what one would expect from English, but there are two types of compound noun which are rare in English but quite frequent in Sinitic and mainland Southeast Asian languages: (i) compounds in which the two elements are parallel, in the sense that neither modifies or describes the other, e.g. *huā-mù* [flower-tree] 'vegetation', *shuǐ-tǔ* [water-earth] 'climate', and *fù-mù* [father-mother] 'parents'; (ii) compounds in which the first element is a "metaphorical description" of the second, e.g. *gǒu-xióng* [dog-bear] 'bear', and *hǔ-jiàng* [tiger-general] 'brave general'. Both of these kinds of compound noun are stylistically valued but non-productive in Mandarin, i.e. they all have to be learnt separately, item by item.

Compound verbs are also common. They can be grouped into several types. One type are parallel compounds, in which the two verbal elements are usually either synonymous, as in the (a) examples, or very similar in meaning, as in the (b) examples:

(27) a. *dān-dú* 'alone' *hán-lěng* 'cold'
     guaī-qiǎo 'clever' *zhì-liáo* 'cure'
     guī-huí 'return to' *pí-fá* 'tired'
   b. *tòng-kǔ* [painful-bitter] 'bitter and painful'
     zhēn-què [real-certain] 'authentic'
     fàng-qì [loosen-abandon] 'give up'
     xiǎn-yǎng [manifest-display] 'show off'

In a second type of compound verb, the first element is a noun and the second an adjectival verb. A third type of compound verb consists of a verb-noun combination, in which, roughly speaking, the noun can be thought of as the "object" of the verb. Examples are given in (28a) and (28b) below.

(28) a. *zuǐ-yìng*   [mouth-hard]   'argumentative'
      yǎn-hóng   [eye-red]   'covetous'
      shǒu-dú   [hand-poisonous] 'vicious'
      mìng-kǔ   [life-bitter]   'unfortunate'
      dǎn-xiǎo   [gall-small]   'cowardly'
   b. *shāng-fēng* [hurt-wind]   'catch cold'
      lǐ-fǎ   [arrange-hair]   'have a haircut'
      sù-kǔ   [tell-bitterness] 'complain'
      jié-hūn   [tie-marry]   'marry (with)'

The examples we have seen so far are all fixed lexical items. On the other hand, compounding is also a productive process, especially for nouns. New noun compounds can be created easily. (Notice the terminological distinction: 'compound noun' for a fixed word; 'noun compound' for a combination formed according to a productive process.) To illustrate the fecundity of noun compounding in Mandarin Chinese, Li and Thompson (1981) list a number of patterns based on the kind of semantic relationships between the elements in the compound. It is probably impossible to list all the possibilities, but Table 3.7 shows some of the more prevalent ones. All these patterns can also be found in English. To emphasize the productivity of noun compounding in Mandarin, Li and Thompson have chosen examples where the connection being illustrated is fairly plain.

In Japanese compounding is the most productive process for creating new words (Shibatani 1990: 237ff., 254–6), particularly new nouns and verbal nouns. (Verbal nouns are a Japanese word class whose members are verb-like but which cannot function without the support of an auxiliary verb.) There are several interesting features. You will recall that aside from its native vocabulary, Japanese has two large strata of borrowed words—Sino-Japanese (S-J) and Foreign. Words from these three different strata can all combine in compounds. For example:

native–native: *aki-sora*   [autumn-sky]   'autumn sky'
               chika-michi [near-way]   'short cut'
               nomi-mizu [drink-water] 'drinking water'
S-J–S-J: *ki-soku*   [regulation-rule] 'rule'
               koo-ri   [high-interest]   'high interest'
native–S-J: *to-kei*   [time-meter]   'clock'
native–foreign: *ita-choko*   [slab-chocolate] 'chocolate bar'
S-J–foreign: *sekiyu-sutoobu* [oil-stove]   'oil stove'

Table 3.7. Noun compounding patterns in Mandarin Chinese (after Li and Thompson 1981): N1 = first noun, N2 = second noun

(i)	N1 denotes a place where N2 is located, e.g. *tái-dēng* 'table lamp'
(ii)	N1 denotes the place where N2 is applied, e.g. *yǎn-yào* 'eye medicine'
(iii)	N2 is used for N1, e.g. *yī-jià(zi)* 'clothes-rack'
(iv)	N2 denotes a unit of N1, e.g. *tiě-yuánzǐ* 'iron-atom'
(v)	N2 denotes a piece of equipment used in a sport N1, e.g. *lánqiú-kuāng(zi)* 'basketball-hoop'
(vi)	N2 denotes a protective device against N1, e.g. *yǔ-mào* 'rain hat'
(vii)	N2 is caused by N1, e.g. *hàn-bān* 'sweat-spot = blemish'
(viii)	N2 denotes a container for N1, e.g. *fàn-guō(zi)* 'rice-pot'
(ix)	N2 denotes a product of N1, e.g. *fēng-mì* 'bee-honey'
(x)	N2 is made of N1, e.g. *mián-bèi* 'cotton-quilt'
(xi)	N2 denotes a place where N1 is sold, e.g. *túshū-guǎn* 'book-tavern = library'
(xii)	N2 denotes a disease of N1, e.g. *fèi-bìng* 'lung-disease = tuberculosis'
(xiii)	N1 denotes a time for N2, e.g. *qiū-yùe* 'autumn moon'
(xiv)	N1 is the energy source for N2, e.g. *qì-chē* 'steam-vehicle = automobile'
(xv)	N2 is a part of N1, e.g. *jī-máo* 'chicken-feather'
(xvi)	N2 is a source of N1, e.g. *yóu-jǐng* 'oil well'
(xvii)	N2 is an employee or an officer of N1, e.g. *gōnsī-jīnglǐ* 'company manager'
(xviii)	N2 denotes a proper name for N1, e.g. *Yángzǐ-jiāng* 'Yangtze River'
(xIx)	N2 denotes a person who sells or delivers N1, *shuǐguǒ-xiǎofàn* 'fruit-peddler'

There are a great many S-J compounds, usually quite semantically transparent (Shibatani 1990: 147). For example, words for various types of machines are compounds with *ki* 'machine' as the second element: *hikoo-ki* 'aeroplane', *sooji-ki* 'cleaner', *syok-ki* 'spinning machine', *hanbai-ki* 'selling machine'; words for various branches of learning have *gaku* 'study' as the second element: *suu-gaku* 'mathematics', *rekishi-gaku* 'history', *kaikei-gaku* 'accounting', *tookei-gaku* 'statistics', *syakai-gaku* 'sociology'.

The main word classes which participate in compounding are nouns (N), adjectives (A), and verbs. Verbs can occur either as stems (V) or, more commonly, in infinitive form (V_i). The most common type of compound has the pattern: N-V_i. For example: *yuki-doke* 'snow melting' and *tsume-kiri* 'nail clipper'. Examples of the A-V_i pattern include: *naga-tsuzuki* 'long lasting' and *haya-jini* 'premature death'; and of the V_i-V_i pattern: *tachi-yomi* 'reading while standing' and *hashiri-zukare* 'fatigue due to running'. There are also quite a few compounds of two verbs. Usually the first verb expresses the manner in which the outcome depicted by the second verb is achieved, or else the second verb can express an aspectual type of modification to the initial verb. Examples are given in Table 3.8.

Table 3.8. Compound verbs in Japanese (from Shibatani 1990)

V1 manner, V2 main		
naguri-korosu	[beat-kill]	'kill by beating'
kiri-taosu	[cut-fell]	'fell by cutting'
kami-kiru	[bite-cut]	'cut by biting'
V1 main, V2 aspect-like modification		
kaki-ageru	[write-raise]	'write-up'
ii-tsukusu	[say-exhaust]	'say exhaustively'
koware-hajimeru	[break-begin]	'begin to break'

There is one interesting difference between native compounds and S-J compounds. It concerns compounds which consist of a verb (V or V$_i$) and a noun (N). In such cases, the noun almost invariably designates the object (or patient) of the verb, as it were. For example, in a compound word with the form 'person-kill' the word for 'person' is the object of the verb 'kill'. The compound refers to killing a person. This reflects the typical situation of verb-noun compounds in languages all around the world. What is peculiar about Japanese is that the order in which the elements occur differs depending on whether they are native or Sino-Japanese. In native compounds the noun comes first: N-V$_i$. In S-J compounds the verb comes first: V-N. This can be readily illustrated with pairs of native vs. S-J compounds with the same meaning, such as *hito-gorosh* [person-kill] and *satu-jin* [kill-person] 'man-killing'; and *iro-zuku* [colour-apply] and *chaku-shoku* [apply-colour] 'colouring'. The explanation lies in the different constituent orders of Japanese and Chinese: Japanese OV vs. Chinese VO. The Chinese VO pattern is so deeply ingrained that even recent coinages follow the same pattern. (Interestingly, a similar phenomenon occurs with Sino-Vietnamese nominal compounds (Nguyễn 1997: 77). Instead of the normal noun–modifier order, Sino-Vietnamese compounds like *quốc-ca* 'national anthem' and *đại-học* [great learning] 'college, university' show the Chinese modifier–noun order.)

As in any language, it often happens that the meaning of the compound is not directly predictable from the constituent forms. Sometimes it is completely obscure unless one has a good deal of cultural and/or historical knowledge. Shibatani (1990: 242) illustrates this with *uguisu-bari* [nightingale-flooring]: this refers to a floor boarding which when people walk on it makes squeaking noises reminiscent of the singing of nightingales, which are supposed to sing as a warning when enemies approach. Another good example is *tai-yaki* 'sea bream-baking'. This refers not to baking sea bream, or to baked sea bream, or even to a pie or other dish with sea bream flesh in it, but rather to a kind of baked snack which is made in the shape of a sea bream.

In other cases, a compound can have one more or less transparent meaning, but has also taken on additional, extended meanings. One common pattern in Japanese is for a compound designating an action also to designate the agent of that action; for example, *hito-goroshi* [person-kill] can refer not only to the act of killing a person, but also to the killer. Sometimes the extension can supersede the original meaning; for example, *e-kaki* [picture-painting] and *sumoo-tori* [sumo-wrestling] do not refer to the act of painting or sumo wrestling, but rather to a painter or sumo wrestler, respectively. In effect, the compound doesn't mean 'doing X' but 'someone who does X'. Aside from the extension from act to agent, other common extensions are (a) from act to instrument (i.e. from 'doing X' to 'something one does X with'); for example, *chiri-tori* [dust-collecting] 'dustpan', *ha-migaki* [tooth-polishing] 'toothpaste', and (b) from act to place where the action is done (i.e. from 'doing X' to 'somewhere one does X'); for example, *mono-hoshi* [thing-drying] 'laundry', *huna-watashi* [boat-crossing] 'ferry terminal'.

3.2.2 Abbreviation and blending

In English, abbreviation (also known as clipping or truncation) is a fairly marginal derivational process, though it does occur and is responsible for the current form of some very common words, such as *fan* (from *fanatic*), *bike* (from *bicycle*), *bus* (from *omnibus*), and *piano* (from *pianoforte*). In some languages, including Japanese and Malay, abbreviation is much more productive, but as one might expect the process doesn't necessarily work the same way as in English. In some languages abbreviation can apply not only to single words but also to whole phrases, so that it brings about a "blending" of several words into a single new word. Japanese often uses these processes to reduce lengthy compounds and phrases down to the preferred word size of two to four moras (for present purposes, two to four syllables; see section 5.4.3 for a more accurate description). Shibatani (1990: 254–6) describes several patterns. The most common is the selection of a mora or two from each member of a compound. This often happens to Sino-Japanese compounds and to expressions borrowed from English (after they have been re-syllabified and otherwise adapted to the Japanese phonological system). For example: *kooyoo-kigyoo-tai* [public-enterprise-body] → *koo-ki-tai; gakusei-waribiki* [student-discount] → *gaku-wari; paasonaru konpyutaa* [personal-computer] → *paso-kon; hangaa-sutoraiki* [hunger-strike] → *han-suto*.

As Shibatani says (p. 255), the process of abbreviation "is sometimes applied ruthlessly, practically mutilating the original forms". For example, the old-fashioned phrase *mune ga kyun to naru* 'the heart aches (for you)' becomes *mune-kyun;* and *natsukashi no merodii* 'long for melodies' becomes *natsu-mero*. Needless to say, abbreviated hybrid words such as *natsu-mero* can be confusing all around, not only to foreigners but also to the Japanese themselves.

3.2.3 Reduplication

Reduplication is more common in East and Southeast Asian languages than in English. In tone languages, it is sometimes accompanied by tonal modification. Vietnamese, for example, has many words which have a reduplicated form. Initially we have to distinguish two types, depending on whether the base exists as an independent word. If it does not, then the reduplicated form can be regarded as a noteworthy fact about the word structure but not as derivational in the strict sense. On the other hand, if the base exists as a word in its own right, and reduplication produces a new word with a modified meaning, then reduplication is correctly termed a derivational process. Notice from Table 3.9 that derivational reduplication in Vietnamese can convey the apparently contradictory meanings of "attenuation" or "intensification". Interestingly, Vietnamese is far from unique in this respect. Both these kinds of meaning change are associated with reduplication in a range of languages around the world. Another meaning frequently expressed by reduplication is "multiplicity"; for example, Thai *dèk-dèk* [child-child] 'children'; Indonesian *lalat-lalat* [fly-fly] 'flies'.

Sometimes reduplication is combined with affixation. In Cantonese, reduplication of adjectives combined with the suffix *-déi*, conveys a meaning somewhat similar to the English suffix *-ish* (Matthews and Yip 1994: 45); for example: *sòh-só-déi* [silly-silly-ish] 'rather silly'; *féih-féi-déi* [fat-fat-ish] 'rather fat'. In these examples, the reduplicated elements don't look exactly the same because reduplication with *-déi* causes a tone change on the second

Table 3.9. Vietnamese reduplications (from Nguyễn 1987: 65; Thompson 1987: 152–3)

Base not an independent word	
ba-ba	'river turtle'
cào-cào	'grasshopper'
đu-đủ	'payaya, pawpaw'
ngấm-ngầm	'secretly'
Base exists as independent word	
đẹp-đẹp	'be rather pretty' (*đẹp* 'be beautiful')
động-động	'move a little' (*động* 'move')
trăng-trắng	'be whitish' (*trắng* 'be white')
quen-quen	'to know slightly' (*quen* 'know')
mau-mau	'very rapidly' (*mau* 'rapidly')
rồi-rồi	'be completely finished' (*rồi* 'be finished')
thường-thường	'usually, regularly' (*thường* 'often')

Table 3.10. Indonesian rhyming and chiming reduplication (Sneddon 1996)

Rhyming reduplication		
sayur-mayur	'vegetables'	(*sayur* 'vegetables')
lauk-pauk	'side dishes'	(*lauk* 'side dish')
kaya-raya	'rich'	(*kaya* 'rich')
ramah-tamah	'hospitable and friendly'	(*ramah* 'friendly')
Chiming reduplication		
bolak-balik	'to and fro'	(*balik* 'return')
asal-usul	'origin, descent'	(*asal* 'origin')
teki-teka	'riddle'	

element (perhaps you remember from section 1.5 that the final *h* in Cantonese words indicates that the word has a low tone).

In another type of reduplication the two parts of the word are not fully identical, but differ in certain consonants or vowels. If consonants differ, the result is that the two parts of the reduplicated word rhyme (as in English *lovey-dovey*). If the vowels differ, the effect is similar but is not rhyming in the strict sense, so the term "chiming" is used instead (as in English *wishy-washy*). Another term for rhyming and chiming reduplication, taken together, is "imitative reduplication". We can see examples of this kind of reduplication in Indonesian (Sneddon 1996: 22; cf. Asmah 1975: 180–2). It is not a productive process in Indonesian, though it is found in a number of common words. Generally speaking, it either indicates variety or emphasizes the meaning of the first component of the word. Often only the first component is recognizable as a word which can appear in its own right; sometimes neither part can appear by itself.

Extensive rhyming and chiming reduplication, often with tonal modification, is characteristic of Thai and Vietnamese. Thompson (1987: 157–68) lists several hundred words of this type in Vietnamese (terming them "emphatics"). He comments (p. 155): "the meanings and usage of the forms are very difficult to get at: dictionary glosses tend to be misleading, and informants are very often hard put to explain the subtle connotations."

3.2.4 Derivational affixation

It would be an exaggeration to say that Sinitic languages and mainland Southeast Asian languages lack derivational affixation altogether. For example, Cantonese (Matthews and Yip 1994: 32ff.) has several prefixes and suffixes for forming nouns from other nouns or other parts of speech. For example: *góng-faat* [speak-way] 'way of speaking', *tái-faat* [see-way] 'point of view', *wá-gā* [picture-ist] 'expert painter', *yàmngohk-gā* [music-ist] 'expert musician', *tói-jái* [table-DIM] 'little table', *māau-jái* [cat-DIM] 'kitten'. Suffix

-fa '-ize, -ify' forms causative verbs from nouns and adjectives, especially in formal registers such as radio broadcasting; for example, *fó-fa* [fire-CAUS] 'incinerate, cremate', *dihnlóuh-fa* [computer-CAUS] 'computerize', *yihndoih-fa* [modern-CAUS] 'modernize', *méih-fa* [beauty-CAUS] 'beautify'. Hakka (Lau 1999) has a set of gender suffixes derived from kin terms which indicate whether a named person, or an animal, is male or female, including *gung¹* [father's father], *po²* [father's mother], *go¹* [elder brother], and *moi⁴* [younger sister]. They also occur in the fixed lexical forms of various words for animals, body parts, and other nouns; for example, *miau⁴gung¹* 'cat', *sa²go¹* 'snake', *ngi³gung¹* 'ear'.

Thai has a number of derivational affixes (Diller 1992), such as the prefix *kaan-*, which forms abstract nouns (e.g. *lên* 'to play', *kaan-lên* 'playing'; *mɨang* 'city', *kaan-mɨang* 'politics'), *khii-*, which forms adjectives from verbs (e.g. *bòn* 'to complain', *khii-bòn* 'given to complaining'), and the suffix *-saat*, which forms nouns denoting a field of knowledge (e.g. *daaraa* 'star', *daaraa-saat* 'astronomy'). Vietnamese has a range of prefixes and suffixes (Nguyễn 1997: 60–6), including the ordinal number prefix *thứ-* (e.g. *thứ-hai* 'second'), *bán-* 'half' (e.g. *bán-cầu* 'hemisphere'), *bất-* 'not, non-' (e.g. *bất-bạo-động* 'non-violent'), and *phản-* 'counter, anti-' (e.g. *phản-kháng* 'to protest', *phản-gián* 'counter-espionage'). Except for the first, these prefixes are all of Chinese origin. They are highly productive and common in newspapers, magazines, and other educated uses of the language. Among the more productive suffixes are *-sĩ* 'ist, expert' (e.g. *hoạ-sĩ* 'artist, painter', *thi-sĩ* 'poet'), and *-học* '-ology, -ics' (e.g. *sinh-vật-học* 'biology', *vật-lý-học* 'physics'). These too are of Chinese origin.

So far we have been concentrating on the languages of mainland Southeast Asia and China. Why? Because these languages are classic examples of isolating languages, i.e. languages in which words do not change their shapes depending on grammatical context. It would be easy to jump to the conclusion that words in isolating languages are mostly morphologically simple, but as you can see by now such a statement would be an exaggeration, even for languages like Thai, Vietnamese, and Mandarin Chinese. Though to a large extent these languages indeed lack inflection, they have a range of derivational morphology.

3.2.5 Productive derivation

Austronesian languages of insular Southeast Asia go beyond the modest derivational morphology we have seen so far. They have extensive and highly productive derivational morphology, which is in fact one of the main distinctive features setting them apart from their northern neighours. For example, Malay (Malaysian and Indonesian) has systems of verbal affixation which involve prefixes, suffixes, and circumfixes (i.e. simultaneous prefixing and suffixing). Each affix can produce several different semantic

Table 3.11. Derivational affixes in Malaysian

ber- derives intransitive stative verbs from noun or adjective: meanings include 'have X', 'wear X', 'produce X'	*ber-isteri* 'have a wife, (of a man) be married', *ber-baju* 'wear a shirt', *ber-telur* 'lay an egg', *ber-payung* 'be using an umbrella', *ber-sekolah* 'attend school'
meN- derives dynamic verbs: meanings include 'move towards X', 'become like X', 'collect or produce X'	*men-darat* 'go ashore', *mem-batu* 'become like rock, harden', *me-rumput* 'cut grass'
ter- derives intransitive verbs: either 'do X suddenly or accidentally' or 'be subject to action or state X'	*ter-tidur* 'fall asleep by accident' *ter-bunuh* 'be killed', *ter-tulis* 'be written, e.g. in English', *ter-buka* 'be open'
-kan suffix used together with *meN-*: (i) derives verbs from adjectives and nouns; meanings include 'cause to become X' and 'treat like X' (ii) derives transitive from intransitive verbs; meanings include 'cause or allow to do X', 'cause to become X'	*mem-bersih-kan* 'to clean', *me-malu-kan* 'embarrass' (*malu* 'embarrassment, shame'), *men-calon-kan* 'nominate' (*calon* 'candidate'), *men-jatuh-kan* 'drop' (*jatuh* 'fall'), *mem-bangun-kan* 'wake someone up' (*bangun* 'stand')
-an a nominalizer, derives nouns from verbs	*nyanyi-an* 'singing', *makan-an* 'food' (*makan* 'eat'), *pukul-an* 'blow' (*pukul* 'hit'), *tulis-an* 'writing' (*tulis* 'write'), *pilih-an* 'choice' (*pilih* 'choose')

effects, depending in part on the nature of the base word. Some of the main derivational affixes of Malaysian are shown in Table 3.11. The prefixes *ber-* and *meN-* also play a non-derivational role in the voice system of Malay, but that need not concern us here. (The capital N in prefix *meN-* indicates that the final consonant of the prefix, if there is one, can be one of several different nasal sounds, depending on the initial sound of the base word: see section 5.3.3).

Korean and Japanese also have a reasonable collection of derivational affixes, though some of them are not very productive. For example, the Korean prefixes *jis-, yeos-,* and *chi-* apply to verbs, deriving verbs with modified meanings; for example, *jis-* + *balb-* [violently-stamp] 'to trample', *yeos-* + *deud-* [secretly-hear] 'overhear', *chi-* + *mil-* [upward-push] 'to push up'. Other derivational affixes, such as the causative suffixes shown in (29), are highly productive. The Korean causative suffix has six phonologically conditioned allomorphs (/-i-/, /-u-/, /-gi-/, /-hi-/, /-li-/, /-hu-/), depending on the final sound of the stem to which it is attached (Lee 1989: 77, 85–6).

(29) *bo-* 'to see'   + *-i-* → *boi-* 'to show'
      chu- 'to dance'   + *-i-* → *chui-* 'to cause (someone) to dance'
      meok- 'to eat'   + *-i-* → *meoki-* 'to feed'
      bi- 'to be empty' + *-u-* → *biu-* 'to empty'

nam- 'to remain'   + *-gi-* → *namgi-* 'to leave behind, make remain'
ip- 'to wear'   + *-hi-* → *iphi-* 'to clothe'
geod- 'to walk'   + *-li-* → *geolli-* 'to make walk'
neuj- 'to be slow' + *-hu-* → *neujchu-* 'to slow down'

Japanese also has a highly productive and regular causative suffix: *-(sa)se*. Some examples follow. The causative suffix applies to the so-called irrealis root of the verb, but we need not worry about this here.

(**30**) a. *mi-* 'look at'   + *-sase* CAUS   → *misase-* 'cause to look at'
   oki- 'wake up' + *-sase* CAUS   → *okisase-* 'make wake up'

   b. *shina-* 'die' + *-se* CAUS   → *shinase-* 'cause to die'
   ika- 'go'   + *-se* CAUS   → *ikase-* 'make go, have go, let go'

In all three languages—Malay, Korean, Japanese—there are a number of irregular causative suffixes of limited productivity. This too is highly typical. Derivational morphology is not always productive, regular, and transparent. One often finds odd quirks (nonproductive sub-regularities) which are confined to very small sets of forms, and often the only explanation that can be given is historical.

3.3 Meaning differences between languages

Everyone knows that any language has certain words for distinctive aspects of the culture, words which lack direct equivalents in other languages with radically different cultures. Obviously, this applies to items of material culture such as food, clothing, shelter, and weapons. For example, it is clearly no accident that Japanese has a word, *sake*, for an alcoholic drink made from rice, whereas English does not. People also expect that there are customs and social institutions which have specific names in one language but not in others. For example, it is no accident that English doesn't have a word corresponding to Japanese *omiai*, referring to a formal occasion when the prospective bride and her family first meet the prospective bridegroom and his family. Later in this chapter, we will see that the same applies to terms for people's emotions, values, and ideals about life, which can differ substantially from culture to culture. After thinking it over, many people find this kind of variation easy to accept, at least in principle (getting used to the idea that other people feel differently and hold radically different values is not as easy as it might sound). What people often do not recognize, and are even often unwilling to accept, is that words for apparently quite simple and basic items and actions also vary in meaning from language to language. This can be a particular trap for language learners.

Before getting started, we have to recognize that describing the meanings of words is no easy task. Most linguists agree that dictionary definitions are usually inaccurate in various ways. The field of linguistics which deals with meanings is known as semantics. We cannot go into the field of semantics in any detail here, but some crucial points are as follows (Goddard 1998). First and foremost, to pin down the meaning of any word we must ensure that our definition is phrased in terms of other words which are relatively simpler and easier to understand. Otherwise we get tangled up in circular and obscure definitions and end up explaining nothing.

A good definition (or set of definitions) should explain the full range of use of a word. It should be a reliable guide to how the word can (and can't) be used and still make sense. However, many words have more than one meaning. In fact, most words have several interrelated meanings, a situation technically known as polysemy. Careful analysis may be necessary to decide whether a particular word has a single general meaning or several more specific, but interrelated, meanings. Without a correct picture of polysemy, we will not be able to understand the correspondences between languages.

3.3.1 Different patterns of polysemy

To illustrate: in English the words *nose, beak*, and *trunk* (of an elephant) are three distinct words, but in other languages the word for 'nose' can be extended to cover the other meanings as well. For example, Russian *nos* may refer to the beak of a bird, and Japanese *hana* may refer to the trunk of an elephant. At first, you might think that this means that *nos* and *hana* do not mean the same as English *nose*, but such a conclusion would be only half-right. Various arguments can be used to establish that the words *nos* and *hana* each have two distinct meanings, i.e. they are polysemous words. Russian *nos* has the meanings: 1. 'nose' 2. 'beak'; Japanese *hana* has the meanings: 1. 'nose' 2. 'trunk'. That is, in both cases one of the meanings (arguably, the primary one) is the same as English *nose*.

Similarly, in Malay (and German, and many other languages) there are two words which correspond to the English verb *live:* one used for 'live' as opposed to 'die' (e.g. to *live for a long time*) and the other used for 'live somewhere' (e.g. to *live in Sydney*). In Malay, the two words are *hidup* ('live' vs. 'die') and *tinggal* ('live somewhere, stay'). The best analysis is that English *live* is a polysemous word with two separate meanings, one of which corresponds to Malay *hidup* and the other to Malay *tinggal*. Most native speakers of English agree (once they have thought about it) that *live* has two meanings. For an example of the same thing the other way around, we can take the Malay word *buat*, which can mean either 'do' or 'make'. Most native speakers of Malay agree, once they have thought about it, that *buat* has two meanings, and that some sentences, e.g. *Apa dia buat?* 'What did he do/make?', are ambiguous between the two meanings.

One of the indicators of polysemy is the existence of different grammatical properties or constraints associated with the separate meanings. For example, *live* in the 'live somewhere' meaning actually requires that a place expression be mentioned, e.g. *Where did she live? She lived in Sydney, He lived in a three-bedroom house.* With Malay *buat*, one indication of polysemy is that the 'make' meaning is compatible with a phrase indicating the "material", whereas the 'do' meaning is not. For example, in the following sentence the word *buat* cannot mean 'do', it has to mean 'make'.

(**31**) *Dengan apa   yang dia buat-nya?*
     with   what LIG he make-it
     'From (with) what did he make it?'

One other common polysemy in East and Southeast Asian languages concerns the meanings 'there is' (existence) and 'have' (alienable possession). In both Malaysian and Mandarin Chinese, for example, the two meanings are expressed by a single word—Malay *ada*, Mandarin Chinese *yǒu*—but they are kept distinct by the fact that they occur in different grammatical frames. 'There is' takes only one obligatory argument, whereas 'have' takes two. Also, 'there is' is compatible with an additional expression indicating a location, whereas 'have' is not. These features can be illustrated from Malay.

(**32**) *Ada*   *dua ekor*   *lembu (di padang tu)*.
     ada (= there are) two CL:ANIMAL cow (in field   that)
     'There are two cows in the field.'

(**33**) *Orang ini ada*   *dua ekor*   *lembu.*
     person this ada (= has) two CL:ANIMAL cow
     'This person has two cows.'

3.3.2 Different meanings for "simple" things and actions

Surprising as it may seem, some languages don't have a word which exactly matches the English word *water*. Japanese is such a language. It has two separate words for 'water'—*mizu* and *yu*—both of which have a reference to temperature built into their meanings. *Yu* (often with an honorific prefix *o-*) is reserved for 'hot water', and *mizu* for 'non-hot water'. One might suspect that *mizu*, the more common of the two words, is really a general term for 'water', but this is not so. *Mizu* cannot be used about hot water; and furthermore, combining the adjective *atsui* 'hot' with *mizu* sounds unnatural (Suzuki (1978: 51–2) calls it "self-contradictory"), though there is no such restriction in relation to other liquids, e.g. *atsui miruku* 'hot milk'. Japanese, then, makes a lexical distinction which is ignored by English.

The same thing can happen with words for events and actions. Many Southeast Asian and East Asian languages have no word corresponding exactly to English 'break', because they differentiate what, from an English speaker's point of view, are different kinds of breaking. For example, Malay has *putus* 'break in two', *patah* 'break but not sever', and *pecah* 'break into many pieces, smash'. Cantonese has *jíng laahn* (roughly) 'break into pieces' (employing *jíng* 'make'), *dá laahn* 'smash into pieces' (*dá* 'hit', implying forceful impact on a fragile object), *dit laahn* 'break by dropping', *ngáauh tyúhn* 'break into two by bending' (*ngáauh* 'bite'). Japanese has *oru* 'break off, bend, fold', *kowasu* 'break, destroy', and *kiru* 'break off, cut off, switch off' (among others). The point being made here is not affected by the fact that English has words like *snap* and *smash* which are more specific than *break*. The point is rather that English has a general word, *break*, which has no counterpart in these other languages. In similar fashion, Khmer has no single general word corresponding to English *carry*; if you look up *carry* in an English–Khmer dictionary (Huffman and Proum 1978) you will find up to fifteen different entries: 'carry under one arm', 'carry on the head', 'carry at one end of a pole', 'carry suspended between two poles', and so on.

Even when languages do seem to have words which match up in meaning, closer scrutiny often turns up subtle (but real) differences. Consider English *drink* vs. Japanese *nomu*. At first they seem the same. However, *nomu* can be used not only about drinking water, tea, coffee, etc. but also for swallowing solid items such as pins and rings, and for smoking a cigarette. Suzuki (1978: 17–19) argues that *nomu* means 'to introduce something into one's body without chewing it'. He also notes that rice is normally something to *taberu* 'eat', but if a fish bone is stuck in someone's throat, one says in Japanese, "You should *nomu* some rice".

Similarly, one often finds that the nearest word for 'come' differs in meaning from the English term. One of the most distinctive things about English *come* is its ability to occur in sentences like *I'm coming to you*, i.e. in contexts in which the "point of view" is not that of the speaker him or herself, but that of the person being spoken to (or even that of a third person). (In the linguistic literature, this phenomenon is often called "deictic projection".) Japanese, Korean and Malay all have words which at first blush seem to mean the same as English *come* (Japanese *kuru*, Malay *datang*, Korean *oda*), but none of them allow the shifting around of the point of view as freely as English *come*. For example, using Japanese *kuru* one cannot adopt an addressee's point of view and say the equivalent of *I'm coming (to you)*. Instead one has to use a different verb and say the equivalent of *I'm going (to you)*. Facts like these are indicators of subtle semantic differences between languages.

3.3.3 Culturally based specialization in the lexicon

Most of the examples we have seen so far don't have any obvious cultural connections, but there are plenty of examples of where semantic specialization (also known as lexical elaboration, i.e. the existence of several words making fine meaning distinctions) is culturally motivated. One of the best-known examples concerns rice, which is a staple food across Asia. Many East and Southeast Asian languages have different words to refer to rice in different states (see list below). Further, the word (or words) for cooked rice often functions as a term for a meal in general. For example, in Japanese, *gohan desu yo* (lit. 'it's cooked rice') means 'It's meal time' or 'Dinner's ready'. In Cantonese, *sihk faahn* (lit. 'eat rice') is an invitation or exhortation to eat a meal, regardless of whether the meal contains rice. In many languages a routine greeting is to ask the equivalent of 'Have you eaten rice?'

	'rice growing'	'raw rice'	'cooked rice'
MALAY	*padi*	*beras*	*nasi* (also: *pulut* 'sticky rice')
VIETNAMESE	*luá*	*gạo*	*cơm*
JAPANESE	*ine*	*kome*	*gohan* or *meshi*

Kinship terminology is a domain which is often reflective of cultural concerns and East and Southeast Asian languages are no exception. Generally speaking, age is an important determinant of social status in these societies. Within the family, the relative age of siblings establishes seniority for life. It is not surprising, therefore, that many languages distinguish between older siblings and younger siblings. This may be done according to various patterns. In Thai, there are words for 'older sibling' and 'younger sibling'. To specify either of them as 'male' or as 'female', one adds an extra word. A second pattern, found in Malay, Lao, and Vietnamese, is for there to be distinct, single words for 'older brother' and 'older sister', but a single word for 'younger sibling'. To specify the gender of a younger sibling one must add an extra word meaning 'male' or 'female'. A third pattern, found in Mandarin Chinese, is for 'older sister', 'older brother', 'younger sister', and 'younger brother' each to have a distinct word of its own. Some of the forms are given in the following list.

	'older brother'	'older sister'	'younger brother'	'younger sister'
LAO	*qaaj⁴*	*qùaj⁴*	*nòòng⁴ (saaj²)*	*nòòng⁴ (saaw³)*
MALAY	*abang*	*kakak*	*adik (lelaki)*	*adik (perempuan)*
MANDARIN	*gē-ge*	*jiĕ-jie*	*dì-di*	*mèi-mei*

Within the family, it is not uncommon for there to be a more specific set of terms, specifying the exact order of birth. There may be expressions meaning 'first brother', 'second brother', 'third brother', etc., 'first sister', 'second sister', 'third sister', etc., as in Mandarin; or a set of "nicknames" for the siblings, based on their order of birth, e.g. Malay *long* 'oldest (sibling/child)', *teh* 'fourth (sibling/child)'.

Terms for the more intangible things in life—feelings, attitudes, and emotions—are equally subject to variation across languages and cultures; (cf. Wierzbicka 1992; 1997; Harkins and Wierzbicka 2001). An interesting feature of the "areal lexicon" of mainland Southeast Asia, first noticed by Matisoff (1986*b*), concerns just this area of meaning. Matisoff coined the term "psycho-collocation" to refer to complex expressions based around a noun translatable as 'heart', 'mind', 'spirit', or the like, often with a separate meaning as a real body part (usually the liver or, less commonly, the heart). Typically such expressions consist of just two words, the "psycho-noun" together with an adjective or a verb, though more complex modifiers are also possible. The interesting thing is that profuse numbers of psycho-collocations are found in languages of different families, including Malay, Hmong, Thai, and Lai (cf. VanBik 1998; Jaisser 1990; Oey 1990; Goddard 2001*a*; Diller and Juntanamalaga 1990).

A small sample of these terms is set out in Table 3.12, which shows languages from three families: Lai or Haka Chin (Tibeto-Burman), Malay (Austronesian), and Thai (Tai-Kadai). Many languages of mainland Southeast Asia have dozens or hundreds of psycho-collocations, providing their speakers with an extremely fine-tuned emotional keyboard for talking and thinking about feelings and other mental states. Psycho-collocations usually overshadow simple one-word terms both in number and in frequency of usage. Diller and Juntanamalaga (1990: 242) comment: "the impression of one approaching the Thai language from an English-speaking background is apt to be amazement that informal Thai conversation so frequently refers to feelings and mental attitudes, and that emotional

Table 3.12. Examples of psycho-collocations in Lai, Thai, and Malay

Lai	Thai	Malay
thin haaŋ	*khu'ang-cay*	*panas hati*
liver become. liquid	be angry-heart	hot liver
'angry'	'feel angry'	'angry, worked up'
luŋ tliŋ	*thùuk-cay*	*puas hati*
heart complete	correct-heart	sated liver
'satisfied'	'please, satisfy'	'satisfied'
luŋ daay	*yen-cay*	*sujuk hati*
heart silent	cool-heart	cool liver
'calm'	'feel relaxed'	'calmed, reassured'
thin/luŋ hneʔm	*plo':p-cay*	*senang hati*
heart/liver soften	pacify-heart	easy liver
'comfort'	'console, comfort'	'contented, relaxed'
luŋ khiak	*khǎeng-cay*	*hati waja*
heart break	hard(en)-heart	liver steel
'determined/decisive'	'steel oneself to'	'resolute, determined'

experience can be so precisely delineated and commented on through *cay* expressions." VanBik (1998: 227) remarks about Lai: "Psycho-collocations are essential in the daily use of Lai. It is impossible to discuss the life of the mind without them."

In the socioeconomic sphere, most traditional Asian societies were based around farming, and, in many cases, fishing. Many of the East and Southeast Asian lexicons are still rather rich in terms for weather (rain, wind, seasons, etc.), for animals, plants and insects, and for fish. According to Inoue (1979: 296–8), Japanese has an unusually rich vocabulary of words which describe and pay tribute to the beauty of nature, including words for the weather phenomena characteristic of different times of the year—different kinds of rain, wind, fair skies, cloudy skies, thunder, summer heat, winter cold, and so on, and a host of seasonally related expressions—flowers, plants, trees, birds and insects, fruit and vegetables, fish, various kinds of household goods, and markets and festivals held at the Buddhist temples and Shinto shrines in all parts of Japan. Inoue links this proliferation of nature-related vocabulary not just with the material conditions of traditional Japanese life, but with other, non-material cultural factors: essentially, a love of nature. "The Japanese literary arts," she remarks, "particularly Japanese poetry, cannot exist without all those expressions about nature and changes in nature."

3.4 Cultural key words

Cultural key words are highly salient and deeply culture-laden words which act as focal points around which whole cultural domains are organized. Exploring these focal points in depth can often bring to light general organizing principles which lend structure and coherence to an entire cultural domain, or have an explanatory power across a number of domains (Wierzbicka 1997). How can we tell that a particular word is one of a culture's key words? To begin with, it will usually be a common word, either in absolute terms or at least within one particular semantic domain, for example, in the domain of emotions or of moral judgments. Often key words are at the centre of a whole cluster of common phrases, as well as occurring in proverbs, in sayings, in popular songs, in book titles, and so on. Likely candidates for key words include salient emotion terms, words for cultural values and standards, and social category terms. Words like *love, work, honesty*, and *friend* are key words for the mainstream Anglo-American culture, and at a finer level of detail words like *mate, dob, whinge*, and even *bloody*, provide cultural keys to Australian culture. But ultimately the question is not how to show whether or not a particular word is one of the culture's key words, but rather to be able to say something significant and revealing about that culture by undertaking an in-depth study of some of them. In a sense, the proof of the pudding is in the eating.

Supposing we find some candidates for cultural key words, then—for example, the kind of words which a language learner finds constantly cropping up in people's explanations about how and why they do things, but which lack clear equivalents in the learner's home language. How can we capture their meanings in a clear and accurate fashion without letting in some culture bias from our home language? Recognizing that there are meaning differences between two languages is one thing. Formulating these differences in an unbiased way is another. In this section we take a brief look at one of the most promising approaches to cross-cultural semantics—the natural semantic metalanguage method (Wierzbicka 1996; 1997; Goddard 1998). We will not have time to justify it fully, but we can cover enough for our purposes.

As mentioned earlier, the cardinal rule when trying to describe the meaning of a word is that the description must be phrased in terms which are simpler and clearer than the word being explained. When we attempt to describe the meanings of words from a language different from our own, there is an additional problem because most words don't have precise equivalents across languages. Meaning variation across languages brings with it the danger of ethnocentrism (culture bias). If we use concepts which are English-specific in describing another language, then our description will inevitably be a distorted one because we will impose our alien conceptual categories onto the other language.

Fortunately, the simpler and clearer a meaning is, the more likely it is to be shared between languages. It appears that the very simplest meanings of all (technically known as semantic primes) are shared by all languages. On current research, up to sixty meanings have a strong claim to being semantic primes (Wierzbicka 1996; Goddard and Wierzbicka 1994; 2002). Examples include SOMEONE, SOMETHING, PEOPLE, THINK, KNOW, WANT, SAY, FEEL, GOOD, BAD, DO, HAPPEN, NOT, and BECAUSE. Semantic primes can be thought of as the basic "atoms of meaning", in terms of which all the thousands upon thousands of complex meanings are composed. If semantic primes are not the "private property" of English, but, as the evidence suggests, are found in all languages, then semantic descriptions composed in semantic primes can be transposed between languages with a minimum of distortion. Just as importantly, because explications composed in terms of semantic primes are easy to understand and easy to translate, they can be tested against native speakers' intuitions and by checking that they account for the actual range of use of the words in question. In the following we use explications in semantic primes as a technique for capturing subtle nuances of cultural meaning.

3.4.1 Some key words of Malay: *malu* and *sabar*

Present-day Malaysia is one of the most industrialized nations in Southeast Asia. It is a multi-ethnic and multilingual country, with Chinese, Indians,

Orang Asli (aboriginal people), and peoples of other ethnicities making up almost 40 per cent of the population. We will focus solely on the Malay people, the largest ethnic group in Malaysia, and in this section I will use the term 'Malay' not only to designate the people and culture, but also to refer to the Malay language as spoken in Malaysia, i.e. as an equivalent to Bahasa Melayu. Traditionally the Malays are a village people, relying on fishing, market gardening, and rice cultivation. They have long been Muslims, though Malay traditions (*adat*) influence their Islamic practices considerably. European observers generally describe Malay culture as valuing "refined restraint", cordiality, and sensitivity. Malays themselves are described as courteous, easy-going, and charming (and, less positively, as fatalistic, indolent, and quick to take offence).

The main external influences on Malay culture have been from India and from the Middle East. As we have seen earlier, the language contains many fully indigenized loanwords from Arabic and Sanskrit. Islam and Malay traditions (*adat*) coexist as powerful influences in contemporary life. Both are deeply concerned with promoting correct behaviour in all facets of life, with the result that moral and ethical themes are more prominent in Malaysian discourse than in contemporary Western societies (cf. Goddard 2000). Among the more important Malay cultural ideals one could count: being considerate and protective of other people's feelings (*bertimbang rasa*); showing respect and deference (*menghormati*) to parents, leaders, and old people; the cultivation of mutual kindness and gentleness (*berbudi bahasa*); and being well-mannered and well-spoken (*bersopan santun*). As with any language, there are many Malay words whose meanings and uses have a lot to say about Malay culture. In this section we will focus on only two of them—*malu* and *sabar*.

Anthropologists and native speakers alike agree on the salience and importance of the feeling designated by the word *malu*. Swift (1965: 76, 176), for instance, says that Malay villagers are "[M]uch concerned with shame (*malu*) in most things they do" and describes it as "a very broad and very important concept". Wilson (1967: 130f.) highlights its importance as the principal disciplinary device in the upbringing of children; more generally, he remarks, "The concept of *malu* is one that acts as a hidden thermostat in interpersonal social relations." In bilingual dictionaries, it is variously glossed as 'ashamed', 'shy', and 'embarrassed'. None of these translation equivalents suggests, however, the moral or social dimension of the concept. In contrast to the negative connotations of 'shame', Malays regard a sense of *malu* as necessary, as a social good—something akin to a 'sense of propriety'.

When could a person feel *malu*? We can illustrate with examples from popular novels and short stories (Goddard 1996). It could follow upon one's having done something wrong or foolish, as in (34) and (35) below, where 'ashamed' or 'embarrassed' often seem to make suitable translations. Sometimes 'shy' or even 'nervous' seem fitting, as in (36) and (37).

(34) *"Tolonglah aku, Lia... aku malu... aku yang silap..." kata Azlin tersedu.*
'"Help me, Lia... I'm ashamed... I've made a mistake (done something stupid)..." said Azlin sobbing.'

(35) *Kalau gagal, buat malu aku saja, getus Sofi Aidura di dalam hati.*
'If I fail, I would be so embarrassed, thought Sofi Aidura.'

(36) *"Ni Inok, cucu Pak Ongah. Inok, salam dengan Amir. Eh! Malu pulak dia!"*
'"This is Inok, my grandchild. Inok, say hello to Amir. Eh! She's shy!"'

(37) *"Malu woii... tak pernah aku jadi orang penting macam ni."*
'"I'm so nervous... I've never been an important person like this."'

You can also feel *malu* on account of a personal characteristic, such as ugliness, a deformity, or poverty. Equally, one may feel it on account of something which is not directly about oneself, but concerns a member of one's family. *Malu* is often felt as a response to being teased or chided, as is commonly done among family and friends, or to criticism or complaints, even of a mild nature.

It is clear that *malu* is vaguer and less specific than any comparable term in English. Essentially, *malu* is just a negative and inhibiting reaction to the idea that other people could think something bad about one. The issue seems to matter little—whether it be something one does, something about one's nature or station in life, something about one's family. In any case, some information has reached or could reach other people, and as a result people could disapprove of one, which is a powerfully unpleasant prospect to Malay sensibilities; Swift (1965: 110) equates *malu* with "hypersensitiveness to what other people are thinking about one". This leads to the final aspect of the concept of *malu*, namely, a desire to avoid or withdraw from other people (cf. Heider 1991: 308), an attitude reflected in the common expression *Tak tahu mana nak letak muka ini* 'I don't know where I can put (= hide) my face.'

These notions are incorporated in the following semantic explication (Goddard 1996) for what it means to say that a person (X) feels *malu*. Of course it looks rather peculiar at first—certainly very different from a normal dictionary definition. One reason is that it is phrased exclusively in semantic primes. The other reason is that the explication reflects a certain approach to the meaning of emotion concepts in general. The basic idea is that emotions are feelings which are linked with certain characteristic thoughts. To convey the quality of an emotion we not only have to identify it as a good feeling or a bad feeling, but we also have to identify the characteristic (or prototypical) thoughts associated with the feeling.

X (*me*)*rasa malu* (X feels *malu*)
X feels something bad because X thinks like this:
  people can know something about me
  people can think something bad about me because of this
  people can say something bad about me because of this
  I don't want this
because X feels like this, X doesn't want to be near other people
it is good if people can feel something like this

This explication tries to do better than merely "matching" *malu* with the nearest English terms (like *ashamed, embarrassed, shy*, etc.), none of which match perfectly anyway. It tries to pin down exactly the complex culture-specific meaning of *malu*. The explication captures the fact that *malu* can be induced by the thought that other people are potentially thinking and saying something bad about an individual, which is a situation the person in question doesn't want. This leads the person to feeling bad and to wanting to avoid other people. Naturally, the implication is that to prevent this scenario from occurring one should avoid doing anything which could incur negative opinions and comments by others; hence the power of *malu* as a force for social conformity. The final component captures the fact that the potential to feel *malu* is viewed as a social good.

Like *malu* in this respect, the word *(ber)sabar* (noun form *kesabaran*) is also extremely common in everyday Malay. Though it is often translated as English *patient*, it is much wider in its semantic range. It certainly can be used about the attitude of someone waiting, as in the expression *sabar menunggu* 'waiting patiently'. But the injunction to *sabar* is often addressed to someone who appears to be annoyed, in which case it approximates English expressions like 'calm down' or 'take it easy'. For example, *Janganlah marah! Sabar! Sabar*! 'Don't be mad! Calm down! Calm down!' It is not unusual to find someone's mood described as *marah dan tak sabar* 'annoyed and not *sabar*'. The advice 'to be *sabar*' is equally appropriate to someone who is grieving or distressed. For example, *Bersabar* . . . was the caption accompanying a newspaper photo which showed a woman being consoled after four of her friends had been killed when a van ran into them as they were jogging (*Utusan*, 26 August 1996, p. 1). In a less serious example, a girl who was distressed about being dumped by her boyfriend was told *Sabar, jangan menangis kuat sangat* 'Be calm, don't cry so loud'. As the last couple of examples suggest, the meaning of *sabar* involves having the self-control to stay calm in the face of suffering or affliction.

The salience of *kesabaran* is explained, in large measure, by the importance of 'forbearance, patience' in Islam. The Koranic saying *Allah sentiasa bersama dengan orang-orang yang sabar* 'Allah is always with people who are patient' is often quoted, as is the saying *Sabar separuh daripada iman* 'Being patient is half the faith'. Muslims need to be *sabar* in order to maintain the strict guidelines of Islamic life (including praying five times a day, and observing the annual month of fasting), and in order to maintain their faith in the face of criticism from non-Muslims. On the Islamic view, misfortunes and sufferings should be seen as tests from God. If we can sustain our *kesabaran*, this will show we are *beriman* 'faithful'. Enduring hardships can even reduce our sins. Aside from the sayings just mentioned, there are linguistic reflections of this attitude in common collocations such as *menguji kesabaran* 'testing (one's) patience' and *mencabar kesabaran* 'challenging (one's) patience'.

The religious perspective helps explain why in difficult personal situations— situations which in Western culture would be likely to attract advice such as 'Do something about it' or 'Express how you feel'—characteristic Malay advice is to 'Endure it, forbear'. Advice columns in newspapers and magazines continually advise people to *bersabar*. It is typical for people who are about to undertake serious action to explain that they are not acting on impulse, but have been 'patient' for a long time. A characteristic expression is *Sampai bila saya harus bersabar?* 'How long am I supposed to be *sabar?*'

Staying calm in troubling situations is fully consistent with major themes of traditional Malay culture. It is only by staying calm that one can follow traditional advice such as *Fikir dulu* 'Think first', *Fikir panjang* 'Think long', and *Sentiasa fikir berhati-hati sebelum melakukan sesuatu* 'Always think carefully before undertaking anything', and so on. Self-control in difficult situations means that one will not make the mistake of *ikut hati* 'following (one's) heart' and acting on impulse; as the saying goes *Ikut rasa, binasa; ikut hati mati* 'Follow (your) feelings, suffer; follow (your) heart, die.' Furthermore, staying calm is conducive to harmonious social relations and reduces the chance that other people's feelings will be unnecessarily aroused or offended, consistent with the injunction to *jaga hati orang* 'mind people's feelings', *memelihara perasaan orang* 'protect people's feelings', and so on.

Lest this review of the high moral standing of *kesabaran* lead us to forget its more mundane uses, recall that one can also use *(ber)sabar* about very minor everyday situations, such as *menunggu sabar* 'waiting patiently/ calmly'. Similarly, if one can no longer resist a desire to do something one has been longing to do, expressions like *Saya tak boleh bersabar lagi* 'I was not able to be *sabar* any longer' become appropriate. Similarly, someone who is too demanding may be told *Sabarlah sikit* (roughly) 'Slow down a bit'.

The meaning of *sabar* can be stated in the following explication (Goddard 2001b). This says that for a person (X) to be *sabar* means that the person 'felt something bad' (an intentionally vague formulation compatible with anything from mild irritation to great suffering) and that this had the potential to bring about an impulse 'to do something now' (again, an intentionally vague formulation but one which highlights the immediacy of the intended action). However, person X did not form such an intention, because 'X did not want to think like this'. In other words, being *sabar* is having a kind of "mental discipline". The final component adds a strong moral endorsement ('it is good if a person can be like this').

> X is *sabar* [at the time]
> at this time, X felt something bad
> because of this, X could have thought:
>> I don't want this
>> I want to do something now
> X did not think like this, because X didn't want to think like this
> it is good if a person can be like this

Notice that, as indicated by this explication, being *sabar* is not simply a matter of external appearances: one can look and act *sabar* without truly being *sabar* (for example, if one is *marah* 'annoyed'). Being *sabar* is a matter of one's true state of mind.

I hope you can see now that these two characteristically Malay words—*malu* and *sabar*—have a surprising amount to tell us about Malay culture, provided we look at their uses and meanings in enough detail. They indicate that Malay culture is concerned with ethical and moral matters, with behaving (or at least, seeming to behave) well. In a sense, they celebrate a person with certain traits and attitudes—someone who is mindful of the views of other people, someone who is prepared to endure discomfort and even suffering without complaint. Of course, the existence of these value concepts does not mean that everyone manages to live up to them, or even that everyone tries to do so. As in every society, there is a wide range of personality types in Malay society, including people who are self-centred, spoilt, nonconformist, etc. What the existence of these (and other) Malay key words indicates is that the particular concepts they designate are a part of the shared cultural and linguistic background: that whether or not particular individuals subscribe to them, these values have an important place in public life.

3.4.2 Some key words of Chinese: *xiào* and *rén*

Despite the antiquity of Chinese civilization, there are today many different "Chinese" cultures—in the People's Republic of China (including now Hong Kong), in Taiwan, in Singapore, and throughout the Chinese diaspora, which over the past 150 years has seen millions of Chinese migrants resettle in Southeast Asia and around the world. Nevertheless, there is also evidence of the resilience of core Chinese values. For example, a recent collection of twenty-two personal stories from Chinese around the world (Djao 2003: 203) concludes that: "*Xiào* ['filial piety or filial devotion'] seems to be a fundamental value held by the narrators ... Although many do not mention it by name, almost every narrator invariably speaks of his or her parents in ways expressing that filial devotion." Other cultural values regarded by the narrators as "the bedrock of Chinese culture" include "forbearance, perseverance, diligence, modesty and frugality", and the high value placed on education. Likewise, despite all the social and cultural upheavals in the People's Republic of China most commentators do not hesitate to say that it too bears the stamp of Confucian thinking. Actually, Chinese has no term corresponding to "Confucianism", referring to the philosophy traceable to Kong Fuzi (Confucius, 551–479 BC) and Meng Zi (Mencius, 371–289 BC) as the *School of Ru*, but this is a side issue. The emphasis of Confucian thinking is on harmonious social relationships and a stable social order; in a nutshell, on how people should live in order to live together well.

In this section we will take a close look at two cultural key words of Chinese; but before that a few words on other core Chinese concepts are in order. Perhaps chief among these is the idea of *guānxì* or network relationships. "Chinese navigate complex networks of *guānxì* relationships which expand, day by day, throughout their lives" (Gabrenya and Hwang 1996: 311). In a sociological study (King 1991: 110) quotes an American Chinese correspondent:

Chinese, on the other hand, instinctively divide people into those with whom they already have a fixed relationship, a connection, what the Chinese call *guan-xi* [kuan-hsi] and those they don't. These connections operate like a series of invisible threads, tying Chinese together with a far greater tensile strength than mere friendship in the West would do.

Second, one should mention the very high value placed on self-control (cf. *han yang* 'capacity to contain oneself'), and on social duties and responsibilities. These far outrank the expression of one's true feelings. Thirdly, cross-cultural studies are unanimous in pointing out the long-term orientation of Chinese culture. The following treatment is based on the work of Zhengdao Ye (2002, in press; cf. 2001).

The noun *xiào* (adjective form *xiàoshùn*) represents an ancient and enduring Chinese virtue, and many people have located it at the very core of traditional Confucian values. *Xiào* is normally rendered into English by way of the curious expression 'filial piety', but this is a highly specialized term, in the sense that most ordinary speakers of English would have only a hazy idea of what it is supposed to convey. Especially they might miss the implications of devotion and duty. Ho (1996) emphasizes that the underlying Chinese concept is an "emic" or culture-specific concept which has no real conceptual equivalent in non-Confucian cultures:

Although some of its component ideas (obedience, for example) are shared by other cultures, filial piety surpasses all other ethics in historical continuity, the proportion of humanity under its governance, and the encompassing and imperative nature of its precepts. (Ho 1996: 155)

Djao (2003: 203) agrees that English has no suitable direct translation for *xiào*:

It expresses the love, respect, obedience, solicitude, devotion, care, and the utter sense of duty of the children towards the parents, with the implicit understanding that the children will look after the parents in their old age. It is the bond that ties the children to their parents, in return for the care, guidance, and devotion, and, above all, life itself that the parents have bestowed on the children.

There are numerous fixed phrases and idioms extolling the importance of *xiào:* for example, *bǎi shàn xiào wéi xiān* 'of the hundred good deeds, *xiào* comes first'. Confucius himself once defined *xiào* as "that parents when alive should be served according to propriety; that, when dead, they should be buried according to propriety; and that they should be sacrificed to according to propriety". This dictum not only emphasizes the lifelong duty imposed by *xiào*, but draws attention also to the traditional Chinese practice of remembering and honouring the family ancestors (normally referred to in English, somewhat misleadingly, as "ancestor worship"). At another place, he characterized *xiào* simply as: "Give your father and mother no cause for anxiety other than illness."

No doubt ideas about the relative importance of the obligations imposed by *xiào* are changing over time. According to one study cited by Ho (1996: 160), the main contemporary obligations are "remembering and worshiping one's deceased parents, minimizing parents' worries, bringing glory to one's parents, and treating one's parents with respectful propriety". Other obligations, such as obedience, staying close to one's parents, and continuing the family line were less strongly held.

At the core of *xiào* is the notion that a person owes a unique lifelong debt to his or her parents. They have given you life, they have raised you, they have educated you, and so on. Especially for a woman, the concept can also be extended to parents-in-law, given that traditional Chinese society is male-dominated, but the prototypical object of *xiào* is *fùmǔ* 'father and mother'. There is a Chinese saying *yǐn shuǐ sī yuán* 'When you drink water you have to think about where it comes from.' How can we forget what our parents have done for us? *Fùmǔ eng bí shān gāo, bí hǎi shēn* 'What our parents give us is higher than a mountain, deeper than the ocean.'

Speaking of *xiào* in terms of indebtedness can be misleading if it draws attention away from the importance of attitude. Adhering to *xiào* is not just a matter of going through the motions of satisfying the material (or mental) needs of one's parents. As Confucius once said: "Nowadays for a man to be filial means no more than that he is able to provide his parents with food. Even hounds and horses are in some way provided with food. If a man shows no reverence, where is the difference?" (Lau 1999: 64; cf. also Goh 1996: 53).

The following explication for *xiào* is based on the work of Zhengdao Ye. The first batch of components, in (a), establishes the focus on one's father and mother and on their special role in bringing an individual into the world and sustaining his or her life, and indicates that the individual has a special emotional attitude towards them. The two components in (b) state that a person should always keep one's parents in mind and maintain a certain attitude towards them, the content of which is spelt out in (c). Overall, they amount to a deep concern for the parents' satisfaction and peace of mind, such that one feels compelled to do certain things to make them feel good, and to refrain from doing certain other things which could make them feel bad. The components in (d) specify that it is considered good if a person puts this attitude into practice in a substantial way, and bad if they do not.

   xiào ('filial piety')

a. everyone can think about some other people like this:
      this person is my father, this person is my mother
      I exist because of them
      because of this when I think about them I feel something very good
      I cannot think about other people like this
b. it is good if a person thinks about these people at all times
      it is good if this person feels something because of this
c. it is good if a person thinks about these people like this:
      I want them to feel something very good at all times
      because of this I have to do many good things for them
      I want to do these things
      I don't want these people to feel anything bad at any time
      because of this I cannot do some things
      I don't want to do these things
d. it is good if a person thinks like this about some people
      it is good if a person does many things because of this
      it is bad if a person doesn't think like this about some people

Notice that the explication does not indicate which particular kinds of action are to be pursued or avoided. These could vary from situation to situation, though obviously looking after the parents' material wellbeing would be a minimum expectation. As for their mental satisfaction and peace of mind, given broader Chinese cultural concerns, this would often include things like achieving success in business or scholarship, bringing honour to the family name, and so on.

The explication does not specify that anything like "obedience" as such is required, taking it for granted that going against one's parents' wishes on a serious matter is ruled out because of the distress this would cause them. On the other hand, the adjective form *xiào-shùn* would presumably contain some such component, since *shùn* means 'to follow, not to go against'. Likewise, the explication does not contain anything which links directly with the idea of remembering and honouring one's ancestors. Perhaps it is sufficiently implied by the logic that just as I think like this about my father and mother, so they must think about their own father and mother—and consequently in order to honour and please them I must honour and please my grandparents, their parents, and so on.

The other Chinese key word we will look at in this section is *rěn*. Paperweights and desk calendars in China often bear a message reminding people of the value of *rěn* 'perseverance, patience'. Confucius is recorded as having said: "The lack of self-restraint in small matters will bring ruin to great plans"; and, as is so often the case, his words resonate with a distinctively Chinese attitude to life. In particular, what is distinctive about this epigram, and the attitude behind it, is the contrast between small, localized concerns and the long-term perspective, i.e. the perspective of one's "great plans".

The celebrated Chinese writer Lin Yu-tang (1935: 47) considered *rěn* one of the key national characteristics of the Chinese people, "deliberately inculcated as a cardinal virtue by Confucian ethics". Lin Yu-tang's description of *rěn* highlights another aspect, namely, the emphasis on the capacity for putting up with other people: "this capacity for putting up with insults has been ennobled by the name of patience." Two common phrases reinforce this point, as well as showing that *rěn* can sometimes be translated as 'to tolerate':

rěn qì tūn shēng (lit. 'tolerate anger swallow sound; to swallow one's anger'); 'to refrain from complaining or protesting even after being unfairly blamed or treated'.

rěn rǔ fu zhòng 'tolerate humiliation in order to fulfil an important task'; (fig.) 'to exercise one's utmost patience and will-power in performing a difficult duty'.

Clearly, neither *patience* nor *tolerance* is an exact match for *rěn*, and neither are other English words such as *forbearance, endurance, perserverance*, and so on.

   rěn

a. everyone can think like this about some things:
   I want these things to happen
   I know they cannot happen if I don't do some things
   I want to do these things because of this

    if I have to do these things for a long time I don't want not to do them
      because of this
    if I feel something bad when I do these things I don't want not to do
      them because of this

b. it is good if a person always thinks like this
c. it is good if a person thinks about this when this person feels something
    bad
d. it is good if a person thinks about this when someone else does something
    bad to this person
e. it is good if a person does many things because this person thinks like this
f. it is good if a person can be like this

As a highly prized attitude and behaviour in Chinese culture, *rěn* is considered a virtue, a source of inner strength that is pertinent to the Chinese idea of a moral person. This is reflected in the last component: "it is good if a person can be like this."

3.4.3 Some key words of Japanese: *amae* and *omoiyari*

Japan is a highly industrialized and technologized country, and one of the economically most important nations in the world. Despite this, and despite the fact that historically Japan has engaged in protracted periods of cultural intercourse with the outside world, many Japanese people regard Japanese culture as unique. There is even a Japanese term, *nihonjiron*, referring to discussions which attempt to define the specificity of Japanese identity, a project which has been the subject of numerous books and articles over the past fifty years. The *nihonjiron* movement, with its flavour of cultural nationalism and conservatism, has provoked a counter-response, both in Japan and in the West, which asserts that there is nothing particularly unique about Japanese culture (see e.g. Dale 1986). The truth is that there are many things about Japanese culture which can be regarded as uniquely Japanese, but this does not make Japanese culture a world of its own, lacking similarities with all other cultures of the world. Perhaps even more importantly, the uniqueness of Japanese culture is itself not unique. Every culture has its own unique peculiarities, its own special configuration of values, attitudes, and traditions. Furthermore, no culture is a monolithic block. Though the idea of a "culture" implies some shared understandings and practices, in any society there is also diversity, internal conflict, and change in progress.

Even so, one could identify a few of the broad themes of Japanese culture as follows: a strong sense of group identity operating at different levels of social organization (family, work, nation), coupled with a sense of duty or obligation to the group; a strong desire for social harmony within the "in-group" and consequent reliance on a variety of strategies to minimize overt conflict and disagreement; and a strong awareness of the "vertical" dimension of the social order, i.e. of a hierarchy of social status and responsibility. Unfortunately, describing Japanese concepts by using English words such as *duty, harmony,* and *hierarchy* can at best be a rough approximation. To unpackage the cultural concepts embodied in the relevant Japanese terms themselves (cultural key words like *giri, wa,* and *on*) requires patient and detailed analysis. In this section, we will give two examples of key word analysis of Japanese taken from Wierzbicka (1997) and Travis (1992; 1997).

One of the most influential books on Japan is Takeo Doi's *Amae no Kozo* (1971; translated as *The Anatomy of Dependence,* 1973). Doi, a psychiatrist, argues that the "peculiarly Japanese emotion" of *amae* is "a key concept for the understanding not only of the psychological makeup of the individual Japanese but of the structure of Japanese society as a whole" (p. 28). But what exactly is *amae?* Doi is convinced that there is no single word for it in English, a fact that the Japanese find hard to believe. As one of Doi's colleagues remarked, "Why, even a puppy does it" (p. 15).

Kenkyusha's New Japanese–English Dictionary (1974) defines *amae* (or more precisely, its verbal form *amaeru*) as 'to presume upon (another's) love' and 'to take advantage of (another's kindness)'. Doi gives glosses like: 'presuming on some special relationship' (1973: 29), and 'to depend and presume on another's benevolence' (1974: 145). Some Japanese–English dictionaries list it as 'coaxing'. Kojima and Crane's *Dictionary of Japanese Culture* (1987) explain it as 'to indulge in a feeling of security as a child feels with its loving mother'.

Roughly speaking, then, we can say that *amae* is a certain emotion linked in a positive way with 'dependence' or 'dependency'. This is the term used in the English translation of Doi's book, and it is a term widely used in cultural commentary on Japan. Many scholars link the importance of dependency (and of *amae*) with specific features of Japanese society, for example, with Japanese child-raising practices, which are characterized by intimate contact with the mother, or with the importance of the *oyabun–kobun* relationship. The senior member of the pair, the *oyabun* (the 'superior', 'leader', 'boss', 'patron'), is the protector and sponsor of the junior *kobun* (the 'subordinate', 'follower', 'protege'), from whom one expects unconditional loyalty. De Vos (1985: 160) makes the link between the *oyabun–kobun* relationship and *amae:*

In the traditional Japanese system there were no "rights" on the part of the subordinate. The only recourse for subordinates in the past, since they had no contractual relationships, was to hope to induce kindness and benevolence in their superiors. These feelings were induced by invoking potential feelings of nurturance and appreciation from them.

As Doi sees it, and most commentators agree, the "psychological prototype" for the concept of *amae* lies in the psychology of the infant in its
relationship to its mother; in particular, the infant's feeling that the mother
is someone indispensable, and the consequent craving for close contact. It is
an emotion that takes the other person's love for granted. According to Doi,
in Japan the kind of relationship based on this prototype provides a model
of human relationships in general.

It has been proposed that the meaning of *amae* can be pinned down as
follows (Wierzbicka 1997: 238–42). This explication tries to spell out in
simple terms the various aspects of the concept of *amae* which have been
described by more complex terms such as 'special relationship', 'self-
indulgence', and 'passivity'.

> X feels *amae* towards Y
> X thinks like this about Y:
>   when Y thinks about me, Y feels something good
>   Y wants to do good things for me
>   Y can do good things for me
>   when I am with Y nothing bad can happen to me
>   I don't have to do anything because of this
>   I want to be with Y
> X feels something good because of this

As for the reasons for the prominence of *amae* in Japanese society,
observers of Japanese society generally link this with a positive attitude
toward the spirit of dependence or interdependence, as opposed to the
emphasis on individual independence or autonomy in the West. In contrast
to the so-called "ego culture" of the West, Japan is often characterized as an
"empathy culture" based on the "maternal principle"; or indeed, as an
"*amae* culture".

The concept designated by the word *omoiyari* has been identified by
numerous cultural commentators as one of the key personal virtues of Japan. It
is variously translated into English with nouns such as 'empathy', 'sympathy',
'compassion', or 'consideration', and with adjectives such as 'thoughtful',
'sensitive', or 'considerate'. Lebra (1976: 38) describes it as follows:

For the Japanese, empathy *(omoiyari)* ranks high among the virtues considered
indispensable for one to be really human, morally mature, and deserving of respect.
I am even tempted to call Japanese culture an 'omoiyari culture'. *Omoiyari* refers
to the ability and willingness to feel what others are feeling, to vicariously experience the pleasure or pain that they are undergoing, and to help them satisfy their
wishes ... without being told verbally.

It is not hard to find evidence to support Lebra's characterization of
Japanese culture as a whole as an "*omoiyari* culture". For instance, in a
reader's column in the newspaper *Shikoku Shimbun*, where readers place a

photo of their child and state their hopes and expectations, one of the most common is *Omoiyari no aru ko ni nattene* 'Please become a person with *omoiyari*.' In education guidelines for teachers, the first one is *Omoiyari no kokoro o taisetsu ni shimashoo* 'Let's treasure the mind/heart of *omoiyari*' (Nakatsugawa 1992). In the *sempai/koohai* "senior/junior" relationship in Japanese companies, *omoiyari* plays a key role: the *sempai* is expected to be able to anticipate the needs of the *koohai* and to satisfy them, for which he or she is rewarded with absolute loyalty.

In a survey conducted among Japanese and Australian people, Travis (1992) asked what kind of personal characteristics the respondents valued most. The top-ranking Japanese words were *yasashii* (roughly, 'gentle'), *akarui* (roughly, 'bright, cheerful'), and *omoiyari*. By way of comparison, Travis found that words most commonly mentioned by Australians were 'honest' and 'intelligent'. The ideal of *omoiyari* is closely linked with the communicative style prevailing in Japanese society, which favours "silent" or "anticipatory" communication.

The burden of communication falls not on the message sender but on the message receiver. Instead of Ego's having to tell or ask for what he wants, others around him guess and accommodate his needs, sparing him embarrassment (Lebra 1976: 123).

Among fellow-members [of an "in-group"] a single word would suffice for the whole sentence. The mutually sensitive response goes so far that each easily recognizes the other's slightest change in behaviour and mood and is ready to act accordingly. (Nakane 1970: 121)

As pointed out by Clancy (1986), "*omoiyari* training" occupies a prominent place in the socialization of children of Japan. She found that "Japanese mothers strongly emphasized sensitivity to the needs, wishes, and feelings of others" (p. 232).

Trying to capture the elusive "spirit of *omoiyari*" in a semantic formula, Travis (1997) proposed an explication phrased in simple terms, justifying each component on the basis of a meticulous analysis of numerous examples. It is presented here in a slightly modified form (cf. Wierzbicka 1997).

X has *omoiyari*
X often thinks like this about other people:
    I can know what this person feels
    I can know what this person wants
    I can do something good for this person because of this
    I want to do this
    this person doesn't have to say anything
because of this, X does something
people think this is good

Key technical terms

calque

cultural key word

ethnocentrism

indigenization

lexical stratum (strata)

loan word

phonological adaptation

polysemy

semantic specialization

CHAPTER 4

Grammatical topics

In this chapter we delve into a selection of grammatical topics in East and Southeast Asian languages. At the noun phrase level, we take up the subject of classifier constructions. Then, in the realm of verbal syntax, we look first at the prevalence of aspect marking in languages of the region, then at the pervasive phenomenon of serial verb constructions. At the level of the sentence we will see that for many East and Southeast Asian languages the traditional notion of grammatical subject has to be augmented with a notion of topic. Finally we look at sentence-final particles, whose use is such an important part of communicative competence in most languages of the region.

4.1 Classifier constructions revisited

When we say that a language has classifier constructions we mean that certain NPs (noun phrases) not only have a slot for modifiers such as demonstratives, adjectives, and quantifiers, they also have a slot for another kind of word: a classifier—a word which categorizes the referent according to some salient social, physical or functional property. In certain kinds of NP, the classifier slot must be filled if the NP is to be grammatical. This applies in particular to NPs which contain a quantifier, such as a numeral: hence the expression "numeral classifier". As noted earlier, this term is not

100 per cent appropriate because in almost all East and Southeast Asian languages classifiers are used not only with numerals but also with vaguer quantifiers like 'many' and 'some', and also because in some languages they can be used without any quantifier.

4.1.1 Classifiers and classifier phrases

We saw in Chapter 1, although the relative order of a noun and quantifier varies across the languages of the region, the classifier always occurs next to the quantifier. Because of this, and also because it is sometimes possible for the classifier and quantifier to occur alone (i.e. without a noun), it is reasonable to assume that these two elements form a grammatical sub-phrase (a classifier phrase) inside the NP. Consider the following questions and answers in Thai and Malaysian. The question-words *kìi* (Thai) and *berapa* (Malaysian), which both mean 'how many', behave as quantifiers. The questions illustrate the fact that the classifier occurs adjacent to the quantifier regardless of whether the quantifier follows the noun (as in Thai) or precedes it (as in Malaysian). The answers illustrate the fact that classifier and quantifier can occur without any noun, because the noun is optional in the answer.

Thai

(**38**) Q. *Mǎa kìi   tua?*
        dog   how.many CL:ANIMAL
        'How many dogs?'

    A. *(Mǎa) sǎam tua.*
        dog   three CL:ANIMAL
        'Three (dogs).'

Malaysian

(**39**) Q. *Berapa   ekor   anjing?*
        how.many CL:ANIMAL dog
        'How many dogs?'

    A. *Tiga ekor   (anjing).*
        three CL:ANIMAL dog
        'Three (dogs).'

As mentioned in section 1.6, classifier constructions are often compared with measure constructions and unit counter constructions. Although this is a useful comparison from a structural point of view, there are significant differences between these constructions and true classifier constructions. Measure constructions allow us to refer to particular quantities of a "mass" substance, e.g. water, butter, or paper, either by means of shape-based units or container units, as in (40a) and (40b), respectively. Unit counter constructions allow us to single out some individual items of a collective type or to refer to groups of items of a particular kind, as in (41a) and (41b), respectively. Both measure constructions and unit counter constructions are found in all languages, including English.

(40) a. *two drops of water*   b. *two cups of water*
        two grains of sand   *two boxes of sand*
        two lumps of butter   *two kilograms of butter*

(41) a. *two items of furniture*   b. *two pairs of shoes*
        two articles of luggage   *two bunches of bananas*
        two pieces of fruit   *two members of the committee*

Though they resemble classifier constructions from a structural point of view, these are not true classifier constructions because they are found only with a limited set of nouns (mass nouns and collectives), and because the measure or unit counter word does not classify, i.e. categorize the nature of, the thing referred to by the noun. True classifier constructions are found with a very wide range of nouns, including count nouns (for example, 'teacher', 'cat', and 'chair'), and above all, true classifier words categorize their referents.

If the referents are people, the classifier may simply categorize them as such—i.e. it may mean little more than 'people'. This happens in Malay, which uses *orang* 'people' as a classifier, e.g. *dua orang guru* [two CL:PEOPLE teacher]. Alternatively, there may be specialized classifiers for highly respected social roles such as royalty, teachers, and monks, as in Korean and Khmer (Aikhenvald 2000). If the referents are inanimate, classifiers usually categorize them according to their physical nature (especially shape and material), or according to their function, or both. Common physical properties involved are: long-thin vs. flat vs. round; curved vs. pointy; straight vs. bent; hard-rigid vs. soft-flexible. Often it makes sense to see classifiers as implicitly referring to material prototypes, as suggested by labels such as 'stick-like', 'rope-like', 'fabric-like,' and 'seed-like'. Size often enters the picture too; in particular, there are often classifiers for very small things. Common function-related properties include: being a tool, a dwelling, a vehicle, an item of clothing. There are often separate classifiers for animals, fish, and birds.

Classifier systems always seem to have one general or neutral classifier which can be used with just about any physical thing. In Cantonese there is *go*, in Mandarin *gè*, in Vietnamese *cái*, in Hmong *lub*. These classifiers are used to count mixed groups (e.g. a collection of a couple of pens, a few marbles, and a knife), and for objects whose specific nature is unknown or irrelevant to the speaker. In casual speech, they are often used in place of more specific classifiers.

In all East and Southeast Asian classifier languages there are many nouns which are counted directly, without classifiers. To put it another way, no language of the region has an exhaustive system, in the sense of having at least one classifier for every noun in the language. This statement applies even to Thai, in which the classifier system is highly developed and deeply entrenched in the grammar. In colloquial Thai, body parts, abstract nouns, institutions, and "big places" (words like 'sky' and 'mountain') are counted directly without any classifier.

In some classifier languages, a word can behave as its own classifier; that is, a phrase meaning 'two X' is constructed as 'two X X', instead of 'two classifier X'. For obvious reasons, this kind of construction is called a "repeater construction". Repeater constructions are often employed with nouns which do not have any specific classifier. It is as if the language "wants" to use a classifier construction, and, in the absence of any real classifier solves the problem by using the noun itself to fill the classifier slot. As just mentioned, in colloquial Thai there are various nouns which are normally not found in classifier constructions. In educated Standard Thai, however, people sometimes use repeater constructions with these nouns, perhaps reflecting a perception that it is incorrect, according to the normative rules of Standard Thai, to count things without any classifier. The following examples are from Lao. In (42) we see that a noun like lot^1 'car', which is covered by an ordinary classifier (namely $khan^2$ lit. 'handle'), cannot be used in a repeater construction. With a noun like taw^4 'vase', the situation is different because there is no ordinary classifier which can be used with vases. As we see in (43), taw^4 'vase' behaves as its own classifier. When it occurs for the first time, in the phrase taw^4 $dòòk^5$-maj^4 (lit.) 'flower vase', taw^4 is functioning as an ordinary noun. The second time it is filling the classifier slot, after the quantifying word cak^2 'how many'.

(42) *Mii^2 lot^1 cak^2 lot^1?
     there.is car how.many car
     'How many cars are there?'

(43) Mii^2 taw^4 $dòòk^5$-maj^4 cak^2 taw^4?
     there.is vase flower-plant how.many vase
     'How many vases are there?'

4.1.2 A closer look

Let's now compare how classifiers work in some well-known languages of the region, starting with Southeast Asia. It seems that in an older stage of Malay, classifiers were used more extensively than in modern Malaysian and Indonesian. In present-day Malaysian a number of classifiers are still in common use and in certain contexts they are obligatory, but many of the specialized classifiers are being lost. In Indonesian, only a handful of classifiers are common and most of the time they are optional. In both languages, classifiers are only used in combination with quantifiers, not with demonstratives. Also, in both languages there are many words which cannot receive any classifier, i.e. these classifier systems are far from exhaustive.

In Malaysian, the following classifiers are in everyday use: *orang* (lit. 'people') for people, *ekor* (lit. 'tail') for animals, birds, and fish, *biji* (lit. 'seed') for fruit, eggs, and other small round items, *helai* for clothing and cloth, *keping* for flat items, and *buah* (lit. 'fruit') for large bulky items. For example: *dua orang guru* [two CL:PEOPLE teacher], *tiga ekor ular/ikan/kucing* [three CL:ANIMAL snake/fish/cat], *empat buah meja/rumah* [four CL:BULKY ITEM table/house], *lima biji telur* [five CL:SMALL.ROUND.ITEM egg]. As you can see, most of the common classifiers also exist as ordinary nouns, though their meanings as ordinary nouns do not necessarily correspond with their meanings as classifiers. More specialized classifiers in Malaysian include: *batang* for trees and stick-like things (especially cigarettes); *kaki* for umbrellas; *pucuk* for letters and for guns; *kuntum* for flowers; *patah* for words. Often the number 'one' (*satu*, or in prefix form *se-*) plus a classifier is used more or less as an indefinite article, i.e. with a meaning corresponding roughly to English *a/an*. Thus *seorang* (lit. 'one-people'), for example, is often used without any real emphasis on the fact that only one person is being referred to.

In Indonesian, there are only three classifiers in common use—*orang, ekor* and *buah*—and they are optional. They are much more likely to occur with the numeral 'one', especially in its prefix form *se-*, than with other numerals (Sneddon 1996: 135). As in Malaysian, there are also more specialized classifiers, but they are not very common. Many other Austronesian languages in insular Southeast Asia (e.g. Javanese, Sundanese, Tagalog) have classifier systems similar to those of Malaysian and Indonesian.

The classifier system of Thai (and of Tai languages generally) is different from that of Indonesian, Malaysian, and neighbouring Austronesian languages in many respects. There are more classifiers in everyday use. Generally speaking, they are not the same in form as any ordinary nouns. Classifier use is obligatory and, notably, classifiers are used with demonstratives as well as with numerals. Some of the earliest linguistic studies of classifiers were based on Thai, in particular, Mary Haas's ground-breaking article of 1942. Table 4.1 lists some of the common Thai classifiers, along with the kind of referents typically covered by each. As well as *khon*, the general classifier for people, there are specialized classifiers for high-status people such as monks and royalty.

Sinitic languages tend to have fairly well-developed classifier systems, though perhaps not quite as elaborate as Thai. Table 4.2 shows some of the classifiers for inanimates in Cantonese. Cantonese has more than a dozen common classifiers based on physical properties such as shape, orientation,

Table 4.1. Some examples of Thai classifiers (after Diller 1992: 154)

Classifier	Referent class
khon	(ordinary) people
ong	monks, sacred objects
phrá-ong	royal persons
tua	animals, shirts, trousers, kites, tables, chairs, etc.
khan	cars, bicycles, ploughs, umbrellas, spoons, etc.
lêm	knives, needles, combs, books, carts, candles, etc.
bay	fruit, jars, pillows, hats, baskets, suitcases, tickets, etc.
phĭin	sarongs, towels, mats, curtains, carpets, etc.
tôn	trees, poles, blades of grass, etc.
duang	stars, lanterns, stamps, seals, eyes, spirits, etc.
an	miscellaneous implements, especially those lacking other classifiers

Table 4.2. Some Cantonese classifiers (adapted from Matthews and Yip 1994: 101–5)

Physical properties: shape, orientation, size
  lāp: round, small things
    e.g. *yāt lāp láu* 'a button', *géi lāp yeuhkyún* 'a few pills'
  jēung: objects with a flat side which typically faces upwards
    e.g. *jēung tói* 'table', *jēung dang* 'seat, bench', *jēung jí* 'sheet of paper'
  fūk: thin flat things with four sides
    e.g. *fūk wá* 'painting', *fūk séung* 'photograph'
  gauh: things which are lump-like or have no fixed shape
    e.g. *gauh sehk* 'stone', *gauh chaatgāau* 'rubber, eraser'
  jī: things which are cylindrical and thin
    e.g. *jī bāt* 'a pen', *jī dék* 'flute', *yāt jī fā* 'a single flower'
  tìuh: things which are long, thin, and not always straight
    e.g. *tìuh louh* 'road', *tìuh sèh* 'snake', *tìuh tàuhfaat* 'a strand of hair'

Function
  ga: vehicles and largish machines with moving parts
    e.g. *ga chē* 'car', *ga fēigēi* 'aeroplane', *ga yī-chē* 'sewing machine'
  bá: tools, weapons, and implements
    e.g. *bá jē* 'umbrella', *bá dōu* 'knife', *bá só* 'lock'

and size. Some of them can also be used as measures or unit counters, when combined with mass nouns. A smaller number of common classifiers are based on function. Cantonese also has more than twenty specialized classifiers; for example, *bouh* for sophisticated books and mechanical devices (e.g. *bouh síusyut* 'novel', *bouh jihdín* 'dictionary', *bouh séunggēi* 'camera'), *gāan* for buildings where people live or gather (e.g. *gāan nguk* 'house', *gāan jáuhlàuh* 'restaurant'), *sáu* for songs and poems. On the other hand, the general classifier *go* can be used about anything—people, animals, and objects. It is also used with abstract nouns and other words which do not have any other classifiers.

Mandarin Chinese, which is furthest from Southeast Asia, has a simpler classifier system than most other Sinitic languages. It has about two dozen classifiers in common use, though dictionaries list a much larger number (Erbaugh 1986). Compared with other Sinitic languages, Mandarin tends to collapse its specialized classifiers into the general classifier *gè*, which in daily usage is hundreds of times more common than any other classifier. Aside from *gè*, common Mandarin classifiers include: *zhī* for animals, *tíao* for long, flexible things, *zhāng* for flat things, *kē* for small, round, hard things, *lì* for tiny, grain-like things, *liǎng* for vehicles, *jiàn* for items of clothing and abstract things, and *bǎ* for movable objects (which can be held in the hand). Among the specialized Mandarin classifiers are the following: *běn* for books, *pǐ* for horses, *jù* for speech, and *shǒu* for verse, as well as *dǐng* for hats and *wèi* for honoured people. As Erbaugh (1986: 403–4) notes: "All these things are highly valued throughout Chinese history; not only is the written word venerated, but horses were the imperial animal while hats displayed official rank."

So far as usage is concerned, there is a big difference between casual and formal speech. In casual speech, people mostly use the general classifier. The other so-called "common" classifiers are not particularly common (even in the speech of people who may insist otherwise). In formal speech, however, the other common classifiers are indeed used. It is only in formal written language that many of the bookish, specialized classifiers are used.

Japanese classifiers are suffixes rather than separate words. Dictionaries and grammars list well over a hundred of them, but (paralleling Mandarin in this respect) studies of real usage show that only about two dozen are in common use, and of these, less than half a dozen are extremely common. Table 4.3 is an extract from a larger table in a book-length study of Japanese classifiers (Downing 1996). It gives the percentage frequencies of the seven most common classifiers in a mixed sample of written works of fiction and recorded conversations. The remaining classifiers have a frequency of 1 per cent or less. They include: *shoku* (colours), *mei* (honorific classifier for people), *tsuu* (letters), *dai* (furniture, machines, vehicles), *men* (flat surfaces), *satsu* (books), *wa* (birds etc.), *joo* (long slender objects), *tsubu* (small, grain-like objects), and many others. As Downing points out, frequency figures like these have to be viewed cautiously, because they are influenced by the genre, context, and style of language. In newspapers, for example, *mei*, the honorific classifier for people, is very much more common than in fiction or ordinary conversation.

Table 4.3. Frequency of some Japanese classifiers (after Downing 1996: 55)

Frequency (%)	Classifier	Referent class
40	*nin*	people
23	*tsu*	inanimates ("general")
6	*hiki*	animals
6	*hon*	long thin objects
6	*mai*	flat thin objects
2	*ken*	buildings
2	*ko*	small, 3-D objects

By the way, even in languages like Mandarin Chinese, Thai, or Japanese, in which most of the classifiers cannot be used as independent nouns, historical studies show that they started their life as ordinary words, which gradually became more and more "grammaticalized" in function, and more and more schematic and polysemic in meaning (cf. Adams 1982; DeLancey 1986; Erbaugh 1986). The Mandarin general classifier *gè*, for example, originally meant 'bamboo-stalk' (Norman 1988: 115). By the second century AD, it was being used as a broad-ranging classifier for many different inanimate things; and subsequently its range extended further to take in people. The present-day 'long-thin' classifier *tiáo* originally meant 'branch'. By the second century AD it was already a classifier for long, slender things. Its further extension to abstract things ('matters', 'affairs', 'items of business', etc.) depended on an interesting detail of cultural history: "In the Han dynasty, documents were often written on slender wooden or bamboo strips. ... [Q]uite naturally *tiáo* was used as a measure for these strips; and from there it was quite easily transferred to the matters written on the strips" (Norman 1988: 116).

4.1.3 Other functions of classifiers

Aside from the classic "numeral classifier" construction, classifiers are often found in other constructions or serving other functions. As a way into this area, we first have to understand what it means to say that an NP is "referential". An NP is referential if it is being used to refer to a specific someone or something. NPs can also be used non-referentially in various ways, and in many languages, including Mandarin Chinese (Li and Thompson 1981: 127–9), non-referential NPs do not take classifiers. In (44), *gōngchéngshī* 'engineer' is used to attribute a description to the subject of the sentence *Xinměi*. It is non-referential. In (45) *shuǐguǒ* 'fruit' is also non-referential. It is not referring to any particular items, but rather to a general kind of thing, i.e. fruit. In (46) *yāzi* 'duck' is non-referential for a similar reason: no particular duck or ducks are being referred to. As you can see, none of these examples has any classifier.

(44) *Xinměi shi gōngchéngshī.*
Xinmei be engineer
'Xinmei is an engineer.'

(45) *Nèi ge shāngrén mài shuǐguǒ.*
that CL merchant sell fruit
'That merchant sells fruit.'

(46) *Tā bu xǐhuan yāzi.*
3SG not like duck
'She doesn't like ducks.'

In some languages classifiers can be used to indicate specificity, i.e. reference to a specific, unique individual (Matthews and Pacioni 1997). An NP which is used "specifically" is normally paraphrasable as 'a certain NP'. In English, NPs with the definite article *the* are usually understood as specific, whereas NPs with the indefinite article *a/an* can be either specific or nonspecific. In the sentence *John wants to marry a rich woman*, for example, the phrase *a rich woman* could refer to a specific known person or merely to a particular category of person. Since Sinitic languages do not have articles, one would expect the specific/nonspecific distinction to go unmarked in Sinitic languages. This is indeed the case in Mandarin Chinese, but in Cantonese classifiers are used to indicate specificity. For example, in (47) the bare noun *chē* 'car' implies a nonspecific interpretation, whereas the classifier + noun combination *ga chē* in (48) implies a specific interpretation.

(47) *Chē hóu wùjòu.*
car very dirty
'Cars are (very) dirty.'

(48) *Ga chē hóu wùjòu.*
CL car very dirty
'The car is (very) dirty.'

Since classifiers can be used to indicate specificity, it is common in Cantonese to find classifiers without any accompanying numeral or demonstrative. In the following example, the presence of classifier *go* in the NP *go hohksāang* 'CL student' signals that the speaker has a specific student in mind.

(49) *Hēunggóng Daaihhohk yáuh   go hohksāang yìhngau*
Hong Kong University there.is CL student   research
Chiúhjàu   Wá.
Chiuchow   language
'At Hong Kong University there is a (certain) student studying
the Chiu Chow language.'

In Hmong, classifiers are used extensively to indicate definiteness or
specificity (Clark 1989: 183; examples slightly modified). For example, in
(50a) *dev* 'dog' is definite because it is preceded by classifier *tus*, whereas
npua 'pig' is indefinite because it appears without a classifier. The reverse
holds in (50b).

(50) a. *Tus   dev tom npua.*
CL:ANIM dog bite pig
'The dog bit a pig.'

b. *Dev tom tus   npua.*
dog bite CL:ANIM pig
'A dog bit the pig.'

For a more interesting pair of examples, compare (51) and (52) below. Note
that there are two homonymous classifiers *tus*, one for animate beings
(already seen in the examples above) and another for long things. (In these
examples, White Hmong and Green Hmong refer to different "tribal"
groups of the Hmong with different characteristic styles of dress.)

(51) *Tus   poj   Hmoob Dawb tus   ntiag tsho   xiav xī:ā li.*
CL:ANIM female Hmong white CL:LONG front jacket blue blue so
'That White Hmong woman's jacket trim is very very blue.'

(52) *Pojniam Hmoob Ntsuab tus   ntiag tsho   muaj xiam*
woman Hmong green CL:LONG front jacket have colour
ntau   ntau yam.
much   much sort
'The jacket trim of Green Hmong women is many coloured.'

Classifiers are also commonly found in a "noun substitute" or anaphoric
function (Downing 1996: ch. 6). When used like this, the classifier appears
with a modifier, but without a noun. It is functioning as a noun substitute,
similar in some ways to English *one* (as in: *a big one*). We saw examples of
question–answer pairs in Thai and Malaysian earlier in the chapter. In a
similar fashion, it is common for classifier phrases to be used to single out
members of groups of referents which have been already mentioned, as in
the second and third sentences of (53) below, or to introduce additional
members of categories which have already been mentioned. The example is
from Japanese (Downing 1996: 162; glosses slightly modified).

(53) *Mae-ni   futari   suwattete   sa,   hitori-wa   taaban-o*
front-LOC 2.person were.sitting PRT CL:I.person-TOP turban-OBJ
maita   indojin de   sa   kore-ga   unten   shiteru   de
wrapped Indian and PRT this-SUBJ driving be.doing and
moo   hitori-wa   arabiajin da   yo   ne.
other CL:I.person-TOP Arab   COP PRT PRT
'There were two people in the front seat. One was an Indian wearing a
turban, and he was driving. The other was an Arab.'

Although in the classic numeral classifier construction, the classifier phrase
occurs adjacent to the noun, it can also occur outside the noun phrase,
elsewhere in the sentence. This kind of construction is sometimes called
"classifier float", the idea being that the classifier phrase has detached from
the noun phrase and floated off to reposition itself elsewhere. This terminology derives from generative grammar, but one can use it as a descriptive
label without believing that there is any actual movement involved. The
examples below are from Thai. In (54) we see an ordinary classifier construction, and in (55) a classifier float construction. Interestingly, the posi-
tioning of the classifier phrase seems to be connected with the information
structure of the sentence. If the number of items is in focus, then the normal
position is adjacent to the noun. (54) would be most likely as an answer to
a question about how many birds were there. However, if the number is not
in focus but is simply an additional, possibly incidental, piece of information,
as in (55), then the float construction is more likely (Diller p.c.).

(54) *Mii   nók   [3   tua]   yuu nay kɔɔmáay.*
there.is bird   3   CL:ANIMAL stay in   bushes
'There are three birds in the bushes.' [with the number in focus]

(55) *Mii   nók   yuu   nay   kɔɔmáay   [3   tua].*
there.is bird   stay   in   bushes   3   CL:ANIMAL
'There are three birds in the bushes.'

4.1.4 Classifiers, prototypes, and polysemy

Classifiers often present a range of uses which is at best confusing and at
worst bizarre. For example, Thai *tua* can be used to classify animals, certain
items of furniture and clothing, and letters of the alphabet. This curious
range of seemingly unconnected uses, added to the general "strangeness" of
classifiers from a European perspective, has given rise to a tendency to
portray them as altogether mysterious from a semantic point of view, but
this impression largely disappears when they are examined in a careful,
culturally informed fashion. One key fact which has to be recognized is that
most classifiers are polysemous. That is, instead of having a single, general

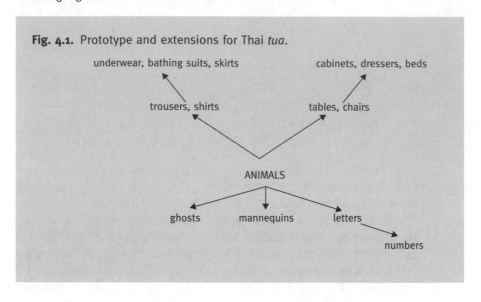

Fig. 4.1. Prototype and extensions for Thai *tua*.

meaning which applies to all instances of use, a typical classifier will have several distinct but interrelated meanings which can best be understood in terms of a "prototype" analysis. Basically this means identifying one use as the central or prototypical meaning, and interpreting the other uses as extensions of various kinds. This concept is best illustrated by example.

A prototype (central meaning) and extensions analysis has been developed for Thai *tua* by Carpenter (1987). It can be diagrammed as in Fig. 4.1, where arrows indicate extensions from more central or prototypical uses to less central ones. This kind of setup is sometimes referred to as "radial polysemy" (Lakoff 1987).

Carpenter (1987) gives the following explanation. Classifier *tua* was first used, she says, "with animals, and the prototype is probably some good quadruped animal such as a dog or water buffalo". Subsequent extensions have meant that it is now applied not only to animals, but to "a wide, but not incoherent, range of things", including various articles of furniture (e.g. tables and chairs, and less often, dressers and beds), items of clothing (e.g. trousers, shirts, jackets, skirts, and, less often, dresses, underwear, and bathing suits), numbers, and letters.

These assignments suggest that it is the presence of limbs, giving these objects a body-like shape, that causes speakers to classify them with *tua*. ... [T]ables and chairs were included on the basis of shape, either because of their general quadrupedal outline or perhaps because of the specific presence of limbs. Other kinds of furniture were added because of their shared function with tables and chairs. Trousers and shirts were included because of their shape, again either because they generally follow the contours of the body of the wearer, or specifically because they have limbs. Other kinds of clothing were included because of their shapes.

Letters (of the alphabet) in Thai is a compound *tua nangseu* 'body book' so a combination of shape and the repetition of the generic compound head caused letters to be classified with *tua*. Numbers were included either on the basis of shape or because of their shared function with letters. (Carpenter 1987: 45–6)

Carpenter also described how classifier *tua* is in the process of being further extended, in the colloquial speech of university students, to cover youth culture items such as guitars, tape recorders, microphones, and university courses. According to Deepadung (1997: 53), it did not take long for these usages to "become more widely accepted in colloquial speech by most of the Thai people... [They are] no longer limited to the youth culture." Deepadung reports that many abstract nouns, commercial and business concepts, and new technological items are now classified with *tua*. For example, words such as: *panhǎa* 'problem', *khwaamkhít* 'idea', *sǐnkháa* 'merchandise, stock', *yaa* 'medicine', *klɔ̂ngthàayrûup* 'camera', and *khrɨ̂angkhɔmphíwtɔ̂ə* 'computer set'. The semantic basis for this latest wave of extensions is not really clear. It looks as if *tua* is starting to behave as a general classifier for abstract and complex items (but not for simple, concrete things, which are still classified using the older general classifier *an*).

The most celebrated example of a prototype analysis of a classifier is George Lakoff's (1987: 104–7) description of the Japanese numeral classifier *-hon*. We will examine *-hon* in the light of a more recent and detailed study by Matsumoto (1993*a*). The treatment follows Goddard (1998). Typical uses of *-hon* are with things like pencils, sticks, fingers, needles, carrots, bananas, ropes, strings, and cords. Both rigid and flexible items are covered. Some examples are given below; notice that *-hon* has several allomorphs, including *-pon* and *-bon*.

(56) *kyuuri   ip-pon   enpitsu ni-hon   himo   san-bon*
      cucumber one-CL:HON   pencil   two-CL:HON   string   three-CL:HON
      'one cucumber'   'two pencils'   'three strings'

Aside from prototypical long-thin referents like these, Matsumoto (1993*a*) discusses such disparate items as: cassette tapes, camera films, rubber bands, liquids in bottles and tubes, telephone calls, letters, movies, theses, TV serials, medical injections, hits and home runs in baseball, and passes and shots in baseball, soccer, and basketball. Like Lakoff (1987), Matsumoto argues that *-hon*'s range of use is best analyzed as the result of radial polysemy, i.e. by assuming that there is one central meaning, from which several extended meanings branch out in different directions. The overall picture can be diagrammed as in Fig 4.2.

There are two sets of extended uses of *-hon* which pertain to concrete objects. The first relates to things like cassette tapes, typewriter ribbons, and camera films—objects that can be seen as consisting of a "*hon*-like" item which is rolled up. Some speakers also apply *-hon* to rubber bands and tyre

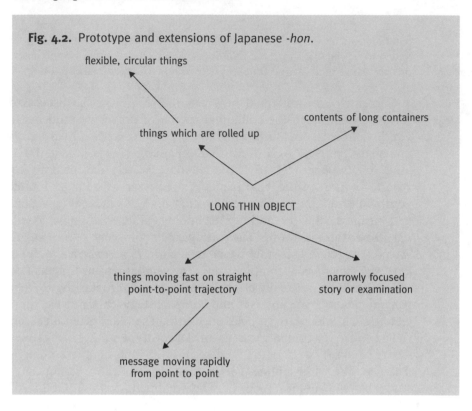

Fig. 4.2. Prototype and extensions of Japanese *-hon*.

flexible, circular things

contents of long containers

things which are rolled up

LONG THIN OBJECT

things moving fast on straight
point-to-point trajectory

narrowly focused
story or examination

message moving rapidly
from point to point

tubes, objects which are normally in a "circular" shape but which, if cut, would assume a more typical *hon*-like shape. The second extended use concerns fluids which come in "closed long-shaped containers" such as bottles, cans, long cartons, tubes, and syringes. Not only the container, but also the fluid inside (be it whisky, coke, milk, paste, or a medical injection) can be classified as *-hon*.

Three further uses of *-hon* relate to non-physical referents. As suggested by Lakoff (1987), the use of *-hon* with home runs, hits and fouls in baseball, passes and shots in soccer and basketball, serves in volleyball, rallies in table-tennis, and so on, seems explicable in terms of a ball travelling along a narrowly defined "trajectory". The extended use is based on a likeness between the image of a long thin object and the trajectory of a moving object. According to Matsumoto (1993*a*), a similar principle explains why telephone calls and letters can sometimes be classified as *-hon*, since they can be seen as involving communication which travels from one place to another. He notes that *-hon* is acceptable when it refers to telephone calls being connected or received, but not when it refers to telephone conversations (even though the same noun, *denwa* 'telephone', is used for both). Similarly, *-hon* is acceptable when speaking of sending a letter, but not when speaking about writing a letter. The key factor seems to be point-to-point transmission.

A third set of non-physical uses is based on what Matsumoto calls "experiential length". Theses, TV serials, movies, and play scripts "form a continuum when we experience (read, write, watch) them in real time, and can therefore be regarded as one dimensional" (1993*a*: 678). This explanation cannot be quite right, however, because it would predict that *-hon* can be applied to a long telephone conversation, which is incorrect. From the range of acceptable referents, however, we might speculate that what is involved is a narrowly focused "story" or an extended examination of a particular topic.

Though this does not exhaust all the possible uses of *-hon*, it should be clear that its apparently bewildering variety of possible referents is not as bizarre and arbitrary as it may at first seem. The key to developing a clear picture is to work patiently through the language-specific facts.

4.2 Aspect

As you know, most East and Southeast Asian languages are isolating in type and lack inflection. For the European language learner, this has the curious implication that verbs are unmarked for tense, i.e. they do not change their form to indicate past, present, or future. On the other hand, verbs in East and Southeast Asian languages are often marked for another less familiar category, namely aspect. Sometimes this is done by way of suffixes, sometimes using auxiliary verbs, sometimes using postverbal particles. To get a clearer idea about aspect, we first have to clarify what we mean by tense. Along the way we will find that English verbs have some marking for aspect, but that in English it is rolled together with the marking for tense.

4.2.1 What is aspect?

Tense is a grammatical category of verbs whose primary function is to indicate the relative time reference of the event or situation being described. English allows us to illustrate some interesting points about tense and tense marking. If we compare the past and future tense forms, we see the past is indicated by suffixation (e.g. *talk, talk-ed*) or by stem modification (e.g. *see, saw*), whereas the future is indicated by means of a separate verb *will* (e.g. *will talk, will see*). When *will* is used in this way, to indicate grammatical information about another verb, we say that it is functioning as an "auxiliary verb". Auxiliary *will* seems to belong to the same set as other auxiliary verbs, such as *can* and *might*, i.e. *will see, can see*, and *might see* all seem to have the same structure. Auxiliary verbs such as *can* and *might* are usually called "modal verbs" (or just modals for short). The general term for the kind of information they convey is modality, which is usually defined in a fairly vague way as a grammatical category whose meanings involve possibility, potentiality, ability, etc. (The 'etc.' here leaves a lot of room for inconsistency between linguists.) Because *will* belongs to the same set of modal verbs as *can* and *might*, and because there is always something uncertain about the future, some linguists say that English doesn't really have a future tense at all.

Notice that although words like *talks* and *sees* are normally said to be "present tense" forms, they are not usually used about events happening at the present time but rather to make generalizations (e.g. *He talks too much*) or to state regularities (e.g. *The bus leaves at ten past the hour*). To describe an event or situation which is happening at the present time, one uses a form of the verb *to be* as an auxiliary together with the '*ing*-form' of the main verb, e.g. *You are talking too much, The bus is leaving*. This is normally called the "progressive" construction. The English progressive construction, however, can occur in any tense. One just changes the tense of the auxiliary; for example, *You are talking too much* (present tense, progressive), *You were talking too much* (past tense, progressive), *You will be talking too much* (future tense, progressive).

The progressive is an English example of the category of aspect. It is a category which is connected with time—but not with location in time. Rather, an aspect category indicates something about the "time structure" (temporal structure) of the event being described. The English progressive, for example, directs our attention to whether or not the event is "in the act of happening", so to speak.

One common type of aspect distinction in the world's languages is the "perfective vs. imperfective" distinction (Comrie 1976). Perfective aspect presents an event in its totality—all bundled up, as it were—without any attention to its internal structure. Imperfective aspect directs our attention to the internal structure of the event. Progressive is a sub-type of imperfective. Other kinds of event structure which also fall under the broad category of imperfective include iterative, durative, and habitual. Iterative refers to events which consist of lots of more or less identical sub-events; for example, *flashing* or *shivering*. Durative refers to any event or action which takes some time; for example, *eat, talk, stand, sit*. Habitual refers to an event or action which takes place regularly or generally. These distinctions are set out in Fig. 4.3.

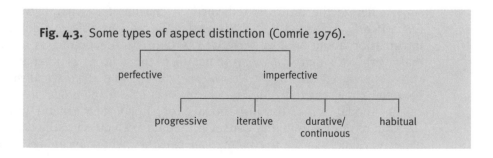

Fig. 4.3. Some types of aspect distinction (Comrie 1976).

Linguists sometimes include under aspect some verbal categories whose meanings don't really focus on the time structure of events, providing that the category has the same grammatical characteristics as other (true) aspects. Consider the construction found in sentences like: *Max has broken his arm, The bus has left, I have never seen him before.* In this construction, often labelled the "perfect" (not to be confused with perfective), an auxiliary verb *have* is used in combination with a special form of the verb (e.g. *broken, left, seen*) which is normally called the "past participle". Many past participles, e.g. *left*, are the same as past tense forms while others have a distinct form: compare *seen* (past participle) vs. *saw* (past tense), *broken* (past participle) vs. *broke* (past tense). The *have* + past participle construction is often referred to as indicating aspect, but it doesn't really meet the ideal definition of aspect. Its function is to signal "present relevance", i.e. that the past event or action is somehow relevant to us (Huddleston 1984). Compare *Max has broken his arm* with *Max broke his arm*: the version with *have* suggests that Max's arm is still broken and that this has some particular consequences for us (it would sound strange to say **Max has broken his arm last year*). In a similar fashion, one finds that Mandarin Chinese is normally described as having an "experiential" aspect, indicating that a situation has been experienced by the subject or the speaker.

One final but important point. There is often something subjective about choice of aspect. I mean, it is often up to the speaker to decide what viewpoint he or she wants to adopt toward a particular event or action—whether, for example, to view it as a single event in its entirety, or as an event which is extended in time, or as an event which has been personally experienced or which has relevance to the present, or whatever. Admittedly, the nature of the verb or some other feature of the sentence structure can limit the speaker's choice in this regard, but often whether to express aspect at all—and if so, which aspect to use on a particular occasion—is up to the speaker.

4.2.2 Aspect marking in Sinitic languages

The aspect systems of the two best described Sinitic languages—Mandarin Chinese and Cantonese—have much in common. It is possible to line up the categories of the two languages, even though different forms are found in each language. After the discussion in the previous section, you will recognize most of the categories shown in Table 4.4. That's a far cry, of course, from knowing exactly how they should be used, but we'll come to that in a moment. Notice that in most cases the marking takes the form of a suffix (for example, Mandarin perfective *-le*, Cantonese perfective *-jó*); but in one case it is done using a separate, preverbal word (i.e. Mandarin

Table 4.4. Aspect markers in Mandarin and Cantonese (after Matthews and Yip 1994: 198, Li and Thompson 1981: 185)

	Mandarin	Cantonese
Perfective	VERB-*le*	VERB-*jó*
Imperfective:		
Progressive	*zài* VERB	VERB-*gán*
Continuous: Durative	VERB-*zhe*	VERB-*jyuh*
Experiential	VERB-*guò*	VERB-*gwo*
Delimitative	VERB-(*yī*)-VERB	VERB-*háh*
Habitual		VERB-*hōi*

progressive *zài*), and in one case it is done by reduplication (i.e. the Mandarin "delimitative").

Now let's look into the usage and meaning of these aspect categories. To begin with, we can note that they can be used regardless of the relative time reference of the event spoken about (i.e. regardless of whether it is in the past, present, or future). Admittedly, there is a tendency for perfective and experiential aspects to be used about events which took place in the past, but this is only a tendency. For example, Mandarin *-le* (interlinear gloss PERF) can be used in sentences about the future, in conditional sentences, and even in imperatives (Li and Thompson 1981: 213).

(57) *Míngtiān wǒ jiu kāichú-le tā.*
tomorrow I then expel-PERF 3SG
'Tomorrow I'll expel him/her.'

(58) *Tā kāi-le   mén, nǐ jiu jìn-qu.*
3SG open-PERF door 2SG then enter-go
'(Once) she opens the door, you go in.'

(59) *Hē-le   tā.*
drink-PERF 3SG
'Drink it up.'

Li and Thompson (1981) explain perfective aspect in Mandarin Chinese as follows:

[I]t indicates that an event is being viewed in its entirety or as a whole. An event is viewed in its entirety if it is bounded temporally, spatially, or conceptually. There are essentially four ways in which an event can be bounded:
A. By being a quantified event
B. By being a definite or specific event
C. By being inherently bounded because of the meaning of the verb
D. By being the first event in a sequence

Under category (A) they include contexts in which the verb occurs in combination with a phrase specifying the overall duration of the event (e.g. 'for three hours', 'for two months'), the number of times it happened (e.g. 'once', 'three times'), or, with transitive verbs, the number of direct objects involved (e.g. 'She bought a lot of books', 'They sent out fifty invitations'). Using quantifying expressions, as in these examples, has the effect of focusing our attention on the overall nature of the event or action.

With appropriate verbs, perfective aspect can be used if the extent to which the event occurred is specified; in (60), for example *yīdiǎn* 'a little' indicates extent. Notice that this example shows a stative verb (semantically equivalent to an English adjective) suffixed with *-le* PERF.

(**60**) *Nǐ gǎo-le   yīdiǎn.*
2SG tall-PERF a.little
'You've got taller (i.e. you "talled" a little).'

Under category (B), Li and Thompson (1981) have in mind sentences in which the identity of the grammatical object is the focus of attention. For example:

(**61**) *Wǒ pèng-dáo-le   Lín Huì.*
I   bump-arrive-PERF Lin Hui
'I ran into Lin Hui.' (where Lin Hui's identity is the important information)

(**62**) *Yīnwéi wǒ kàn-le   xīn chūbǎn de   zīliào.*
because I   see-PERF new publish GEN material
'Because I looked at the newly published figures.' (e.g. to answer the question 'How did you know?')

Li and Thompson (1981: 195) stress that the choice of perfective *-le* "depends on what the speaker judges to be the significant information the sentence is conveying in the context in which it is used". To help dramatize this point they refer to the following sentence (from Spanos 1977: 45):

(**63**) *Tā wèn wǒ zuótiān   wǎnshang zuò(-le)   shénme?*
3SG ask I   yesterday evening   do(-PERF) what
'She asked me what I did last night.'

When thirty-nine speakers were asked to say whether *-le* should be included, only seven said it should be, while thirty-two said it should not be. On further investigation it emerged that the seven who favoured using *-le* were thinking of a situation in which the questioner was asking for a specific list of activities; for example, if *tā* 'he/she' in sentence (63) were a nurse in charge of making sure the speaker didn't do too much.

The reason speakers disagree when they are presented with sentences in isolation is because they have to imagine what the real conversational situation might be, and they might come to different conclusions on this point. (Li and Thompson 1981: 195)

Under their category (C), Li and Thompson refer to verbs which are "inherently bounded" by virtue of their meanings, for example, verbs like *wàng* 'forget', *sĭ* 'die', *huài* 'broken', and *miè* 'go out' (of a fire). (However, Li and Thompson do note that these verbs do not necessarily take perfective *-le* when they are the complements of verbs like 'want', 'hope', 'prefer', etc. They explain this apparent discrepancy by saying that in these contexts the verbs are not depicting real events.)

Finally, to Li and Thompson's category (D): "first event in a sequence". This refers to sentences in which an event is bounded by the fact that it is the first in a sequence: "what is important is that after one event has taken place, another one happens or a whole new state materializes. In such cases, the first event is of interest as an unanalyzed whole" (1981: 198). In the following examples, notice that neither of the first clauses contains an explicit conjunction corresponding to English *when* or *after*. This is very typical.

(**64**) *Wŏ kàn-wán-le   bào,   jiu   shuì.*
I   read-finish-PERF paper then sleep
'(When) I finish reading the paper, I will go to sleep.'

(**65**) *Zĕnme pèng-le   bēizi   yĕ   bù   hē?*
how   bump-PERF glasses also not drink
'How come (after) you touched the glasses, you still don't drink?'

We have looked at Mandarin perfective aspect in some detail for two main reasons. First, because it is one of the most difficult features of the language for English-speaking learners to understand—and hence to use properly. Second, to emphasize the way in which aspect marking often depends on the speaker's communicative intentions in the on-going flow of discourse.

We will illustrate the other Sinitic language aspect categories in less detail, using Cantonese as our example language (Matthews and Yip 1994: 198ff.). The "progressive" *-gán* indicates ongoing actions, often in the present. The "continuous" *-jyuh* indicates a state of affairs, typically present or timeless. Both these categories can be regarded as subtypes of imperfective aspect.

(**66**) *Wòhng síujé góng-gán dihnwá.*
Wong miss talk-PROG telephone
'Miss Wong is talking on the phone.'

(**67**) *Dī wàhn jē-jyuh   go taaiyèuhng.*
CL cloud block-CONT CL sunlight
'The clouds are blocking out the sunlight.'

The "experiential" aspect implies that the situation took place before the time of speaking, but this is not its primary meaning. Its primary meaning is difficult to state clearly, but has to do with the relevance of the past event. For example:

(**68**) *Kéuih duhk-gwo daaihhohk, yīnggōi hóu yùhngyih wán dóu gūng.*
she   study-EXP university   should very easy   find PRT job
'She's been to university, so she should be able to find a job easily.'

(**69**) *Ga dihnlóuh waaih-gwo géi chi.*
CL computer break-EXP few time
'This computer crashed a few times before.'

The Cantonese experiential aspect is a bit like the English "perfect" described in the previous section (and the perfect often makes a good translation), but there is an important difference. The English perfect suggests that a state or result persists until the current time, but Cantonese *-gwo* tends to convey the opposite assumption: that the events being described are all over. When this happens, the English perfect cannot be used as a translation. Consider, for example, the following sentence with the experiential aspect:

(**70**) *Léih hái Hēunggóng jyuh-gwo géi loih a?*
you   in Hong Kong live-EXP how long PRT
'How long did you live in Hong Kong?'

It suggests that the speaker assumes that the subject (*léih* 'you') is no longer in Hong Kong. The experience is over. (To express the opposite assumption the perfective *-jó* would be used.)

As the name suggests, the Cantonese "habitual" *-hōi* indicates a habitual customary activity. It is often found in reference to the present situation, as in (71) below. To specify that the customary or habitual activity took place in the past, we have to add an adverb such as *yíhchìhn* 'before', as in (72).

(**71**) *Kéuih jouh-hōi jūngdím ge.*
she   work-HAB part.time PRT
'She normally works part-time.'

(**72**) *Kéuih yíhchìhn jā-hōi Bēnsí ge.*
she   before drive-HAB Benz PRT
'She used to drive a Mercedes.'

Finally, the so-called "delimitative". This is formed with the suffix *-háh*, and conveys a meaning something like 'to do for a while'. Often it can be rendered into English with the *have a V* construction, e.g. *tái-háh* 'look for a while, have a look', *hàahng-háh* 'walk for a while, have a walk', *yāusīk-háh* 'rest a while, have a rest'.

Interestingly, there is an alternative way of expressing this meaning (or something very similar to it) employing reduplication. The construction is: verb–*yāt*–verb, i.e. a reduplication with the morpheme *yāt* 'one' inserted between the two verb forms. For example, *kīng-yāt-kīng* 'have a chat', *lám-yāt-lám* 'have a think'. This corresponds to a pattern also found in Mandarin, where verb–*yī*–verb is the relevant form (*yī* 'one').

Before we leave the Sinitic languages, we can draw out one further observation. Some of the aspect suffixes are identical in form to ordinary verbs. The Cantonese continuous suffix -*jyuh* is identical with the verb *jyuh* 'to live', and the experiential suffix -*gwo* is identical with the verb *gwo* 'to cross'. Presumably their aspectual functions have evolved from their ordinary lexical uses. Notice that we can still discern some similarity in meaning between *jyuh* 'to live' and "continuousness": namely, that 'living' is by its nature a continuing state. Similarly, we can sense a similarity in meaning between "experiential" -*gwo* and verbal *gwo* 'to cross': having an experience can be thought of something one has 'been through' or 'crossed through' (which incidentally helps explain why experiential -*gwo*, unlike the English perfect, implies that the experience is all over). The same phenomenon—grammatical words or affixes evolving from ordinary verbal words—can be found in language after language in East and Southeast Asia. They often appear to follow parallel pathways of development even in the absence of language contact. For example, progressive markers have developed from verbs meaning 'to live or be somewhere' in languages as different as Lahu (Tibeto-Burman), Vietnamese, and Hmong, where the verbal forms are *chê* 'dwell, be in a place', *ở* 'be somewhere', and *nyob* 'be somewhere', respectively (Matisoff 1991*a*: 415–17). How and why does this happen? We will see the beginnings of an answer in section 4.3, when we look at serial verb constructions.

4.2.3 Aspect marking in Lai Chin and Malaysian

To make the point that aspect systems may differ significantly in both their formal and semantic characteristics, we will take a quick look at two other languages: Lai Chin (Tibeto-Burman) and Malaysian (Austronesian).

Aspect in Lai Chin (Kavitskaya 1997, cf. Singh 1999) is achieved mainly by particles which either precede or (more commonly) follow the verb. The preverbal particles seem to signal both aspectual and tense-like meanings and (in some cases) directional meanings. For example, *rak* can indicate either past perfective or motion directed towards the speaker. It seems to originate historically from the verb 'come'. Particle *von* indicates immediateness of action or motion. Examples of aspectual uses follow. Notice that the particles appear after the pronominal subject-marking prefix.

(73) *Nii kum ʔaʔ ka-law ka-(rak)-thloʔ.*
last year LOC my-field 1SG-PAST.PERF-plough
'I ploughed my field last year.'

(74) *ʔa-von-kal.*
    3SG-right.away-go
    'He went straight away.'

There are more than a dozen postverbal particles, including completive *tsang* (from lexical verb *tsang* 'happen, become'), habitual *toon*, experiential *bal*, and progressive *liaw*. Another postverbal particle, *laay*, indicates irrealis (unreal condition), which is required for future contexts. Aspectual and temporal adverbs also occur postverbally. Some examples follow. Notice that (75) shows perfective *tsang* and lexical verb *tsang* 'happen, become' in the same sentence. (76a) and (76b) show the contrast between habitual *toon* and experiential *bal*.

(75) *Ngaa ʔaʔ ʔa-tsang-tsang.*
    fish   LOC 3SG-become-PAST.PERF
    'He had become a fish.'

(76) a. *Falaam ʔaʔ ka-kal-toon.*
       Falaam LOC 1SG-go-HAB
       'I used to go to Falaam.'

    b. *Falaam ʔaʔ ka-kal-bal.*
       Falaam LOC 1SG-go-EXP
       'I had the experience of going to Falaam.'

(77) *ʔa-law   ʔaʔ Tsewmang rian ʔa-ʈuan-liaw.*
    3SG-field LOC Tsewmang work 3SG-do-PROG
    'Tsewmang is/was working in his fields.'

In Malaysian, aspect is marked not by suffixes or verbal particles, but by separate words which precede the main verb. The word *sudah* (often shortened to *dah*) is often said to indicate perfective aspect, and *sedang* (or *tengah*) to indicate progressive or continuous (Koh 1990: 203).

(78) *Saya pun   sudah beritahu juga semalam, terlupa?*
    I   FOCUS PERF   tell   also yesterday forget
    'I already told (you) yesterday, (have you) forgotten?'

(79) *Besok   dah besar, besok   kamu tahu-lah!*
    tomorrow PERF big   tomorrow you   know-EMPH
    'In future (after) you grow up, then you'll understand.'

(80) *Bila   saya masuk, dia sedang membaca.*
    when I   enter, he PROG   read
    'When I came in, he was reading.'

As we would expect of a perfective marker, Malaysian *sudah/dah* tends to be used about events in the past, but it is not confined to such contexts—as we can see, in fact, from example (79) above. In this, and in other ways, Malaysian resembles its perfective counterpart in Mandarin. However, there are also differences in the behaviour and properties of the two markers. One difference is that Mandarin *-le* is not used in negative sentences, but *sudah*—or rather, its negative counterpart *belum*, roughly, 'still not'—is. Malaysian *sudah* also differs from Mandarin *-le* in that it exists independently as a particle, meaning roughly 'That's enough! no more of that', and as a stative verb meaning 'complete, ready' (cf. Koh 1990: 207). Examples follow. Similarly, the progressive marker *tengah* can function as a separate word with a meaning of its own, namely 'middle'; for example, in expressions like *tengah hari* 'middle of the day'. The other progressive marker *sedang* can be used as an adverb meaning 'moderate, medium'.

(**81**) *Sudah!   Berhenti dulu.*
complete stop   first
'That's enough. Stop before (you do anything else).'

(**82**) *Surat itu   pun   sudah-lah.*
letter that FOCUS complete-EMPH
'The letter was finally ready.'

Before leaving aspect in East and Southeast Asian languages, a reminder—as always—that there are many systems which differ from the few which we have considered here. The differences may be in how aspectual categories are marked and/or in the nature of the categories themselves. For example, in Tagalog, one means of marking perfective aspect is to replace an initial /m/ in the infinitive form with an /n/ (e.g. infinitive *magwalis* 'to sweep', perfective *nagwalis* 'swept'); imperfective aspect is marked by reduplicating the first consonant and vowel of the following syllable (e.g. imperfective *nagwawalis* 'is/was sweeping') (Schachter 1987: 226–7). These morphological techniques are quite different from those we have seen so far, but the categories (imperfective/perfective) are not unfamiliar. On the other hand, Tagalog also has an additional aspect, the so-called "contemplated aspect", for events which are hypothetical rather than real. There are also languages which have little or no marking of aspect. For example, neither Acehnese (Austronesian) nor Khmer (Mon-Khmer) have much in the way of aspect marking, and what there is is optional (Durie 1985).

4.2.4 Other verbal categories

As mentioned earlier, modality refers to meanings which are connected with potentiality, ability, obligation, permission, and so on. In English, one way in which modality meanings are expressed is by means of a special kind of auxiliary verb, the so-called modal verbs such as *can, may*, and *must*. English modal verbs have some special properties which set them apart from other verbs; for example, they don't show "agreement" with a 3SG subject in the present tense e.g. *He can/*cans do it.* Modality meanings can also be expressed by other, more elaborate verbal expressions (e.g. *be able to, have to, need to*), and in other ways.

All languages have ways of expressing modality meanings, and East and Southeast Asian languages are no exception in this respect. It is quite common to find verbal particles (i.e. words which occur with verbs but which are not themselves particularly verb-like), and/or modal auxiliary verbs. These possibilities are illustrated below with the modal particle *boleh* 'can' in Malaysian, and the Mandarin modal auxiliary *néng* 'can' (Norman 1988: 166), in (83) and (84) respectively.

Malaysian

(**83**) *Dia tak boleh buat.*
    3SG not can do
    'He can't do it.'

Mandarin

(**84**) *Tā bù néng zǒulù.*
    3SG not can walk
    'She can't walk.'

It is also common to find the verb for 'get' being used as an auxiliary and/or as a verbal particle, with meanings such as 'to get the chance to' and 'be able to'. These usages are not as exotic as they may sound: (American) English has something similar, e.g. *I got to see the movie after all*. But they are much more extensive and more deeply embedded in the grammar of many East and Southeast Asian languages than the comparable use of *get* is in English (Enfield 2003; cf. Clark 1989: 217). For example, the Lao word *daj⁴* 'get' can not only function as an ordinary verb, as in (85). It can also occur as a preverbal marker, conveying a meaning associated with accomplishment, as in (86), and—even more commonly—as a postverbal marker meaning 'can', as in (87). These examples are from Enfield (2003), who shows that *daj⁴* has several other functions as well. A similar pattern is found in Thai, Vietnamese, Khmer, Hmong, and Cantonese, among other languages.

(**85**) *Lang³ caak⁵ nan⁴ laan³   kaᵒ daj⁴ pùm⁴.*
    back from that grandchild then get book
    'After that, his grandchild got his book.'

(**86**) *Laaw² bòò¹ daj⁴ beng¹.*
    3SG   not get look
    'He didn't get a look at it.'

(**87**) *Qaan¹ bòò¹ daj⁴.*
    read   not get
    'He couldn't read it.'

The term "irrealis" refers to a verbal category for events and situations which are not being presented as real or actual, but rather as hypothetical, conditional, or potential. Many languages around the world have special irrealis verbal forms which are used when talking about possible future events or hypothetical situations (in European grammars a somewhat similar category is known as "subjunctive"). The converse term, by the way, is realis. Some East and Southeast Asian languages mark irrealis status by means of verbal particles, e.g. Thai *ca*, Lao *si⁰*.

4.3 Serial verb constructions

In this section we are going to get acquainted with an aspect of grammar which may seem at first rather strange and unfamiliar, but which is extremely widespread, not only among the languages of East and Southeast Asia but also in many other places in the world. I am talking about serial verb constructions, also known as verb serialization. Verb serialization was first observed and discussed in relation to African languages, but has subsequently been recognized in the languages of Asia, the Pacific, Papua New Guinea, and Australia. Unfortunately, there is a lot of theoretical disagreement about the nature of verb serialization, and even about what range of constructions are entitled to be called serial constructions. As in this book generally, we will largely steer clear of theoretical debate and adopt a basically descriptive approach. The definitions and explanations we will use are fairly conservative, but you should be aware that there are other, broader, definitions of serialization around; for example, Li and Thompson's (1981) grammar of Mandarin Chinese employs a much broader definition of serialization than we will.

As we saw back in Chapter 1, serial verb constructions are a pervasive feature of languages in this region, especially in the isolating languages of mainland Southeast Asia and China. A serial verb construction involves two or more verbs, all of them sharing a single grammatical subject, packed into a single clause without any intervening conjunctions. In this section we will see that there are different kinds of serial construction, and will investigate the range of grammatical functions they can serve. Though we are treating these separately for the sake of clarity, the different types can—and often do—occur combined in one sentence.

4.3.1 Loose vs. tight serialization

Loose serialization is illustrated in example (88) below. As suggested by the term itself, the connection between the verbs is fairly loose. Often they simply represent a string of actions and events which occur one after another, and which all concern a single, shared subject. The Lao example (88)

contains three verbs: *paj³* 'go', *sùù⁴* 'buy', and *maa²* 'come' (Enfield 2002).
The final element *lèèw⁴* (lit. 'finish'), glossed as PERF, is an aspect marker
which applies to the sentence as a whole. Notice that the individual verbs have
some arguments peculiar to themselves (e.g. *talaat⁵* 'market' belongs with
paj³ 'go', *khùang¹* 'stuff' belongs with *sùù⁴* 'buy') and that these arguments
occur in their normal positions, intervening between the verbs.

(88) *Dèèng paj³ talaat⁵ sùù⁴ khùang¹ maa² hùan² lèèw⁴.*
Deng go market buy stuff   come house PERF
'Deng went to market, bought some stuff, (and) came home.'

Some linguists maintain that loose serialization should not be regarded as
serialization at all, but merely as "fortuitous multi-verb sequences" created
by ellipsis of subjects (cf. Matisoff 1973). On this interpretation, example
(88) is derived by ellipsis from an underlying sentence in which each of the
verbs has a separate subject, which just happens to be identical to the one
before. For me, this is a somewhat implausible interpretation. It doesn't
explain why the perfective aspect marker *lèèw⁴* 'finish' applies to the sentence as a whole. Nor can it account for the difference between (88) and a
comparable sentence such as (89) below, which has the coordinating conjunction *lèka⁰* 'and' separating the verb phrases. The key fact is that while
sentence (88) may not represent a "unitary event" (in the way that tight
serialization arguably does: see below), it does present the sequence as a
single episode, in a way which (89) does not.

(89) *Dèèng paj³ talaat⁵ lèka⁰ sùù⁴ khùang¹ lèka⁰ maa² hùan² lèèw⁴.*
Deng go market and buy stuff   and   come house PERF
'Deng went to market, and bought some stuff, and came home.'

It is also possible to have loose serialization where the verbs refer to
events which happen at the same time, as in (90) below, or to different
aspects of the same event, as in (91). These examples are from Hmong
(Jarkey 1991: 172, 165). Notice again that in both examples the individual
verbs have some arguments peculiar to themselves, and that these arguments intervene between the verbs.

(90) *Nws sawv ntsug   ntawm qhov cub ua   mov noj.*
3SG stand be.upright near   kitchen   make rice eat
'She stood in the kitchen making rice to eat.'

(91) *Cov Hmoob hla   dej Na-Koom dim   hauv Nplog teb*
CL Hmong cross river Mekong escape inside Laos
mus Thai teb.
go   Thailand
'The Hmong crossed the Mekong River, escaping from Laos
and going to Thailand.'

In tight serialization, the syntactic bond between the verbs is stronger, and so is the conceptual connection. Usually there are only two verbs involved, and they can be regarded as depicting a single "unitary event", i.e. something which happens all at the same time, despite the fact that we can separate this event into component parts if we wish. Often one of the verbs is a verb of posture or of motion. The following example from Lao is from Enfield (2002: 243), and the example from Thai has been adapted from Clark (1989: 204).

Lao

(92) *Laaw² nòòn² lap².*
    3SG   lie   sleep
    'She is already asleep (lying asleep).'

Thai

(93) *Dèk   wîng   pay   sɨɨ   khanŏm.*
    child   run   go   buy   candy
    'The child ran (and) bought candy.'

Tight serialization is also sometimes found in combinations in which the second verb describes the successful accomplishment or achievement of the action or event depicted by the preceding verb. In such cases both verbs can be transitive, with a common object (as well as subject). The examples below are from Hmong (Jarkey 1991: 214). Notice that the two verbs occur back-to-back (with the object NP, in the case of transitive verbs, coming after both).

(94) *Kuv nrhiav   tau kuv nti nplhaib.*
    1SG search.for   get 1SG CL ring
    'I found my ring.'

(95) *Nws mus txog   tom   khw   lawm.*
    3SG go   arrive over.there market PERF
    'She has arrived at the market.'

(96) *Kuv mus raws   cuag   lawv.*
    1SG go   pursue reach 3PL
    'I caught up with them.'

Because tight serialization calls upon the listener to recognize the occurrence of a single event (at some level), there are limits on what verbs can be combined with one another in tight serialization. Normally, the combination has to be readily recognizable in the cultural context as a single typical event (Enfield 2002). Sometimes this leads to puzzling outcomes—for the cultural outsider, that is. For example, sentence (97) below is deemed acceptable and normal, but example (98) is rejected by Hmong informants as unnatural. The explanation (Jarkey 1991: 169–70) is that whenever the *qeej* pipes are played, the performer dances along with the music. So it is culturally natural to recognize "dancing-while-playing" as a single event. On the other hand, dancing and listening are considered to be distinct events.

(97) *Nws dhia   tshov qeej.*
    3SG   dance blow bamboo.pipes
    'He dances playing the pipes.'

(98) **Nws dhia   mloog qeej.*
    3SG   dance listen   bamboo.pipes
    'He dances listening to the pipes.'

   A study by Enfield (2002) illustrates how the use of serial verb constructions can be sensitive to cultural factors. The Lao *lanaat⁴* is a traditional instrument, which is usually played on the ground in a seated position, as in Fig. 4.4. As one might expect, the serial verb construction in (99) is immediately recognized and judged as acceptable by Lao consultants (note that the verb *tii³* 'beat, hit' is the most common verb used to speak about 'playing' the *lanaat⁴*).

(99) *nang¹ tii³   lanaat⁴*
    sit   beat lanaat
    'play the lanaat sitting'

But what happens if we try to form analogous constructions using the verbs *jùùn³* 'stand' and *nòòn²* 'lie down'? If speakers were presented with example (100), without any context, it "was met with some hesitation, but in most cases judged to be acceptable, usually with a comment to the effect that 'one *could* play a *lanaat⁴* standing up, if it were on a table, say, but people don't do that'" (Enfield 2002: 248). When presented with example (101), the reaction was even more negative. A number of consultants rejected the example, with a comment like "you can't play the *lanaat¹* lying down". Essentially, the idea depicted by (101) has no ready "explanation" out of context. It doesn't make cultural sense.

Fig. 4.4. Playing the *lanaat⁴* in normal position.

Fig. 4.5. Playing the *lanaat⁴* in an unusual position.

(**100**) *jùùn³ tii³   lanaat⁴*
stand beat lanaat
'play the lanaat standing'

(**101**) *nòòn² tii³   lanaat⁴*
lie   beat lanaat
'play the lanaat lying down'

However, when presented with Fig. 4.5, "*every* informant spontaneously produced the structure [in (101)]..., a string which most informants in elicitation sessions found difficult to accept, and which some had rejected outright" (Enfield 2002: 248). In other words, when a situation depicted by a serial construction is culturally non-typical (and so, non-salient), this can affect the way speakers react to the construction. But when a context is given to them, such as a musician practising or playing for fun at home, they do not have to search their "cultural catalogue" to find a suitable situation. In this context the very same construction is not only completely natural, but optimal.

4.3.2 Quasi-adverbs and verb-prepositions

In many East and Southeast Asian languages verbs like 'go', 'come', 'return', 'go up', 'go down', 'go in', and 'go out' function not only as independent verbs, but also in an apparently "adverbial" fashion, adding a specification of direction to another verb. For example, in the Thai sentences below, the main verb is *klàp* 'return'. The difference in meaning is conveyed by the words *maa* and *pay*, which used independently mean 'come' and 'go', respectively (Clark 1989: 198). From a grammatical point of view, these sentences qualify as serial verb constructions (since they combine more than one verb into a single clause), but it is worth identifying them as a distinct type of serial construction on account of the "quasi-adverbial" function of the serial verbs.

Thai

(102) a. *Khǎw klàp   maa   léɛw.*
       3SG   return hither(=come) PERF
       'She came back already.'

    b. *Khǎw klàp   pay   léɛw.*
       3SG   return away(=go) PERF
       'She went back already.'

In Thai and Lao, serial verb constructions of the directional type can consist of three verbs—the main verb, and two serial verbs with an adverbial function (Enfield p.c.). In the first slot, immediately following the main verb, comes a verb which indicates "absolute direction", i.e. direction oriented to the environment, not to the speaker or some other arbitrary point; for example (Lao forms), *khùn⁵* 'go up', *long²* 'go down', *khaam⁵* 'go over', *lòòt⁴* 'go under', *qòòk⁵* 'go out', *khaw⁵* 'go in'. In the second slot, choices are limited to verbs which indicate direction relative to the speaker (or to some other point of reference established in the discourse): namely *paj³* 'go', *maa²* 'come', and *mùa²* 'return'. For example:

Lao

(103) *Laaw² ñaang¹ khùn⁵ maa².*
     3SG   walk   go.up come
     'She walked up here.'

(104) *Khòòj⁵ lèèn¹ khaam⁵ paj³.*
     1SG   run   go.over go
     'I ran across there/away.'

In examples like these, the three motional verbs each describe different aspects (manner of motion, absolute direction, relative direction) of a single motion event.

In many languages which have serial verb constructions, one finds that certain verbs (especially verbs with meanings like 'go', 'give', 'reach', 'arrive', 'use', and 'take') have taken on a grammatical function: they provide the normal way of marking the optional arguments and adjuncts of other verbs. In effect, they perform the same kind of grammatical role as adpositions (prepositions and postpositions). Different linguists use different terminology to describe serial verbs in this kind of function. We will adopt the term "verb-prepositions".

The following examples are from Lao (Enfield p.c.). In (105) the verb *haj⁵* 'give' functions as a verb-preposition indicating a beneficiary role (i.e. a meaning corresponding to that expressed by English 'for'). In (106) the verb *nam²* 'accompany' indicates a comitative role (i.e. a meaning corresponding to that expressed by English 'with').

(**105**) *Laaw² nùng¹ khaw⁵ haj⁵   khòòj⁵.*
    3SG   steam rice   for(= give) I
    'He steamed some rice for me.'

(**106**) *Khan² haw² juu¹ nam²   mèè¹-thaw⁵, ...*
    if   we   live with(= accompany) mother-old
    'If we live with your mother, ...'

The quasi-prepositional status of *haj⁵* 'for' and *nam²* 'with' is shown by the fact that in this function they cannot take any of the aspect or mood markers (e.g. the experiential marker *kheej²* or the irrealis marker *ca⁰*) which they can take when they function as main verbs. Nor can one break up a combination of a main verb and *haj⁵* (or *nam²*) by inserting the coordinating particle *lèka⁰* 'and'.

The examples below show the verb for 'reach, arrive at' used to indicate the "locutionary topic" (i.e. the person or thing spoken about) in Vietnamese and Hmong, respectively (Clark 1989: 191–2).

Vietnamese

(**107**) *Chúng tôi   nhắc đến   anh   luôn.*
    PL   I(EXCL.) recall about(= arrive) brother often
    'We often speak about you.'

Hmong

(**108**) *Txhob poobsiab   txog   ntawn kuv cov   khoom.*
    don't be.worried about(= arrive) place I   group thing
    'Don't worry about my things.'

Other serial verb-prepositions found in East and Southeast Asia include the verb for 'use' functioning as instrumental 'with' (e.g. He did it use stick = He did it with a stick), and the verb for 'go' functioning as allative 'to' (e.g. She ran go shop = She ran to the shop).

4.4 Subject and topic

Linguists tend to get excited when they start talking about whether or not there are languages which don't have "subjects". So before we start to do just that, it might be a good idea to go over the background to the issue and get an idea of what is at stake. What is a subject? The easiest way to approach this question is to look at the way the grammar of an English sentence is organized. If we do this, we will find that there are a range of grammatical processes and properties which indicate that the NP immediately preceding the verb has a special, privileged status in English grammar.

For example: (i) With a few exceptions, all English sentence types have at least one NP, and that NP comes before the verb (even if it is a "dummy" element like *it*, as in *It's raining* or *It seems that...*). (ii) Most English pronouns have a distinctive form when they come before the verb (e.g. *I* as opposed to *me, they* as opposed to *them*). (iii) The present tense form of most verbs gets a suffix *-s* when the NP before the verb is third person singular (e.g. *She knows the answer, He seems upset*). (iv) It is possible to rearrange the grammar of a transitive sentence (e.g. *The committee elected Maxine*) into a so-called "passive" form; this involves putting the NP which was after the verb into the preverbal position (e.g. *Maxine was elected*).

Because all these properties converge on the preverbal NP, linguists recognize the preverbal NP in English as having a special, premier grammatical function, i.e. "subject". Crucial to this conclusion is the fact that the preverbal NPs have these properties regardless of their semantic role in the sentence, i.e. regardless of whether the NP is an agent (a "do-er"), a patient or undergoer (a "do-ee"), an experiencer, an instrument, etc.

The particular properties just listed are specific to the English language, but in other European languages and in many languages around the world, we can find a similar basketful of special properties which justify identifying one NP in any sentence as the grammatically most important NP, the subject of the sentence. For example, in most European languages verbs show extensive "agreement" with the subject of a sentence; that is, the form of a verb changes depending on the person/number category of the subject. The German verb *gehen* 'go', for instance, in the present tense has the following forms when it occurs with a singular subject: *gehe* (with 1SG subject), *gehst* (with 2SG subject), *geht* (with 3SG subject). Furthermore, most European languages have a system of "case" according to which nouns and other elements of an NP change their form depending on their grammatical function; and the simplest case is usually the "subject case" (known as "nominative" case). There are grammatical constructions analogous to the English passive in most European languages as well.

Up till now in this book we have been taking the notion of subject for granted. For example, when we describe the constituent order of sentences using the symbols S (subject), O (object), and V (verb), we are taking for granted that all languages have subjects—or, putting it another way, that the grammatical function of subject is a universal of human language. In fact, the assumption that all languages have subjects is one of the oldest assumptions about universal grammar. Perhaps now it is easier to understand why linguists get excited at the proposal that there are some languages which lack the grammatical function of subject. Such a proposal challenges a cherished assumption about universal grammar.

Before we can start to explore whether there are languages in East and Southeast Asia which do not have subjects, I have to explain another related and important notion, that of "topic". Basically, a topic is what the sentence is about; for example, *Cats eat mice* is about *cats, Susie went to Guyra* is about *Susie*, etc. Notice that this definition of topic is not based on grammatical criteria. It is based on discourse and semantic criteria: a topic is an expression which has a certain role in the ongoing communication between the speaker and his or her interlocutors. Even so, you will probably say that there is not much difference between subject and topic, and you would be right—at least for English. The fact is that in English there is a strong tendency for subjects to be topics, and vice versa. That is, in English the NP which comes in front of the verb (i.e. the grammatical subject) strongly tends to be the NP which the sentence is about (i.e. the topic).

In many East and Southeast Asian languages, however, subject and topic do not align in this regular and reliable fashion, and it is much easier to separate the two notions. Furthermore, in many of these languages the notion of topic is apparently more important than that of subject in describing how the language works. In fact, some linguists believe that languages can be grouped (roughly) according to whether they work primarily in terms of topic or in terms of subject: i.e. whether they are "topic-prominent" or "subject-prominent" languages.

4.4.1 Topic prominence

In this section we will look into three languages which have been described as topic-prominent: Thai, Mandarin Chinese, and Japanese. We will see that although topic is undoubtedly a very important notion in all three of these languages, they also differ significantly in their treatment of topics—specifically, in the extent to which the marking of topic (and related discourse notions) is explicit. At one extreme there is colloquial Thai, whose syntax seems at first almost anarchic in nature, the consequence of flexible word order combined with extensive ellipsis. At the other end is Japanese, in which subjects and topics are each neatly and explicitly marked by separate grammatical particles. In between, there is Mandarin Chinese, which resembles Thai in many ways but which has also developed some explicit topicalizing constructions.

Thai is normally described as an SVO language, but in informal conversation other orders are very common (Diller 1988). If a noun phrase is topical, it often precedes the verb (or verbs), resulting in orders such as OSV and SOV. For example, in (109) the O *khâaw* 'rice' comes before the S *raw* 'we': the order is OSV. In (110), the O *kaanbâan* 'homework' comes after the S, but it still precedes the verb *tham* 'do': the order is SOV. Notice that example (109) also has a peripheral NP (*Pàakphanang*, the name of a town) in topical preverbal position. (Peripheral NPs are those which

describe the setting of the event, as opposed to NPs which are arguments of
the verb.)

(**109**) *Pàakphanang khâaw raw kin ngâay.*
Pakphanang rice   we   eat simple
'(In) Pakphanang we ate (our meals) simply.'

(**110**) *Dèk hɔ̂ng níi kaanbâan mây khəəy tham sàk thii!*
child room this homework not ever do   even time
'The kids in this room have never once done their homework!'

In informal conversation it is also very common in Thai for the S to come
after the verb, with varying degrees of pause separating the verb from the postposed S. This gives rise to orders like VS and VOS, as in (111) and (112)
below. (Example (112) also has a preposed peripheral NP *ráan nán* 'that shop'.)
Of course, it is fair to point out that in English we also sometimes "postpose"
subjects, often with a kind of "afterthought" effect, but as Diller (1988: 275)
points out, sentences of this type have a rather marginal status in English
grammar: "In Thai conversation they seem to play a more important role."

(**111**) *Phɛɛng   mamûang mɨang níi.*
expensive mangoes town this
'Expensive, the mangoes in this area.'

(**112**) *Ráan nán nâ mây phɔɔ-cay aahǎan ləəy phûak raw.*
shop that PRT not satisfied food at.all group we
'That shop—we weren't at all satisfied with the food there.'

The flexible, topic-oriented word order possibilities of Thai combine with
another notable characteristic of the language—widespread ellipsis—in a
very common construction which is roughly equivalent, in functional terms,
to an English (agentless) passive. Consider a sentence like (113) below,
which is taken from a recorded conversation. In the context, this sentence
had the interpretation given in (i). That is, the initial NP *phûu-chaay* 'men'
was understood as the O, because in the context this was the topic of the
sentence. The speaker was correcting the addressee's mistaken assumption
that only women were being taught. The sentence does not contain
any explicit S, but this is quite typical of Thai in cases where the identity of
an NP can be understood from context. Notice that this interpretation
depends crucially on the surrounding linguistic and conversational context.
If sentence (113) is presented in isolation to Thai speakers, they tend to
favour the interpretation given in (ii). That is, they assume that the initial
NP *phûu-chaay* 'men' is the S (subject) of the verb.

(**113**) *Ɔɔ, phûu-chaay kɔ̂ sɔ̌ɔn.*
oh men   also teach'
(i) 'Oh, (they) also teach <u>men</u>.'
(ii) 'Oh, men also teach.'

Admittedly, the possibility of ambiguity in (113) is connected with the fact that it is semantically plausible either way. In many cases, there is no potential ambiguity because, for example, the preposed NP is not capable of acting as the subject. For example:

(114) *Nǎngsɨ̌ lêm nán khǐan maa lǎay pii lɛ́ɛw.*
book   CL   that write come many year already
'That book (someone) wrote many years ago (= that book was written many years ago).'

(115) *Kày   nîi thɔ̂ɔt con mây sǐa   lɛ́ɛw.*
chicken this fry   until burn spoil already
'This chicken has been fried so long it's burnt.'

In summary, informal Thai shows strong tendencies towards what Diller (1988) calls "pragmatically organized syntax", especially in everyday conversation among less educated speakers who know each other well. The situation is rather different in formal Standard Thai. What Diller means by "pragmatically organized syntax" is that the principles which determine the arrangement of phrases do not work primarily in terms of grammatical relations such as subject and object. Rather, the order of phrases is largely determined by pragmatic factors, such as topicality and the highlighting of new information.

The question then arises: If notions such as subject (S) and object (O) are not very important in describing the grammar of informal Thai, is it even justified to assume that they are "there" in Thai, in the same way that they are there in English? Diller seems to think not:

Although these labels are useful on the level of practical description, in any rigorous theoretical sense it would be difficult to defend such notions as autonomous grammatical relations for Thai along the lines that such relations have been argued for in English. (Diller 1988: 277)

In their description of Mandarin Chinese, Li and Thompson (1981) draw a clear distinction between subject and topic, explaining that it is the latter notion which is more important in the grammar of Mandarin. "[T]he concept of subject seems to be less significant, while the concept of topic appears to be quite crucial in explaining the structure of ordinary sentences in the language" (p. 16). In referring to the structure of ordinary sentences, Li and Thompson have in mind, above all, constituent order (word order). In Mandarin the topic is always the first constituent of a sentence, regardless of grammatical role. For example, in (116) the expression *Zhāngsān* comes first because it is the topic, even though it is not the subject of the sentence (it is the object).

(116) *Zhāngsān wǒ yǐjīng   jiàn-guo le.*
Zhangsan I   already see-EXP CRS
'Zhangsan, I've already seen (him).'

A similar constituent order is possible in English too, as shown by the translation, but an English sentence of this form is stylistically unusual whereas the Mandarin sentence is perfectly ordinary.

Of course, in many sentences the topic and the subject will be same. But if they are not the same, in Mandarin it is the topic which claims the sentence-initial position.

Aside from sentence-initial position, another formal characteristic of Mandarin topics is that they can optionally be separated from the rest of the sentence (called the "comment") by a pause or by one of several "topic-marking" particles, such as *a/ya, me, ne*, or *ba*. From a semantic point of view, Li and Thompson maintain that topics can be thought of as "setting the frame" for the rest of the sentence. Here they follow a definition of topic given by Chafe (1976): "the topic sets the spatial, temporal or other framework in which the predication holds."

As in Thai, subjects can be omitted in Mandarin under various conditions. Sentence (117) gives one kind of example. Here the omission of an overt subject conveys an effect similar to that of an English indefinite pronoun (i.e. 'someone'). It implies that some unspecified person is responsible for the action. The expression *nèi běn shū* 'that book' is the topic.

(117) *Nèi běn shū   chūbǎn le.*
       that CL   book publish PERF
       'That book (is) published.'

Aside from noun phrases two other kinds of constituent which often occur in sentence-initial position in Mandarin are time phrases and locative phrases, as in the examples below. Li and Thompson (1981: 94–5) regard these as topics too, because they literally "set the frame" for the event or situation described in the rest of the sentence, and because, like other topics, they can be followed by topic particles.

(118) *Shàng ge yuè   tiānqì   fēicháng   mēn.*
       last   CL month weather extremely humid
       'Last month the weather was extremely humid.'

(119) *Zài Táiběi kéyi chī de hěn hǎo.*
       at   Taipei can eat CSC very good
       'In Taipei one can eat really well.'

Li and Thompson stress that the topic-comment structure of a Mandarin sentence is extremely flexible. "As long as the comment expresses something about the topic in the perception of the speaker and the hearer, the sentence will be meaningful" (1981: 95). In English translation, this often gives rise to an apparently disjointed effect, as illustrated in the following examples—but in Mandarin these sentences sound quite ordinary.

(120) *Mián   wǒ zuì   xǐhuān chī là   de.*
noodle I   most like   eat spicy NOM
'Noodles, I like spicy (ones) best.'

(121) *Nèi chǎng huǒ xìngkuī   xiāofáng-duì lái   de kuài.*
that CL   fire fortunate fire-brigade come CSC fast
'That fire, fortunately the fire brigade came fast.'

Sometimes the topic can be a verb or a verb-phrase functioning as a noun-phrase. For example:

(122) *Zhù Táiběi zuì   fāngbiàn;   chī háishi Xiānggǎng   hǎo.*
live Taipei most convenient eat still   Hong Kong good
'Housing, Taipei is most convenient; eating, Hong Kong is still better.'

The distinction between topic and subject allows us to understand one of the most puzzling features of Mandarin grammar, the so-called "double-subject construction". Actually this term is a misnomer, dating from the time before the distinction between topic and subject was clearly recognized, but it continues in usage till the present day. The term refers to sentences like those below in which topic and subject are closely connected, e.g. in a part-whole relationship, so that what is said about the subject can be seen as a comment on the topic (Li and Thompson 1981: 92–3).

(123) *Xiàng   bízi   cháng.*
elephant nose long
'Elephants, (their) noses are long.'

(124) *Zhèi ge nǚhái yǎnjing hěn dà.*
that CL girl   eye   very big
'That girl, (her) eyes are very big.'

In Japanese too it is necessary to distinguish topic from subject, but in Japanese we find an even clearer and more explicit grammatical demarcation between the two notions. In fact, in Japanese it is arguable that "topic" has been so completely grammaticalized that it is literally part of "sentence-level" grammar, and no longer a discourse notion. The stand-out feature of Japanese, so far as topic and subject are concerned, is the existence of two grammatical particles—*wa* and *ga*—either of which can mark what would appear (on the basis of comparisons with English) to be the subject of a sentence. Our treatment will follow that of Shibatani (1990: 262–80), who remarks that explicating the differences between sentences like (125a) and (125b) below has been a "major task for Japanese grammarians" (p. 262). (I will diverge from Shibatani, however, in glossing the *ga* particle as SUBJ, for subject, rather than as NOM, for nominative.) Consider sentences (125a) and (125b) below. Although they are often given an identical English translation ('The sun rises') most grammarians agree that they differ semantically and structurally. To hint at the meaning difference, extra translations are supplied in each case.

(**125**) a. *Hi   wa   nobor-u.*
sun TOP rise-PRES
'The sun rises. or: The sun is something that rises.'

b. *Hi   ga   nobor-u.*
sun SUBJ rise-PRES
'The sun rises. or: (Look) The sun is rising. or: It is the-sun-rising.'

One immediate indication that *wa* and *ga* are not interchangeable is that, generally speaking, in subordinate clauses *wa* is not possible: only *ga* occurs.

In trying to grasp the difference between the *wa* construction and the *ga* construction, it is easiest to begin with *wa*, and specifically with the observation that sentence (125a), with *wa*, can be used to make a generic statement, i.e. a generalization about the sun. Essentially, the function of *wa* is to establish something (in this case, the sun) as the "object of judgment" (i.e. a sentence topic). Early Japanese grammarians described it as "separating" an entity from the rest of the sentence, in order to allow the rest of the sentence to function as a judgement upon that entity (the topic). In a certain European philosophical tradition (the Bretano-Marty theory; see Sasse 1987), the kind of sentence in which *wa* is found is called a "categorical judgement".

As Shibatani and others point out, *wa* is very much at home in contexts in which the referent of the NP is being contrasted with another referent, as in (126). It is also appropriate where a contrast is implicit. In (127), for example, the second occurrence of *wa* (following *hon* 'book') is appropriate because of the expectation that at a library Taroo would have read a book. Notice also that in sentence (127) the *wa*-marked NP is not the subject of the verb.

(**126**) *Ame wa hutteiru ga   yuki   wa   hutteinai.*
rain TOP falling   but snow TOP falling:NEG
'Rain is falling but snow isn't falling.'

(**127**) *Taroo wa toshokan ni itta   ga,   hon   wa   yomanakatta.*
Taroo TOP library   to went but book TOP read:NEG:PAST
'Taroo went to the library but he didn't read a book.'

Some analysts, such as Kuno (1973), say that *wa* used in clearly contrastive sentences is a different *wa* ("contrastive *wa*"), but it is probably better to say that *wa* always indicates a conceptual contrasting of an item, and that this contrasting effect merely becomes more pronounced when there is a contrasting proposition in the immediate discourse context.

Coming now to the *ga* construction, the basic idea is that such sentences do not imply the same kind of "analytical" perspective as we have been discussing in relation to *wa*. Instead, "a state of affairs is grasped as a whole", as if in a single act of recognition of an event and its participants. (In the Bretano-Marty theory, this is called a "thetic" judgement.) This is why, it is claimed, a sentence like *Hi ga noboru* [sun SUBJ rise:PRES] is appropriate if one is actually watching a sun rise. This kind of use is sometimes called "descriptive *ga*" (cf. Kuno 1973).

Another way of looking at the difference between a *wa*-marked NP and a *ga*-marked NP is in terms of the distinction between "given" and "new". A topic NP is, in some sense, "given" or "presupposed": its identity and its relevance is taken for granted. Thus, in a clause with a *wa*-marked NP, the speaker's interest is focused on the rest of the clause, i.e. on the "comment". Shibatani (1990) illustrates with the two sentences below, which come from a classic work of Japanese grammar by Matsushita (1977). In the case of (128), the speaker's presence is taken as "given" and the focus of interest is on what is being said about the speaker. Example (129), on the other hand, is used when the addressee is aware (or is assumed to be aware) that someone is the trustee but does not know who it is. It could be used, for example, in response to a question 'Who is the trustee of this organization?' Thus, the predicate part of the sentence is, in a sense, given, and the subject part is new. Notice that example (129) shows a second kind of use or context for *ga* (aside from the "descriptive" use already mentioned above). In this second use the *ga*-marked NP supplies a referent which fills in a missing piece of information; that is, it "answers a question", either explicit or implied.

(128) *Watashi wa honkai no rijidesu.*
'I am a trustee of this organization.'

(129) *Watashi ga honkai no rijidesu.*
'I am a trustee of this organization. or: The trustee of this organization is me.'

As in Mandarin, there are certain sentences in which the difference between topic and subject becomes particularly clear. These are sentences which contain both *wa*-marked and *ga*-marked NPs, as in the examples below. If you compare these Japanese sentences with the Mandarin examples given earlier, you will see that they are very similar. As indicated by the bracketing, in sentences like these the entire second part (which could be an independent sentence in its own right) is functioning as a comment upon the *wa*-marked topic.

(130) *Zoo   wa [hana ga   nagai].*
elephant TOP   nose SUBJ long
'An elephant's nose is long. or: An elephant is such that its nose is long.'

(**131**) *Tori wa [mesu ga tamago o umu].*
bird TOP female SUBJ egg   OBJ lay
'A bird is such that a female (bird) lays eggs.'

(**132**) *Huyu wa [sukii ga tanoshii].*
winter TOP ski SUBJ enjoyable
'Winter is such that skiing is enjoyable.'

Also as in Mandarin it is possible for adverbial phrases of various kinds to appear as topics, i.e. marked by *wa*. Compare the following examples with the Mandarin examples given earlier.

(**133**) *Kyoo wa [boku ga ryoorishiyoo].*
today TOP I   SUBJ cook:TENT
'Today I will cook.'

(**134**) *Hayaku wa hashirenai.*
fast   TOP run:POTEN:NEG
'(I) can't run fast.'

Some linguists believe that adverbial topics, like those in the sentences above, are quite different in nature from NP-topics. Shibatani (1990) draws a sharp distinction, saying that adverbial topics are basically superficial, "stylistic" variants of ordinary simple sentences. They do not reflect a particular mode of human judgment (categorical judgments) as NP-topic sentences do. Despite their formal similarity, Shibatani (1990: 277) says, the difference between NP-topic constructions and adverbial topic constructions is "deep". As we have already seen in relation to Mandarin, however, there is another view which sees adverbial topics (at least when they specify time, place, or other aspects of the "setting") as simply ordinary "topics". We will leave this issue open here.

One question which we cannot leave hanging, however, concerns the status of subject in Japanese—and, for that matter, in Mandarin. If both languages are so "topic-prominent", are we entitled to recognize the existence of any grammatical category of subject at all? As Shibatani (1990: 281) acknowledges: "Within the tradition of Japanese grammar, the status of the subject is highly controversial, some scholars taking its existence for granted, and others vehemently denying the usefulness of the concept." For his part, Shibatani has no doubt that subject is a useful notion even in Japanese, mainly because of its participation in various syntactic phenomena. We will only look at two of these here: control of "gapping" in coordinate constructions and control of reflexivization. Consider sentence (135) below, looking at both the Japanese and the English translation. You will see that the second clause has no explicit subject. Now one might expect from the content of the first clause ('The mother scolded the child') that if anyone was going to cry it would be the child. But as a matter of fact, this interpretation is not available either in Japanese or in English. In both languages the gapped position must be interpreted as coreferential with the subject of the first clause.

(135) *[Hahaoya ga   kodomo o   shikat]-te ø naita.*
      mother   SUBJ child   OBJ scold-and   cried
      'The mother scolded the child and ø cried (i.e. the mother cried).'

One might perhaps suspect that the property which controls the interpretation of the gapped position is not subject-hood, but "actor-hood". But if this were so, it wouldn't matter whether the first clause was active or passive. In fact, however, if the first clause is turned into a passive, the interpretation of the gapped position in the second, coordinate clause changes: see (136) below. This shows that to state the generalization about the referent of a gapped position, we have to make reference to the concept of subject.

(136) *[Kodomo ga   hahaoya ni shikarare]-te   ø naita.*
      child   SUBJ mother   by scold:PASS-and   cried
      'The child was scolded by the mother and ø cried (i.e. the child cried).'

A second syntactic phenomenon which is controlled by the subject is the interpretation of the reflexive form *jibun* 'self'. The Japanese reflexive form is neutral for person, gender and number, but when there are two or more possible antecedents, as in (137) below, it turns out that *jibun* can only refer to the subject.

(137) *Taroo ga   Hanako ni Ziroo o   jibun no ie   de shookaishita.*
      Taroo SUBJ Hanako to Ziroo OBJ self of house in introduced
      'Taroo$_i$ introduced Ziroo to Hanako in his own$_i$ (lit. self's) house.'

4.4.2 Trigger constructions in Austronesian languages

In this section, we will look at some Southeast Asian languages which have made linguists rethink the notion of subject. Our focus will be on Philippine languages, which have played an important role in the evolution of linguistic thinking about subject-hood. As part of the exercise, we will examine a rather unusual and very flexible grammatical system possessed by various Philippine languages, including Tagalog, which enables practically any of the NPs in a sentence to be featured as the grammatically most important NP in the sentence. Many other Western Austronesian languages have systems of this type, though usually not as elaborate as in Philippine languages.

In an influential article, Paul Schachter (1976) argued that Philippine languages may have a "unique contribution to make to our understanding of the nature of subjects" (in the grammatical sense). I will summarize the main points here using a somewhat different terminology. The main difference is that I will use the term "trigger" in place of Schachter's "topic". The term trigger had not been coined back in 1976, but it has since been widely adopted in grammatical studies of Austronesian; indeed, Schachter himself uses it in later works. Also, I will use the term "patient" for Schachter's (1976) "goal".

What, then, is a "trigger"? The easiest way to appreciate this notion is to study the three Tagalog examples below. As you will see from the translations, the three sentences depict essentially the same event but in each sentence one of the three arguments (child, toy, and box) is preceded by a grammatical particle *ang*, glossed as TRIG (for "trigger"). The trigger NP has a special status. For one thing, it is always understood as "definite", i.e. as denoting a referent whose identity is, in some sense, presupposed or "taken-for-granted" by the speaker. Thus *ang bata* in (138) has to be glossed as 'the child', *ang laruan* in (139) as 'the toy', and *ang kahon* in (140) as 'the box'. Otherwise, definiteness is not marked in Tagalog, so the other NPs could be glossed with either the definite article 'the' or the indefinite article 'a', depending on the context.

More striking than the implied definiteness of a trigger NP is the fact that its semantic role, e.g. whether it denotes an agent, a patient, a location, etc., is marked on the verb. The verb in (138) has an "actor trigger" (AT) prefix *mag-*, which signals that the trigger NP is an actor (i.e. someone who does something). The verb in (139) has a "patient trigger" (PT) suffix *-in*, which signals that the trigger NP is a patient (i.e. someone or something which is the undergoer of an action). The verb in (140) has a "direction trigger" (DT) suffix *-an*, which signals that the trigger NP is a directional expression (i.e. a source or a goal of motion). The semantic roles of the other (non-trigger) NPs, are marked by grammatical particles: *ng* (pronounced [naŋ]) for both actors and patient, and *sa* for directionals.

(138) *Mag-aalis   ang bata ng laruan sa kahon.*
AT-will.take.out TRIG child PAT toy   DIR box
'The child will take a toy out of a/the box.'

(139) *Aalis-in   ng bata ang laruan sa kahon.*
will.take.out-PT ACT child TRIG toy   DIR box
'A/the child will take the toy out of a/the box.'

(140) *Aalis-an   ng bata ng laruan ang kahon.*
will.take.out-DT ACT child PAT toy   TRIG box
'A/the child will take a toy out of the box.'

Incidentally, aside from the fact that the verb normally comes first, the ordering of the constituents is quite free. According to Schachter (1976: 495), "there does not even seem (surprisingly enough) to be any clearly preferred ordering of the postverbal constituents in Tagalog".

Notice that there are various other allomorphs (i.e. variants) of the AT (actor-trigger), PT (patient-trigger), and DT (direction-trigger) verbal affixes, aside from *mag-*, *-in*, and *-an*, respectively. To simplify the glossing, from now on I will not bother to segment the verbs into distinct morphemes, but simply indicate in the interlinear glosses whether they occur in an AT, PT, or DT form. For example:

(**141**) *Humiram* <u>*ang babae*</u> *ng pera sa bangko.*
AT:borrow TRIG woman PAT money DIR bank
'<u>The woman</u> borrowed money from a/the bank.'

(**142**) *Hiniram ng babae* <u>*ang pera*</u> *sa bangko.*
borrow:PT ACT woman TRIG money OBL bank
'A/the woman borrowed <u>the money</u> from a/the bank.'

(**143**) *Hiniraman ng babae ng pera* <u>*ang bangko.*</u>
borrow:DT ACT woman PAT money TRIG bank
'A/the woman borrowed some money from <u>the bank</u>.'

I should perhaps mention that a number of other semantic roles, including beneficiary, can also be indicated on the verb. Some verbs are said to have up to seven different forms that indicate seven different semantic roles for a trigger NP. But there are some additional complications involved, which we will steer clear of here.

At this point you may be wondering: Why use the term "trigger"? Why not just call the trigger NP the "subject" of the sentence? Or, if that's no good, why can't we call it the "topic"? The answer—or at least, the answer which is often given within Philippine linguistic studies—is that trigger NPs aren't very "good" subjects, i.e. they lack certain properties which we would normally expect of subjects, and they are not very "good" topics either, i.e. they lack certain properties which we would normally expect of topics. The value of the term "trigger" is that it gives us a useful label for the particular configuration of properties we find in Tagalog (and in many other Philippine languages) without forcing us to commit ourselves as to whether a trigger is a subject, a topic, or neither.

The main thrust of Schachter's (1976) article is to argue that Tagalog triggers don't fit our preconceptions of either subjects or topics. Let's begin with topic: Why isn't a Tagalog trigger a topic, in the sense that we have been using the term in our previous treatment of Thai, Mandarin, and Japanese? The main difficulty is that a Tagalog trigger does not have to be the "centre of attention" in the discourse context. That is, the sentence is not necessarily *about* the referent denoted by the trigger NP. Schachter (1976: 496) gives example (144) below, in which the initial phrase (translated as 'As for Maria') seems to establish that *Maria* is the topic of the sentence. Yet *Maria* is not the trigger NP: the NP *mga pinggan* 'the dishes' is the trigger. (One detail relevant to this particular sentence is that pronouns have special actor forms; unlike nouns, they do not occur with the particle *ng*.)

(**144**) *Kung tungkol kay Maria, hinuhugasan   niya   <u>ang mga pinggan</u>.*
     if about   Maria is.washing:PT ACT:she TRIG   dishes
     'As for Maria, she is washing <u>the dishes</u>.'

Also very telling is the fact that the main clause of the example above, i.e. *Hinuhugasan niya ang mga pinggan* 'She is washing the dishes' (with 'the dishes' as the trigger NP), can be used as an answer to the question 'Where's *Maria*?'. A question like this surely establishes *Maria* as the topic, but in the answer *Maria* does not have to be the trigger NP. In short, a Tagalog trigger NP cannot be identified as the topic of the sentence, in the standard linguistic sense of the term.

(It is unfortunate that many linguistic writings about Tagalog do routinely refer to trigger NPs as "topics", including not only Schachter's early work, but also influential books such as Foley and Van Valin (1984). Essentially, the usage is—or was—a terminological peculiarity of Philippine linguistics: cf. Manaster-Ramer (1992). To make matters worse, the system of trigger-marking is often referred to in Philippine linguistics as a "focus system", which is a further terminological peculiarity, since the term "focus" has a different meaning in general linguistics. We do not have to pursue these matters here; they are only being mentioned in case you intend to do some follow-up reading on Tagalog.)

What about subject then? Why can't we say that a trigger NP is the subject of the sentence in which it occurs? Some linguists would be quite happy with this proposal, but, as Schachter (1976: 502–5) points out, despite the undoubted grammatical importance of trigger NPs, they do lack some characteristics which one might expect of subjects. His most persuasive argument is that trigger NPs do not control certain grammatical processes in the way one might expect they would if they were truly subjects. For example, consider reflexives, i.e. expressions corresponding to 'himself', 'herself', 'themselves', etc. Normally one expects reflexives to be "dependent" expressions, whose interpretation usually depends on the subject of the sentence (which provides the antecedent, as it is termed in traditional grammar). In Tagalog, reflexive expressions are formed with a possessive pronoun and the nominal *sarili* 'self'. If you study the two following examples, I think you will be able to see that they seem quite peculiar—if we assume that a trigger NP is a subject. In both sentences, the reflexive NP is itself the trigger!

(**145**) *Sinaktan ng babae <u>ang kaniyang sarili</u>.*
     hurt:PT ACT woman TRIG her   self
     'A/the woman hurt <u>herself</u>.'

(**146**) *Iniisip   nila   ang   kanilang sarili.*
think.about:DT ACT:they TRIG   their   self
'They think about <u>themselves</u>.'

Of course, if we look upon the actor NP as the subject in the above sentences, then everything makes sense again. But if the actor is the subject, then presumably the trigger cannot be.

Another kind of grammatical construction which poses a challenge to the idea that a trigger NP is a subject concerns complements of verbs like 'want'. Consider the two English sentences:

(**147**) a. *Max wants —— to borrow some money.*
       b. *Max wants Charles to borrow some money.*

In example (147a), the complement of *want* does not have any explicit subject. In a sense, we understand that the "missing" subject is the same as the subject of the verb *want* itself (i.e. the "wanter", Max). In generative grammar, one interpretation of this situation is that the "underlying structure" of a sentence like (147a) does contain a subject in the complement clause, but that this subject is deleted by a transformational rule if it is coreferential with the subject of the main verb. Notice that these processes are phrased in terms of "subjects".

Now consider the following Tagalog sentences (Schachter 1976: 504) (which, unfortunately, do not use the verb 'want'). To make the examples easier to read, I have separated the main clause from the complement clause by the symbol ‖, and I have inserted a dash (——) in the complement clause to indicate that something is missing. The sticky thing about these sentences—on the hypothesis that trigger NPs are subjects—is that although both the complement clauses are missing something, they are not missing trigger NPs. In (148) the trigger of the complement clause is *ang pera* 'the money', and in (149) it is *ang bangko* 'the bank'.

(**148**) *Nagatubili   siyang ‖ hiramin   ——   ang   pera   sa   bangko.*
AT:hesitated TRIG:he   borrow:PT   TRIG money DIR bank
'He hesitated to borrow <u>the money</u> from the bank.'

(**149**) *Nagatubili   siyang ‖ hiraman   ——   ng   pera   ang   bangko.*
AT:hesitated TRIG:he   borrow:DT   PAT money TRIG bank
'He hesitated to borrow money from <u>the bank</u>.'

The missing NPs in the complement clauses of these examples are, of course, the actor NPs. The generalization seems to be that the complement clause is missing an actor NP which is coreferential with the actor NP of the main clause. All well and good, but this makes it look as though it is the actor NP which is the subject (and if the actor is subject, then the trigger cannot be).

I realize that this may seem all very confusing. In a sense, that's the point. For many linguists, Tagalog seemed to provide an example of a language in which neither the traditional concept of "subject" nor yet the newer concept of "topic" seemed to fit neatly. Schachter's (1976) summation, which has proved very influential, is that instead of thinking in terms of discrete categories such as subject and topic, we would do better to recognize the existence of two different kinds of properties: reference-related and role-related. The reference-related system is concerned with identifying and keeping track of particular persons, places, and things which are being spoken about. In Philippine languages, the category of "trigger" (which, as mentioned, implies a definite, presupposed or taken-for-granted referent) is a reference-related category. The role-related system, on the other hand, is concerned with "who does what to whom"; that is, with identifying actors (agents), patients, locations, and other semantic roles which participate in various kinds of events. Schachter wrote (1976: 513–14):

Since in most languages these two different kinds of properties are associated with a single syntactic category [i.e. subject—CG], linguists have generally not been led to sort the properties out. In Philippine languages, however, the properties are conveniently sorted out by the grammatical systems themselves, so that one is given a clearer view than usual of the basis for the properties, and the properties are seen to make a kind of sense one might not otherwise have attributed to them.

This basic idea has since been elaborated into a significant new theory of grammar, known as Role and Reference Grammar (Foley and Van Valin 1984; Van Valin and LaPolla 1997).

4.4.3 Actor vs. undergoer marking in Acehnese

For our final example of a language which resists analysis in terms of the conventional, European-based concept of subject, we turn to Acehnese (Durie 1985; 1987). Acehnese is a regional language of Indonesia, spoken by over 3 million people in the province of Aceh on the northern tip of Sumatra, the area devastated by the tsunami in December 2004. Acehnese is an Austronesian language, but not a typical one, because it has many features in common with the Mon-Khmer languages of mainland Southeast Asia. It seems likely that the ancestors of the present-day Acehnese once lived on the mainland, as part of the same group as the ancestral speakers of the Chamic languages (which presently form an Austronesian "pocket" in southern Vietnam and Cambodia).

One unusual feature of Acehnese is that verbs take affixes (strictly speaking, clitics) which "cross-reference" the person category of one of the arguments of the verb. For example, in (150) the prefix *geu-* on the verb *mat* indicates third person (it is neutral as to number). In (151), the verb *mat* has two cross-referencing affixes: prefix *lôn-* indicating 1SG, and suffix *-geuh* indicating third person. Notice that the 1SG prefix is identical in form with the independent pronoun for 'I'. Also, the suffix *-geuh* is essentially the same as the prefix *geu-*. It just gets the *-h* at the end for phonological reasons which we need not go into here.

(**150**) *Gopnyan geu-mat lôn.*
     3SG   3-hold   1SG
     'He/she holds me.'

(**151**) *Lôn lôn-mat-geuh.*
     1SG   1SG-hold-3
     'I hold him/her.'

Whenever the same information is signalled by both an independent pronoun and by an affix on the verb, the independent pronoun is optional. In other words, in (150) we could omit *gopnyan* 'he/she' and the sentence would still have the same meaning; and similarly, we could omit *lôn* 'I' from (151). This aspect of the grammar of Acehnese does not really concern us here, however.

Verbal affixing in Acehnese, as described so far, might seem to be quite straightforward. There are cross-referencing affixes which can be either prefixes or suffixes. As prefixes, they cross-reference the subject, as suffixes they cross-reference the object. This simple picture, however, is completely upset once we look at how things work in intransitive sentences, like the examples below. Since intransitive sentences have only one core argument, which presumably must be the subject of the sentence, one would expect to find intransitive verbs carrying cross-referencing prefixes. But as you can see from comparing (152) and (153), this is not always the case. Some verbs take prefixes, and others take suffixes.

(**152**) *Geu-jak.*
     3-go
     'He/she goes.'

(**153**) *Lôn rhët-lôn.*
     1SG fall-1SG
     'I fall.'

What explains the difference in grammatical behaviour between verbs like *jak* 'go' and verbs like *rhët* 'fall'? It turns out that the governing principle is a semantic one. If the verb is a "doing" verb, under the volitional control of the NP, it will take a cross-referencing prefix. But if it is a "happening" verb, not under the control of the NP, it will take a cross-referencing suffix. Put another way, the principle is that actor NPs are cross-referenced by prefixes, and undergoer NPs are cross-referenced by suffixes.

Essentially, this means that, contrary to initial impressions, the cross-referencing system of Acehnese does not work on a "subjects and objects" basis. We can explain the distribution of the affixes on the basis of a single, purely semantic, generalization. Furthermore, the fact that intransitive "subjects" are not treated in a uniform way (actor subjects being marked by prefixes, undergoer subjects being marked by suffixes) brings into question the assumption that there is any unitary grammatical category of subject in Acehnese.

This impression becomes stronger when we look into some of the grammatical constructions of Acehnese where one would expect to find "subjects". Consider the verb *tém* 'want' and its complement clause. In Acehnese, as in English (and, as we have seen in the previous section, Tagalog) the verb for 'want' can take a complement which is missing an NP. The omission of the NP is indicated by the absence of the cross-referencing affix on the complement verb. See example (154) below, where the verb *taguen* 'cook' lacks the expected prefix *geu-*. The referent of the missing NP is understood to be the 'wanter' him or herself.

(154) *Gue-tém* ‖ *taguen bu.*
     3-want   cook   rice
     'He/she wants to cook rice.'

When we look into how intransitive complement clauses are formed, however, we discover that the rule is not so simple. If the verb is an "actor" verb, such as *jak* 'go', the expected cross-referencing affix (prefix) can—indeed, must—be omitted and the sentence is grammatical, as shown in (155a). However, if the verb is an "undergoer" verb, such as *rhët* 'fall', the expected cross-referencing affix (suffix) cannot be omitted, as shown by the ungrammaticality of (155b).

(155) a. *Gopnyan   geu-tém* ‖ *jak.*
        3SG   3-want   go
        'He/she wants to go.'

     b. **Gopnyan geu-tém* ‖ *rhët.*
        3SG   3-want   fall
        ≠'He/she wants to fall.'

Once again, the language is not treating all putative "subjects" in the same fashion. To describe 'want' constructions in Acehnese we need to use the semantic notions of actor and undergoer, but we do not need to use the notion of subject.

Durie (1987) examines a wide range of other construction types in Acehnese, and for all of them the outcome is the same. The fundamental grammatical distinction in the language is between actors and undergoers (rather than between subject and object). All the grammatical constructions which one might expect to work in terms of a "subject" actually distinguish between two kinds of subject, as it were, actor-subjects and undergoer-subjects. In the end, there is very little motivation for recognizing the notion of subject in Acehnese. Bowden (2001) makes a similar argument for Taba, an eastern Indonesian language.

4.4.4 Reprise

In this section, we have canvassed some facts about East and Southeast Asian languages which have led linguists to rethink and revise their ideas about the nature and universality of the traditional (European-oriented) concept of grammatical "subject". I have to conclude by emphasizing, however, that there is still a great deal of controversy surrounding this issue. In general terms, many linguists would now accept that "subject" in English (and other European languages) is best looked upon as a composite category which typically combines the properties of (true) grammatical subject and of topic. That is, many linguists now accept that the concept of "topic" deserves to be incorporated—in some shape or form—into a general theory of grammar. However, there are widely differing views on how this should best be done.

A more radical position (descending from Schachter 1976) is that neither subject nor topic are universal categories of grammar, equally valid in all languages, but that these labels are just convenient terms for commonly-found configurations of role-related and reference-related properties. On this view, it would be possible to have a language which, for instance, simply lacks the category of grammatical subject altogether. This is the position Durie (1987) takes on Acehnese. Some linguists, e.g. LaPolla (1993; 1995), take a similar stance in relation to Mandarin. It is beyond the scope of this book to follow up on theoretical debates like these. What is clear, however, is that facts about East and Southeast Asian languages such as Mandarin, Japanese, Thai, Tagalog, and Acehnese have been, and will continue to be, pivotal to these debates.

4.5 Sentence-final (illocutionary) particles

The term "illocutionary particles" refers to little words which express a speaker's immediate "here-and-now" emotions, thoughts, and desires towards what he or she is saying. Often words of this kind occur at the end of sentences (or more precisely, utterances), hence the term sentence-final particle. A rich inventory of illocutionary particles is an areal feature of mainland Southeast Asia. In languages like Thai, Vietnamese, and Cantonese, particles distinguish different kinds of speech-acts (requesting, questioning, persuading, advising, reminding, instructing, and so on), and express the speaker's emotional responses (surprise, doubt, impatience, reluctance, hesitation, and so on). In English, similar functions tend to be expressed by intonation.

We will illustrate from Cantonese, mainly because sentence-final particles are one of the most well-studied aspects of Cantonese grammar (cf. Luke 1990; Kwok 1984). There are more than thirty basic particles in Cantonese which can yield over 100 combinations, each with its own special nuance of

Table 4.5. Sentence-final particles in Cantonese (Matthews and Yip 1994: 340)

ā	lively statement, question or request
a	softening statement or question
àh	disapproving, surprised or suspicious
áh	seeking confirmation
ak	abrupt (dis)agreement
ge	affirmative: 'this is the case'
gé	tentative or uncertain affirmation seeking sympathy, etc.
ga	(*ge* + *a*)
gá	(*ge* + *ā*)
gak/gaak	(*ge* + *ak*)
gàh	(*ge* + *àh*)
jē	playing down a fact: 'that's all'
je	'just, only'
jēk	cheeky, intimate
ja	(*je* + *a*)
já	(*je* + *ā*)
jàh	(*je* + *àh*)
lā	requesting, seeking common ground
la	current relevance; advice
làh	(*la* + *áh*)
lak/laak	current relevance + finality
lō	seeking agreement, settlement, etc.
lo	emphasizing current situation
lòh	impatient: 'of course'
lok	definitive: 'that's the way it is'
bo/be	exclamatory, appreciative
wo	informative (noteworthiness)
wòh	discovery
wóh	evidential (hearsay, reported speech)
āma	indicates obvious reason, excuse, etc.
amáh	as above, negative or impatient
gāma	(*ge* + *āma*)
jāma/jīma	(*je* + *āma*)

meaning. Matthews and Yip (1994) tabulate the particles in Hong Kong Cantonese as in Table 4.5. You can see that some of them can be analyzed as contracted versions of particle combinations, e.g. *ga* ← *ge* + *a*, *gak* ← *ge* + *ak*.

A few examples follow. The first three examples (from Matthews and Yip 1994) show particles in questions: *áh* suggests surprise, scepticism, or disapproval, *há* presupposes the addressee's agreement or compliance (much like an English tag question), while *mē* expresses surprise, especially in rhetorical questions.

(**156**) *Léih gú   gam yúhngyih áh?*
      you guess so   easy   PRT
      'You think it's that easy, do you?'

(**157**) *Léih gwāai   ngóh jauh góng gújái béi léih tēng há?*
      you behave I   then tell   story for you listen PRT
      'If you're good, I'll tell you a story, OK? (to children)'

(**158**) *Kéuih hóu lēk   mē?*
      he   very clever PRT
      'As if he was so clever!'

The following pair show directive particles. *La* emphasizes a point of current relevance. *Lō* invites agreement, cooperation or sympathy.

(**159**) *Taai chóuh la, ngóh fan   m̀h dóu.*
      too noisy PRT I   sleep not PRT
      'I can't sleep (you know), it's too noisy.'

(**160**) *Gám jauh dāk   lō.*
      so   then okay PRT
      'That'll be all right, won't it?'

Needless to say, these few examples can hardly convey any real impression of the subtlety and vibrancy which particles add to Cantonese conversation. Aside from the size of the particle inventory, their sheer frequency is remarkable. According to Luke (1990: 10–11): "An informal count reveals that an utterance particle is found in continuous talk on the average every 1.5 seconds."

A similar statement could no doubt be made in relation to languages like Thai and Lao, which also have large particle inventories, even if the rate of particle use may not be quite as impressive. Even in Mandarin Chinese, which has a much smaller inventory than Cantonese (only seven are at all common), particles are highly typical of ordinary conversation. Chappell (1991: 40) estimates one every six or so seconds. She also notes, however, that particle use is much less frequent outside familiar, conversational settings; and that in scientific and historical texts, they are actually quite rare. Particles are also an extremely common and important part of ordinary Japanese conversation (Asano 2003).

Key technical terms

aspect
classifier
classifier float
double subject construction
imperfective
loose serialization
measure construction
modality
perfective
progressive
prototype
radial polysemy
referential (non-referential)

repeater construction
sentence-final particle
serial verb construction
specific (non-specific)
subject
tense
tight serialization
topic
topic-prominent
trigger
unit counter construction
verb-preposition

CHAPTER 5

The soundscape of East and Southeast Asia

In this chapter we first compare phoneme inventories in a sample of languages, and look at the patterns which govern how sounds can be combined to form syllables and words. Then we revisit the question of lexical tone. Finally we survey some ways in which phonology and morphology interact.

5.1 Phoneme systems

A word of caution at the onset. Linguists sometimes give the impression that identifying the phonemes of a language is a straightforward matter, but in reality there is often room for disagreement on matters of phonemic analysis. In the literature on certain languages of East and Southeast Asia the same phonemes are sometimes described in quite different terms and written with completely different symbols. Opinions can differ even about the number of phonemes in a particular language.

5.1.1 Insular Southeast Asia

Austronesian languages such as Indonesian and Malaysian (referred to collectively as Malay), Javanese, and Tagalog, tend to have phoneme inventories which are small to medium in size. Malay, for example, has eighteen indigenous consonant phonemes, plus five additional fricatives which occur only in loan words, in the speech of educated people. They are

Table 5.1. Indigenous Malay consonants (additional phonemes in recent loans: f, v, z, ʃ (spelt sy), and x (spelt kh))

	Labial	Alveolar	Palatal	Velar	Glottal
Stops					
voiceless	p	t	c	k	*k [ʔ]
voiced	b	d	j [ɟ]	g	
Nasals	m	n	ny [ɲ]	ng [ŋ]	
Fricatives		s			h
Lateral		l			
Trill		r			
Semi-vowels	w		y [j]		

shown in Table 5.1. In the standard orthography (spelling system) of Malay most of the consonants are written using the same symbols as they would have in the International Phonetic Alphabet (IPA). Where the orthography differs from the IPA, the corresponding IPA symbol is placed in square brackets next to the ordinary Malay spelling. Notice that several of the Malay phonemes are spelt using combinations of two letters. The letter combination *ny*, for example, indicates not an *n*-sound followed by a *y*-sound, but a single sound: the palatal nasal symbolized by the IPA symbol /ɲ/. When two letters are used to indicate a single sound they are referred to as a digraph. English spelling uses several digraphs, including *ng* for /ŋ/, *sh* for /ʃ/, and *th* for both /θ/ and /ð/.

The glottal stop ʔ is asterisked in Table 5.1 because in traditional and village Malay it is not a separate phoneme, just a pronunciation variant (allophone) of the phoneme /k/ when it occurs at the end of words and syllables, and as a transition sound between two vowels, e.g. *kakak* [kakaʔ] 'older sister', *rakyat* [raʔyat] 'citizenry', *maaf* [maʔaf] 'pardon'. Recent loan words from English do not conform to this pattern, however, which means that in the speech of educated people there is now a contrast between the *k*-sound and the glottal stop (though both are still spelt with the letter *k*); for example, Indonesian *fisik* [fisik] 'physics' vs. *bisik* [bisiʔ] 'whisper'; *maknit* [maknit] 'magnet' vs. *makna* [maʔna] 'meaning' (Prentice 1987: 189).

Tagalog has the same indigenous consonant phonemes as Malay, except that it lacks the palatal stops and palatal nasal. Like Malay, Tagalog has some phonemes which are found only in loan words.

The vowel systems of both Tagalog and Malay are also rather small, with five and six vowels, respectively; see Table 5.2. The extra vowel in the Malay system is a tense central vowel. This is often symbolized in linguistic descriptions using the IPA symbol /ə/ (schwa), but really this symbol should

Table 5.2. Vowel phonemes of Tagalog and Malay

Tagalog vowels				Malay vowels		
Front	Central	Back		Front	Central	Back
i		u		i		u
e		o		e	ə/ɨ	o
	a				a	

Table 5.3. Acehnese vowels (after Durie 1985)

Front	Back-central unrounded	Back rounded
i	ɯ	u
e	ə	o
ɛ	ʌ	ɔ
	a	

be reserved for a reduced or unstressed vowel (such as we find in English). Another symbol which is sometimes used is IPA /ɨ/ though strictly speaking this designates a high central vowel. The most appropriate IPA symbol, from a strictly phonetic point of view, is /ɜ/ but this is almost never used in linguistic descriptions of Malay.

Even counting the foreign phonemes the total number of phonemes in Malay and Tagalog does not exceed thirty. Not all Austronesian languages have such small vowel inventories. For example, Acehnese (northern Sumatra), has ten simple vowels, as shown in Table 5.3, and a number of diphthongs as well. Typologically this resembles the Mon-Khmer languages of the mainland. Things are also a bit different on the eastern side of the Indonesian archipelego (Klamer 1998; 2000), where implosive and pre-nasalized consonants can be found.

5.1.2 Mainland Southeast Asia

Phoneme systems in mainland Southeast Asia typically range from about thirty to forty or more in number. Among consonants, voicing is usually not distinctive, but aspiration often is; i.e. there are often two series of stops: aspirated vs. unaspirated. To English speakers, unaspirated stops usually sound voiced (since English voiced stops are less aspirated than their voiceless counterparts). Quite a few languages have three series of stops, the third series often having a distinctive phonation, such as stiff or creaky voice (see section 5.3.1). We will run through some mainland phoneme systems in

Table 5.4. Thai consonants (after Hudak 1987: 32)

	Labial	Alveolar	Palatal	Velar	Glottal
Stops					
voiceless unaspirated	p	t	c	k	[ʔ]
voiceless aspirated	ph [pʰ]	th [tʰ]	ch [cʰ]	kh [kʰ]	
voiced	b	d			
Nasals	m	n		ng [ŋ]	
Fricatives	f	s			h
Rhotic		r			
Lateral		l			
Semi-vowels	w		y [j]		

Table 5.5. Thai vowels (Hudak 1987: 32)

	Front	Back unrounded	Back rounded
High	i	ɨ	u
Mid	e	ə	o
Low	ɛ	a	ɔ

increasing order of complexity (segmental phonemes only at this point; tones will be dealt with later).

Thai has a moderately sized system, with twenty consonant phonemes and nine vowels. The two Thai voiced stops tend to be pronounced with a degree of stiff voice. Though Thai is normally written in Thai script (see Chapter 6), in linguistic descriptions one commonly sees Thai words written in roman letters using the conventions shown in Table 5.4. As before, when these differ from the appropriate IPA symbols, the IPA symbols are placed in brackets.

Notice that Thai has a series of unrounded back vowels, as shown in Table 5.5. Something which should be pointed out about this table, which represents a common system for transcribing Thai, is that some of the symbols (particularly /ɛ/ and /ɔ/) are not used according to their IPA values.

Vietnamese has a somewhat larger phoneme inventory, with some additional consonants, notably a series of voiced fricatives, a couple of retroflexes, and two extra vowels in the low front-central area of the vowel space. It has twenty-three consonants and twelve vowels, making thirty-five phonemes in all.

Burmese has a larger consonant inventory. As shown in Table 5.6, there are thirty-four consonants, though three are marginal or rare (r, ʍ, ð).

Table 5.6. Burmese consonants (after Wheatley 1987; Watkins 2001)

	Labial	Alveolar (Dental)	Palatal	Velar	Glottal
Stops					
voiceless unaspirated	p	t	c	k	[ʔ]
voiceless aspirated	ph [pʰ]	th [tʰ]	ch [cʰ]	kh [kʰ]	
voiced	b	d	j [dʒ]	g	
Nasals					
voiced	m	n	ɲ	ŋ	
voiceless	hm [m̥]	hn [n̥]	hɲ [ɲ̥]	hŋ [ŋ̥]	
Fricatives					
voiceless		s / θ	hs, sh [ʃ]		h
voiced		z / ð			
Approximants					
voiced	w	l	y [j]		
voiceless	hw [ʍ]	hl [ɬ]			
Rhotic		r			

Unusually from a typological point of view, Burmese has a full set of voiceless nasals (one corresponding to each of the plain nasals) and two voiceless approximants (a semi-vowel and a lateral). As well, there are three series of stops (plain, aspirated and voiced), each with members at the four main places of articulation, and a variety of fricatives. There is no settled system for romanizing Burmese script, but the roman letters and digraphs in Table 5.6 are in common use. The vowel system of Burmese is open to competing interpretations, basically because a different range of vowel contrasts are found in open and closed ("checked") syllables. Nine to ten vowel phonemes would appear to be the minimal reasonable number.

Another well-described Tibeto-Burman language is the minority language Lahu (Matisoff 1973). Although it belongs to the same Lolo-Burmese subgroup as Burmese, its phoneme inventory has a couple of notable differences. It lacks voiceless nasals and approximants, it has two additional stops (plain and aspirated) at the postvelar place of articulation, and, most strikingly of all from a typological perspective, it lacks a phoneme /s/ even though it has several other fricative phonemes, both voiced and voiceless (including /f/, /v/, /ʃ/, /h/ and /ɤ/.)

Mon-Khmer languages are known for their large vowel inventories. Table 5.7 shows the full range of vocalic nuclei (simple vowels and diphthongs) in Khmer, as spoken in the Battambang province, according to the analysis of Diffloth (1992). All twenty-seven occur

Table 5.7. Khmer vocalic nuclei (simple vowels and diphthongs) (Diffloth 1992: 273)

Long	iː			ɯː			uː
	ie̤			ɯə̤			uɔ̤
	eɛ̤		ɛɛ̤	ʌe		ɔo	oɔ̤
		aɛ̤		aʌ			aɔ̤
			aː		ɒː		
Short	ɪ			ɤ		Ŭə	U
			ĕa			ŏa	
		ɛ		ʌ			ɔ
			a		ɒ̆a		

contrastively in major syllables (see section 5.2.2) preceding a final consonant. Diffloth recognizes five degrees of vowel height, though as you might expect with a system of this complexity, there are a number of rival analyses. Notice that modern Khmer has a length contrast (long vs. short), whereas many other Mon-Khmer languages, including modern Mon, have a register or phonation type distinction (clear vs. breathy). The modern Khmer system evolved historically from an earlier register distinction, and the conservative Khmer script works as if the register distinction still existed (which has been the cause of some confusion in the linguistic literature).

Vowel systems with more than twenty units are common in Mon-Khmer languages generally. If all types of vocalic nuclei are counted, including those distinguished by nasalization and phonation type, one variety of Bru (a minority language of central Vietnam) has been claimed to have sixty-eight contrastive vocalic nuclei. As Diffloth and Zide (1992: 14) remark, this is probably a world record.

The largest consonant inventories in all of East and Southeast Asia occur in the languages of the Hmong-Mien family. Hmong itself has four stop series: unaspirated, prenasalized unaspirated, aspirated, prenasalized aspirated. All of these are phonetically voiceless, except for the nasalized portions of the prenasalized series (Ladefoged and Maddieson 1996: 124–5). The four series occur in six different positions: labial, dental, retroflex, palatal, velar, and uvular. There are also affricated dentals, affricated palatals, and both voiced and voiceless nasals. In addition, the language has a set of labial stops with lateral release, a set of voiceless and voiced fricatives, a pair of glottalized dental stops, and a voiceless lateral (Heimbach 1969; Clark 1989; Strecker 1987). The number of consonant phonemes is in the mid to high fifties.

Table 5.8 is given solely in IPA symbols mainly for reasons of space. There is a well-established romanization, the Romanized Popular Alphabet,

Table 5.8. White Hmong stops and nasals (incomplete; after Heimbach 1969; Strecker 1987)

	Labial	Dental	Dental affricated	Retroflex	Palatal	Palatal affricated	Velar	Uvular	Glottal
Unaspirated	p	t	ts	ʈ	c	tɕ	k	q	ʔ
Aspirated	pʰ	tʰ	tsʰ	ʈʰ	cʰ	tɕʰ	kʰ	qʰ	
Prenasalized									
unaspirated	^{m}p	^{n}t	^{n}ts	^{n}ʈ	^{ɲ}c	^{n}tɕ	^{ŋ}k	^{N}q	
aspirated	^{m}pʰ	^{n}tʰ	^{n}tsʰ	^{n}ʈʰ	^{ɲ}cʰ	^{n}tɕʰ	^{ŋ}kʰ	^{N}qʰ	
Nasals									
voiced	m	n			ɲ		ŋ		
voiceless	m̥	n̥			ɲ̥				

used in the linguistic literature and elsewhere in this book, but it uses many three-letter and even four-letter combinations.

5.1.3 Sinitic languages

Mandarin Chinese (Modern Standard Chinese) has twenty consonant phonemes, which all contrast word-initially. The stops and affricates have two series: unaspirated and aspirated. Mandarin is unusual in having retroflex consonants (affricates and fricatives). In China, the language is normally written using Chinese characters (see Chapter 6), but there is a well-established system—pinyin (lit. 'spell-sound')—for writing in roman letters. Table 5.9 shows both pinyin symbols and IPA symbols.

As shown in Table 5.9, Modern Standard Chinese (in the standard pronunciation based on the Beijing dialect) differentiates between dental affricates and fricatives, on the one hand, and retroflex affricates and fricatives, on the other. Speakers from elsewhere in the country, however, often have difficulty making these distinctions (Norman 1988: 140). They tend to pronounce *shān* 'mountain' the same as *sān* 'three', *chí* 'late, slow' the same as *cí* 'word', *zhēng* 'to steam' the same as *Zēng* 'a surname', and so on. Being able to make these distinctions is considered one of the hallmarks of elegant pronunciation.

Although they are listed in Table 5.9, the palatal sounds of Mandarin are not separate phonemes because they are not contrastive. They are only found preceding high front vowels, which puts them in complementary distribution with no fewer than three sets of other sounds: the dental affricates, the retroflexes, and the velars. The palatals have been regarded, by different analysts, as allophones of each of these other sets. Chao (1968) claims that native speaker intuition favours interpreting them as allophones of the velars.

Table 5.9. Mandarin Chinese consonants, Beijing dialect (adapted from Li and Thompson 1981)

	Labial	Dental	Retroflex	Palatal	Velar	Uvular
Stops						
unaspirated	b [p]	d [t]			g [k]	
aspirated	p [pʰ]	t [tʰ]			k [kʰ]	
Affricates						
unaspirated		z [ts]	zh [tʂ]	j [tɕ]		
aspirated		c [tsʰ]	ch [tʂʰ]	q [tɕʰ]		
Fricatives	f	s	sh [ʂ]	x [ɕ]		h [χ]
Nasals	m	n			ng [ŋ]	
Liquid		l				
Rhotic			r [ɻ]			
Semi-vowels	w		y [j]			

According to many linguists Standard Chinese has five phonemically distinctive vowels (Norman 1988): three high vowels (IPA /i/, /y/, /u/; pinyin: *i, ü, u*) and two non-high vowels (IPA: /ɤ/, /a/; pinyin: *e* and *a*). The following set of words shows this five-way contrast: *lì* 'profit, benefit', *lǜ* 'green', *lù* 'road', *lè* 'happy', *là* 'pungent, hot'. The situation is more complex than a simple five-way contrast, however. There are a dozen or so two-vowel combinations (e.g. in pinyin: *ie, ia, iu, ua, ui, üe, ai*), and even a couple of three-vowel combinations. Most of the vowel phonemes have a wide range of allophonic variants depending on adjacent consonants and vowels. On account of these complications, authorities differ on the correct analysis of the vowel system. Some recognize an additional vowel (IPA /o/). This is also the analysis assumed by the pinyin system, which has a vowel written as *o*.

Cantonese has a smaller inventory of consonants than Mandarin— eighteen altogether. It lacks the retroflex series, has no rhotic (r-phoneme), and lacks a distinction between /n/ and /l/. Unlike Mandarin, however, Cantonese has a small set of labiovelar stops. There is no standard romanization for Cantonese. In recent years, the system recommended by the Linguistic Society of Hong Kong has been gaining widespread recognition, but the best reference grammar of Cantonese is Matthews and Yip (1994), which uses a slightly different system. The roman letter symbols given in Table 5.10 are those used in that work.

From a phonemic point of view, the Cantonese simple vowel inventory (eight vowels in all) is larger than that of Mandarin, mainly because some (though not all) of the vowel-vowel combinations of Mandarin have been merged into single vowels in Cantonese.

Table 5.10. Cantonese initial consonants (after Matthews and Yip 1994)

	Labial	Dental	Palatal (affricated)	Velar	Labiovelar	Glottal
Stops						
unaspirated	b [p]	d [t]	j [ts]	g [k]	gw [kw]	
aspirated	p [pʰ]	t [tʰ]	ch [tsʰ]	k [kʰ]	kw [kwʷ]	
Fricatives	f	s				h
Nasals	m	n/l		ng [ŋ]		
Semi-vowels	w		y [j]			

5.1.4 Korean and Japanese

The most noteworthy feature of the Korean consonant inventory is that there are three series of stops, and that the nature of the phonetic differences between them is disputed. In Korea, the language is usually written in the unique Korean writing system Hangeul (Han'gŭl) (see Chapter 6). There are several competing systems for writing Korean in roman letters. In this book we use the official Revised Romanization of Korean (National Academy of the Korean Language 2000).

One series of stops is normally described as aspirated—heavily aspirated, in fact. To English ears, they sound similar to English voiceless stops like *p, t,* and *k,* which are usually aspirated in initial position. The other two series are often labelled as "lax" and "tense". The lax series are voiceless and unaspirated, sounding to English ears like weak or soft versions of voiced sounds *b, d,* and *g.* The tense series are produced with some kind of muscular tension (causing a stiffening of the vocal folds), and so they do sound quite tense. They can be described as "glottalized", and this description accounts for the choice of IPA symbols in Table 5.11; but it has to be borne in mind that the term "glottalization" normally describes an articulation which is quite different from that of Korean. For the purposes of romanization, Table 5.11 represents the aspirated stops as *p, t, c, k* and the lax series as *b, d, j, g.* The tense consonants are given double letters, i.e. as *pp, tt, cc, kk, ss.* This has the advantage of corresponding (if only loosely) with the Korean writing system, which uses doubled letters for these sounds.

The differences between the lax, aspirated, and tense series do not show up in many positions in a word. Word-finally or before another consonant (i.e. in syllable-final position), all stops and fricatives are pronounced as unreleased stops, so that the differences between the series are neutralized. These changes (and there are many more) might look at first as if they are rules of allophony, but this is not so. Allophonic rules do not change one phoneme into another, they merely determine which of several different

Table 5.11. Korean consonant phonemes (after Kim 1987)

	Labial	Dental	Palatal	Velar	Glottal
Stops					
lax	b [p]	d [t]	j [c]	g [k]	
aspirated	p [pʰ]	t [tʰ]	c [cʰ]	k [kʰ]	
tense	pp [p']	tt [t']	cc [c']	kk [k']	
Nasals	m	n		ng [ŋ]	
Fricatives					
lax		s			h
tense		ss [s']			
Liquid		l/r			
Semi-vowels	w	y [j]			

Table 5.12. Korean simple vowels (after Lee 1996: 53)

	Front unrounded	Central	Back rounded
High	i	eu [ɨ]	u
Mid	e	eo [ʌ]	o
Low	ae [ɛ]	a	

pronunciations a particular phoneme adopts in particular circumstances. The kind of neutralization process just mentioned is more properly called "morphophonemic" (see section 5.4). A genuine rule of allophony affects the Korean liquid sound. This has one variant [l] in syllable-final position, and a second variant [r] elsewhere, i.e. in word-initial and intervocalic positions.

As for vowels, there is disagreement about the exact number. The Revised Romanization recognizes ten simple vowels, but two of them (the front rounded vowels), are more realistically described as diphthongs. This leaves eight simple vowels as shown in Table 5.12 (cf. Lee 1996).

Compared with other languages of East Asia, and even with Korean, Japanese has a rather small phoneme inventory, similar to the Austronesian systems. This is one reason (not a particularly good one) that some scholars believe that there is a distant genetic relationship between Japanese and Austronesian. Standard Japanese has a simple five-vowel system, as shown in Table 5.13, in the same configuration as Tagalog. There is a lot of dialectal variation in Japanese, however, and some regional dialects have as few as three or as many as eight vowel phonemes. Two notable features of Japanese vowels are that the articulation

Table 5.13. Japanese vowels
(Shibatani 1990: 159)

Front	Central	Back
i		u [ɯ]
e		o
	a	

Table 5.14. Japanese consonants (Shibatani 1990: 137)

	Labial	Dental	Postalveolar	Velar	Postvelar
Stops					
voiceless	p	t		k	Q
voiced	b	d		g	
Nasals	m	n		N	
Fricatives					
voiceless		s			h
voiced		z			
Liquid			r		
Semi-vowels	w		j		

of the high back vowel is unrounded [ɯ], and that, except in slow careful speech, the two high vowels lose their voicing when they occur in a voiceless environment, such as between voiceless consonants, e.g. [kɯ̥tsɯ] 'shoe', [haʃi̥] 'chopstick'.

Except for the mysterious phonemes Q and N, which we'll come to in a minute, the Japanese consonant inventory, as shown in Table 5.14, looks straightforward. Voicing is phonemic, there are only three main places of articulation (labial, dental, velar), only two nasals, and only three fricatives.

A notable feature of Japanese is that the dental phonemes are "palatalized" before the high front vowel /i/. This means that /s/ is often pronounced as [ʃ], /z/ as [dʒ], /t/ as [tʃ], and /d/ as [dʒ]. Except for /s/, the dental phonemes are also affected by a phonetic process of "affrication" when they occur before the high back vowel /u/. This means that /t/ is often pronounced as [ts], and that /d/ and /z/ are often pronounced as [dz]. In a fully phonemic transcription these differences would not be shown, but Japanese is usually transcribed according to the Hepburn system (see Chapter 6), which does indicate the allophonic pronunciation; for example, *watashi* instead of *watasi* 'I', *uchi* instead of *uti* 'inside', *tsunami* instead of *tunami* 'tidal wave'.

To explain the Japanese consonants indicated as N and Q, we have to take account of the most celebrated feature of Japanese phonology—the phenomenon of the mora. In principle, the concept of a mora (plural: moras or morae) is based on the time it takes to pronounce a certain sound or sequence of sounds. Each mora is supposed to take roughly the same duration in time. Moras are used as units of rhythm in Japanese poetry. In Japanese a mora may be: a consonant plus vowel, a vowel alone, a so-called moraic nasal, or certain other moraic consonants. Leaving this last category aside for a moment, we can illustrate with the words *hachimaki* 'headband' and *shinbun* 'newspaper'. *Hachimaki* consists of four syllables (*ha-chi-ma-ki*), and because none of these syllables ends with a consonant, each of them corresponds to a single mora. The word *shinbun* consists of two syllables (*shin* and *bun*), but because each of the syllable-final nasals also counts as a mora, this word also consists of four moras: *shi-n-bu-n*. In the Japanese kana scripts (see Chapter 6), *hachimaki* and *shinbun* are both spelt with four letters.

Syllable-final nasals are normally regarded in Japanese phonology as belonging to a different phoneme to ordinary (non-moraic) /n/. In Table 5.14 the moraic nasal is symbolized as N, which in the IPA script stands for a uvular nasal. This is because a moraic nasal at the end of a word tends to be pronounced, in careful speech, as a uvular nasal. In casual speech it is usually realized as nasalization on the vowel. When it precedes a consonant, it assimilates in place of articulation to the following consonant; so *shinbun*, for example, is pronounced more like [ʃimbɯN].

The remaining kind of moras are non-nasal consonants which occur syllable-finally. The basic structure of the Japanese syllable is very restricted—essentially CV. The only way a non-nasal can occur at the end of a syllable is if it is the first of two identical consonants (a so-called geminate cluster), e.g. the first /k/ in *hakkiri* 'clearly', the first /p/ in *yappari* 'as expected', the first /t/ in *tatta* 'stood'. The tradition in Japanese phonology is to regard the first element of a geminate cluster as an "underspecified" consonant which gets its full pronunciation (e.g. as /k/, /p/, or /t/) from the following sound. The underspecified moraic consonant is symbolized as Q. We will come back to the topic of Japanese moras in section 5.4.3.

5.2 Word shapes: phonotactics

Phonotactics concerns the patterns governing how sounds can be combined to form syllables and words.

5.2.1 Insular Southeast Asia

In the western part of peninsular and insular Southeast Asia, the indigenous vocabulary of languages such as Malay and Tagalog tends to have disyllabic lexemes of the form: $(C)V_1(C)(C)V_2(C)$. Monosyllabic forms exist but they are mostly exclamations (e.g. *nah!* 'take this', *wah!* 'gee!'), or shortened forms of disyllabic words (e.g. *tak* 'not' from *tidak*, *mak* 'mother' from *emak*). Most polysyllabic words are compounds or morphologically derived, at least historically, e.g. *matahari* [eye-day] 'sun'; *setuju* 'agree' from *se-* 'one' + *tuju* 'aim, goal'. A few polysyllabic words appear to be indigenous, e.g. *telinga* 'ear', and there are various polysyllabic loans, e.g. *sekolah* 'school' from Portuguese.

Without further specifications, the template (C)V$_1$(C)(C)V$_2$(C) tends to overrepresent the actual diversity of word shapes. In V$_2$ position in Malaysian, for example, there is no contrast between the high vowels /i, u/ and their mid counterparts /e, o/. Only the high vowels occur in open final syllables and only the mid vowels occur in closed final syllables. In the dialects spoken on the east coast of peninsular Malaysia, distinctions between final consonants are greatly reduced: continuants are lost altogether, the only obstruent is the glottal stop, and all final nasals are realized as /ŋ/ or as nasalization on the vowel.

In the eastern parts of insular Southeast Asia, medial consonant clusters and final consonants are less common (Klamer 2000). That is, the preferred root form is the simpler structure: CVCV.

5.2.2 Mainland Southeast Asia and Sinitic languages

In most languages of mainland Southeast Asia, simple words are typically monosyllabic, with disyllabic words resulting mainly from compounding or reduplication. The exception to this statement are Mon-Khmer languages, which typically have the so-called sesquisyllabic ("one and a half syllable") or iambic pattern (Matisoff 1973; Haiman 1998). In these languages there are plenty of simple disyllabic words, but the first syllable is prosodically weak (e.g. invariably unstressed and centralized) and has restricted phonotactic possibilities compared with the main syllable. Such "half syllables" are usually termed minor syllables. The Khmer sesquisyllabic word has a structure like this: C(r)V$_1$(N) – C(C)V$_2$(C). Only three vowels can occur in the unstressed V$_1$ position, while the entire (very large) inventory is found in the V$_2$ position. The range of consonants in the minor syllable is also sharply reduced. As shown, the final consonant of the minor syllable (if present) can only be a nasal (N), whereas the final consonant of the main syllable can be any one of thirteen or fourteen different consonants. In casual speech, the minor syllable is often further reduced by the vowel being pronounced as a schwa or omitted altogether, or by the loss of voicing contrast in the initial consonant, or by simplification of the cluster (if there is one). These processes make the minor syllable phonologically unstable compared with the major stressed syllable (Haiman 1998).

In contrast to other language families of the region, Mon-Khmer languages usually permit numerous word-initial consonant clusters, especially of the form stop + sonorant, or stop + /h/; and at the beginning of major syllables, an even greater range can be possible. In this environment, Khmer, for example, permits unusual combinations like those in the following words (Haiman 1998: 604): *mcul* 'needle', *mnuh* 'person', *lbaeŋ* 'game', *lʔɔɔ* 'good', *pkaa* 'flower', *tbooŋ* 'south', *sʔaek* 'tomorrow', *ckae* 'dog', and many more. The minority language Chrau permits up to three consonants in a sequence, e.g. *prhɔː* 'red', *khlɔːm* 'to blow' (Sidwell 2000: 5).

Burmese is also sesquisyllabic, probably having acquired the pattern from Mon many hundreds of years ago. The Burmese sesquisyllabic pattern (Wheatley 1987) looks like this : $C_1 ə – C_1 (w/y)V(C_2)$. The vocalic nucleus of the major syllable allows numerous contrasts, but the vowel of the minor syllable is always lax, mid central and toneless. As in most mainland Southeast Asian languages, the maximum range of contrasts between consonants is found in the syllable-initial position. No clusters are permitted in word-initial position and the range of consonants in final position is heavily restricted: C_1 can be any of the thirty-plus consonants, but the only possible C_2 is *n* (the glottal stop can also appear finally, but it is best regarded as a tone, since it precludes any other tone and always produces a very short, high, and even pitch contour).

For many mainland Southeast Asian and Sinitic languages, phonotactic factors make it convenient to analyze syllable structure by dividing the syllable into two parts: the initial segment and the remainder, which many linguists term the rhyme (namely, the vowels plus final consonant, if there is one). The possibilities for each part are then tabulated. This is the traditional approach in Chinese linguistics, in which the rhyme is often termed the "final". For example, the syllable structure of Mandarin Chinese (Beijing dialect) has the form: (C)(V)V(V/N). This means that every syllable has a nuclear vowel, which may occur with a preceding vowel to form a two-vowel combination (diphthong), or with two other vowels to form a three-vowel combination (triphthong). Initial and final consonants are optional, except that no final consonant can occur after a three-vowel combination. Furthermore, only nasals (more specifically, /n/ and /ŋ/) may occur as final consonants. No clusters are permitted at all. Table 5.15 lists all the finals (i.e. rhymes) of Mandarin Chinese.

Vietnamese has a very similar phonotactic structure to Mandarin, except that there is a maximum of two vowels, and the final consonant can be a voiceless stop as well as a nasal. In addition there may be a semi-vowel /w/ before the vocalic nucleus: (C)(w)V(V)(C). The possibility of numerous vowel-vowel combinations in the nucleus of Mandarin and Vietnamese syllables compensates, in a sense, for the relative simplicity of the periphery of the syllable.

The phonotactic structure of Hmong-Mien languages is also fairly simple. Most words are monosyllabic, and there are severe restrictions on syllable-final consonants. In Hmong itself, for example, the only consonant possible at the end of a syllable is the velar nasal (Clark 1989). (A curious detail of

Table 5.15. Modern Standard Chinese finals, i.e. rhymes, based on Beijing pronunciation (adapted from Chen 1999: 35)

Pinyin				IPA			
	i	u	ü		i	u	y
a	ia	ua		a	ia	ua	
o		uo		o		uo	
e				ɤ			
ê	ie		üe	ɛ	iɛ		yɛ
ai		uai		ai		uai	
ei		uei		ei		uei	
ao	iao			au	iau		
ou	iou			ou	iou		
an	ian	uan	üan	an	iɛn	uan	yɛn
en	in	uen	ün	ən	in	un	yn
ang	iang	uang		aŋ	iaŋ	uaŋ	
eng	ing	ueng		əŋ	iŋ	uəŋ	
ong	iong			uŋ			yŋ
er				ɚ			

the Hmong orthography is that word-final ŋ is indicated not by the letters *ng,* but by doubling the vowel. Also, a set of orthographic word-final consonants are used as a device for indicating tone. Thus in its own orthography, the name of the language is spelled *Hmoob,* with the final *-b* indicating high-level [55] tone.)

5.2.3 Korean and Japanese

Korean syllable structure is a bit more complex than in Sinitic languages: (C)(V)V(C)(C). The language allows some syllable-final consonant clusters, but not in word-final position. A word like *gaps* 'price', for example, is pronounced as *gap* when it occurs in isolation, though the second consonant of the cluster shows itself if a vowel-initial suffix or clitic follows, e.g. *gaps-i* [price-nominative]. An interesting characteristic of Korean is that although the syllable structure allows for complex vowels, most morphemes in the language have simple vowels. The complex vowels arise when vowel-initial suffixes join onto vowel-final stems (remember that Korean is an agglutinating language, with numerous suffixes). When vowels come together in this way, they often undergo various modifications, which we will look into shortly (section 5.4.1).

As mentioned, the basic pattern of Japanese is CV, with the added possibility of a syllable-final moraic nasal (N), or, if the syllable is not word-final, a moraic consonant homorganic with the initial consonant of the following syllable. This is probably the most restrictive phonotactic pattern to be found among the languages of East Asia. Naturally, when Japanese adopts loan words from languages like English, which have much more complex syllabic patterns, extensive phonological adaptation is often necessary.

5.3 Tones and allotones

It can be helpful to look at tones using the same kind of framework as we use for phonemes. This means that we have to identify those aspects of tone pronunciation which are contrastive, i.e. which serve to make distinctions between words. This procedure leads to the conclusion that languages can have "allotones", i.e. non-contrastive variants of particular tones. As we work our way towards this subject, we first have to look in a little more detail at the phonetic qualities of tones, and at aspects of their distribution.

5.3.1 Phonetic qualities of tones

When we speak of "pitch", we are referring to the perceptual correlate of the fundamental frequency of the sound wave. The fundamental frequency of a speech sound is determined by the rate of vibration of the vocal folds. Speakers can control this by varying the tension in the vocal folds, and by varying the rate of airflow through the glottis. The precise mechanisms of pitch control are not perfectly clear, and it is probably done somewhat differently in different languages. One thing which is known is that qualities other than pitch contribute to the phonetic identity of tones in some languages. Naturally enough, these tend to be voice qualities controlled by the same part of the vocal apparatus which controls pitch, i.e. the larynx (Ladefoged and Maddieson 1996). They include stiff voice, an effect achieved by stiffening the muscle of the vocal folds, and creaky voice, done by tightly closing the cartilages at the back of the larynx so that only the front part of the vocal folds can vibrate, producing a very low-pitched vibration. There is a continuum between stiff and creaky voice, both of which depend on tension in the larynx. Stiff voice and creaky voice tend to be associated with low tones. For example, in Cantonese the low-falling tone is often accompanied by creaky voice, especially in male speakers. A third kind of voice quality, breathy voice (also called murmur), is achieved by a looser form of vibration of the vocal cords than with normal voicing, allowing a faster rate of air flow through the glottis.

Phonetic studies of tone assist us in understanding tonogenesis—the process by which languages develop tones. While Sinitic languages have been tonal since ancient times, many of the present-day tone languages of Southeast Asia, including Burmese, Thai, and Vietnamese, have developed tones more recently, probably under the influence of neighbouring tonal languages. The details are complex, but basically it depends on the fact that, in an older stage of the language, certain types of syllable tended to be pronounced with particular pitches on account of their initial or final consonants. For example, words beginning with voiceless stops tended to be pronounced at a slightly higher pitch than words beginning with voiced stops. (This happens in present-day English too, though of course speakers are completely unaware of it.) Originally these pitch distinctions were not contrastive: they were just phonetic effects associated with particular consonant types, e.g. voiced vs. voiceless, glottalized vs. plain. But subsequent sound changes merged the consonants, and the functional load of the original consonant distinctions was taken over by the pitch distinctions. What had been allophonic distinctions in pitch had become phonemic. The language had developed tones.

5.3.2 Distribution of tones and allotones

The distribution of tones is often dependent on the shape of the syllable (Hudak 1987: 34). In Thai, for example, any of the five tones can occur in syllables ending in a long vowel, a semi-vowel, or a nasal. For example:

mid tone	*khaa*	'to be lodged in'
low tone	*khàa*	'a kind of aromatic root'
falling tone	*khâa*	'servant, slave'
high tone	*kháa*	'to do business in'
rising tone	*khǎa*	'leg'

Other syllable types have a restricted range of tones. For example, syllables with a short vowel and a final stop (or no final consonant) can only have a low or high tone (or occasionally a falling tone). Syllables with long vowels followed by a stop can only have low or falling tones (or occasionally a high tone). The mid and rising tones are not possible in either of these syllable types.

In many languages, contour tones are not found in syllables with short vowels, because the short duration of the vowel does not allow much time to shift the pitch. It is possible in some languages, however, if the vowel is followed by another voiced sound, preferably a nasal. It should also be noted that, in some languages, unstressed or weak syllables may have no lexical tone, i.e. no contrastive tonal identity. This is the case in Mandarin Chinese. Grammatical particles or suffixes (e.g. the genitive marker *de*), which are usually unstressed, have a so-called "neutral tone" whose pitch varies depending on the tone of the previous syllable. It has no inherent tone of its own. In other tone languages, e.g. Cantonese, there is no such thing as neutral tone, and every morpheme has a distinctive tonal quality.

The realization of tones may change depending on adjacent tones or on the shape of the syllable. Let's see some examples of each kind. In Mandarin Chinese the falling-rising tone is not normally pronounced as such in ordinary speech. If a morpheme with falling-rising tone is followed by a tone of any other kind, the falling-rising tone (214) is replaced by a tone with pitch contour (21). For example, if *mǎ* (*ma²¹⁴*) 'horse' is followed by the word *chē* (*che⁵⁵*) 'vehicle', the sequence is pronounced as *ma²¹ che⁵⁵*. In other words, the contours (214) and (21) are allotones—alternative pronunciations of the same element. The version we hear on a particular occasion is determined by the phonetic environment: (214) in isolation or followed by a neutral tone, (21) otherwise. (This rule is sometimes referred to as a rule of "tone sandhi", but it is better to reserve this term for rules which actually change one tone into another; see next section.)

A different kind of example of allotones comes from Cantonese. As mentioned, Cantonese is usually described by linguists as having six contrastive tones; but you will also see it described as having nine tones. What's going on? In fact, the three extra tones only occur in closed or "checked" syllables, i.e. syllables which end with a stop (/p/, /t/, and /k/ are the only possibilities). In this same environment, however, the normal level tones (high level, mid level, low level) are never found. Furthermore, the tones found in checked syllables are phonetically equivalent to shortened versions of the normal high, mid, and low level tones. It is therefore more sensible to interpret the extra "tones" which are confined to checked syllables as allotonic variants of the level tones.

A similar allotonic analysis may be possible for some of the six tones usually recognized for Lao. If you examine the following set of examples from a dialect spoken in the Laos capital Vientiane (Enfield 1994: 9–10), you will see that it illustrates a five-way contrast on the syllable *phaa* (recall that *ph* stands for an aspirated stop). The low level tone (33), however, is illustrated with a different syllable, *paa*.

high level	44	*phaa* 'split'
high falling	51	*phaa* 'machete'
high rising	34	*phaa* 'lead'

low level	33	*paa* 'fish'
low rising	213	*phaa* 'cliff'
low falling	21	*phaa* 'cloth'

In fact, the low level tone (33) and the low rising tone (213) are in complementary distribution. The (33) tone is found only when the initial consonant is a non-aspirated stop /b, p, d, t, c, k, ʔ/ or the palatal glide /j/. The (213) tone is never found in syllables with these initial consonants. Thus they can be regarded, in this dialect of Lao anyway, as allotones of a single tone.

5.3.3 Tone sandhi

If a language has contour tones (as most tone languages in East and Southeast Asia do), there are usually some rules which bring about a change in certain tones when they are juxtaposed to certain other tones. These rules of tone change are known as "tone sandhi". Often they can be understood as processes of assimilation or dissimilation. In Modern Standard Chinese, for example, there are two main tone sandhi rules. One concerns high rising tone, and the other concerns falling-rising tone. Li and Thompson (1981: 8f.) describe them as follows:

(i) If a high rising tone (35) follows either another high rising tone (35) or a high level tone (55), it changes into a high level tone (providing it is also followed by a tone-bearing syllable). In a shorthand notation: 35/55 35 → 35/55 55. This is assimilatory. The starting point of the second tone changes to match the final level of the preceding tone.

(ii) When a falling-rising tone (214) is followed by another falling-rising tone, the first one changes to a high rising tone (35). For example, *gǎn* 'to chase' and *guǐ* 'demon' both have falling-rising tones when pronounced separately in isolation, but if they are combined to form a phrase meaning 'to exorcize demons', *gǎn* is pronounced with a high rising tone. In a shorthand: 214 214 → 35 214. This is dissimilation. The first tone changes to become different from the one following it.

The complexity of tone sandhi differs markedly from language to language. For example, Tianjin is another dialect of Mandarin Chinese with four basic tones, but it has more complex rules of dissimilation. The Tianjin basic tones are: 21, 45, 13, 53. When two tones are juxtaposed, the following changes take place (Yip 1995: 491; Milliken et al. 1997):

```
21 21  →  13 21
13 13  →  45 13
53 53  →  21 53
53 21  →  45 21
```

On the other hand, Cantonese does not have any tone sandhi in the strict sense. There are some morphological processes which alter tones (e.g. reduplication, mentioned in Chapter 3), but few—if any—purely phonological processes which do this.

This has been a very sketchy account of tone sandhi. We have not even mentioned another type of tone sandhi, which changes tones when they appear in certain positions, especially phrase-finally.

5.3.4 Issues in tonal phonology

To conclude our treatment of tones, it is interesting to take a broader perspective. In world terms, tone languages are by no means rare. As many as one-third of the world's languages, including most of the sub-Saharan languages of Africa and many languages in Mesoamerica, have lexical tone. Understanding how tones work in different languages is therefore an important challenge to phonological theory. One big issue is whether it is possible to produce a universal system of distinctive features which can account for the range of tonal distinctions found in the world's languages. Various proposals have been made. Though we cannot go into the details here, most of them agree that contour tones should be analyzed as combinations of level tones. In recent years, the study of tones in African languages has played an important role in generative phonology. It has been the catalyst for the development of the new-style "autosegmental phonology".

The tonal systems in East and Southeast Asian languages, however, are rather different from those of African and Mesoamerican languages (Yip 1995). Those other tone languages tend to have smaller tonal inventories, with fewer levels and fewer contour tones. Furthermore, in African and Mesoamerican languages the tone-bearing unit tends to be the word as a whole (rather than the syllable or morpheme). That is, there is only one tone per word, and often this tone shifts around from syllable to syllable depending on affixes, etc. In view of these differences, there may be some fairly fundamental phonological principles or parameters which operate differently in the tonal systems of East and Southeast Asian languages. As the study of these tone languages deepens and develops (cf. e.g. Yip 1990; Wang and Smith 1997), it would not be surprising if important phonological discoveries are made.

5.4 Shifting sounds: morphophonemics

Under this heading, linguists deal with processes in which morphemes change their phonemic shape under various conditions. It is usual to assume that there is a single "underlying form", and that the alternative forms arise through the operation of various rules which apply in specific conditions. A simple example from English concerns the plural suffix, which appears in three different forms, /-s/, /-z/, and /-əz/, depending on the final segment of the base. The form /-əz/ is found after a fricative or affricate (e.g. *horses, matches*), /-z/ after a voiced sound of any other kind (e.g. *dogs, tools, flies*), and /-s/ after voiceless sounds of other kinds (e.g. *cats, slips, clicks*). A common analysis is that underlyingly the plural suffix has a single form, either /-s/ or /-z/, and that the other forms arise as a result of regular, natural rules. A vowel /ə/ is inserted to break up unacceptable fricative-fricative or affricate-fricative clusters; and a rule of voicing assimilation ensures that the suffix adopts a voiceless form after voiceless segments, and a voiced form after voiced segments (after all, we could hardly pronounce final clusters such as /gs/, /ls/, /kz/, or /pz/). Taking things a step further, it can be argued that the underlying form of the suffix is unspecified for voicing and just picks up this feature from adjoining sounds.

5.4.1 When sounds collide

Most of the examples in this section will be drawn from languages of the agglutinating type, such as Malay, Korean, and Japanese. This should not be surprising because languages which employ affixation tend to "need" morphophonemic processes. For example, affixation can bring together a sequence of vowels or consonants which is not allowed by the phonotactic rules of the language. When this happens, the language will have special rules to deal with the illegal combinations.

We can see this kind of morphophonemic rule in Korean, which has several general rules to deal with situations in which sounds "collide" as a result of affixation or compounding. There are several common Korean suffixes which begin with a vowel, for example: -*ess* the 'experiential/contrastive' aspect, causative -*i* (one of several allomorphs), and passive -*i*. What happens when one of these suffixes has to attach itself to a base which ends with a vowel, thus bringing two vowels together? Often the two vowels merge, as shown in the following examples with passive and causative affixes (Kim 1992). For the phonetic values of the vowel symbols, see Table 5.12 above. (In the Korean orthography such changes are not indicated, and transliterations into English usually do not indicate them either; but for illustrative purposes we will do so in this section of the book.)

$$o + i \rightarrow oe; \text{ e.g. } bo\text{-}i\text{-}da \rightarrow boeda \quad \text{'be seen'}$$
$$eo + i \rightarrow e; \text{ e.g. } seo\text{-}iu\text{-}da \rightarrow seuda \quad \text{'raise'}$$
$$a + i \rightarrow ae; \text{ e.g. } ja\text{-}iu\text{-}da \rightarrow jaeuda \quad \text{'make sleep'}$$
$$u + i \rightarrow wi; \text{ e.g. } bakku\text{-}i\text{-}da \rightarrow bakkwida \text{ 'be changed'}$$

If a verbal base ending in *eu* is followed by a suffix beginning with *eo*, then the *eu* is deleted; for example, *sseu-eo* 'write' → *sseo*. If a verbal base ending in *i*, *o* or *u* is followed by a suffix beginning with *eo* or *a*, the vowel of the base can optionally become a glide (and usually does in ordinary speech); for example, *gi-eo* → *gieo* or *gyeo* 'crawl', *du-eoseo* → *dueoseo* or *dwoseo* 'leave', *bo-aseo* → *bo-aseo* or *bwaseo* 'look at'.

Affixation often brings together clusters of consonants which are not permitted by Korean phonotactics, inducing further morphophonemic changes. A simple example is when a suffix like -*gwa* 'and' is added to a base which already ends in a cluster. This creates a sequence of three consonants in a row, when only two are allowed. The solution, in this case, is that the second consonant of the base is deleted (notice that the glide *w* does not count as a consonant for the purposes of this rule). For example: *gabs-gwa* → *gabgwa* [price-and], *dalk-gwa* → *dalgwa* [chicken-and]. Other consonant-initial suffixes include the verbal honorific -*si*, the 'retrospective' past -*deo*, the interrogative -*kka*, and imperative -*ra*; and among nominal suffixes there is the plural marker -*deul*.

Another rule converts a stop to a nasal before another nasal. This rule is mostly needed as a result of compounding (Sampson 1985: 137). For example: *bueok + mun* → *bueong-mun* 'kitchen door', *jeob-neun-da* → *jeom-neun-da* 'folded', *dad-neun-da* → *dan-neun-da* 'closed'. There are several other rules whose motivation is less obvious. For example, the second obstruent in a cluster becomes tense; for example: *ip-da* → *iptta* 'wear-past', *gagsi* → *gagssi* 'bride'. Also, the /r/ sound (sometimes spelled as /l/) becomes /n/ unless it follows a vowel.

Often several morphophonemic rules apply to a single word. For example, in the following words the /r/ first converts to an /n/ because it is not following a vowel; after this, the preceding stop changes to nasal (Kim 1992: 284).

baeg + ri → *baeg + ni* → *baengni*   'a hundred miles'
sueobryo → *sueobnyo* → *sueomnyo* 'tuition'

After hearing about all these processes (and there are more!) you will not be surprised to find that Korean has one of the most complicated morphophonemic systems of all the languages of East Asia.

Finally, a note on the existence of lexical strata. You will recall from Chapter 3 that a lexical stratum is a set of loan words with special stylistic, phonological, and morphological status, like that of the Latinate vocabulary of English, the Indic vocabulary of Burmese, Thai, and Lao, and the Sino-Japanese and Foreign vocabulary of Japanese. The interesting thing is that particular phonological and morphological rules may (or may not) apply within lexical strata, differently from the rest of the vocabulary. For example, Sino-Japanese words in Japanese are exempted from certain phonological rules, such as the rule traditionally known in Japanese as *Rendaku* 'sequential voicing' which ensures that the initial consonant of the second element of a compound word is voiced (hence, *yu* 'hot water' + *toofu* 'tofu' → *yudoofu* 'boiled tofu', *de* 'leave' + *kuchi* 'mouth' → *deguchi* 'exit'). Similarly, there is a rule prohibiting sequences like *bb, dd, gg*, and *zz,* i.e. geminate (doubled) sequences of voiced obstruents, and though this does apply to strongly indigenized Foreign loans, in many other Foreign loans the constraint is ignored, e.g. *doggu* 'dog', *beddo* 'bed' (Itô and Mester 1995).

5.4.2 The "nasal alternation" in Austronesian languages

As you know from Chapter 3, Malay and Tagalog (and other related languages of peninsular and insular Southeast Asia) have productive systems of derivational morphology. Equally characteristic of these languages is the existence of prefixes (and sometimes, infixes) containing a nasal which is realized differently depending on the following sound, i.e. the initial sound of the base. (Usually it is symbolized as N, but with no relation to IPA [N], which stands for a uvular nasal.) In Indonesian there are two prefixes which

Table 5.16. Nasal alternation with prefix *meN-* in Indonesian

a. *meN-* + *beli* → *membeli*	*peN-* + *beli* → *pembeli*
meN- + *dengar* → *mendengar*	*peN-* + *dengar* → *pendengar*
meN- + *ganggu* → *mengganggu*	*peN-* + *ganggu* → *pengganggu*
b. *meN-* + *pakai* → *memakai*	*peN-* + *pakai* → *pemakai*
meN- + *tulis* → *menulis*	*peN-* + *tulis* → *penulis*
meN- + *kirim* → *mengirim*	*peN-* + *kirim* → *pengirim*
c. *meN-* + *ajar* → *mengajar*	*peN-* + *ajar* → *pengajar*
meN- + *urus* → *mengurus*	*peN-* + *urus* → *pengurus*
d. *meN-* + *lihat* → *melihat*	*peN-* + *lihat* → *pelihat*
meN- + *rasa* → *merasa*	*peN-* + *rasa* → *perasa*
meN- + *nyanyi* → *menyanyi*	*peN-* + *nyanyi* → *penyanyi*

end with N, namely *meN-* and *peN-*. Both have derivational functions: *meN-* derives dynamic verbs from nouns and adjectives, *peN-* derives agentive and instrumental nouns from verbs. In addition, *meN-* can function as a marker of "agent focus" with transitive verbs. For present purposes we do not have to go into these functions in any detail.

With both prefixes the final consonant of the prefix can be one of several different nasal sounds, depending on the initial sound of the base word. Oversimplifying a bit, the rules are as follows: (a) if the initial sound of the base is a voiced stop, or /f/, or /c/, N appears as a homorganic nasal; (b) if the initial sound is a voiceless stop (other than /c/) or /s/, N appears as a homorganic nasal which is substituted in place of the voiceless sound; (c) if the initial sound is a vowel, N appears as /ŋ/; (d) if the initial sound is a sonorant (i.e. a liquid, nasal, or semi-vowel), N is realized as ø (i.e. as nothing). This process is often referred to as nasal alternation. Some examples are given in Table 5.16. They are written in normal Malay orthography, in which /ŋ/ is spelt as *ng*, and /ɲ/ is spelt as *ny*.

Many Austronesian languages have prefixes which involve a similar kind of nasal alternation. For example, Javanese has a morphological process which prefixes a voiced stop with a homorganic nasal, replaces a voiceless stop with a corresponding nasal, and prefixes an /ŋ/ in front of liquids (i.e. /r/ and /l/) and vowels. This can be interpreted as a prefix which consists of a single archiphoneme N-. Tagalog has verbal prefix *maN-* which shows similar behaviour. Examples are given in Table 5.17.

5.4.3 Japanese moras and archiphonemes

As mentioned earlier, the traditional analysis of Japanese phonology posits the existence of two archiphonemes, Q and N. These are the only two

Table 5.17. Nasal alternation in Javanese (Robson 1992) and
Tagalog (Schachter 1987: 211)

Javanese (in standard orthography)

a. *N-+pinggir* → *minggir* 'move to the side'
   N-+tengen → *nengen* 'move to the right'
   N-+kebak → *ngebaki* 'to fill up'

b. *N-+bocah* → *mbocahi* 'to act childishly'
   N-+duwé → *nduwèni* 'to have, get something in particular'
   N-+godhog → *nggodhog* 'to boil'

c. *N-+lenga* → *nglenga* 'to glisten like oil'
   N-+resik → *ngresiki* 'to clean'

d. *N-+uyuh* → *nguyuh* 'to urinate'
   N-+awak →*ngawaki* 'to do by oneself'

Tagalog

   maN-+pi:liʔ → *mami:liʔ* 'choose'
   maN-+ta:kot → *manata:kot* 'frighten'
   maN-+kaʔilaŋan → *mangaʔilaŋan* 'need'

---

consonants which can close a syllable, and each counts as a mora in its own right. Q is always non-nasal and N is always nasal, but otherwise their phonetic identities in a particular word are determined by the following sound. Q is only found preceding another obstruent, and it leads to the creation of a cluster of two identical consonants (a geminate cluster). For example (Shibatani 1990: 168):

(161) *jaQpari* → *yappari* 'as expected'
      jaQto → *yatto* 'finally'
      juQkuri → *yukkuri* 'slowly'
      aQsari → *assari* 'dry'

The phonetic identity of N also depends on the following sound. Preceding a stop, it is realized as a homorganic nasal, as in the (162a) examples; preceding other consonants it appears as a nasalized version of the following sound, as in the (162b) examples. It is also found at the end of some words where, as mentioned, it is generally realized as a uvular nasal, or as vowel nasalization, as in (162c)

(162) a. *eNpitsu* → *empitsu* 'pencil'
         keNdoo → *kendoo* 'kendo'
         eNgi → *eŋgi* 'performance'
         aNkoku → *aŋkoku* 'dark'

b. *jaNwari*   → *jaw̃wari* 'softly'
   hoN-jaku → *hojjaku* 'translation'
   haN-seN   → *hass̃eẽ* 'anti-war'

c. *hoN*   → *hõõ*   'book'

So far so good. However, there is a problem with the traditional Japanese analysis. It concerns geminate clusters which arise in other ways. For example, when a verb stem ending in *t*, *r*, or *w* is followed by a suffix beginning with *t*, e.g. the past tense suffix -*ta*, a geminate cluster is produced because *r* or *w* assimilate to the following *t*. See the examples in (163a) below (the underlying stem-final high vowel *i* drops out). A similar situation occurs in certain compound words, where the final high vowel of the first element drops out and the exposed consonant assimilates to the initial consonant of the second element; see the example in (163b).

(163) a. *tat-i + ta* → *tatta* 'stood'
         tor-i + ta → *totta* 'took'
         kaw-i + ta → *katta* 'bought'

      b. *hati + seN* → *hat seN* → *hass̃eẽ* 'eight thousand'

In one of the traditional Japanese spelling systems (*hiragana*), the words for 'stood' and 'eight thousand' are written, in effect, as *taQta* and *haQseN*. The rationale for this is that the first member of the clusters count as moras, and that Q and N are the "letters" for moraic consonants. One can see the sense of it from a spelling point of view; but from a phonological point of view, it creates a contradiction to say that the final consonant in the stem for 'stand', for example, is *t* in certain inflected forms, but Q in others.

5.5 Pitch-accent in Japanese

In phonology, the term "accent" refers to a system which distinguishes the prominence of one syllable, e.g. by making it louder, or longer, or by giving it the peak pitch of the word. In Japanese, most words have an inherent pitch pattern, and some words are distinguished from others purely by pitch pattern. If we use the symbols H and L for relatively high pitch and relatively low pitch, respectively, the following contrasts apply (in the Tokyo and Kyoto dialects, respectively) (Shibatani 1990: 177):

(164) Tokyo
      a. *ame* (LH) 'candy'
         ame (HL) 'rain'

   Kyoto   Tokyo
   b. *hashi* (HH) 'edge'
      hashi (LH) 'chopsticks'   *hashi* (HL) 'chopsticks'
      hashi (HL) 'bridge'   *hashi* (LH) 'bridge'

The system differs from the tonal system of Sinitic languages in several ways. First, although most words have a characteristic pitch pattern the functional load is not high, i.e. there are relatively few minimal or near minimal pairs. Second, the domain of the pitch contour is the full word, not individual syllables. Third, when a large number of words are examined, it becomes clear that the range of attested pitch patterns can be predicted if we know, for any word, when the first pitch fall occurs. In other words, it makes sense to identify, for each word, an "accented" syllable. The full pitch pattern can be predicted by rules, once the location of the accent is known.

Consider the following set of words in Tokyo dialect (Shibatani 1990: 177–8). The left-hand column gives the phonemic form, with an apostrophe indicating the accent (if there is one) on the preceding syllable. The middle column gives the pitch pattern of the entire word, syllable by syllable. The first thing to note is that if a word has no accent, as in the group of words in (165a), the first syllable will have a low pitch and all subsequent syllables will have a high pitch—i.e. words of this kind don't have any pitch fall and the initial low pitch is completely predictable. If a word does have an accent, as in the examples in group (165b) and (165c), the accented syllable has H pitch and everything after it has L pitch.

(165) a. *ame*   LH   'candy'
      sakura   LHH   'cherry'
      shirakaba   LHHH   'white birch'
    b. *a'me*   HL   'rain'
      za'kuro   HLL   'pomegranate'
      ka'makiri   HLLL   'mantis'
    c. *koko'ro*   LHL   'heart'
      iro'gami   LHLL   'colour paper'
      kagari'bi   LHHL   'torch'

The difference between the (165b) and (165c) examples concerns the situation of the syllables preceding the accent. This too is governed by a rule. One way of stating it is to say that any syllable before the accented syllable will be H, except that if the second syllable of a word is H the initial syllable is changed to L. Essentially, the idea is that all syllables have H pitch unless this is changed for some reason. One reason for a pitch change is the presence of the accent: after the accent, the pitch falls and it stays down for the rest of the word. The only other situation in which a low pitch syllable is found is predictable from the pitch of the second syllable: if the second syllable has H pitch, the first has L pitch. (Or, putting it another way, words start with L unless the second syllable is L.)

This discussion has been oversimplified in some ways. We have not taken account of the difference between syllable and mora, nor described various differences between different dialects of Japanese. Even so, it should be enough to convey the general idea of the accent system, and to clarify the difference between the tone systems of Sinitic and mainland Southeast Asian languages and the pitch-accent system of Japanese.

Key technical terms

Students who have not studied linguistics will have to do some catching up with the meanings of some of the phonetic terms. The Glossary should help.

affricate	nasal alternation
allophone	phoneme
allotone	phonotactics
aspiration	pitch-accent
fricative	stop
initial + rhyme	tone sandhi
mora	toneme
morphophonemics	tonogenesis
nasal	voice quality (phonation)

Writing systems

Western linguists have often been disdainful of the written language. They have regarded language itself as primarily the spoken word, and writing merely as a medium for capturing the spoken word in a visible and stable form. For many people, however, especially in East Asia, the written form of a language *is* the language, and speech is regarded as an imperfect rendition of written words. In this book we take the view that people's writing practices, and their ideas about writing, are an important part of the language culture of any society, and, as such, are worthy of study in their own right. We will also find that learning about East and Southeast Asian writing systems can bring insights into cultural history; and that it can extend and deepen our thinking about the sound systems of languages.

6.1 Types of writing system

Writing systems can work according to two basic principles: logographic and phonographic (Sampson 1985: 32ff.). In a logographic system each symbol stands for a separate meaningful unit in the language, i.e. for a particular word or bound morpheme. In a phonographic system, each symbol stands for a sound unit of the language, e.g. for a particular phoneme or syllable. The English writing system is primarily phonographic (i.e. it records sounds), but we have a few symbols which are logographic—for example, the digits *1, 2, 3, 4*, and symbols such as & (for 'and') and % (for 'per cent').

Sampson (1985) further distinguishes five subcategories, depending on the particular kind of meaningful unit or phonological unit on which the writing is based. He maintains that while it is theoretically possible to have a logographic system which is purely "word-based"—i.e. having a separate, independent symbol for each and every word—in practice no real-life writing system works this way. Logographic systems are always based primarily on morphemes rather than words, Sampson argues, for reasons of efficiency. The other four types of writing system are found, however, and we can find examples of each type among the languages of East and Southeast Asia.

I have reproduced Sampson's scheme in Fig. 6.1 as a framework for discussion; but as a matter of fact we will find reasons to revise his interpretation on a couple of points. First, the Korean writing system is really better analyzed as a special kind of alphabetic script, rather than as a "featural" script; and second, it is not really true to say that the Chinese system is based on recording morphemes in the strict linguistic sense. Also, as Sampson himself points out, there are some "mixed" logographic-phonographic systems, such as we find in Japanese.

It is helpful to note another distinction which Sampson draws—between "motivated" and "arbitrary" letters. This distinction applies to the individual symbols in a system, rather than to the system as a whole. A symbol is motivated to the extent that there is some kind of natural or logical relationship between the form of the symbol and what it stands for; otherwise it is arbitrary. Both phonographic and logographic symbols can be motivated. Most English letters are not motivated in the slightest. There is no connection whatever between the letters *k* and *g*, on the one hand, and the sounds that begin the word *cat* and *got*, respectively. But in Pitman shorthand, the symbols for the sounds /k/ and /g/ are partly motivated. /k/ is written as a thin horizontal line —, and /g/ is written as thicker bold line ▬, reflecting the fact that the two sounds are very similar phonetically, having the same place and manner of articulation and differing only according to

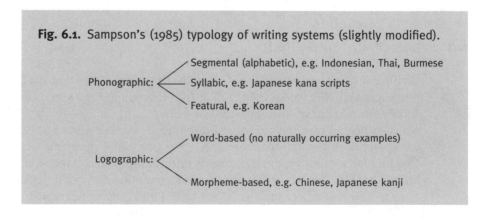

Fig. 6.1. Sampson's (1985) typology of writing systems (slightly modified).

Phonographic:
— Segmental (alphabetic), e.g. Indonesian, Thai, Burmese
— Syllabic, e.g. Japanese kana scripts
— Featural, e.g. Korean

Logographic:
— Word-based (no naturally occurring examples)
— Morpheme-based, e.g. Chinese, Japanese kanji

whether they are voiceless (as with /k/) or voiced (as with /g/). Notice that, in this example, there is no direct relationship between the sounds and the symbols. Rather, the similarity between the symbols corresponds to a similarity in the sounds. Actually, one could perhaps claim that the main English letter-symbols for nasal sounds—i.e. *n* and *m*—are partially motivated, because they have a particular kind of shape (with vertical uprights and a rounded top) shared by no other letters. To find a familiar example of motivated logographic symbols we can refer to the digits *0* and *1*. The symbol for 'zero' could be seen as resembling an empty hole, and the symbol for 'one' consists of a single stroke.

As these examples show, motivation is a matter of degree, and a symbol can be partly motivated in subtle ways which might not be obvious, especially to people who are very familiar with the system and use it more or less automatically.

6.2 Alphabetic systems

In this section we look at several writing systems from Southeast Asia and East Asia which are segmental (alphabetic). That is, they are phonographic—they record sounds—and more specifically they break sounds down into individual speech segments (phonemes). One more piece of terminology: the ordinary letters we use in writing English and other European languages are known as "roman" letters; a writing system which uses these letters is called a "romanization".

6.2.1 Malaysian and Indonesian: from *jawi* to *rumi*

The traditional writing system for Malay and related languages is known as Jawi. It is based on Arabic letters introduced along with Islam in the fourteenth century, the time when the great Malay empire centred on Malacca converted to Islam. As the sacred language of the Koran, and the language of the Muslim heartland of the Middle East, Arabic enjoyed tremendous prestige for centuries—and still does. The Jawi system (so-named after the island of Java) is designed to be written with a brush, and so the letters are smooth-flowing, and most have somewhat different forms depending on their position in words (see Table 6.1).

When several letters are joined together, some of them in a reduced shape, it can look as if the system is syllabic but it is not. It is alphabetic. There is an example of Jawi writing in Figure 6.2. You can probably tell from the layout that Jawi is written from right to left.

Versions of the Jawi script were the main vehicle for writing Malay until well after the European colonization. The Dutch introduced a romanization into the region which is now Indonesia, and the British introduced a slightly different system into what is now Malaysia, but the real ascendancy of

Table 6.1. Some letters from the Jawi script (Kaye 1996: 761)

Transliteration	Transcription	Isolated	Final	Initial	Medial
_	[Ø]	ا	ـا	–	–
b	[b]	ب	ـب	بـ	ـبـ
t	[t]	ت	ـت	تـ	ـتـ
th	[s]	ث	ـث	ثـ	ـثـ
j	[dʒ]	ج	ـج	جـ	ـجـ
ch	[tʃ]	چ	ـچ	چـ	ـچـ
ḥ	[h]	ح	ـح	حـ	ـحـ
kh	[x, k]	خ	ـخ	خـ	ـخـ
d	[d]	د	ـد	–	–
dz	[dz]	ذ	ـذ	–	–
r	[r]	ر	ـر	–	–
z	[z, dʒ]	ز	ـز	–	–
s	[s]	س	ـس	سـ	ـسـ
sh	[ʃ, s]	ش	ـش	شـ	ـشـ
ṣ	[s]	ص	ـص	صـ	ـصـ
ḍ	[z, dʒ]	ض	ـض	ضـ	ـضـ
ṭ	[t]	ط	ـط	طـ	ـطـ
ẓ	[z]	ظ	ـظ	ظـ	ـظـ
ʿ	[Ø]	ع	ـع	عـ	ـعـ
gh	[ɣ, r]	غ	ـغ	غـ	ـغـ
ng	[ŋ]	ڠ	ـڠ	ڠـ	ـڠـ

roman letters (and the decline of Jawi) did not take place until well into the twentieth century. There is still one Malaysian newspaper published in Jawi, and learning the basics of Jawi is still part of the Malaysian school curriculum.

Until 1972, the romanizations used in Indonesia and Malaysia differed from one another in various ways, a result of differences between the Dutch and British systems. In that year, both countries modified their systems to create a common orthography. Many proper names (e.g. the former Indonesian president Soeharto, the author Pramoedya Ananta Toer) still retain

Fig. 6.2. Part of a TV guide from the newspaper *Utusan Melayu*.

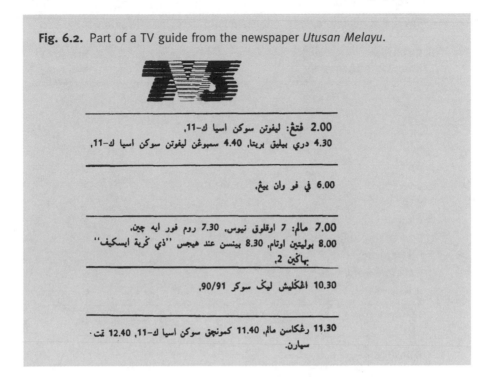

their older spellings. Table 6.2 shows the main differences in the pre-1972 systems.

Malaysian/Indonesian orthography is largely phonemic, i.e. there is a one-to-one correspondence between sounds and letters (or digraphs), but there are a few exceptions. There is "under-differentiation" in the spelling of vowels, because the phonemes /e/ and /i/ are both spelt as *e*. In the old British system /i/ was distinguished by means of a diacritic (called a pepet): *ĕ*. This convention is still used in bilingual dictionaries. The spelling system also makes provision for various fricatives which are "loan phonemes", i.e. sounds which are only found in words borrowed from Arabic, English, or other languages. These include *f* for /f/ as in *fikir* 'think', *sy* for /ʃ/ as in *syaitan* 'Satan', and *kh* for /x/ as in *khiatan* 'connection'. People without much formal education tend to pronounce these in their indigenized versions, i.e. /p/, /s/, and /k/, respectively. In this respect there is "over-differentiation".

An interesting problem for Malaysian/Indonesian spelling is posed by the fact, mentioned in the previous chapter, that in final closed syllables the contrast between /i/ and /e/ is neutralized, as is the contrast between /u/ and /o/. There is no need for maintaining a choice of letters in this position. In principle, either letter of each pair could be chosen. For example, in principle the words below could be spelt in either of the

Table 6.2. Malaysian and Indonesian orthographies (Prentice 1987: 191)

Post-1972 Common orthography	Pre-1972 Indonesia	Pre-1972 Malaysia
c	tj	ch
j	dj	j
kh	ch	kh
ny	nj	ny
sy	sj	sh
y	j	y
e (ə)	e	e, ĕ
e (e)	e, é	e
i (before word-final h, k)	i	e
i (elsewhere)	i	i
u (before word-final h, k, ng, r)	u, oe*	o
u (elsewhere)	u, oe*	u

* The spelling 'oe' was replaced by 'u' in 1946.

following ways:

(166) 'white'   *putih*   *puteh*
      'to wet, wash'   *basuh*   *basoh*
      'more (than)'   *lebih*   *lebeh*
      'sleep'   *tidur*   *tidor*

Before the 1972 spelling reform both systems were in use. The Indonesians used the convention in the right-hand column and the Malaysians the version in the left-hand column. It has now been standardized to follow the left-hand column.

6.2.2 Thai

The writing systems for Thai, Lao, and Khmer all derive from Indic scripts originally designed to represent the sounds of Sanskrit. The Burmese script was adapted from Mon, which also ultimately went back to Indic origins. We will consider only the Thai system, which has its origins in the late thirteenth century as an adaptation of Old Khmer script (Diller 1996; Danvivathana 1987). The top line in (167) is an example of modern Thai writing. Notice that the words are run together, i.e. they are not separated by spaces, as in English. Although not obvious to the untutored eye, a notable feature of the system is that the main letters stand for consonants, with the vowels being indicated by diacritics which can occur after, over, under or before their associated consonant letter.

(167) คำ ภาษา ไทยให้เขียนตานหลักเกณฑ์นิรุกติศาสตร์

คำ	ภาษา	ไทย	ให้	เขียน	ตาน	หลัก	เกณฑ์	นิรุกติศาสตร์
kham	*phaasǎa*	*thay*	*hây*	*khǐan*	*taam*	*làk*	*keen*	*nirúktisàat*
word	language	Thai	let	write	follow	basis	rule	etymology

'Words in the Thai language should be written on the basis of principles of etymology.' (Diller 1996: 466)

For various reasons, especially the intervention of sound changes which have taken place in spoken Thai since the spelling system was stabilized, the relationship between sounds and letters in the modern script is rather indirect. There are many sounds which can be represented in writing by one of several letters. However, the choice of letter for any particular word is not arbitrary, but depends on the tone of the syllable. Putting it the other way around, the choice between alternative ways of spelling the same sound helps to indicate the tone.

To get an idea of what's involved, look at the display in Table 6.3 (from Smalley 1994: 184). It shows a set of words beginning with the same phoneme /kh/. In the top row, initial /kh/ is represented by the letter ข. In the bottom row it is represented by the letter ค. The words shown have various tones, indicated in the romanization by the following diacritics: rising tone /ˇ/, falling tone /ˆ/, low tone /ˋ/, high tone /ˊ/; and mid tone is indicated by the absence of a diacritic. Take a look first at the leftmost column. You will see that the two words have different tones *khǎa* 'leg' vs. *khaa* 'embedded', and that this is indicated in the Thai spelling purely by the choice of letter ข as opposed to letter ค.

Things get more complicated in the second and third columns. The appropriate tones for these words are indicated by the combination of the choice of initial letter and one of two Thai tone diacritics: /ˋ/ in the second column and /ˊ/ in the third column. The diacritics occur above the initial letter. So for example, letter ข with diacritic /ˋ/ indicates low tone, as in *khàa* 'galangal' (a type of plant), but the same letter with diacritic /ˊ/ indicates falling tone, as in *khâa* 'slave'. Study the table for a minute, concentrating

Table 6.3. Thai words with initial /kh/ (Smalley 1994: 184)

ขา	ข่า	ข้า	ขาด	ขัด
khǎa	*khàa*	*khâa*	*khàat*	*khàt*
'leg'	'galangal'	'slave'	'lack'	'obstruct'
คา	ค่า	ค้า	คาด	คัด
khaa	*khâa*	*kháa*	*khâat*	*khát*
'embedded'	'cost'	'trade'	'to strap'	'be clogged'

just on the first three columns, and make sure you can see what we are talking about here.

The situation is still more complex, however, as you can see if you now look at the two rightmost columns. These show words which have a final consonant, either with a long vowel preceding, as in the fourth column, or a short vowel preceding, as in the fifth column. If you study the table as a whole, you can see that no tone is indicated in a completely uniform way. The combination of choice of letter for the initial consonant, plus tone mark, if any, plus presence of a final consonant, if any, plus the length of a vowel preceding the final consonant—all of these factors work together to indicate the appropriate tone.

In Thai tradition, written letters for consonants are divided into three groups or classes, depending on how they help to represent tone in the writing system. For example, ข is a so-called "high-class consonant" and ค is a "low-class consonant" (there are also "middle-class consonants"). What we have seen illustrated above is that: (a) choosing a letter from one or other of the three classes contributes to symbolizing the tone, and (b) the relationship between the classes and tone is not straightforward but depends also on the phonotactic shape of the word. Nevertheless, despite its complexity, the system is essentially consistent (with one exception). That is, once one has mastered the appropriate rules, which we will not attempt to describe any further, Thai spelling provides a unique way for indicating the tone of any word. (The one exception is that some words with falling tone can be spelt in two ways. When this is possible only one spelling is correct for a given word. Even this exception can be exploited to distinguish homophones, as in ข้า *khâa* 'slave' and ค่า *khâa* 'cost'.)

The explanation for the peculiarities of the Thai spelling system is historical. It is believed that old Thai had a broader range of consonants than the modern language. In this ancestral stage of the language (spoken around 1400 AD or BCE) letters like ข and ค actually stood for different consonants. Over time, however, these differences were lost and replaced by tonal distinctions (as mentioned in Chapter 5). The exact process whereby this happened has been subject to a great deal of historical reconstruction and speculation in Thai linguistics, but we need not go into that here.

As we have just seen, for many sounds Thai writing provides several different letters. A further source of mismatch between letter and sound in Thai concerns certain words which originated from Sanskrit, as much of the formal vocabulary of Thai does. The spelling system continues to distinguish between Indic sounds which are pronounced the same in modern Thai—specifically, there are still separate letters for what were originally retroflex stops, even though they are now pronounced with alveolar articulation.

6.2.3 Korean: featural or alphabetic?

The Korean writing system, known as Hangeul (or Hankul), is unique among the world's writing systems. It has even been called "the world's best alphabet" (Vos 1964: 31, cited in Sampson 1985: 120). Hangeul was invented by the Korean King Sejong (Seycong) in the mid-fifteenth century, as part of a general set of language reforms. Sejong's motivation was to provide a logical and linguistically sound method of writing Korean, to supersede the previous inefficient and tedious practice of recording Korean words by means of Chinese characters: see example (168). For various reasons, the Hangeul system was not widely adopted until hundreds of years after its invention—not until the twentieth century, in fact, but it is now firmly established as the main way of writing Korean in both North Korea and South Korea.

(168) 우리 나라의　　말은　　　중국의　　말과
　　　uri naraui　　maleun　　junggukui malgwa
　　　our   country-'s language-TOP China-'s   language-with

　　　달라서　　　한자와는　　　　　　서로　　잘
　　　dallaseo　　hanjawaneun　　　　seoro　　jal
　　　different-so characters-with-contrast mutually well

　　　통하지
　　　tonghaji
　　　communicate-COMP

'Our country's language is different from that of China and thus does not correspond well with characters.' (The first lines of King Sejong's language reform proclamation (from Kang 1990, quoted in King 1996: 225–6).)

Aside from being the only national script which is the product of wholly original planning, Hangeul has a number of interesting features. It is basically a phonemic system, i.e. each of the letters represents a separate phoneme, but the letters are arranged in syllable blocks rather than just being lined up side by side as in roman writing. In a sense, therefore, the script presents both a phonemic and a syllabic breakdown of a word. For example:

(169) 바다　　<ba-da>　　'sea'
　　　나무　　<na-mu>　　'tree'
　　　하늘　　<ha-neul>　　'sky'
　　　바람　　<ba-ram>　　'wind'

Even more remarkable, the design of the individual letters (for the consonants, at least) is based on an analysis of how the sounds are pronounced. There is a stylized letter shape for each place of articulation. As shown in

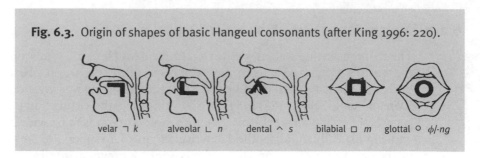

Fig. 6.3. Origin of shapes of basic Hangeul consonants (after King 1996: 220).

velar ㄱ *k*   alveolar ㄴ *n*   dental ᄉ *s*   bilabial ㅁ *m*   glottal ㅇ *ϕ/-ng*

Figure 6.3, the basic letter shapes were derived from graphic depictions of the speech organs involved.

The manner of articulation is also indicated in a systematic way. For example, the letters for the lax and aspirated stop series are derived by adding additional strokes to the basic letter shapes. One horizontal stroke indicates a lax stop and a second, smaller, horizontal stroke represents an aspirated stop. (The bilabials are an exception, probably because the symbol for /m/ already has two horizontal lines and additional ones would be visually confusing.) The tense consonants are written by doubling the basic shapes. Another "linguistically aware" aspect of the Hangeul system is that the vowel symbols (being based on vertical strokes) are graphically quite different from the consonants.

Table 6.4 sets out the Korean symbols for the basic phonemes. On account of the systematic aspects of letter design, Sampson (1985) does not recognize it as an alphabetic writing system, but describes it as a "featural" writing system—the only naturally occurring featural script in the world. Despite the analytic design of the letters, however, it is questionable whether Hangeul deserves to be seen as completely different from other alphabetic scripts. For one thing, the letter designs are not completely systematic and transparent in their design but more importantly, in ordinary writing and reading, Korean people seem to "process" each letter as a single unit, without breaking it down into featural aspects. For this reason the Korean system is best seen as a "motivated" set of alphabetic symbols.

One final aspect of Korean writing: though we have referred to it as "phonemic", it would be more accurate to term it "morphophonemic" (cf. section 5.4). Recall that Korean is a language which has numerous automatic rules which change the phonemic identity of particular sounds when they are brought together in combination with other sounds (for example, by suffixation). If the spelling were strictly phonemic all these sound changes would be indicated, which would mean that many words would have multiple spellings—one spelling for the word pronounced in isolation (the "original" form, as it is termed in Korean), another when followed by (say) the nominative suffix, another when followed by (say) the comitative suffix, and so on. In earlier times, the phonemic approach was

Table 6.4. The Korean alphabet (adapted from King 1996: 221–2)

Consonants (columns follow Fig. 6.3)

ㄱ k	ㄴ n	ㅅ s	ㅁ m	ㅇ ø/ŋ
	ㄷ t	ㅈ c	ㅂ p	
ㅋ kʰ	ㅌ tʰ	ㅊ cʰ	ㅍ pʰ	ㅎ h
ㄲ kk	ㄸ tt	ㅆ ss	ㅃ pp	
		ㅉ cc		
	ㄹ l/r			

Simple vowels

ㅣ i	— ɨ	ㅜ u
ㅔ e	ㅓ ʌ	ㅗ o
ㅐ ɛ	ㅏ a	

widely used, but since the 1930s each root or suffix has been spelt in a uniform way, regardless of any pronunciation changes which occur due to the way roots and suffixes are combined. Opinions differ as to which approach makes for easier reading and writing.

6.2.4 The pinyin system for Mandarin Chinese

The traditional writing system for Mandarin Chinese is the logographic "character system" which we'll look at shortly, but Chinese scholars have experimented with romanized scripts for a long time. After the founding of the People's Republic of China, the new government inaugurated a programme of script reform. The main effort was directed at simplifying the traditional characters, but another aspect was the development and promotion of a system of romanization. Pinyin (lit. 'spell-sound') was introduced in 1957—not as an orthography, in the sense of a widely used writing system, but as an auxiliary scheme with two main objectives: first, to provide a precise system of "sound annotation" for characters, especially for use in education; second, to promote the pronunciation style of the Beijing dialect, which was designated as the official standard pronunciation of Putonghua (Chen 2001: 78–80). In the first objective at least, it has been an outstanding success. Pinyin is now an indispensable tool for the learning of Chinese characters, not only for non-native learners in classrooms around the world, but for native speakers as well. It is learnt in the first year of primary school and used extensively as an aide to character learning and in the teaching of Putonghua. A newer role for pinyin is to provide a way of accessing characters stored on computer (see section 6.4.5).

Internationally pinyin has been widely accepted, e.g. by the United Nations and the ISO, superseding the earlier Wade–Giles system. The changeover explains why well-known Chinese names like Beijing and Mao Zedong were once spelt as Peking and Mao Tse Tung. We are using pinyin spelling for Mandarin Chinese throughout this book, so you have seen plenty of examples of it. We have already noted, in the previous chapter, that pinyin over-differentiates some sounds, e.g. it has distinct letters for several sets of allophones. There is still no universally accepted romanization for writing other Sinitic languages, such as Cantonese.

6.3 A logographic system: Chinese

The writing system of Chinese is not only fascinating and unique. It is of enormous cultural importance to Chinese civilization. The character system has its roots in very ancient times, with the earliest surviving forms (on oracle-bones, used in divination) dating back to the Shang dynasty of the mid to late second millennium BC. By the year 1200 BC it was already highly elaborated, and similar in most essentials to what it is today. It has served as a medium for the evolution of Chinese culture, and as a vehicle for some of the world's finest literature. The existence of a common writing system spanning the whole of China has been a powerful force for cultural and political unification, muting the divisive potential of linguistic and ethnic differences between speakers of the various Sinitic "dialects". Chinese script, like Chinese culture generally, has had an important and prolonged influence outside the boundaries of China proper, especially in Korea and Japan.

6.3.1 The Chinese writing system

The Chinese character system of writing has been a topic of fascination for Europeans ever since Marco Polo brought back reports of his travels to China. Unfortunately it has often been misunderstood, partly through a tendency to oversimplify, and myths about characters still abound. One of these myths, which we may as well knock on the head right away, is that characters are "pictograms", i.e. idealized pictures of the things they stand for. It is true that the system started this way in ancient times, just as ancient Egyptian writing started with pictorial hieroglyphics, but with the passing of

Fig. 6.4. Chinese characters: some changes over time.

Shū 'book' or 'to write'. The first form was used in the Bronze Age around 2000–1000 BC. The middle form shows the character as it was standardized in the Tang Dynasty. In this period, complex characters were aesthetically valued. At the right is the modern simplified character. It is not directly descended from the traditional design, but instead originated as a "folk character" (*shūzì*).

Yuè 'moon'. The first form is one of the very earliest attested forms, found on ancient bone oracles and inscriptions on turtle shell. It was standardized early, adopting the form shown in the middle panel, and has remained much the same up till now.

Chè 'vehicle, cart'. The ancient form on the left still shows its pictographic origins. The other panels show the traditional and simplified modern forms, respectively. In this case the simplified form is based on the old "running hand" version of the traditional character.

the centuries, and the proliferation of thousands upon thousands of characters, the original pictorial basis of the system has changed. There are still a
small number of pictorial elements, but the vast majority of characters have
no recognizable pictorial basis.

Though it doesn't show up very well in printed books, characters are
designed to be written with a brush. This accounts for aspects of the shape
of the strokes. To write a character correctly one has to make the strokes in
the right order, and in the right directions. The diagrams in Figure 6.5
illustrate this well. Every character, whether it takes one stroke or sixty-
four, is designed to fit into the same square frame.

In premodern times, characters were written from top to bottom, and
from right to left, in long strips. These days they are mostly written hori-
zontally and from left to right. But as in olden times, modern character

Fig. 6.5. The stroke progression for some Chinese characters. The first and
second characters mean 中 'middle' and 国 'kingdom'—when
combined they mean 'China'. The third character 语 is 'language'
and the fourth 雷 is 'thunder'.

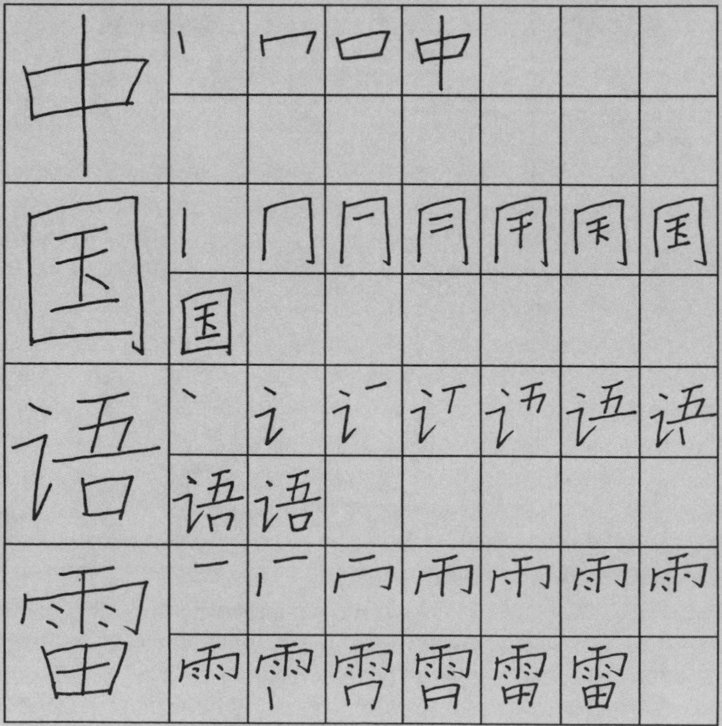

writing still does not group syllables into word units, nor does it separate one word from the next.

A second fallacy about characters is that they are "ideograms", i.e. that each character stands for a separate "idea". This implies that a character represents an idea directly, as it were, rather than a specific word of Mandarin Chinese. This is false: Chinese characters represent units of a particular spoken language, i.e. Mandarin Chinese, with all its quirks and illogicalities. One quick way to confirm this is to look at how near-synonyms are written. For example, consider the characters for *zhīdào* 'know' and *dǒngde* 'understand'. The meanings are similar, but the characters are completely different. The same applies to *shìjiè* 'earth, world' and *dìmiàn* '(on) ground'. If characters represented ideas (meanings) directly, we would expect that words with similar meanings would always be written using similar characters—but they are not.

(170) 知道 *zhīdào* 'know'   懂得 *dǒngde* 'understand'
      世界 *shìjiè* 'earth, world'   地面 *dìmiàn* '(on) ground'

Linked with the idea that characters are ideograms are two other mistaken assumptions: first, that there is no phonographic component to Chinese writing; and second, that it is possible to identify a distinct "idea" (meaning) for every character. Contrary to these misconceptions, most characters have a compound structure, with both a phonetic and a semantic component. Furthermore, many characters do not have a specifiable, constant meaning which they maintain across all instances of use. We will take these points one at a time.

6.3.2 The makeup of characters

For the time being, let's assume that a typical character represents a morpheme (i.e. a meaningful unit) of Mandarin Chinese. This is an idealization we will revise shortly, but it will make things easier for the time being. Also, for convenience and subject to later revision, we will further assume that morphemes are typically monosyllabic in their phonological shape. At this level of approximation, we can say that each character represents a single monosyllabic morpheme. How exactly is this done? The system is far from consistent or uniform. In fact, any modern character is the product of a long period of evolution and adaptation, which in many cases has obscured the motivation for its original design. Plus, there are several different techniques of character design which are sometimes used together.

To begin with, there are some so-called simple characters, which consist of only one graphic element. Often these characters have very ancient, pictographic origins, though this is usually not obvious in their modern form. A simple character identifies a particular morpheme with a particular monosyllabic form. Most characters, however, have a two-part structure.

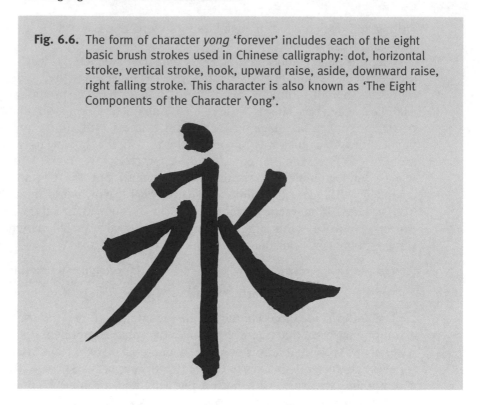

Fig. 6.6. The form of character *yong* 'forever' includes each of the eight basic brush strokes used in Chinese calligraphy: dot, horizontal stroke, vertical stroke, hook, upward raise, aside, downward raise, right falling stroke. This character is also known as 'The Eight Components of the Character Yong'.

One part, often called a "phonetic" (abbreviated as P), gives an indication—often little more than a clue—to the intended pronunciation. Usually a P is a modified version of a simple graph, being used not on account of its meaning but purely on account of its pronunciation. For example, in the character 油 for *jóu* 'oil' the P is 由, which when it is used as a simple character indicates *jóu* 'cause, by/from' (Sampson 1985: 158). This technique of using a meaningful symbol solely to indicate a sound is sometimes called the "rebus principle". We can find sporadic examples in English, in racy or "smart" spellings like B4 for 'before' or CU for 'see you'.

In the case of 油 the P is the character for an actual homophone of the morpheme which the full character represents. That is, the P precisely indicates the intended pronunciation. More commonly, the P component is only an approximation, often a pretty rough one, to the intended pronunciation. For example, in the character 狼 for *láng* 'wolf', the P is *liáng* 'good' (an archaic word, but still found in certain compounds) (Norman 1988: 60). The correspondence between the P and the actual intended pronunciation is not exact, but it is fairly close. In the character 召 *zhāo* 'summon', on the other hand, the P is 刀 *dāo* 'knife'. In this case, the phonetic correspondence is not so close.

The other part of most characters, often called a "radical" or, less commonly, a "signific" (S), gives a clue to the intended meaning. For example, in 狼 'wolf' the radical or S is 'dog'. In 召 'summon', the radical or S is 口 'mouth'. You can already see from these examples that radicals vary in how specific they are. Names for animals, plants, birds, and so on, usually have a predictable radical for their category, but many words have unpredictable radicals.

In short, neither component of a compound character (phonetic or semantic) gives an exact indication (of the intended sound, or of the intended meaning). Thus, although characters can be analyzed into two different functional elements from a graphic point of view, in practice one still has to learn the combination by heart. Sampson (1985: 156–7) sums it up as follows:

A Chinese-speaker who learns to read and write essentially has to learn the graphs case by case; both significs and phonetics will give him many hints and clues to help him remember, but the information they supply is far too patchy and unreliable to enable him to *predict* what the graph for a given spoken word will be, or even which spoken word will correspond to a graph that he encounters for the first time. From the point of view of a modern speaker, the most important benefit of the phonetic/signific structure is that graphs involving many brush-strokes can be seen as groupings of familiar visual units, rather than having to be remembered stroke by stroke.

6.3.3 Character = morpheme?

According to many experts, ancient Chinese was a language in which most words consisted of a single monosyllabic morpheme (Li 1996), but, as we have noted a couple of times already, modern Mandarin Chinese is not like this. Though there are plenty of monosyllabic words (just as there are in English), there are also numerous disyllabic and polysyllabic words. Probably most words in modern Mandarin have two or more syllables. Here are some common examples:

(171) *zhīdào* 'know', *fāshēng* 'happen', *yīnwèi* 'because', *yǐqián* 'before', *yǐhòu* 'after', *xuéxiào* 'school', *yóuqī* 'paint', *kěshì* 'but', *liánhé* 'join'

All of these disyllabic words are written with two characters, one for each syllable. Obviously, therefore, from a linguistic point of view we have to reject the equation: 1 character = 1 word. (Chinese people will often tell you that each character does represent a separate "word", but they are not using the term "word" in a strict linguistic sense, i.e. to designate a minimal linguistic form which can be pronounced in isolation.) But what about another equation: 1 character = 1 morpheme? This equation is much more viable because it is quite reasonable to suppose that many of the disyllabic words consist of two morphemes. This is uncontroversially true, if both the compounding elements exist as independent items, and the meaning of the compound is clearly related to the meaning of its components, whether directly (as with English compounds such as *bookshelf* and *underarm*) or figuratively (as in English examples like *heartfelt* and *brainwash*). There were lots of Mandarin Chinese examples in section 3.2.1. Here are a few more: *fēi-jī* [fly-machine] 'aeroplane', *jìn-bù* [advance-step] 'make progress', *mǎn-zú* [full-sufficient] 'be content', *kāi-guān* [open-close] 'switch', *tiān-qī* [heaven-breath] 'weather', *rù-shén* [enter-spirit] 'fascinated' (Li and Thompson 1981: 47–50).

But there are numerous borderline cases of different kinds. Sometimes both elements exist as independent items but the semantic connection between these items and the compound form is obscure (as with English words like *understand* and *return*). Sometimes only one of the two elements can be used as an independent item and the other is a "one-off" (as with English *cranberry*). There are also elements which recur in various compounds but are not found as independent items (as with *con* in English *converse* and *consider*). Some Mandarin Chinese examples are given in (172a). There are even some disyllabic words where both syllables are unknown in the contemporary spoken language, as in (172b).

(**172**) a. *shāng-fēng*   [hurt-wind]   'catch cold'
        xīn-shuǐ   [fuel-water]   'salary'
        fǒu-zé   [other-]   'otherwise'
      b. *qū-zú*   'chase'
        pú-táo   'grape'

As one might expect, these examples normally have historical explanations. For example, in Classical Chinese *qū* and *zú* were separate morphemes, meaning 'drive' and 'pursue', respectively, but neither has survived into the modern spoken language; and *pútáo* is an old loan word from Iranian *badag(a)* (Li and Thompson 1981: 45–6). But in linguistics we do not normally let historical facts (which are often unknown to ordinary speakers) play a role in analytic decisions about a present-day language.

Even setting aside examples like those in (172b), examples like those in (172a) are enough to pose a problem for the idea that "1 character = 1 morpheme". The key question is: how exactly do we decide whether a particular form in a particular word deserves to be called a morpheme? This is not the easy question it might seem (despite the impression conveyed in some introductory linguistics courses), and it is a question which is relevant to English, as much as to Chinese. How many morphemes are there in *understand*, or in *converse*? In order to preserve the key idea about a morpheme (i.e. that it is a minimal form with an identifiable meaning), many linguists introduce a new term—"formative"—at this point. They say that recurrent forms like *under-, con-*, and *-verse* are not morphemes in the strict sense, but formatives, i.e. recurrent morphological building blocks which lack clearly specifiable meanings. Using this terminology, we can say that many Chinese characters indicate morphemes, but that many others can indicate either morphemes or formatives (depending on the words in which they are found). A smaller number indicate formatives alone. Linguists who write about Mandarin Chinese at an introductory level often gloss over the morpheme/formative distinction. Perhaps they feel that it is difficult enough describing the structure of characters without taking on this additional complication; or perhaps they are influenced by the Chinese linguistic tradition, which has a strong historical/etymological orientation. In any case, although you will often see Chinese described as a "morphemic" writing system, I hope you can now see that this is an oversimplification.

6.3.4 Reformed characters

The new Chinese government in 1949 began a programme of simplification of the traditional characters. The problem was that too many characters required a great number of strokes to complete. This not only made writing time-consuming and demanding, it made learning to read and write much more difficult. Actually, even before 1949, the unnecessarily complicated nature of the script was widely recognized. A large number of simplified "folk characters" (*shūzì*) had been created and were used among the common people for everyday purposes, such as writing accounts, personal correspondence, or medical prescriptions. But these characters were not officially recognized: in fact, they were banned for any official or public use.

Since 1949 thousands of simplified characters have been introduced, some of them based on the existing unofficial simplifications, others created afresh. Table 6.5 shows some characters in their "before" and "after" versions. (Sometimes the old forms are still used, but the government does not encourage it.) There are also a large number of simplified characters in

Table 6.5 Examples of traditional and simplified characters (adapted from Norman 1988: 81)

(雲) 云	*yún*	'cloud'	(潔) 洁	*jié*	'clean'
(禮) 礼	*lǐ*	'ritual'	(裡) 里	*lǐ*	'inside'
(後) 后	*hòu*	'behind'	(撲) 扑	*pū*	'pounce'
(醫) 医	*yī*	'doctor'	(歷) 历	*lì*	'undergo'
(門) 门	*mén*	'door'	(讓) 让	*ràng*	'allow'

common use in the People's Republic which have not yet received official approval.

Outside the People's Republic of China, the older complicated characters are still used. People outside China, especially in Taiwan, can find it difficult to read and write in the simplified script, while the people of mainland China can find it hard to follow the old complicated script.

6.3.5 Using the Chinese script for other Sinitic languages

Contrary to what one sometimes hears, it is no easy matter to employ the character system to write languages other than Mandarin Chinese. The first problem is that the phonetic clues do not necessarily work with other languages, though this is not in itself an insurmountable problem, given the amount of sheer memory work needed to master the system even in Mandarin. To the extent that it is possible to match words one to one between Mandarin and (say) Cantonese or Taiwanese, one can use the Mandarin script to write Cantonese or Taiwanese. This assumes, of course, that the literate Cantonese or Taiwanese person will also know Mandarin, but this is a reasonable assumption given the Chinese educational tradition. In effect one has to learn Mandarin, in its written form at least, in order to be literate.

The real problem is that many of the other Sinitic languages have words and grammatical morphemes which have no equivalents in Mandarin. This means that there are no standard characters for these words. To deal with this, writers in these other languages resort to various strategies and conventions. We will illustrate from Hong Kong Cantonese. Bauer (1988: 246) describes the situation as follows:

> [T]he writer bears in mind that the person who will read what he has written speaks Cantonese, understands standard (written) Chinese, and "reads" (silently or aloud) the text with (standard or non-standard) Cantonese pronunciation. The writer thus attempts to bridge the (primarily) lexical gap that exists between Cantonese speech and standard written Chinese.

Bauer's reference to "standard or non-standard" pronunciation alludes to another relevant consideration, namely, that there are different "registers" in Cantonese depending on the formality of the situation. In a formal situation, the style of Cantonese one uses is much closer to standard Chinese (Mandarin) in grammar, lexicon, and pronunciation, than the style used in an informal or intimate situation. Because of this, formal Cantonese is easier to render in standard characters.

Bauer (1988) identifies ten different strategies used in Hong Kong to write distinctively Cantonese words and bound morphemes. He stresses that these strategies have not been imposed or organized by any official body, but have simply developed through the efforts of ordinary people. Three of the most useful, and most interesting, strategies are: (i) using special Cantonese characters which have no equivalents in Mandarin, (ii) using standard characters to indicate Cantonese morphemes on a principle of phonetic resemblance, (iii) using English letters to represent Cantonese morphemes, also by phonetic resemblance.

As an example of category (i) we can look at a text like the following, which was part of an advertisement for 'Raid' insect spray in a popular Hong Kong magazine. In the interlinear gloss, the items in capital letters stand for elements written with specifically Cantonese characters. Some other common Cantonese characters (with their nearest standard equivalents) are given in Table 6.6.

(173) 即 刻　　睇 吓　　你 用　開 嗰 隻 殺
jīk hāk　　*TÁI-HÁH néih yuhng HŌI GÓ jek saat*
immediately look-PRT you use　　-ing that kind kill

虫　　劑 有 乜 成 分
chùhng jí　　*yáuh MĀT síhng fahn*
insect drug has what components
'Immediately go look at the insecticide you are using and see what's in it!' (*Affairs Weekly*, No. 348, 19 September 1986)

A particularly interesting and productive method for "coining" new Cantonese characters relies on phonetic resemblances. It works by joining the 'mouth' signific 口 to a standard character, with the meaning 'sounds like (this character)'. For example, the Cantonese pronominal plural suffix is *-deih* (also romanized as *-de*). The character for it is: 哋. It consists of the 'mouth' sign 口 joined to the standard character 地 'earth, dirt' which is also pronounced as *deih* in Cantonese. Sometimes standard characters are used in Cantonese purely on account of their phonetic resemblance to Cantonese words (without this being marked by the 'mouth' sign 口). For example, the characters 埋 and 俾 are used in Cantonese writing to indicate the words *màaih* 'near' and *béi* 'by (passive)', respectively. But in Mandarin these characters stand for *mái* 'to bury' and *bǐ* 'in order to', respectively (Bauer 1988: 252).

Table 6.6. Cantonese characters with their Standard Chinese equivalents

Cantonese character	Standard Chinese character equivalent	English gloss
佢	他	'he'
冇	沒有	'not have'
嗰 (or 個, 果)	這	'this'
唔	不	'no, not'

English letters are also borrowed into written Cantonese for their phonetic value. The most prominent is the letter D, which is used to represent two (homophonous) Cantonese morphemes: plural classifier *dī* and comparative marker *dī*. The following example is taken from a newspaper.

(174) 後　　面　　D　位　　平　　　D　　呀
　　　hauh　*bihn*　*dī*　*WÁI*　*PÈHNG*　*dī*　　*a*
　　　back　　　PL　seat　cheap　　COMP　QUES
　　　'Are the seats in the back cheaper?'
　　　(東方日報 *Oriental Daily News*, 30 December 1983)

On account of local writing conventions such as these (and others), a text written in Hong Kong Cantonese can be difficult for a non-Cantonese to follow, especially if the style is very informal and colloquial.

6.4 Japanese: a multiscriptal system

Though the Chinese writing system is formidably complicated, the Japanese writing system is even more so. This is because it uses both logographic characters (*kanji*, each standing for a lexical root), and phonographic symbols (*kana*, each standing for a separate syllable). Further complications come from the fact that many of the logographic characters can be read in two or more completely different ways, and from the existence of not one but two systems of syllabic "letters"—*hiragana* and *katakana*. The explanation for this situation is historical. Before we go any further, it is probably a good idea to get clear on what is meant by a system of syllabic letters—a "syllabary", as it is called.

6.4.1 The syllabaries: *hiragana* and *katakana*

You may remember from the previous chapter that Japanese has a very small range of possible syllable structures, most of which have the shape CV—i.e. a single consonant followed by a single vowel. Since the number of consonants and vowels is also quite modest, it is possible to list every possible syllable: *ka, ki, ku, ke, ko; sa, si, su, se, so; ta, ti, tu, te, to*, and so on. A syllabary is simply an "alphabet" whose letters each stand for a separate syllable (without breaking the syllable down any further into its individual segments). The most widely used, *hiragana* 'plain kana', has rounded letter shapes; the other system, *katakana* 'partial kana', has squarish letter shapes. Both systems have the same number of letters, forty-six in all (plus some diacritics), and do exactly the same job. Anything that can be said in Japanese can be written in either of the kana syllabaries; see Table 6.7.

Table 6.7. Japanese *kana* syllabaries (Shibatani 1990: 127)

	a	ka	sa	ta	na	ha	ma	ya	ra	wa	
Hiragana	あ	か	さ	た	な	は	ま	や	ら	わ	
Katakana	ア	カ	サ	タ	ナ	ハ	マ	ヤ	ラ	ワ	
	i	ki	si	ti	ni	hi	mi		ri		
Hiragana	い	き	し	ち	に	ひ	み		り		
Katakana	イ	キ	シ	チ	ニ	ヒ	ミ		リ		
	u	ku	su	tu	nu	hu	mu	yu	ru		
Hiragana	う	く	す	つ	ぬ	ふ	む	ゆ	る		
Katakana	ウ	ク	ス	ツ	ヌ	フ	ム	ユ	ル		
	e	ke	se	te	ne	he	me		re		
Hiragana	え	け	せ	て	ね	へ	め		れ		
Katakana	エ	ケ	セ	テ	ネ	ヘ	メ		レ		
	o	ko	so	to	no	ho	mo	yo	ro	wo	n
Hiragana	お	こ	そ	と	の	ほ	も	よ	ろ	を	ん
Katakana	オ	コ	ソ	ト	ノ	ホ	モ	ヨ	ロ	ヲ	ン

Voicing oppositions, where applicable, are indicated by diacritical dots on the upper right-hand corner of each *kana*, e.g. *gi* ぎ, ギ as opposed to *ki* き, キ. を and ヲ, used only for writing the accusative particle *o*, are pronounced the same way as お and オ, which are used for all other instances of the *o* sound. は and ハ are pronounced as *wa* when they are used to write the topic particle *wa*. へ and ヘ are pronounced as *e* when used to write the directional paticle *e*.

Both *kana* systems have their origins back in the ninth century, when Japanese scholars were struggling to find better ways of writing their language using Chinese characters. As the Cantonese do today, one strategy was to employ Chinese characters not for their meanings but purely for their phonetic value. This was particularly handy for writing the various suffixes and grammatical particles which are found in Japanese (an agglutinating language) but have no equivalents in Chinese (an isolating language). Over time the Chinese characters which were coopted in this way for their phonetic value alone were simplified and, eventually, standardized.

An interesting fact about *kana* is that one of Japan's greatest literary masterpieces, the *Genji monogatari* (*The Tale of Genji*), was written entirely in *hiragana*. This was in the eleventh century, at a time when *kana* were generally regarded as a mere supplement to the *kanji* mode of writing. The explanation? *The Tale of Genji* was written by a woman, Lady Murasaki, and at that time women were largely excluded from learning the *kanji* system, which was the medium of scholarship and officialdom. The *kana* system, being easier to learn, allowed an alternative for Japanese women writers.

In contemporary Japan, the language is usually written in a combination of *kanji* and *kana*, primarily *hiragana*. *Hiragana* is used for particles, auxiliary verbs, and suffixes of nouns, adjectives, and verbs—in short, for the grammatical morphemes. *Katakana* is mainly used for borrowings from other languages (other than Chinese, that is), for mimetic words, and for foreign names. It has a more angular appearance, which makes it stand out from surrounding text, a bit like italics. Young people are likely to mix more *katakana* into their writing to give a more "conversational" tone. *Kanji* are used for the lexical elements: nouns, verb stems, adjective stems, and so on.

6.4.2 The world of *kanji*

The ancestors of the *kanji* characters entered Japan in the third century. They were Chinese in origin, but at that time (and for many centuries afterwards) Chinese was the preeminent language of scholarship in Korea and in Japan (much as Latin used to be in medieval Europe). Japanese scholars all knew Chinese, though their pronunciations of many words were probably somewhat "Japanized". For these ancient scholars, steeped in Chinese influence, the characters would have seemed the natural way of representing words, and they could be pressed into service for this purpose. Writers relied on finding Chinese equivalents to the Japanese words they wanted to write: they wrote the Chinese characters as a way of indicating Japanese words. Readers had to do the same thing in reverse: recognize the Chinese words and convert each back to Japanese. A fairly clumsy system, you might think—and you'd be right. But there were many further complications.

One complication came from the fact that at the same time as the *kanji* were being adopted into Japanese, the language was also borrowing countless words of Chinese (as we have seen in Chapter 3). Naturally these words of Chinese origin were written using their original characters, even if the same characters were also used for writing indigenous Japanese words. Often the meanings of the Japanese terms and the Chinese loans diverged over time. This has led to the situation where many *kanji* now have two quite different meanings and pronunciations: an "*on*-reading" based on the Chinese word at the time of borrowing, and a "*kun*-reading" representing an indigenous Japanese morpheme. To read and write Japanese properly, one has to know both meanings and be able to recognize which is intended in context.

Take, for example, the well-known Japanese word *kimono* 'clothing' (Sampson 1985: 177). It is a compound of two native Japanese roots *ki* 'wear' and *mono* 'thing, stuff', and is written with two *kanji*:

(175) 着 物
　　　ki   mono

The first of these *kanji* descends from the Chinese word /zāu/ 'to place, put' and the second from Chinese /ù/ 'thing'. But both these Chinese words also exist as loans in Japanese, in words such as *chaku-shu* 'to start' (from 'put-hand') and *doo-butsu* 'animal' (from 'move-thing'). The current Japanese pronunciations, of course, differ markedly from the Chinese originals (compare *chaku* and *zāu; butsu* and *ù*), for reasons we cannot go into here. The main point is that the words *chaku-shu* 'to start' and *doo-butsu* 'animal' employ the same *kanji* as appear in *kimono*, but with different pronunciations and meanings (*on*-readings) in the different words.

(176) a. 着手 'to start'　　b. 動物 'animal'
　　　　 chaku-shu　　　　　 *doo-butsu*

There is no way of telling from the written form alone whether an *on*-reading or *kun*-reading is intended. The reader just has to know which of these alternatives is right. Furthermore, there are many *kanji* which have more than one *on*-reading.

With all these complications, why not just write everything in one of the phonographic *kana* scripts? For the Japanese there are powerful cultural and aesthetic reasons for holding on to *kanji*, but it has been suggested that *kanji* has at least one purely functional advantage over *kana*. The mass borrowing of words from Chinese has resulted in what Sampson (1985: 178) calls "a truly colossal degree of homophony" in Japanese. This came about because many of the original pronunciation differences between Chinese words were lost as they were adapted to Japanese phonology. Sampson illustrates this point with the Japanese form *kankoo*, which corresponds to at least seven different (homophonous) words. In a *kana* script, they would all be written the same way, but they have different, individual *kanji*.

6.4.3 Writing in a mixed system

As an example of the multiscriptal nature of Japanese writing, consider the Japanese sentence 'He suddenly gave her a kiss' in (177). The written sentence runs vertically downwards. Notice that *kanji* (with either *kun*-readings or *on*-readings) are used for the lexical roots, *hiragana* for the suffixes, and *katakana* for foreign loan words (in this sentence, only one word: *kisu* 'kiss', is borrowed from English). The abbreviations NJ and

S-J identify "native Japanese" words and "Sino-Japanese" words, respectively. This example also shows another interesting characteristic of Japanese writing: there is no formal means of indicating word boundaries. Each written symbol follows the one before with equal spacing, regardless of whether it represents a suffix or a new word. The transition from *hiragana* to *kanji*, however, generally serves as a visual indication of the onset of a new word.

(177) 彼   kun for NJ *kare* 'he'

が   hiragana *ga*, nominative case marker

彼 ⎫
女 ⎬ kun for NJ *kano* 'that' + on for S-J *jo* 'she'
    ⎭

に   hiragana *ni*, dative case marker

突 ⎫
然 ⎬ on for S-J–S-J *tostsu-zen* 'thrust-nature'
    ⎭

キ ⎫
ス ⎬ katakana *kisu*, borrowed from English 'kiss'
    ⎭

を   hiragana *o*, accusative case marker

し   hiragana *shi* 'do'

た   hiragana *-ta*, past tense marker suffix

'He suddenly gave her a kiss'.

6.4.4 *Romaji*

As if three scripts were not enough, Japanese also employs the roman alphabet and numerals for various purposes: to write train station names, street and highway signs, names of stores and firms on signs and advertisements. Capital letters are used to produce acronyms like OL 'office lady' and 2DK 'two [rooms] plus a dining-kitchen'. As mentioned earlier, there are two recognized systems for transcribing Japanese into the roman alphabet. The older system, first published in 1886, goes back to an American missionary, James Curtis Hepburn. As one might expect, it is designed to assist English speakers in pronouncing Japanese. The Hepburn system is known in Japan as *Hebon-shiki*. The other system, known as *kunreishiki*, is phonemic. The main difference is that Hepburn indicates certain allophonic variations; for example, it writes *shi* (not *ti*)

Box 6.1. Learning to write in Japanese: 'The winter holiday starts from tomorrow'. Japanese children first learn to write using *hiragana* exclusively, as illustrated in the top line. As they begin to learn *kanji*, they replace *hiragana* with *kanji* forms where possible, as on the bottom line: *ashita* 'tomorrow', *fuyuyasu* 'winter holiday', and *haji* 'start' are written in *kanji*.

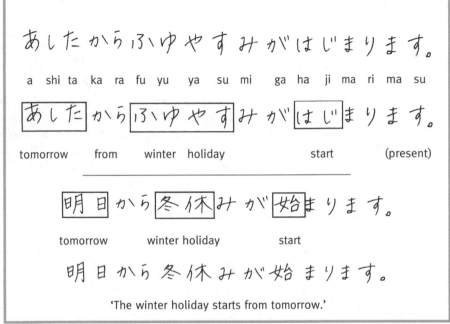

a shi ta ka ra fu yu   ya su mi   ga ha ji ma ri ma su

tomorrow   from   winter holiday   start   (present)

tomorrow   winter holiday   start

'The winter holiday starts from tomorrow.'

and *tsu* (not *tu*), even though the palatalization of /t/ to [ʃ], and the affrication of /t/ to [ts] are predictable from the following vowel (cf. section 5.1.4).

Official policy is that *kunreishiki* should generally be used except when there are special reasons for preferring the Hepburn system, mainly for use by foreigners, e.g. to write proper names, book titles, and the names of railway stations, and in passports and many official application forms. Despite this, the Hepburn system is still widely used in Japan and is perhaps more popular than the *kunreishiki* system.

6.4.5 Parting comments

On account of its many complexities, the Japanese writing system has often been described by outside commentators in extremely negative terms (as has the Chinese writing system, but criticism of Japanese has been even harsher). It has been claimed that the multiple scripts and the intricacies of *kanji* are unnecessary and that they impose an onerous learning task on

Japanese children, not to mention foreign language learners. One of the standard reference works on Japanese grammar (Miller 1967) argues that the complexity can be blamed on the leisured aristocracy of ancient Japan, who had no motivation to develop a functionally efficient writing system but indulged themselves instead in aesthetic and intellectual elaborations. Calls continue for both Japanese and Chinese to abandon their traditional logographic systems in favour of more "efficient" alphabetic writing (Hannas 1997).

Ironically, a quintessentially modern development—the advent of powerful and affordable personal computers—may help to give character writing a new lease of life (Gottlieb 2001; Chen 2001). Desktop, portable, and handheld computers can now store large character sets, and characters can be accessed and written (either on the printed page or in electronic messages) at the press of a button. One consequence, already evident in highly technologized Japan, is that the range of characters in everyday use is increasing. Some of the older complex characters are making a comeback, now that there is a reduced need to write them by hand. At the same time, the new computer-mediated character literacy requires a different balance of skills. Being able to recognize a larger set of characters, and to access a desired character quickly and efficiently, is becoming more important, and being able to write characters by hand is becoming less so.

In the past, locating a desired *kanji* or Chinese character in a dictionary could be a tricky task. Because a phonographic principle such as alphabetical order is not applicable to logographic scripts, some other method of ordering and indexing the entries had to be used, such as listing first by radical and then by the number of strokes per character. These days, computer-based dictionaries increasingly use a "look-up" system based on phonographic principles; for example, one keys in the pinyin spelling of a Chinese word and gets presented with a set of possible characters to select from. (Remember: because there are many homophones in Chinese and Japanese, any single phonetic form usually corresponds to several different words, with different individual characters.) In short, the transition from pen to keyboard is likely to favour the retention of character-based scripts.

Despite all the criticism and condemnation, character-based scripts do not seem to be in any imminent danger. Indeed:

The Japanese writing system... is associated with a highly literate and successful society, with a rich written tradition which makes full use of its multiscriptal potentialities for the creation of nuanced, graphically vital texts. The high degree of literacy in Japan and the high consumption of written material suggest that the writing system is fully functional. (Smith 1996: 214)

6.5 A note on calligraphy

It would be wrong to conclude this survey of writing systems without mentioning the art of calligraphy, which is an essential element of many traditional East Asian cultures (cf. Sampson 1985: 191–3; Stevens 1996: 244–51; Qu 2002). In traditional Chinese culture, calligraphy was considered the highest art form, more valued than painting. Japan too has a rich calligraphic tradition. (There is also an Islamic calligraphic tradition, which we will not consider here.) Calligraphy places an aesthetic value on the handwritten form of language. Whereas Western tradition tends to value clarity and legibility for its own sake, the calligraphic sensibility looks to the beauty, artistry, grace, or individuality expressed by the manner in which the brush is wielded, in trained hands. Although each character has a

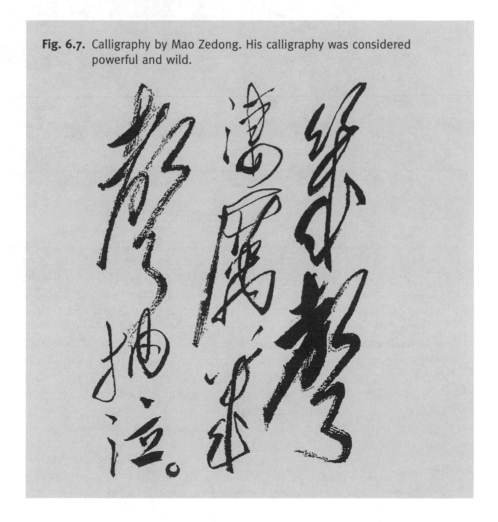

Fig. 6.7. Calligraphy by Mao Zedong. His calligraphy was considered powerful and wild.

Fig. 6.8. Calligrapher Cuncun Wu at work. She is writing in standard script (*kǎi shū*) the traditional aphorism *dū shū* 'read book', i.e. study. Calligraphy scripts are always written in the traditional right to left order; the calligrapher's signature and seal will be added on the left. The equipment (the Four Treasures: brush, ink, paper, inkstone) is placed to the right of the calligrapher. Good calligraphy requires the brush to be held upright and unsupported. The design must be fully formed in the mind at the outset and executed in a single, steady, and continuous effort, demanding great coordination of hand and mind.

defined structure, the tip of the brush never moves in exactly the same way twice, so no two characters in calligraphy are ever exactly the same.

From early times in China it was held that "Calligraphy *is* the person"—that is, that a person's character is revealed in the brushstrokes. Specimens of calligraphy by statesmen, philosophers, scholars, generals, famous beauties, monks and nuns were more highly valued than pieces by professional calligraphers (Stevens 1996: 247). Various styles of calligraphy were recognized, each with its own flavour, so to speak: bold and elegant *zhuàn shū* 'seal script', dignified and serious *lì shū* 'clerical script', formal and controlled *kǎi shū* 'standard script', graceful and polished *xíng shū* 'running script', and the fluid, individualistic *cǎo shū* 'grass script'.

In traditional China, calligraphy was everywhere—in shop signs and banners, on wall hangings in people's homes, in offices and restaurants, and, of course, in official uses. Calligraphy was, in Chiang's (1973: 17) words, "the most popular of the arts... a national taste, a common aesthetic instinct nourished in every Chinese from childhood up". With the advent of the People's Republic and the consequent simplification of characters, the status of calligraphy has diminished somewhat, but it is still recognized as a vital part of the Chinese cultural tradition.

In Japan, as in China, a good style of handwriting was traditionally admired, not only in artistic works but also in everyday use among educated people. The so-called "grass style" was held in highest regard. This goes beyond simply fusing together separate strokes into smooth continuous motions of the brush (as in the *xíng shū* 'running script'), but also involves radical simplifications so that characters normally written with a dozen or more strokes may be reduced to a few sketchy hints. Needless to say, this calls for special skills by readers as well as by writers. An extension of 'grass style', dynamic Zen calligraphy (sometimes termed "brushstrokes of enlightenment"), has had a profound impact on Japanese aesthetics.

Key technical terms

alphabetic/segmental	logographic
calligraphy	phonographic
featural	syllabic

The art of speaking

Speaking any language well calls for a lot more than mere grammatical knowledge. It means having command of a whole range of possible ways of speaking and knowing how to choose between them depending on the social circumstances. To make this point clearer, linguists often distinguish between narrow "linguistic competence" and broader "communicative competence". In this chapter we sample some of the dimensions of communicative competence in East and Southeast Asian languages. We will start at the level of individual expressions, looking at aspects of "word skills" in various languages. After that we look at speech styles, i.e. more or less codified ways of speaking appropriately in different social situations. Then we will spend some time examining one of the most elaborate honorific systems in East Asia—or, indeed, anywhere in the world—that of Japanese. Finally, we will deal with some even broader concerns under the heading of "communicative style".

7.1 Word skills in East and Southeast Asian languages

7.1.1 Proverbs and sayings

In many East and Southeast Asian languages, proverbs, traditional sayings, and traditional verses play an incomparably more important role in effective communication than they do in English. For example, in Malay there are literally hundreds, if not thousands, of traditional *peribahasa* 'sayings' and *pepatah* 'maxims' which encapsulate correct behaviour according to custom (*adat*) or which sum up social situations in colourful, if often oblique, images (cf. Brown 1989; Sheppard 1992). Many of the images reflect the traditional village lifestyle of fishing, market gardening, and rice farming. As Chee (1993: 89–90) remarks: "It may rightly be said that proverbs and proverbial sayings are the distillation of a people's genius... they provide an insight on Malaysian life and thought at the level of the ordinary folk."

Some sayings (*peribahasa* in the true sense) express a moral message or offer advice on how to cope with everyday situations. There are a few examples in (178). Other sayings (sometimes called *kiasan* 'innuendo, insinuation') are similes or allusions which convey a feeling or characterize a situation. There are some examples in (179).

(**178**) *Ada hujan, ada panas, ada hari boleh balas.*
'There is rainy weather, there is hot weather, there is a day of repayment' (i.e. every action, whether good or bad, will be repaid in kind).
Sedikit-sedikit lama-lama jadi bukit.
'Little by little it becomes a mountain' (i.e. small, patient actions can bring big results in the end).
Perlulah ikut resmi padi. Jangan ikut resmi lalang.
'(We) have to follow the way of the paddy rice. Don't follow the way of the long grass' (i.e. stay low and humble, don't raise yourself up high).
Mati semut kerana gula.
'Ants die because of sugar' (i.e. people can be ensnared by sweet words).

(**179**) *Seperti aur dengan tebing.*
'Like bamboo by a riverbank' (depending on something else for one's survival).
Seperti kakak di bawah tempurung.
'Like a frog beneath a coconut shell' (someone who is narrow and isolated, a country bumpkin).
Durian runtuh.
'Durians [a highly prized kind of fruit] fall [from the tree]' (i.e. a windfall of good fortune).
Seperti tikus membaiki labu.
'Like a mouse fixing a pumpkin' (someone who makes matters worse by trying to fix up something which is beyond his or her skill).

Having a large stock of traditional sayings on hand enables one to comment on social situations or to offer advice, without the comment or advice seeming to come exclusively from oneself. Producing an appropriate *peribahasa* can "de-personalize" the comment, allowing it to appear as a piece of traditional wisdom, and thereby deserving of being taken seriously. Many sayings are so well known that one needn't quote the whole thing in order to be understood.

A single word or phrase may be enough to evoke the intended meaning. By skilfully weaving these suggestive words or phrases into one's speech a great deal can be conveyed in an indirect and allusive fashion.

In Malay many *peribahasa* come in the form of a *pantun* 'quatrain' (Sim 1987; Daillie 1988). Perhaps the most famous is the *pisang emas* 'golden banana' *pantun* shown in (180) below, which deals with the obligation to repay what is known as *hutang budi* 'a debt of gratitude/kindness' to someone who has helped out in a serious time of need. This illustrates traditional *pantun* form. The first couplet portrays a "suggestive image"; roughly: 'golden bananas (a variety of banana) on a sailing ship, one ripens on my seaman's chest'. The second couplet gives the message of the *pantun* in a more straightforward form: 'a debt of gold can be repaid, a debt of gratitude goes to the grave' (Sim 1987: 30). As with most *pantuns*, it is difficult to convey the full effect in translation.

(**180**) *Pisang emas bawa belayar,*
     Masak sebiji di atas peti;
   Hutang emas boleh di bayar,
   Hutang budi di bawa mati.

As Sim (1987: 12) observes: "As a poetical form the *pantun* is remarkably crisp, often extremely colourful and passionate, sometimes bitterly cynical, and it says a great deal in a very small space." To understand many *pantuns* and *peribahasa*, one needs to know a lot of symbols. For example, that a flower *bunga* represents a girl, that a bee *kumbang* is her lover or suitor, that the squirrel *tupai* is a village playboy. As these examples suggest, the majority of *pantuns* are concerned with affairs of the heart, though many address other aspects of the human condition.

In traditional rural life, *pantuns* were a major part of Malay verbal culture, as Fauconnier (1990: 82) reports:

It is the play on words, the equivocations, the tenuous allusions, that constitute their special charm for the Malays. ... [T]hey all know a large number of pantuns and are constantly inventing new ones. Their conversation is full of these poetic insubstantial images.

One can easily appreciate how an abundance of *pantuns*, and other evocative sayings, are a very serviceable resource for alluding to potentially sensitive matters. In traditional-style courtship they play a special role, providing the young man and woman with a compact written medium in which their feelings may be expressed with acceptable restraint. Karim (1990: 32) describes how a series of veiled messages in *pantun* form will often be passed between the pair by a go-between. She comments:

Like Japanese haiku, the brevity of verse attempts a controlled elegance over emotion. It is in this sense a mode of communication which guides passion into acceptable poise and restraint.

Although many of the traditional *peribahasa* and *pantuns* are no longer in daily use, dozens (perhaps hundreds) are still known and used. Partly as a reflection of the resurgence of Malay cultural pride, learning *peribahasa* now forms a significant part of the school language curriculum in Malaysia.

7.1.2 Elaborate expressions

The term "elaborate expression" refers to a special kind of compounding. An elaborate expression is usually a four-syllable expression achieved partly through repetition of one of the elements and partly by the addition of a new element. It is an areal feature of Southeast Asia (Hudak 1987: 39–40).

The repeated element usually occurs in first and third position, or otherwise in second and fourth position, i.e. in the patterns ABAC or ABCB. Sometimes there is no repetition, but there is a rhyme between second and third syllables. Table 7.1 shows examples of each of these types in Thai. As Hudak (1987: 40) says: "for the Thai, the ability to use elaborate expressions is an essential part of speaking well and fluently (*phayrɔ́*)." The same could be said about Lao, Vietnamese, and many other language communities of mainland Southeast Asia.

In Chinese, elaborate "four-character expressions" (*chéng yǔ* 'set phrases') are regarded as "the cream of the Chinese language" (Xu 1998: 71). Knowing and using them is considered the "height of culture", and teaching how to use them elegantly is one of the main goals of literacy education. *Chéng yǔ* dictionaries are common. Many rely on shared knowledge of classical literature and history. For example, the phrase "to have the shadow of the third man" means something like 'being happy in solitude'. It is derived from one of the poems of Li Bai (Li Taibo) from the eighth century AD. The poem speaks of a contented man with a kettle of wine, drinking in solitude.

Table 7.1. Examples of elaborate expressions in Thai

tɨ̀n-taa-tɨ̀n-cay	*thii-khray-thii-man*
wake-eye-wake-heart	time-who-time-it
'to be full of wonder and excitement'	'every dog has its day'
hǔu-pàa-taa-thɨan	*phûut-yàang-tham-yàang*
ear-forest-eye-forest	speak-kind-do-kind
'to be ignorant of what is going on'	'say one thing and do another'
náam-sǎy-cay-cing	*càp-cháang-klaang-plɛɛng*
water-clear-heart-true	catch-elephant-middle-field
'sincerity'	'to do something which will never be accomplished'

jǔ bēi yāo míng yuè   If I lift the cup and invite the bright moon
duì yǐng chéng sān rén   my shadow becomes the third man of the company
(Karlgren 1962, cited in Pickle 2001: 26–7)

The expression *Yè gōng hào lóng* [Ye lord love dragon] 'a professed love for what one really fears' goes back to a story recorded in a Han dynasty text, about a man, Lord Ye, who loved to draw, carve, and write about dragons—until visited by the real dragon of heaven, who scared him out of his wits (Xu 1998: 72). On a more contemporary note, the film *Crouching Tiger, Hidden Dragon* takes its title from a four-character expression *wò hǔ cáng lóng* [crouching tiger hidden dragon]. The tiger and dragon refer to people who have hidden talents. The expression reminds one never to underestimate people. Some simpler examples include: *mù dèng kǒu dāi* [eye open-wide mouth dumbstruck] 'overcome with fear or amazement', *huà shé tiān zú* [draw snake add feet] 'making unnecessary addition to something, wasting time and effort'.

Chéng yǔ are not just a fixed inventory, since new expressions on the same pattern can be coined. Mao Zedong was a master of this. Some of his memorable examples are: *hǔ fù wú quǎn zi* [tiger father not dog son] 'Tigers do not breed dogs', *niú guǐ shé shén* [cow demon snake spirit] 'bad elements', i.e. undesirables to be imprisoned, *yī qióng èr bái* [one poor two blank] 'poor and blank', describing the situation of China.

7.1.3 Auspicious and inauspicious words in Chinese

An interesting aspect of verbal culture in Sinitic languages is based on the belief that using certain words can foster good fortune, while other words must be avoided in order to avert misfortune. The auspicious or inauspicious associations come from resemblances in form to other words explicitly linked with good or with ill fortune. Writing in relation to Cantonese, Bauer and Benedict (1997: 304–7) say:

[S]peakers of Chinese dialects . . . believe that a person must be very careful about his or her use of words, because malevolent spirits are everywhere listening to what he or she is saying. Uttering the wrong word can arouse the wrath of evil spirits and bring down bad luck on oneself and one's family. Speaking auspicious words, on the other hand, can placate the spirits and invite good fortune into one's life. Superstition among Cantonese speakers about their spoken language is based on the homonymy or near homonymy between the names of certain common things, such as foods, numbers, animals, and the names or abstract states or occasions which are regarded as highly desirable.

For example, the Cantonese word *baat* 'eight' rhymes with *faat* 'to become (rich)'—cf. the expression *gūng héi faat chòih* [congratulations make wealth] used at Chinese New Year. Hundreds of people in Hong Kong decided to get married on 8 August 1988, because the confluence of so many 8s would surely bring good luck. Attention to lucky numbers also carries over to number plates and telephone numbers. For example, number plates with many 8s and 3s (*sāam* 'three' almost rhymes with *sāang* 'life') can attract high prices at auctions.

Table 7.2. Auspicious rhyming words in Cantonese (adapted from Bauer and Benedict 1997: 305)

baat 八 'eight'	*faat* 發 'become (rich)'
daaih gāt 大橘 'large tangerine'	*daaih gāt* 大吉 'greatly auspicious'
dóu 倒 'to turn upside down'	*dou* 到 'to arrive' (as good fortune)
gām 柑 'mandarin orange'	*gām* 金 'gold'
gáu 九 'nine'	*gáu* 久 'long time'
faat-choi 髮菜 'fine black seaweed'	*faat-chòih* 發財 'become rich'
[pīn] fūk [蝙]蝠 'the bat'	*fūk* 福 'good fortune'
sāam 三 'three'	*sāang* 生 'give birth; life'
sāang-choi 生菜 'lettuce'	*sāang chòih* 生財 'make money'
hòuh-sí 蠔豉 'dried oysters'	*hóh sih* 好事 'good affairs' or
	hóu síh 好市 'good market'
ché fu 扯褲 'pull out trousers'	*ché fu* 扯富 'pull out wealth'
jí 子 'seeds'	*jí* 子 'sons'
léih 鯉 'carp'	*leih* 利 'advantage'
leih 脷 'tongue'	*leih* 利 'advantage'
lìhn-jí 蓮子 'lotus seeds'	*lìhn-jí* 連子 'successive sons'
yú 魚 'fish'	*yùh* 餘 'surplus'

Table 7.3. Inauspicious rhyming words in Cantonese (adapted from Bauer and Benedict 1997: 306)

sei 四 '4'	*séi* 死 'to die, be dead'
sei-sahp 四十 '40'	*séi saht* 死實 'die surely'
sahp-sei 十四 '14'	*saht séi* 實死 'surely die'
siht 舌 'tongue'	*siht* 蝕 'to lose'
syū 書 'book'	*syū* 輸 'to lose'
hūng 空 'empty'	*hūng* 凶 'unlucky, inauspicious'
	hūng 兇 'fierce'

Table 7.2 lists some sets of auspicious Cantonese words. During the Chinese New Year, Cantonese speakers eat various foods, such as carp, duck tongue, dried oysters, and mandarins because the names of these things are homophonous with auspicious words and phrases, as shown in Table 7.2. For similar reasons, good luck posters at this time of year are often bordered with small pictures of bats, because the syllable *fūk* in *pīn-fūk* 'bat' is the same as *fūk* 'good fortune'.

As examples of inauspicious words, one can take the number 4 *sei*, which rhymes with *sei* 'die', and *syū* 'book', which is homophonous with *syū* 'to lose'. Other examples of inauspicious words are given in Table 7.3.

7.2 Speech styles

In many East and Southeast Asian languages one can identify a number of more or less distinct speech styles (sometimes called registers) which are appropriate in different social contexts. Speech styles express respect, social distance, solidarity, or familiarity by various means including: pronunciation style, special vocabulary items, special particles, and special morphology and syntax. Sometimes the language itself has quite fixed, traditional names for the speech styles, as in Javanese and Korean (see below), but this is not necessarily so. For example, Smalley (1994) identifies three major speech styles in Thai—the public, the consultative, and the personal—but there are no terms in Thai which correspond precisely to Smalley's three-way classification, although Thai people are highly aware of the need to employ different words, forms of address, particles, and so on in different social situations.

Thai provides a good example of how different linguistic features can tend to co-occur, to constitute a recognizable speech style. For example, in the so-called consultative style (used with people one doesn't know well), speakers continually exchange messages of mutual deference and respect bundled up compactly in the form of the social status particles *khráp* and *khâ* (cf. section 4.5). These particles, interestingly, depend on the gender of the speaker. Men use *khráp* or a variant, and women use *khâ* or a variant. The particles occur either at the end of an utterance or phrase, or by themselves to signal agreement or to show that one is paying attention. But speaking in this style requires more than simply repeated use of particles. One should also employ a careful style of pronunciation, use elegant or high-level

Fig. 7.1. Variations on the *wai*, the traditional Thai way of greeting: (1) student to teacher, (2) gentlemen on an equal level, (3) student to Buddhist monk. As a rule the higher the higher-ranked person is, the higher his/her head can be and the more relaxed the hands can be. Just as with verbal etiquette, there are many subtle variations which are sensitive to social nuances.

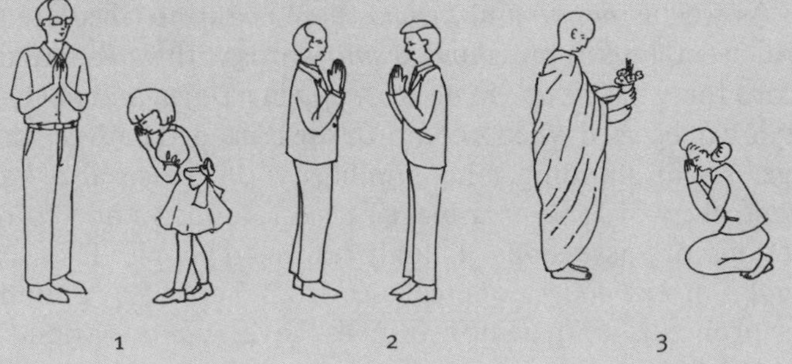

vocabulary (loan words from Sanskrit, Pali, or Khmer: see section 3.1.3), and avoid negative, confrontational or abrupt replies. To speak too briefly or curtly, *phûucaa mây miihǎang sǐang* 'to speak without sounding the tail', as the saying goes, is considered impolite (Khanittanan 1988*a*).

7.2.1 Javanese and Sasak speech styles

The phenomenon of different levels of vocabulary is particularly well developed in some of the Western Austronesian languages of Indonesia, such as Javanese, Sundanese, Madurese, and Balinese. In Javanese and Sundanese up to 1,000 and 800 words, respectively, have different style-level variants. The elaboration and codified nature of these systems reflects the fact that these societies have been highly stratified for hundreds of years. Let's take a closer look at Javanese. The basic style is called *ngoko*. This is the first way of speaking acquired by the young child at home, the style in which one thinks to oneself, and the style one uses with one's close family and friends of the same age or younger: "no refinements are called for and one's feelings can be expressed without inhibition" (Robson 1992: 15).

In order to speak to someone socially superior, however, or to a stranger, linguistic etiquette requires one to substitute higher-level vocabulary items whenever they are available. This forms the speech style called *basa* 'polite speech' or *krama* 'proper conduct'. *Krama* speech also requires a certain style of delivery ("stately" and "measured", in Robson's words), and a high degree of indirectness and sensitivity to the addressee's sense of self-esteem. The "tone" in which one speaks *krama* should be very different to ordinary *ngoko*. It is full of polite set phrases and stereotypical remarks. Westerners tend to find this inhibiting or even "thought stultifying", but Keeler (1984: p. xvii) says that for the Javanese it is "gracious, comfortable, [and] indicative of the desire to make every encounter smooth and effortless for all concerned." As Robson puts it (1992: 14):

The underlying idea seems to be that a highly placed person, someone who deserves respect, is refined and sensitive, so that his feelings would be hurt by hearing coarse or blunt expressions.

As well as *ngoko* and *krama* there is an intermediate style called *madya*, which employs abbreviated *krama* words with *ngoko* affixes; for example, the word for 'what' is *apa* in *ngoko*, *napa* in *madya*, and *punapa* in *krama*. *Madya* style can be used when a compromise is needed between conflicting criteria of age, social standing, and familiarity. Javanese also has several hundred honorific words (*krama inggil*) used to address and to refer to the person, actions, or possessions of highly respected people. These can be used in either *ngoko* or *krama*. As one can see from Table 7.4, grammatical words such as pronouns and demonstratives have *krama* variants, as do locational and directional words, and some of the more common auxiliaries and

Table 7.4. Javanese speech styles (adapted from Errington 1998: 37)

Ngoko	*Iki*	*apa*	*ya*	*dhuwèk*	*-mu?*
Low Basa (Madya)	*Niki*	*napa*	*nggèh*	*gadhahan*	*sampéyan?*
High Basa (Krama)	*Punika*	*punapa*	*inggih*	*kagungan*	*panjenengan?*
	this	QUES	yes	possession	your
	'Is this yours?'				

Table 7.5. Examples of Javanese speech style variants (Robson 1992)

		Ngoko	**Krama**
Nouns	'house'	*omah*	*griya*
	'person'	*wong*	*tiyang*
	'bird'	*manuk*	*peksi*
Adjectives	'young'	*enom*	*enèm*
	'old'	*tuwa*	*sepuh*
	'small'	*cilik*	*alit*
	'heavy'	*abot*	*awrat*
Verbs	'go'	*lunga*	*késah*
	'say'	*celathu*	*wicanten*
	'get'	*éntuk*	*angsal*
	'have'	*duwé*	*gadhah*
	'die'	*mati*	*pejah*
Adverbs	'now'	*saiki*	*sapunika*
	'shortly'	*mengko*	*mangké*
	'far'	*adoh*	*tebih*
	'near'	*cedhak*	*celak*

prepositions, e.g. *ngoko ora, krama mboten* 'not'; *ngoko saka, krama saking* 'from'. Generally speaking, however, the grammar of the two varieties is the same. One exception is that in *ngoko* there are first person and second person clitic pronouns (*-ku* 'I, my', *-mu* 'you, yours') as well as the free forms (*aku* 'I', *kowé* 'you'), but *krama* speech only has free forms (*kula* 'I', *panjenengan* 'you'). This difference is consistent with the tendency for *krama* to be slow, measured, and long-winded, and for *ngoko* to be fast, terse, and pithy.

Table 7.5 gives a few examples of *ngoko* and *krama* variants from open word classes. As you can see, they are typically common items of core vocabulary. One must bear in mind, however, that many common words have no special *krama* forms.

In a true sense, *ngoko* is a Javanese person's "first language". It is purely personal, making no adjustments or special concessions to the presence of an

Table 7.6. Sasak speech styles

Low	Wah-m	mangan	kamu?
Mid	Wah-m	medaran	side?
High	Sampun-m	majengan	pelinggih?
	already-you	eat	you
	'Have you eaten?'		

addressee. *Krama* can be regarded as a kind of "second language" (cf. Siegel 1986: 17), both in the sense that it is learned after *ngoko* and also in the sense that it is an "other-oriented" way of speaking. As one might expect from this analogy, not every Javanese gains the same level of mastery of refined, high *krama*. In practice this is the prerogative of the educated and aristocratic. In many villages a low *basa* variant is fully adequate for the purposes of polite conduct (cf. Errington 1998: 44–6).

Speech levels also exist in smaller and less well-known languages, such as Sasak, spoken by about 2.5 million speakers on the Indonesian island of Lombok (Austin and Nothofer 2000). As in Javanese, many common Sasak words have up to three variant forms at different speech levels (high, mid, and low), so that some common sayings, such as 'Have you eaten?', appear in three quite different forms; see Table 7.6. Again as in Javanese, there is some overlap between the levels. For example, the word *wah* 'already' is shared between low and mid levels, and clitic endings (such as -*m* 'you') have a neutral status, being used with all three levels.

In Sasak, there are different style-level forms for only about 180 words, so from a formal point of view the Javanese and Sundanese systems are much more complex. On the other hand, in the larger languages the usage conditions for the different style levels are a bit simpler and more uniform. For example, though the choice of high level is primarily conditioned by the need to show respect for the addressee, once this level is chosen it remains constant in Javanese and Sundanese, even when speaking about one's own actions and possessions; but in the Sasak system, high words are never used about one's own actions and possessions. Another important difference is that in Java the speech-level system is supposed to be known and used by everyone, whereas in Sasak it is primarily used by the *menak* (noble) class. Differences like these remind us that similar linguistic features can serve rather different social purposes in different cultures and societies.

7.2.2 Speech styles in Korean

Korean is notable for the fact that its speech styles (*che*) are distinguished primarily by a large set of verb-final endings (suffixes) which have different forms for different sentence types—declarative, imperative, interrogative.

Table 7.7. Korean speech styles

hayla-che—plain *Bi ga o-nda* 'it is raining'	Used by parents to children, by elders to children up to high-school age, with close friends except if they are middle-aged or older.
banmal-che—banmal *Bi ga o-a* (→ *wa*) 'it is raining'	Very similar to plain style but doesn't imply that the addressee is young; it shows a little more social distance and reserve than plain style.
hage-che—familiar *Bi ga o-ne* 'it is raining'	Used when addressee is below the speaker in age or social rank but not enough to use *banmal* or plain; the speaker is showing his authority but at the same time indicating that he wants to treat the addressee with 'consideration and courtesy'; used almost exclusively by and with males.
haeyo-che—polite *Bi ga o-ayo* (→ *wayo*) 'it is raining'	Used when addressee is a superior or someone else one wishes to treat with reserve; it is the most frequently heard style, used 'in almost any situation where polite language is called for'; also used by teachers addressing the class as a whole; morphologically, an addition *-yo* to *banmal* style.
hapsyo-che—formal *Bi ga o-bnita* 'it is raining'	Used in sharply asymmetrical power situations, e.g. with much older relatives, in a job interview, reporting to a superior officer. Also used in speeches to large audiences, news and weather reports, and in much advertising; it can be mixed with polite style.

Our description in this section is based on Lee and Ramsey (2000: 249–72). There are five speech styles (*che*) in common oral use, as shown in Table 7.7, and another style, *hao-che* (semi-formal), not shown in the table. Except for *banmal* (literally 'half language'), the Korean names for the speech styles are based on imperative forms of the verb *hada-* 'do'. These names have not been made up by linguists but are traditional Korean ones, still in daily use. For example:

(**181**) *Uri neun seoro hage-haneun sai.*
'We have a *hage*-speaking relationship with each other.'

(**182**) *Nugu hante banmal eul haneun geo ya?*
'Who do you think you're speaking *banmal* to?'

People who have used polite language with each other switch to *banmal* when they become close. This is called *mal eul noh neunda* 'putting down the language' or *neo-na haneun sai ga doenda* 'getting on *neo-na* (you-I) terms'.

In spoken Korean, the polite style and *banmal* style have been described as "the twin pillars of the speech-style system of modern Korean" (Lee and Ramsey 2000: 260). No doubt this is partly because the form of the polite style is derived from that of *banmal* by simply adding *-yo*. In written Korean, the main contrast is between plain style and formal. Plain is used when writing to a general audience, though the endings used in the written form are not always the same as those used in speech.

As for the usage conditions, they are complex and shifting rapidly with changing social attitudes and values. Generally speaking, age is a dominant factor. "In Korea," as Lee and Ramsey (2000: 268) put it, "age influences not only the language, but all aspects of life." A few years are enough to make a difference; one could not speak *banmal* style with someone more than three or four years older than oneself. It makes sense then, that:

[t]o a degree that can be embarrassing to Westerners, Koreans are interested in knowing a person's age. Koreans ask and freely reveal their ages and they make a display of seniority. In a fight, a frequently used retort is *myeoch sal inde, geonbang-jige guneunya* 'How old are you, that you're acting like such a smart-aleck?'

It's not just a matter of relative age differences either. As they grow older, even siblings begin to use polite language between each other. The age of marriage is an important benchmark, so that as the age of marriage gradually goes up there is a delay in the age at which Koreans become more "serious and formal".

Choice of speech style essentially depends on the speaker's relationship to the addressee, or more precisely on the attitudes a speaker wishes to "project" about the addressee. As mentioned in Chapter 1, Korean also has a well-developed system of honorification, i.e. a system for expressing respectful attitudes towards third parties; but we will not describe this in any further detail here.

7.3 The Japanese honorific system

The Japanese honorific system is deserving of special treatment for three main reasons. From a formal point of view, it is one of the most elaborated honorific systems in any language, comparable in complexity to that of Korean. From a sociolinguistic point of view, the details of the system show fascinating differences and similarities vis-à-vis Korean, reflective of the values and structures of Japanese society; plus, the changing patterns of usage in honorific speech can be seen to reflect changes in Japanese society. Finally, the Japanese system has been extensively studied and described, both in indigenous Japanese scholarship and in Western-inspired socio-linguistic models. The treatment in this section is heavily indebted to Inoue (1979), Coulmas (1992), and Maynard (1997).

7.3.1 Outline of the system

As shown in Figure 7.2, three major types of Japanese honorifics are normally identified: *teinei-go* 'polite expressions', *sonkei-go* 'honouring expressions', and *kenjoo-go* 'humbling expressions'. As with Korean, the polite expressions are addressee-related and expressed primarily by the form of the verb. The copula verb has a special polite form, *desu* (as well as *da* and *dearu*), and there is a polite suffix (-*masu*, in present tense) which can be used with any other verb. Because of these morphological features, the polite style is often referred to as "*desu/masu* style".

We will concentrate here on the "referent-related" honouring and humbling expressions. Despite the high-flown terminology—Coulmas (1992) describes labels like 'honouring' and 'humbling' as "pompous"—it is essential to realize that honorifics are an integral part of everyday usage in Japanese. They are not just stylistic frills which can easily be left out. Speakers may not always use them "correctly" according to the normative standards (see below), but they simply cannot omit them, if only because to do so would render many utterances incomprehensible or provoke misunderstanding. The two main social factors which determine the proper use of honorifics are relative status (interrelated with gender) and group membership, i.e. the distinction between one's "in-group" and "out-group" (Japanese *uchi* 'inside' vs. *soto* 'outside'). Status and gender are social parameters which are familiar enough, but the same cannot be said of the in-group/out-group or *uchi/soto* distinction. Nonetheless, it is of great importance to the operation of the honorific system and to Japanese society at large (cf. Bachnik and Quinn 1994).

One way of thinking about the *uchi/soto* distinction is to see it as analogous to the distinction between one's own family and everyone else. The family is probably the prototypical, and the strongest, in-group in Japanese

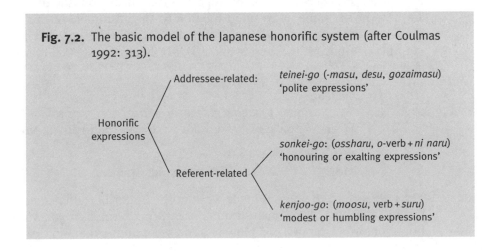

Fig. 7.2. The basic model of the Japanese honorific system (after Coulmas 1992: 313).

Honorific expressions

Addressee-related: *teinei-go* (-*masu*, *desu*, *gozaimasu*) 'polite expressions'

Referent-related

sonkei-go: (*ossharu*, o-verb + *ni naru*) 'honouring or exalting expressions'

kenjoo-go: (*moosu*, verb + *suru*) 'modest or humbling expressions'

society. We identify with the members of our own family. The implication is
that as far as honorifics are concerned, one treats members of one's own
family in the same way as one treats oneself. Hence, just as one uses modest
or humble forms when referring to oneself, so one uses modest or humble
forms when referring to members of one's own family. In Japan the notion
of in-group extends well beyond the family, taking in also the following
main groups: teachers and their students (school and university), and
salaried workers (blue-collar and white-collar) in business and industrial
firms of all sizes. Hence, a teacher would use modest expressions to talk
about his or her own students to teachers from other schools or to prospective employers (while the students are enrolled, that is, not after
graduation). Similarly, a company employee would use modest expressions
to talk about people in the same company to a person who works
for another company. Interestingly, not all occupations consider themselves
as belonging to in-groups, so far as honorific language is concerned. For
instance, doctors who work at hospitals are full-time salaried employees,
but they are not group-oriented. Similarly, though university professors
regard their students as members of their in-group, they do not necessarily
consider other staff at their universities as part of their group. We cannot
pursue the basis for these distinctions here.

The general principles behind the honorific system can be summarized as:
(i) use modest (humbling) expressions about people in one's own in-group
and respectful (honouring) expressions about outsiders, and (ii) use
respectful (honouring) expressions about those of higher status or social
position than oneself. For example, within an in-group one would use
respectful expressions for people who are older than oneself or who are
higher up in the hierarchy of an organization. What happens if these two
principles conflict? For example, how does a secretary refer to his or her boss
in response to a customer's query? The boss is higher in the hierarchy of the
organization (hence deserving of respectful treatment), but the two of them
are both in the same in-group in relation to the customer. In this kind of
situation, the in-group vs. out-group distinction takes precedence. For
example, supposing the boss's name is Mr Mori, the secretary's answer
might be:

(183) ⎰ a. *Buchoo*
       ⎱ b. *Mori*

⎰ a. *Buchoo*
⎱
          wa   tadaima gaishutsu shite   ori-mas-u.
          TOP   now   go out   do:GER be:HUM-POL-NONPAST

⎰ a. The department head
⎱ b. Mori   is out at the moment.

The reference to the boss is made without the honorific suffix -*san*, i.e. it is
just plain *buchoo* 'department head' or *Mori* (not *buchoo-san* or *Mori-san*).
For a junior person in a company to address a senior person in this fashion

would imply unacceptable intimacy and equality, but referring to some-one using a bare name merely indicates group membership. Similarly, suppose I want to tell someone from outside my family about my father's state of health. Although my father is older than and senior to me, I will not refer to him using an honouring expression. Because we belong to the same group, a humbling expression is called for. So I might say, for example, the sentence in (184) below, where the verb *ori-* 'be' is a humble form.

(184) *Chichi wa   genkide ori-mas-u.*
father TOP healthy be:HUM-POL-NONPAST
'(My) father is healthy.'

To ask about the health of your father, I would have to say either (185) or (186) below. Sentence (185) can be used between two friends, and (186) would be used if the hearer is, for example, my teacher or supervisor.

(185) *O-too-san   wa o-genki   des-u   ka.*
RESP-father-HON TOP RESP-health be:POL-NONPAST QUES

(186) *O-too-san   wa o-genkide   irasshai-mas-u   ka.*
RESP-father-HON TOP RESP-healthy be:HON-POL-NONPAST QUES
'Is (your) father healthy?'

As with Korean, gender is also relevant to honorific use. Generally speaking, women are expected to use more elaborate honorific expressions. Put another way, to achieve the same level of honorific effect, women are required to use a higher degree of linguistic formality than men (cf. Ide et al. 1986). However, it should also be noted that the differences between male and female speech decrease as one goes up the social hierarchy and as the overall politeness level increases (Coulmas 1992: 312).

Control over the complex honorific system is by no means automatic or effortless for the Japanese. As with Korean, it is difficult for native speakers too, and is the subject of countless popular guide books, official memorandums, in-service training, "speech clinics", and even radio and television shows, all of which are designed to help people improve their mastery of honorific speech. Many regional dialects of Japanese don't have the very elaborate honorific system described in section 7.3.2 below.

Honorific speech is heavily subject to prescriptive or normative attitudes; and interestingly enough, many Japanese linguists and other highly quali-fied language academics actively support and participate in the norm-setting exercises. Coulmas (1992: 301) notes in this connection:

there is a long-standing tradition of language cultivation in Japan which has always been supported by language experts who have never been affected by the modern Western credo that linguists should discover rather than stipulate norms, and who believe that language is both a natural asset and a deliberately created instrument. This tradition is associated with the notion of *gengo seikatsu* 'the life of language'. ... [L]anguage guidance and the normative attitudes towards linguistic usage are integral parts of the sociolinguistic landscape of Japan.

Appropriate use of honorific language is considered to be the mark of good education and good upbringing. An opinion poll by the national broadcasting station NHK revealed that 75 per cent of the Japanese respondents wished to improve their command of honorific language (Coulmas 1992: 302).

7.3.2 The mechanics of honouring and humbling

We will now see how the system works by taking a sentence and changing parts of it using honouring and humbling expressions. Sometimes the effect is achieved by lexical differentiation. That is, there may be two or more words which convey essentially the same meaning except that one is neutral and the other(s) honouring or humbling. Many kinship terms exist in pairs, with the honouring variant being used for people outside the speaker's own family. Table 7.8 lists a few of the verbs which have different forms.

When no lexical differentiation is available, the same distinctions can be signalled by morphosyntactic means: by using an auxiliary verb—*naru* (lit. 'become') for honouring, *suru* (lit. 'do, make') for humbling—and simultaneously adding an honorific prefix *o-* to the main verb stem. Thus, the pattern [*o*-verb + *ni naru*] functions as an honouring form, and [*o*-verb + *suru*] functions as a humbling form. There are also more complex variants which employ passive verb forms and auxiliary uses of the words for 'give' and 'receive'.

Inoue (1979) starts her description with the straightforward example in (187), which assumes that the speaker is equal in status to the people being talked about. Here is no need for either honouring or humbling expressions. The speaker simply adds the respectful suffix -*san* to the names of the referents. Depending on the relationship to the addressee, the speaker can either use the polite verb ending -*mashi* or be informal and not use it (e.g. if the addressee is a good friend).

Table 7.8. Lexical differentiation of referent-related honorific levels (after Coulmas 1992: 314)

Meaning	Neutral	Honouring	Humble
'say'	*iu*	*ossharu*	*moosu*
'go'	*iku*	*irassharu*	*mairu*
'do'	*suru*	*nasaru*	*itasu*
'eat'	*taberu*	*meshiagaru*	*itadaku*

(187) *Sakai-san   ga   Suzuki-san   ni   chizu-o*
Sakai-HON SUBJ Suzuki-HON for map-OBJ
{
a. *kaki-mashi-ta.*
draw-POL-PAST
b. *kai-ta.*
draw-PAST
}

'Mr Sakai drew a map for Mr Suzuki.'

If the speaker has considerably lower status than Sakai, for instance, if he or she is much younger than Sakai, it would be appropriate to use a more respectful honouring expression. The verb phrase *o-kaki ni nari-mashi-ta* consists of a respectful prefix *o-* followed by the verb *kak-* 'write/draw', which is followed by *ni* 'for/to', and *nar-* (lit. 'to become') with the polite verb ending in the past tense *-mashi-ta*. Again, the speaker can omit the polite verb ending if the addressee is someone with whom he or she can be informal.

(188) *Sakai-san   ga   Suzuki-san   ni   chizu-o*
Sakai-HON SUBJ Suzuki-HON for map-OBJ

o-kaki   ni   {
a. *nari-mashi-ta.*
become-POL-PAST
RESP-draw   for   b. *nat-ta.*
become-PAST
}

'Mr Sakai came to draw a map for Mr Suzuki.'
(or: 'It came about that Mr Sakai drew a map for Mr Suzuki.')

When Sakai, the person who did the drawing, has considerably lower status than Suzuki, the speaker would use a humbling expression *o*-verb stem *su-*. The expression *o-kaki shi-mashi-ta* consists of the respectful prefix *o-*, *kak-* 'draw', and the irregular verb *su-* 'do' (which takes the form *shi-* before *mas-* or *-ta*). The speaker is showing respect toward Suzuki by humbling Sakai, rather than honouring Suzuki. Such a sentence sounds more natural if the high status of Suzuki is made explicit using an honorific title such as *sensei* 'teacher' or *shachoo* 'president'.

(189) *Sakai-san   ga   Suzuki-san   ni   chizu-o*
Sakai-HON SUBJ Suzuki-HON for map-OBJ

o-kaki   {
a. *shi-mashi-ta.*
do-PAST
RESP-draw   b. *shi-ta.*
do-PAST
}

'Mr Sakai undertook the drawing of a map for Mr Suzuki.'

These options can be further elaborated by use of so-called "donatory verb" constructions (Maynard 1997: 124–9; Tsujimura 1996: 334–44). These are auxiliary verb constructions using various words for 'give' and 'receive', which allow the speaker to convey a sense of affinity with either

Table 7.9. Verbs of giving and receiving in Japanese

	Plain	Honorific
'give to me'	kureru	kudasaru
'give to someone'	ageru	sashiageru
'receive'	morau	itadaku

the actor or the undergoer individual. The system depends on the exist-ence of the set of verbs listed in Table 7.9. In standard Japanese (though not in all dialects), a distinction is drawn between 'giving to me' (*kureru*) and 'giving to someone' (*ageru*). Both these verbs, as well as *morau* 'receive', have honorific variants. There is also a humbling verb (*yaru*) for giving to a person (or animal) lower in status than oneself (not indicated in the table).

Interestingly, the verbs for 'giving to me' are extended to situations in which someone from my in-group is given something by someone from an out-group. For example, one would use *kureru* or *kudasaru* not only to say that someone outside the family gave me some sweets, but also to say that this person gave my brother or sister some sweets (the choice between *kureru* or *kudasaru* depending on the status of the giver). Similiarly, one would use *ageru* not only to say that I gave something to a friend, but also to say that my mother or father gave something to my friend.

The verbs for giving and receiving can be used as auxiliary verbs, with the main verb appearing in the gerundive *-te* form. When this happens, the choice of a verb for 'give to me' reflects the speaker's sense of identifi-cation or affinity with the recipient. For example, in (190) the use of *kureta* (lit. 'gave to me') is due to the speaker's identification with his or her younger sister. In this case the family provides an obvious in-group. In (191), the situation is the same except that the giver is a high-status person (a teacher) who warrants honorification; hence the honorific variant of the auxiliary is used. In both cases, the polite verb suffix *-mashi* could have been used preceding the past tense ending, depending on one's relationship with the addressee. The following examples are from Tsujimura (1996), with interlinear glosses and orthography adjusted to suit the conventions of this book.

(**190**) *Tanaka-san   ga   imooto   ni   okashi o   tukutte*
Tanaka-HON SUBJ younger.sister DAT sweets ACC make:GER
kure-ta.
give.to.me-PAST
'Mr Tanaka made some sweets for my younger sister.'

(191) *Sensei   ga   musuko ni   hon   o   misete*
teacher SUBJ son   DAT book OBJ show:GER
kudasa-tta.
gave.to.me:HON-PAST
'The teacher showed my son the book.'

The verbs for giving in general (*ageru* or *sashiageru*) are used when the speaker does not wish to show any special identification with the recipient, as in the following examples. The choice between them depends on whether the recipient is deserving of special honorification.

(192) *Tomodati ni   zisyo   o   misete   age-ta.*
friend   DAT dictionary OBJ show:GER give-PAST
'(I) showed my friend a dictionary.'

(193) *Haha   ga   sensei   ni   keeki o   tukutte   sashiage-ta.*
mother SUBJ teacher DAT cake OBJ make:GER give:HON-PAST
'Mother made a cake for my teacher.'

The verb for 'receive' also exists in two versions (*morau* and *itadaku*, plain and honorific, respectively), but the situation is a bit different, because even as a main verb it implies that the subject is oneself or someone from one's in-group; in a sense therefore the meaning is closer to 'I receive something from someone'. The choice of plain vs. honorific version depends on the status of the giver. The honorific form *itadaita* 'received' is used in (194) because the giver is my son's teacher. The overall meaning is difficult to convey in translation, because it implies that the subject (my son) benefited from the teacher's act.

(194) *Musuko ga   sensei   ni   sakubun   o   naoshite*
son   SUBJ teacher DAT composition OBJ correct:GER
itadai-ta.
receive:HON-PAST
'My son received his essay being corrected from this teacher.'
'From his teacher, my son received the correcting of his essay.'

7.3.3 Some social situations

Now let's look at a few cases where the situation establishes a power relationship between the interlocutors. In a customer–salesperson relationship the former has decisive power over the latter. The following would be a typical conversation at a department store. Notice how the asymmetry in power influences the language. The customer has a choice of three styles of speaking, from a very courteous style to a rather rude one, whereas a well-trained salesperson must remain courteous regardless of the customer. Here the salesperson is using *o*-verb stem *itas-* (using the humble form of *suru* 'do'). The same principle holds in the relationship between a doctor and a patient. The latter will always speak deferentially but the doctor has the option of speaking casually.

(195)

Customer: *Kore (wa)*
this   TOP

> a. *o-ikura*   *des-u*   *ka.*
>   RESP-how.much   be:POL-NONPAST   QUES
> b. *ikura*   *des-u*   *ka.*
>   how.much   be:POL-NONPAST   QUES
> c. *ikura.*
>   how.much

'How much is this?'

Salesperson: *Sore wa ichi-man-en   degozai-mas-u.*
that TOP ten-thousand-yen be:HUM-POL-NONPAST
'That is ten thousand yen.'

Customer: *Todokete*
deliver:GER

> a. *itadak-e-mas-u*   *ka.*
>   receive:HUM-POT-POL-NONPAST   QUES
> b. *kure-mas-u.*
>   give-POL-NONPAST
> c. *kure-ru.*
>   give-NONPAST

'Will you deliver?'

Salesperson: *Hai. O-todoke   itashi-mas-u.*
yes   RESP-deliver do:HUM-POL-NONPAST
'Yes, (we) will deliver.'

The next case is a situation in which a higher status person asks a person of lower status to do a personal favour. Instead of saying something like (196), which is a polite request, he or she would put his request in the form of a negative question such as (197), which is even more polite:

(196) *Kono tegami o   dashite   kudasa-i.*
this   letter   OBJ dispatch:GER give-NONPAST
'Please mail this letter.'
(lit.: 'Please give the dispatching of this letter.')

(197) *Kono tegami o   dashite   kudasai-masen ka.*
this   letter   OBJ dispatch:GER give-POL:NEG   QUES
'Won't you please mail this letter?'
(lit.: 'Won't you please give the dispatching of this letter?')

It is interesting to look at a social relationship which has undergone a big change of image in postwar Japan: the relationship between government officials and the public. Until the end of WW II, Japanese government officials, from top bureaucrats to police on the beat, were regarded as keepers of the power and authority of government, and thus they had a strong tendency to speak down to the citizens of the country. Since the end of the war, government officials have become public servants. While people speak to them using polite expressions because they receive services, the government officials are expected to speak courteously in return. They use polite expressions, although they need not use humbling ones.

Seniority (respect for age and rank) is another aspect of Japanese society where there has been a considerable change in the attitudes over the past thirty years, along with changes in family structure itself. Traditional Japanese families had a vertical structure based on seniority. A large number of family members lived together, with children relating not only to their parents but also to grandparents and other relatives as well. The oldest son was the principal inheritor of family property and had a special responsibility to oversee family affairs. Today, only 25 per cent of Japanese households live with grandparents and other relatives. Over 60 per cent are nuclear families. The average size of those nuclear families is between three and four, and the oldest son no longer has the privilege or responsibility of being the principal inheritor. Ironically, while the corporate structure, which is modelled after the family, retains a highly vertical structure, the family itself has lost much of its traditional hierarchy. The style of speaking adopted by the younger people to their elders, within the family and to society in general, has become much less deferential and far more egalitarian in recent years. Between husband and wife, too, there is variation, but with the younger generation, styles of speech are much more equal.

7.4 Communicative styles

Everyone knows that in different societies people not only speak different languages and dialects but use them in radically different ways. Throughout this book, we have seen numerous examples of speech practices in East and Southeast Asian languages which have no direct counterparts in English. However, it is also possible to see cultural factors influencing how people speak at a much broader level; as, for example, when we say that in many contexts Japanese people speak in a more "indirect" way than English speakers, or that in some contexts Chinese people will speak in a more "direct" way than English speakers. When we try to describe culturally preferred ways of speaking at this level, we are entering the area which is often referred to as the study of communicative style or discourse style.

7.4.1 What are cultural scripts?

As in all cross-cultural studies, we are immediately faced with a problem. How is it possible to describe a culture from the outside, using a foreign language, without that foreign language (e.g. English) imposing its own conceptual categories on the culture being described? To get around this problem we will adopt the "cultural scripts" approach, which has emerged from the cross-linguistic semantic research of Anna Wierzbicka and colleagues (Wierzbicka 1994a; 1994b; 1994c; 2003; Goddard and Wierzbicka 1997; 2002). The main idea is that we should frame our descriptions in maximally simple terms (semantic primes) which are shared between languages, e.g. meanings like PEOPLE, SOMEONE, SOMETHING, THIS, SAY, THINK, WANT, KNOW, GOOD, BAD, NOT. As we will see, it is possible to achieve a surprising degree of precision using this apparently simple metalanguage.

A "cultural script", then, is a hypothesis about culture-specific attitudes, assumptions, or norms which is spelt out in semantic primes. For example, the script below is intended to capture a cultural norm which is characteristically (though not exclusively) Japanese.

[people think like this:]
if something bad happens to someone because of me
I have to say something like this to this person:
    'I feel something bad because of this'

This describes the often noted tendency of the Japanese to "apologize" very frequently and in a broad range of situations, but it does not rely on the English-specific verb 'apologize' which has no exact equivalent in many languages, including Japanese. The English word 'apologize' would also be misleading in implying a meaning component like 'I did something bad to you'. The so-called "Japanese apology" does not presuppose such a component. One is expected to do it whenever one's action has led to someone else suffering harm or inconvenience, no matter how indirectly. The script above is therefore more accurate, as well as being readily translatable into Japanese. Cultural scripts are an improved method for stating the kind of "rules for speaking" which are invoked in other traditions in discourse and culture studies, such as the ethnography of communication and cross-cultural pragmatics (Gumperz and Hymes 1972; Bauman and Sherzer 1974; Blum-Kulka et al. 1989; Clyne 1994).

In the rest of this chapter we will look at a case study of communicative style in the Malay culture of Malaysia (Goddard 1997; 2000). I hasten to add that Malay culture has not been chosen because it is a typical East Asian or Southeast Asian culture. There is no "typical" East Asian or Southeast Asian culture. The communicative styles of Malay, Chinese, and Japanese (for example) are as different as those of English, French, and German.

7.4.2 High-level cultural scripts of Malay

As described in section 3.1.2, the primary cultural influences on mainstream Malay culture in Malaysia are the Islamic religion and the indigenous *adat* 'custom, rules for life' tradition. Islam is noted for its insistence on absolute submission to the will of God (Allah) and for offering its followers a complete system of guidance for behaviour and morality. *Adat* too is deeply concerned with what is *patut* 'proper' or *sesuai* 'appropriate, fitting' in different everyday life situations. The twin influences of Islam and *adat* largely explain why one of the most prominent concerns of mainstream Malay culture is knowing how to behave in particular circumstances. We can see this concern reflected in the high profile of *nilai* 'values' in Malaysian public discourse (quite striking from an Australian perspective) and in the didactic themes of Malay literature, both classical and modern (Muhammad Haji Salleh 1991: 20–1; Banks 1987). Political and religious leaders are a constant source of advice (*nasihat*) and guidance (*panduan*), whether at the mosque or through newspaper columns, TV programmes, and the like. Within the family, *orang tua* 'old people' such as grandparents and other older relatives, and one's *ibu bapa* 'mother (and) father', are a specially valued source of advice.

A very general or high-level script of Malay culture (shared, no doubt, by many other cultures) can be stated as below (Goddard 1997; 2000). At first glance, this script might appear obvious or even tautological, but really it embodies an "absolutist" orientation about ethics and morality which is quite different from that of mainstream Western culture.

> [people think like this:]
> it is good if a person knows at all times what it is good to do
> it is not good if a person doesn't know at all times what it is good to do

There is also abundant evidence for a number of scripts concerned with the concept of *balasan*, a noun derived from the verb *balas* 'to return (to someone), return in kind'. Numerous *peribahasa* convey the message that a person's deeds, whether good or bad, will be repaid "in kind" (cf. section 7.1). A school compendium of *peribahasa* on *nilai-nilai* 'values' sums up the message as: *Setiap perbuatan, baik atau jahat, akan ada balasan* 'Every deed, whether good or wrong, has its *balasan*' and *Budi baik dibalas baik, jahat dibalas jahat* 'Good treatment of others is *balas* with good, bad is *balas* with bad' (Abdullah and Ainon 1995: 17–18, 28). From sayings like these, and from consultations with native speakers, we arrive at the following script. One particular way in which good behaviour is likely to be rewarded derives from the cultural imperative to *balas budi* 'return good treatment, return kindness'; but as the script suggests, good and bad behaviour can be rewarded or punished by all kinds of events.

> [people think like this:]
> good things will happen to a person if this person does good things
> bad things will happen to a person if this person does bad things

Now consider the script below. It corresponds to the common sayings *fikir dulu* 'think first', *fikir panjang* 'think long', *fikir dua kali* 'think twice', etc. It is easy to see how this makes perfect sense against the background of the *balasan* script given above. It is also connected with, and in a sense supported by, the cultural importance attributed to *kesabaran* 'patience, forbearance', described in section 3.4.1.

[people think like this:]
I don't want something bad to happen because I do something
because of this, when I want to do something
it is good if I think about it for some time before I do it

An immediate consequence for communicative style is the imperative to be careful about what one says: *Berhati-hati bila bercakap* 'be careful when you speak'. One should *jaga mulut* 'mind/guard (one's) mouth', lest *rosak badan kerana mulut* 'the body suffers because of the mouth' (Abdullah and Ainon 1995: 14, 73, 75). In particular, one should think about what one is going to say before speaking. *Kalau cakap fikirlah sedikit dulu* 'if you're going to speak, think a little first'. All this implies the following script:

[people think like this:]
it is not good if when I say something to someone, this person feels
    something bad
because of this, when I want to say something to someone it is good to
    think about it for some time before I say it

This script is connected with the fact, invariably remarked upon by cultural commentators, that Malay culture greatly values the capacity of a person to be sensitive, considerate, and understanding of others, and therefore always to speak with care lest the other person has his or her feelings hurt (*tersinggung*). Wilson's (1967: 131f.) list of Malay values includes: "showing consideration and concern, anticipating the other... and, above all, being sensitive to the other person". Many traditional sayings enjoin people to watch over or look after other people's feelings. Australian insensitivity on this score has been identified by Malaysia's former Prime Minister, Dr Mahathir Mohamad, as one cause of the perennially strained relations between the two countries. In "Asian culture", Dr Mahathir remarked, "people are reluctant to pass comment on others. ... [We] have a way of making our views known, without hurting feelings" (ABC Radio, 2 December 1995).

Obviously this makes it very difficult to voice criticisms directly. At a simple everyday level, suppose that I have done something to hurt a Malay friend's feelings and she wants to say something about it to me (instead of putting it aside). The most explicit thing she might feel comfortable saying would be something like the sentence (198) below (the name is used in place of a pronoun). Notice that the evaluation of my behaviour is indirect (terms like *buruk* 'bad' and *tak baik* 'not good' are not used), and balanced by the favourable evaluation that I am usually *ramah* 'agreeable, affable'.

(198) *Malam Cliff lain dari biasa. Selalunya Cliff tak macam begitu selalunya Cliff lebih ramah.*
'Yesterday you [Cliff] were different from normal. You're usually not like that, you're usually more agreeable.'

At a more public level, the prospect of *malu* 'shame, embarrassment' (section 3.4.1) rears its ugly head, along with a whole cluster of associated concepts concerned with what other people think about one, such as *maruah* 'dignity', *nama* 'reputation', and *air muka* 'face' (lit. 'water face'). Observers of Malay culture have often remarked on the salience of such concepts in interpersonal interaction and in public discourse. For example:

The social value system is predicated on the dignity of the individual and ideally all social behaviour is regulated in such a way as to preserve one's own amour propre and to avoid disturbing the same feelings of dignity and self-esteem in others. (Vreeland et al. 1977: 117)

The cultural history of *nama* as a key concept in the development of modern Malaysian politics has been traced in persuasive detail by Milner (1982; 1995). One is well-advised to be careful about saying anything publicly which could lower another person's *maruah* or *nama*, especially if that person is in a position to retaliate (or has supporters who are likely to do so). An offence against a person's *maruah* or *nama* is not likely to be forgotten or forgiven. There is a connection here with the potent Malay concept of *dendam* 'revenge, payback' (Goddard 1996). To capture this piece of cultural common knowledge, we can propose the following script:

[people think like this:]
it is not good to say something about someone if other people might think something bad about that person because of it
if I do this, something bad might happen to me because of it

7.4.3 Scripts about expressing what one wants

An area of potential conflict in any culture has to do with what individuals want (or don't want) each other to do. What if A wants to do something, but B doesn't want A to do it? What if A wants B to do something which B doesn't want to do? Different cultures have evolved different "solutions" to such potential problems. In some parts of the world, the solution is that

people don't mind an overt clash of wills. It may even be welcomed in the
interests of some other cultural value, such as intensity or truthfulness in
personal interaction, or because openness of expression is valued for its own
sake. In traditional Malay society, an overt clash of wills is something to be
avoided. Part of being brought up Malay is learning to anticipate others'
wishes and, as far as possible, to accommodate them. Conversely, people
feel constrained from voicing their own wants. For a Malay it can be hard to
say outright what he or she wants even if it is obvious that the interlocutor
wants to know. A Malay friend illustrated this for me by relating how she
once unintentionally offended her husband's grandfather, who is European.
He had offered her some food and when she did not accept it at once, he
asked her pressingly "Do you want it or not?" Though she did in fact want
it, the closest she could come to saying so was "not really", which he mis-
took for diffidence.

The following script seems indicated. The phrasing inhibits only the
expression of self-interested wishes. There is no proscription against
expressing wishes of other sorts; for instance, giving directions to children or
junior family members, helping to organize communal activities, or in giving
instructions in accordance with one's role as a teacher, superior officer, or
the like.

> [people think like this:]
> when I want someone to do something good for me it is not good to say to
>   this person:
> 'I want you to do this'

Consider also the following scenario, volunteered by the same Malay
consultant, about how she might speak to her husband if she wanted him to
make dinner that evening. Rather than a direct request, or an Anglo-style
hint such as saying how much she enjoys her husband's cooking, she might
say something like: "Are you hungry?" It was explained that this would be
effective because her husband would realize that if she had intended to do it
herself she would have simply said "What would you like for dinner?" From
an Anglo point of view this is pretty subtle stuff, but it makes sense on the
assumption that Malay interlocutors are actively "tuned in" to divining each
other's desires.

The cultural imperative to avoid friction, i.e. not to do or say anything
which would clash with or interfere with the other person, creates an obvious
problem when you don't want to do something your interlocutor wants you
to do. Ideally such difficult moments do not arise, but when they do, the
basic strategy is to avoid saying the uncomfortable thing while still saying
something else. As one Malay informant put it: "Don't say it straight,
go around." The other person will understand and not press the matter.
This strategy is summed up in the following script.

[people think like this:]
when someone wants me to do something
   if I don't want to do it, it is not good to say to this person:
     'I don't want to do it'
   it is good to say something else

7.4.4 *Menghormati* 'showing respect'

It is very important in Malay culture to *menghormati* 'show respect' for parents (*ibu bapa*), old people (*orang tua*) generally, and for anyone who has a higher ranking in society. This concept—a cultural key word—is so revealing that it will repay an excursion into lexical semantics. Grammatically *(meng)hormati* is a verb formed from the root *hormat*, which exists as a noun in expressions such as *memberi hormat* 'give respect', *menerima hormat* 'receive respect', and *tanda hormat* '(a) sign of respect'. It can be appropriately translated not only as 'respect' and 'respectful behaviour', but also as 'deference' and 'proper politeness'; as Kessler (1992: 147) puts it, "deference that is owed to a social position". Among the *tanda hormat* 'signs of respect' there are gestures such as *tunduk kepala* 'bowing the head', *tabik* 'greeting with an honorific term of address', and *undur ke tepi dan memberi jalan lalu* 'moving to one side and giving way'. There are also certain linguistic proprieties to be observed, such as avoiding the first person pronoun *aku* 'I', and second person pronouns *kau* and *awak* 'you' in favour of kin-terms, names, and honorifics (cf. section 1.8). In a range of other ways too, the junior person is supposed to be on their "best behaviour", including speaking in a soft and even tone of voice, not saying too much, not opposing or contradicting what the other person says. All these ideas are encapsulated in the following semantic explication: that one recognizes the "respected" person's higher standing, that one thinks well of him or her, and wants to avoid his or her disapproval, and that to this end one behaves in a deliberately selective way in terms of what one does, what one says, and how one says it.

   X *menghormati* person-Y
   X thinks good things about Y
   X thinks things like this about Y:
     Y is someone above me
     I don't want Y to think anything bad about me
   X wants Y to know this
   because of this, when X is with Y
     X does some things, X doesn't do some other things
     X says some things, X doesn't say some other things
     X says some words, X doesn't say some other words

(The phrasing 'Y is someone above me' reflects the natural Malay idiom for speaking about differences in social standing, which is based around a vertical dimension; for example, people can be said to occupy a *tinggi* 'high' or *rendah* 'low' position; rulers and leaders are said to be *di atas* 'above' their subjects or followers, who are in turn *di bawah* 'below' them.)

The normative scope of the *hormati* concept extends even wider than people of higher social standing and those who are older. Children are taught that it is important for people generally to *hormat-menghormati* 'respect each other'. How can this be explained? Partly, it seems, on the basis of another important traditional cultural principle—the injunction to *merendah diri* 'be humble' (lit.'lower oneself') before others, and, correspondingly, to avoid appearing *sombong* 'arrogant' at all costs. The following script is an attempt to make explicit the meaning behind this injunction. It is a bit tricky to state the conditions on this script. It doesn't apply within the family, because within the family the overriding principle is age: obviously, parents are not supposed to *merendah diri* with their children. Nor would it apply between a member of the aristocracy and one of the common people (*rakyat*); or between a boss and his or her subordinate. It seems to be a kind of default script, telling us what attitude to adopt in public with the vague category of *orang lain* 'other people'.

[people think like this:]
when I am with other people
it is good if these other people think like this about me:
  this person thinks good things about other people
  this person thinks like this:
    I am someone below these other people
    I don't want these people to think anything bad about me

In effect, this script enjoins one to deliberately *menghormati* 'show respect/deference' to *orang lain* 'other people' (an expression which would normally exclude people who live in the same household or others with whom one feels a strong sense of solidarity). It does not necessarily mean that one must actually think of oneself as 'below' others—only that one should try to convey this impression. Admittedly, this is a traditional value which is changing in modern times. An example from one of the works of the esteemed Malaysian cartoonist Lat (1980: 4–13) illustrates this well. Titled 'Brave New World', the story tells of a *kampung* 'village' boy who, like thousands before him, goes to stay with his cousin in the capital city, Kuala Lumpur. As he leaves the village his parents impress upon him: "You should NEVER be arrogant! Always be humble" and "Uphold the good name of our folks... always be humble." On his first night in KL, his cousin tells him "... and another thing, Mat. Don't be too soft... too humble! That's the trouble with our folks back home—too humble! Where does it get them? They're down with inferiority complex... In this town, if you're too humble... they're going to step on you."

7.4.5 Concluding remarks

Generally speaking, Malay discourse style tends to strike Westerners as pleasantly good-natured—even charming. Commentators often identify values such as "consideration", "sensitivity", "respect", "cooperation", and "harmony" as particularly important to the Malays. Many of the same terms, as it happens, are used about Japanese people and culture; and there is much more written in the pragmatics literature about Japanese than about Malay. In view of the similarities at the "global" level of description, it would be easy to jump to the conclusion that the underlying values and motivations are similar, but this would be a mistake, for Malay discourse style is rooted in Islamic values and in Malay tradition (*adat*), both of which are altogether alien to Japan.

A parting caveat should be made about the use of the term "script". Despite the possible connotations of the word, it is important to acknowledge that cultural scripts are not binding on individuals. Cultural norms may be followed by some of the people all of the time, and by all of the people some of the time, but they are certainly not followed by all of the people all of the time. Whether or not they are being followed in behavioural terms, however, cultural norms are always in the background as an interpretive framework against which people make sense of and assess other people's behaviours.

Key technical terms

auspicious words	humbling expression
cultural script	illocutionary particle
elaborate expression	*peribahasa*
honouring expression	speech style

Exercises

Chapter 1

1.1 Brush up on your geography. Identify the countries labelled 1–13 in map E.1 on the next page.

1.2 Examine these two sentences from Vietnamese. What typical features of mainland Southeast Asian languages do they show?

a. *Tuy   nghèo, nhưng anh thích giúp bạn.*
  though poor yet   he like help friend
  'Though he's poor, he still likes to help his friends.'

b. *Đêm qua ra   đứng bờ   ao.*
  night last go.out stand edge pond
  'Last night, I went to stand on the edge of the pond.'

1.3 Examine the following sentences from one of the minority languages of East Asia. (i) What do they show about the word order of this language? (ii) The examples show two features which are not typical of East Asian languages. What are they?

a. *Poro cise   ta horari.*
  big   house in live
  'He lives in a big house.'

b. *Tampe huci   orun ku-kore.*
  this   grandmother to   1SG-give
  'I gave this (to) grandmother.'

c. *Pon   pewrep tup ci-hok.*
  small bear   two 1PL-buy
  'We bought two small bears.'

1.4 On the basis of the following examples, describe how questions are formed in Tetum (Tetun Dili). (i) The data in A show information questions ("wh-questions"): identify the interrogative pronouns and say where they

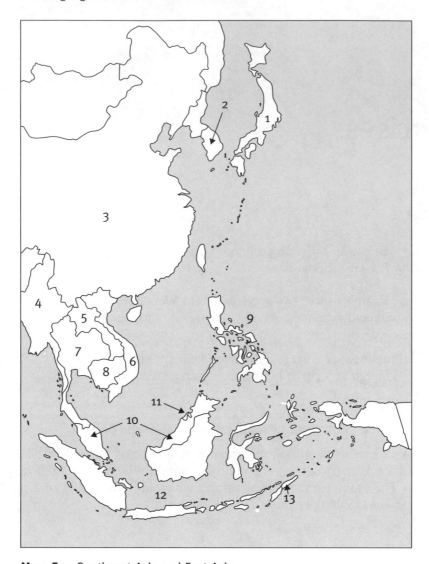

Map. E.1. Southeast Asia and East Asia.

are positioned in the sentence. (ii) The data in B show several different ways of forming polar ("yes/no") questions. Describe them.

A. information questions

a. *Sé   mak fó   hán imi?*
   who FOC give eat 2PL
   'Who fed you?'

b. *Nia iha   nebé?*
   3SG LOC where
   'Where is he?'

c. *O   hakarak saida?*
2SG want   what
'What do you want?'

d. *Ita   koalia ho sé?*
2SG:HON speak with who
'Who were you speaking with?'

B. polar questions

e. *Nia la   tanis?*
3SG not cry
'Didn't she cry?'

f. *Apá iha né ka?*
Dad LOC this or
'Is Dad here?'

g. *Ita   bót nia oan bele kose nehan ka lae?*
2SG:HON big POSS child can brush tooth or not
'Can your child brush her teeth?'

h. *Isin   manas la   iha?*
body hot   not there.is
'Is there no fever?'

i. *Ita   diak ka lae?*
2SG:HON good or not
'Are you well?'

j. *Imi sai ka lae?*
2PL exit or not
'Are you leaving?'

k. *Imi beik   ka?!*
2SG stupid or
'Are you stupid?!'

1.5 Examine the following sentences from Language Z. (i) Identify the classifier constructions. (ii) Identify the measure constructions. (iii) Describe the word order of a noun-phrase in Language Z, using the following labels: Adjective, Classifier, Measure, Demonstrative, Noun, Numeral. You will have to make some assumptions about combinations which do not appear in the data.

a. *Tua² maa⁴ hao¹ te¹ taai¹-taau⁵ kwa⁵.*
animal horse white that dead-return ASP
'That white horse has been very sick.'

b. *Haa³ buŋ¹ hou⁴-hon¹ moot⁶ lieu.*
five   basket grain-seed mouldy ASP
'The five baskets of grain have all gone mouldy.'

c. *Pi⁴   pai¹ su̱⁴ dai⁴ saam¹ som¹   maan¹ piaŋ¹.*
   sister-in-law go   buy ASP three armspread cloth beautiful
   'Sister-in-law bought three armspreads of beautiful cloth.'

d. *Te¹ kaai¹ saam¹ tua²   mu¹ te¹ pai¹ le.*
   he sell   three animal pig that ASP PRT
   'He sold those three pigs.'

1.6 The following passage shows some interactions in a Thai household. It is presented in English, except that the expressions used for addressing or referring to people are given in Thai (with English "translations" in parentheses). The characters are: *Jaew*: a girl in her last year of high school, Jaew's father, *Jate*, and mother, *Amporn*, Jaew's teacher, *Weera* (who is visiting the house), and *Jack*, Jaew's young brother. Study the usage of pronouns, kin-terms, and other expressions for personal address and reference. (i) Summarize the usage patterns for addressing or referring to someone while showing respect. (ii) Summarize the usage patterns for addressing or referring to someone junior or younger. (iii) Describe the usage of the Thai term *phîi*. (iv) Identify three ways in which the usage patterns in this passage differ from the description given in section 1.8. Note the following Thai words: *phɔ̂ɔ* 'father', *mêɛ* 'mother', *khruu* 'teacher'.

Father: Hullo *khun khruu* (teacher). What is *khun* (you) up to?
Teacher: Hullo, *khun* Jate. *Phŏm* (I) have come to talk with *khun* (you) about Jaew.
Father: Sure, come in.
Mother: Jaew, get a glass of water for *khun khruu* (teacher).
[Jaew goes to the kitchen. Her little brother is there.]
Jaew: Jack, *khun khruu* (teacher) came to see *phîi* (me).
Jack: Really. Does *phîi* (you) want *nŭu* (me) to go outside?
Jaew: Yes.
[Jaew goes back to the living room with the water.]
Jaew: *Khun khruu* (teacher), here's water.
Teacher: Jaew, we have been talking about *nŭu* (you). *Khruu* (I) told *phɔ̂ɔ nŭu* (father (of) you) and *mêɛ nŭu* (mother (of) you) about giving *nŭu* (you) a scholarship.
[A little later.]
Mother (to Jaew's father): *Phîi* Jate, can *phîi* (you) go and see what Jack is doing outside?
[Outside. Jack is playing ball with a friend.]
Father: Jack, can *nŭu* (you) come inside?
Jack (to his friend): *Chăn* (I) have to go now. You (*kɛɛ*) can keep the ball.

Chapter 2

2.1 Consider the following words from Language B. (i) What can one say about the phoneme inventory of the language? (ii) What can one say about the morphology of the language? (iii) Which language family is Language B most likely to belong to? Explain your reasons.

paredde	'singer'	*parmuruk*	'one who is angry'
edde	'sing'	*muruk*	'be angry'
parsuliŋ	'flute player'	*las*	'hot'
suliŋ	'play the flute'	*lumas*	'hotter'
sonaŋ	'happy'	*hicca*	'cheerful'
sumonaŋ	'happier'	*humicca*	'more cheerful'
daŋgur	'to throw'	*poŋgol*	'to break'
daŋguri	'to throw repeatedly'	*poŋgoli*	'to break several
bereŋ	'to look at'		things off, e.g. twigs
bereŋi	'to gaze at'		off a branch'

2.2 Examine the following phrases and sentences from Lao, Cantonese, and Hmong, from the point of view of the word order in the various constructions shown. (i) Describe the orderings found in these three languages. (ii) Are these orderings typical of the language families to which these languages belong?

Lao

khon² suung³	*huan² (khòòng³) khòòj⁵*		*juu¹ theng² phuu²*
person tall	house of I		at top mountain
'tall person'	'my house'		'on top of the mountain'

maa³ dam⁰ too³ khòòng³ khòòj⁵
dog black CL of I
'my black dog'

Cantonese

dākyi gáujái	*ngóh (ge) sailóu*		*jēung tói hahbihn*
cute puppy	I LP younger-brother		CL table underneath
'a cute puppy'	'my younger brother'		'under the table'

ngóh ge hāk gáu
I LP black dog
'my black dog'

Hmong

koj lub tsev	*zaub ntsuab*	*rau hauv vaj*
you CL house	vegetable green	at inside garden
'your house'	'green vegetable'	'in the garden'

kuv tug dev dub
I   CL   dog black
'my black dog'

2.3   Here are three sentences from a little-known minority language. What language family do you think it comes from, and why?

a. *Ka-nùu   niʔ ròol ʔa-tshúan.*
ISG:POSS-mother ERG food 3SG:S-cook
'My mother cooked the food.'

b. *Ka-fàr   niʔ thày ʔa-ka-kheʔ.*
ISG:POSS-sister ERG fruit 3SG:S-ISG:O-peel.for.INV
'My sister peels the fruit for me.'

c. *Hakha-ʔaʔ ʔa-ka-kal-piak-mii   ka-philʔ.*
Hakha-LOC 3SG:S-ISG:O-go-BENEF-REFL ISG:S-forget:INV
'I forgot that he went to Hakha for me.'

2.4   Examine the data below from Language M. It is given in IPA symbols, except that *y* stands for IPA /j/, i.e. a palatal glide, and *j* stands for IPA /ɟ/, i.e. a voiced palatal stop. The left-hand column gives a list of verb roots, while the right-hand column shows corresponding derived nominal forms. The derived forms all result from the application of a "nominalizing" affix with several allomorphs. (i) List the allomorphs of the nominalizing affix and explain the conditioning factors which determine when each is used, along with any other morphological process which may be involved. (ii) From a typological point of view, the data suggest that Language M comes from what region of East or Southeast Asia? Explain your reasons.

	Verb root		Derived nominal	
a.	*ŋuy*	'wear, use'	*nuŋuy*	'apparel, something used'
b.	*bantu*	'help'	*bunantu*	'help'
c.	*puɡɨt*	'make, fix'	*punuɡɨt*	'thing made'
d.	*tət*	'burn'	*tunuutət*	'something burnt'
e.	*pɔh*	'hit'	*punupɔh*	'hitting'
f.	*daom*	'roar, purr'	*dunaom*	'purr'
g.	*leŋ*	'pour'	*nuleŋ*	'something poured'
h.	*ɲuə*	'stretch out legs'	*nuɲuə*	'an extended, long part of a spinning wheel'
i.	*ba*	'bring'	*bunuba*	'something brought'
j.	*tumpoʔ*	'stack'	*tunumpoʔ*	'stack of rice sheaves'
k.	*nɔh*	'put in stocks'	*nunɔh*	'stocks'
l.	*canɛ*	'whet'	*cunanɛ*	'sharpness of a blade'
m.	*kɔh*	'cut, harvest'	*kunukɔh*	'cutting, harvesting'
n.	*publɔə*	'sell'	*punublɔə*	'thing sold'
o.	*siə*	'cut'	*sunuusiə*	'a cut'

p.	*maɲaŋ*	'be high'	*muɯnaɲaŋ*	'height'
q.	*yuə*	'order'	*nɯyuə*	'an order'
r.	*jawɯəp*	'answer'	*junawɯəp*	'an answer'
s.	*jaʔ*	'go'	*juɯnɯjaʔ*	'a way, path'

Chapter 3

3.1   A minority Language X has the following loan words from French. (i) In what part of East or Southeast Asia is this language most likely to be found? (ii) From the nature of the loan words, what can you deduce about the nature of the cultural contact between the French and speakers of Language X?

Language X		French	
bɵrô	'office'	*bureau*	'office'
kɵnong	'artillery'	*canon*	'artillery'
kɵphẽ	'coffee'	*café*	'coffee'
lɵgat	'map'	*la carte*	'map'
pɵtŏu	'boat'	*bateau*	'boat'
xɵlat	'lettuce'	*salade*	'salad'
prang	'French'	*français*	'French'
rɵdiô	'radio'	*radio*	'radio'
xak	'bag'	*sac*	'bag'
xup	'soup'	*soupe*	'soup'
buat	'canned food'	*boîte*	'can'

3.2   The data show some loan words which Language F has borrowed from a certain Sinitic language (Language E). Examine the data and answer the questions below. The symbol *c* stands for a palatal stop. Tone markings have not been shown for Language E, since tones were lost when the borrowing occurred. (i) Language E has some consonant phonemes—k^h, *c*, and c^h—which are not found in Language F. What happened to these consonants when they were adapted into the phonology of Language F? (ii) From the nature of the loan words, what can you deduce about the nature of the culture contact?

	Language F	Language E	
a.	*kintsai*	$k^h in\text{-}c^h ai$	'celery'
b.	*ditse*	*di-ci*	'second elder sister'
c.	*mami*	*maʔ-mi*	'soupy noodle dish with meat'
d.	*petsai*	$pe\textipa{ʔ}\text{-}c^h ai$	'Chinese cabbage'
e.	*humba*	*hoŋbaʔ*	'spicy meat dish'
f.	*sutsua*	$c^h o\text{-}cua$	'medicinal paper'
g.	*hikau*	*hi-kau*	'gold earring'
h.	*utau*	*o-tau*	'soy bean'
i.	*siyanse*	*cian-si*	'frying instrument'

j. *lumpia?*   *lun-pia?*   'vegetable and shrimp wrapped in dough'
k. *santo*   *c^{h}an-to*   'bamboo fishing raft'
l. *tiho*   *te-ho*   'gold bars'
m. *gintsam*   *gin-cam*   'goldsmith's chisel'

3.3 The following complex words and expressions are from Dehong Tai, a minority Tai language spoken in the Sino-Burmese border area of southwestern China. It contains examples of items from the following categories: (i) parallel compounds, (ii) head-modifier compounds, i.e. where one element modifies the meaning of the other, (iii) elaborate expressions, (iv) psycho-collocations. Allocate the words into these categories (some may be in two categories at the same time).

kaan^{6}xɔŋ^1 [work affair] 'work, affair, matter', *kɨp^1 mɨ^2* [nail hand] 'fingernail', *kə^{6}waan^1* [salt sweet] 'sugar', *po^{3}tsaɨ^6* [happy heart] 'be happy', *sop^{3}kat^5* [mouth capable] 'have a glib tongue', *məŋ^{2}kaŋ^{4}taŋ^{5}loŋ^1* [country wide mouth. of.river big] 'big place', *tso^{6}kɔn^{3}mɔn^{3}len^1* [life before pass ancestor] 'ancestors', *laat^5 taap^3* [speak.to answer] 'to answer', *tsaɨ^{6}yaau^2* [heart long] 'to be broad minded', *tsɔm^{2}tsaɨ^6* [put heart] 'to mind (doing), to take to heart', *kaaŋ^{6}wan^2* [middle day] 'during the day, daytime', *tsɔɨ^{6}thɛm^1* [to.help to.aid] 'to help, aid', *laɔ^{6}la^{1}pha^{1}tsan^2* [hill thick cliff steep] 'sheer precipice and overhanging rocks', *kaŋ^{6}tsaɨ^{6}laɨ^{2}xo^2* [centre heart inside throat] 'heart, innermost being'.

3.4 Examine the following data and describe how the future tense is formed in Tagalog.

	Non-future		Future	
a.	*lakad*	'walk'	*lalakad*	'will walk'
b.	*tawag*	'call'	*tatawag*	'will call'
c.	*sakay*	'ride'	*sasakay*	'will ride'
d.	*lubog*	'sink'	*lulubog*	'will sink'
e.	*bukas*	'open'	*bubukas*	'will open'
f.	*upo*	'sit'	*uupo*	'will sit'
g.	*lipad*	'fly'	*lilipad*	'will fly'
h.	*hiram*	'borrow'	*hihiram*	'will borrow'
i.	*tayo*	'stand'	*tatayo*	'will stand'
j.	*iyak*	'cry'	*iiyak*	'will cry'

3.5 Dulong/Rawang is a Tibeto-Burman language spoken on both sides of the China/Myanmar border, in Yunnan province and Kachin state, respectively. Consider the morpheme *-shì* in the following data. How would you describe its range of uses or functions? For your information, *v* stands for schwa, *ø* for an unrounded high back vowel, and *q* for glottal stop, but this is not relevant to the question.

a. *àng vdip-shì-ē*
   3SG hit-*shì*-NONPAST
   'He is hitting himself.'

b. *àng mýr zýl-shì-ē*
   3SG face wash-*shì*-NONPAST
   'He is washing his face.'

c. *àng nōl   tut-shì-ē*
   3SG fingernail cut-*shì*-NONPAST
   'He is cutting his fingernails.'

d. *àng vhō-shì-ē*
   3SG laugh-*shì*-NONPAST
   'He is laughing/smiling.'

e. *àng shvmō   shvt-shì-ē*
   3SG mosquito kill-*shì*-NONPAST
   'He is killing a mosquito on his body.'

f. *àng laqtūn   wīn-shì-ē*
   3SG clothing buy-*shì*-NONPAST
   'He is buying himself clothing.'

3.6   The following data from Ainu (Shizunai dialect) show the operation of a particular derivational morpheme. (i) What kind of words are produced by this derivational morpheme? (ii) The data show several variant forms (allomorphs). List them. (iii) What factors condition the occurrence of the different allomorphs?

	Base word		Derived word	
a.	*kore*	'give'	*korere*	'make (someone) give'
b.	*epakasnu*	'teach'	*epakasnure*	'make (someone) teach/tell'
c.	*nu*	'hear'	*nure*	'tell'
d.	*e*	'eat'	*ere*	'serve'
e.	*hopuni*	'get up'	*hopunire*	'wake/make someone get up'
f.	*nukar*	'see'	*nukare*	'show'
g.	*kor*	'have'	*kore*	'give'
h.	*kar*	'make'	*kare*	'make someone make'
i.	*ek*	'come'	*ekte*	'make someone come'
j.	*ahup*	'enter'	*ahupte*	'make someone enter'
k.	*wen*	'be bad'	*wente*	'destroy, ruin'
l.	*rikip*	'ascend'	*rikipte*	'make someone ascend'

3.7   Khmer (Cambodian) has a number of prefixes which appear on the verbal bases of many causative verbs. The prefixes are no longer productive. (i) On the basis of this data, describe the morphology of causative verbs in Khmer. (ii) What other changes take place when causative prefixes are added?

a. *rìəy* 'scattered'   *pra:y*   'to scatter'
b. *rìən* 'to learn'   *priən*   'to teach'
c. *ŋu:t* 'to bathe'   *pʰŋo:t* 'to bathe'
d. *caɲ*   'defeated'   *pʰcaɲ*   'to defeat'
e. *de:k* 'to go to bed'   *pʰde:k* 'to bed (someone)'
f. *rùəm* 'to gather'   *pʰrùəm* 'to round up'
g. *ŋɔəs* 'to hatch'   *pʰɲɔəs* 'to hatch (something)'
h. *cut*   'close'   *pʰcut*   'to join'
i. *cùm*   'to unite'   *prəcùm* 'to cause to unite'
j. *beh*   'to pick'   *prəbeh* 'to keep on picking'
k. *kʰam* 'to bite'   *prəkʰam* 'to bite one another'
l. *mɤl*   'to look'   *prəmaɤl* 'to estimate'
m. *haɤ*   'to fly'   *bəŋhaɤ* 'to fly (trans.)'
n. *kʰos* 'be in error'   *bəŋkʰos* 'cause a mistake'
o. *kɔəp* 'pleased'   *bəŋkɔəp* 'to please'
p. *co:l* 'to enter'   *bəɲco:l* 'to cause to enter'
q. *to:c* 'small'   *bənto:c* 'to diminish in power'
r. *doh*   'to grow'   *bəndoh* 'to plant'
s. *bak*   'broken'   *bəmbak* 'to break'

3.8 Examine the Language D data below, which gives base forms and "expressive" reduplicated forms of some words (tones omitted). Work out rules to account for the forms taken by the reduplicated versions. There are three separate rules. For your information, here is a chart of vowel phonemes in Language D.

	FRONT	CENTRAL	BACK
HIGH	i		u
	e		o
MID		ə	
	ε		ɔ
LOW		a	

	Original form	Reduplicated form
a.	*cɔɔk* 'drinking glass'	*cɔɔk cεεk*
b.	*khu* 'bucket'	*khu khi*
c.	*pet* 'duck'	*pet pət*
d.	*pheet* 'sex'	*pheet phəət*
e.	*pum* 'book'	*pum pim*
f.	*nangsuu* 'books'	*nangsɔɔk nangsuu*
g.	*hoong luaj* 'timber mill'	*hoong lɔɔk hoong luaj*
h.	*to* 'table'	*to te*
i.	*kɔɔng* 'camera'	*kɔɔng kεεng*
j.	*kua* 'salt'	*kua kia*
k.	*hua* 'fence'	*hua hia*

l. *cia* 'paper'   *cia cəa*
m. *tip* 'rattan rice container'   *tip təp*
n. *sɛk* 'cheque'   *sɛk sək*
o. *nam saa* 'tea'   *nam sɔɔk nam saa*

3.9 Describe how causative verbs are formed in the following data from Hakha Lai, spoken in Chin state of Myanmar (Burma). The data has been slightly regularized. The symbols *t*, *ts*, and *k* represent stops; *th*, *tsh*, and *kh* are aspirated stops. The digraphs *hl* and *hm* represent voiceless *l* and *m*, respectively. *ʔ* is the glottal stop.

A. *káaŋ*   'burn' (intr.)   *kháaŋ*   'burn' (trans.)
    mit   'go out'   *hmit*   'extinguish' (trans.)
    láw   'disappear'   *hláw*   'erase'
    tsat   'be severed'   *tshat*   'sever' (trans.)
    trúm   'descend'   *thrúm*   'put down' (trans.)

B. *raŋ*   'be fast'   *ranʔ*   'rush' (trans.)
    saaw   'long'   *sawʔ*   'make longer'
    thlùm 'sweet'   *thlumʔ* 'sweeten'
    dàm   'be healthy'   *damʔ*   'heal' (trans.)

C. *tsat*   'be severed'   *tsaʔ-tèr* 'cause to split'
    ríl   'roll'   *rilʔ-tèr* 'cause to roll'
    rook   'break down'   *rʊʔ-tèr*   'cause to break down'
    kàaŋ   'burn'   *kaŋʔ-tèr* 'cause to burn'
    mit   'go out'   *miʔ-tèr*   'cause to extinguish'

3.10 Reread the description of Malay *sabar* in section 3.4.1. Identify ways in which it is different from English *patience*.

3.11 Reread the description of Japanese *omoiyari* in section 3.4.3. Identify ways in which it is different from English *empathy*.

Chapter 4

4.1 Consider the following list of phrases from Malaysian. For convenience, they all employ the same numeral, *dua* 'two'. (i) Separate out the true classifier constructions from the measure constructions and unit counter constructions. (ii) Consider just the classifier constructions. Can you figure out the semantic basis for the classifications?

dua ekor kuda 'two horses', *dua helai kertas* 'two sheets of paper', *dua keping kertas* 'two sheets of stiff paper', *dua keping syiling* 'four coins', *dua anggota keluarga* 'two members of the family', *dua biji telur* 'two eggs', *dua bakul beras* 'two baskets of rice', *dua potong roti* 'two slices of bread', *dua kilo beras* 'two kilos of rice', *dua ekor ikan* 'two fish', *dua biji mata* 'two eyes', *dua buah rumah* 'two houses', *dua sikat pisang* 'two hands of bananas', *dua keping surat* 'two letters', *dua helai baju* 'two shirts', *dua ahli parti* 'two members of the party', *dua helai kain* 'two pieces of cloth', *dua biji guli* 'two marbles', *dua ekor ayam* 'two chickens'.

4.2 One of the most common and versatile classifiers in Hmong is *lub*. Examine the following list of phrases, and describe its range of use as economically as you can. Be aware that *lub* could have a radial polysemy structure.

a. *lub thoob* 'bucket', *lub tshuaj* 'pill, medicine', *lub kahub hnab* 'ball', *lub lwj* 'blacksmith bellows'
b. *lub qhov* 'hole', *lub quiv rooj* 'door', *lub quov raj* 'window', *lub ncauj* 'mouth'
c. *lub xauv* 'neck ring', *lub laj kab* 'fence, hedge'
d. *lub tsheb* 'car', *lub dav hlau* 'airplane', *lub nees zab* 'bicycle', *lub nkoj* 'boat', *lub tshuab* 'engine, machine'
e. *lub tsev* 'house', *lub zos* 'village', *lub teb chaws* 'country, region'
f. *lub cev* 'body', *lub taub hau* 'head', *lub pob ntseg* 'ear', *lub quov muag* 'eye', *lub plawv* 'heart', *lub duav* 'waist', *lub siab* 'liver'
g. *lub tsho* 'shirt', *lub ris* 'trousers'

4.3 Study the following data from Hmong. It shows various kinds of noun-phrase in which classifiers are either obligatory or prohibited. An asterisk next to a form means that the sentence is unacceptable, a slash indicates an alternative, and the symbol ø (zero) means that a form is missing. So item (a), for example, tells us that classifier *tus* is possible in this context, and that omitting it is unacceptable. (i) In what kinds of NP are classifiers obligatory in Hmong? Try to generalize. (ii) In what kinds of NP are classifiers not found in Hmong?

a. *Tus/*ø tsov tshaib   tshaib   plab.*
   CL   tiger hungry hungry stomach
   'The tiger was very hungry.'

b. *Muaj ib   tus/*ø tsov.*
   be   one CL   tiger
   'There was one tiger.'

c. *Tus/*ø txiv   neeb tau txhia tus/*ø mob.*
   CL   shaman cure can all   CL   illness
   'The shaman can cure all illnesses.'

d. *Lawv lub/*ø zos   puas deb?*
   their CL   village QUES far
   'Is their village far?'

e. *Lub/*ø tsev   no*
   CL   house this
   'this house'

f. *Ntau lub/*ø tsev*
   many CL   house
   'many houses'

g. *Tus/*ø tswj lub/*ø tsev*
   CL   chief CL   house
   'the chief's house'

h. *Lawv muaj pes tsawg tus/*ø menyuam?*
   they have how much CL   child
   'How many children do they have?'

i. *Tus/*ø npua ntawd siab.*
   CL   pig that happy
   'That pig is happy.'

j. *Tooj tus/*ø dev*
   Tong CL   dog
   'Tong's dog'

k. *Lawv muaj rau tus/*ø menyuam.*
   they have six CL   child
   'They have six children.'

l. *Kuv ntshai ø/*tus tsov.*
   I   fear CL   tiger
   'I'm afraid of tigers'.

m. *ø/*tus mob tsis tu.*
   CL   illness not go.away
   'Disease never disappears.'

4.4 Aspect in Language B. The following data from Language B show two aspect markers, both glossed ASP. From the examples given, what is the apparent difference in meaning or function between them?

a. *ʐa³¹maŋ³¹ ʐa³¹ki³³ ʐaŋ³³ taŋ³¹an³¹ kuaŋ³¹ne³¹ na⁵⁵ çi⁵⁵ ne⁵⁵*
   old.men   children he   story   tell   listen like ASP
   'Old men and children all like to listen when he tells stories.'

b. *ni⁵⁵ ʐa⁵⁵ ko³³ kha³³ ne⁵⁵*
   this field rice grow ASP
   'Rice is growing in this field.'

c. *gu³³ tas³¹ pɤn³³ne⁵⁵*
   we   eat ASP
   'We're eating.'

d. *ʐa³¹ki³³ tshaŋ⁵⁵ pɤn³³ne⁵⁵*
   children sing   ASP
   'The children are singing.'

e. gu^{33} $\underset{}{z}um^{55}tun^{31}$ fu^{33} xan^{55} sha^{33} ne^{33}
   we   family   CL four there.are ASP
   'There are four members in our family.'

f. $na\eta^{33}$ $a^{55}ma\eta^{55}$ xa^{33} $p\gamma n^{33}ne^{55}$ γ^{31}
   you   what   do   ASP   PRT
   'What are you doing?'

g. ni^{55} u^{55} $ka\eta^{31}pha^{31}$ $a^{55}me^{33}$ xau^{55} ne^{55}
   this kind vegetable how   call ASP
   'What is this kind of vegetable called?'

4.5 The four examples given below show tight serialization and quasi-adverb serials in Language M. Decide which is found in each sentence, explaining your reasons.

a. *Lajis berjalan keluar.*
   Lajis walk   go.out
   'Lajis walked out.'

b. *Leman, pegi ambik ayam   tu.*
   Leman go get   chicken that
   'Leman, go get those chickens.'

c. *Aku lepak   jaga   kambing kat tepi padang.*
   I hang.out look.after goat   at side field
   'I was hanging out minding the goats beside the field.'

d. *Aku bawak balik.*
   I bring go.back
   'I brought (it) back.'

4.6 Consider the data below from Khmer, which show serial constructions employing the verbs *nɨw* 'be at', *tɨw* 'go' and *mɔɔk* 'come'. What kind of serial construction do they exemplify? Explain.

a. *Yɔɔk qǝywan nih tɨw bǝntup.*
   take thing this go room
   'Take these things to the room.'

b. *Yɔɔk qǝywan nih mɔɔk pteǝh.*
   take thing this come house
   'Bring these things to the house.'

c. *Look Sok twǝǝ kaa nɨw kǝnlaeŋ nɨn.*
   sir Sok do   work be.at place that
   'Mr Sok works at that place.'

d. *Nɨw psaa   nih miǝn   mǝnuh craǝn nah.*
   in market this there.are person many very
   'There are a lot of people in this market.'

e. *Koət   tuul   səmlaa cəñ tɨw srae.*
   he/she head.carry stew   out go rice.field
   'She carried (on her head) the stew to the ricefields.'

4.7   The examples show the so-called "double subject" construction in Korean, which is comparable to similar constructions in Mandarin and Japanese, described in section 4.4.1. There is a topic NP at the beginning of the sentence (marked by *-neun/-uen*), then comes a second NP (with the subject marker *-i* or *-ga*) which functions as the immediate subject of the verb. All the examples would remain grammatical if the initial topic NP were omitted, i.e. the subject NP and the verb together form a self-contained grammatical clause which functions as "comment" on the topic NP. There can be various different kinds of semantic relationship between the comment and the topic NP. Summarize those occurring in the data.

a. *Suni-neun don-i   manh-da.*
   Suni-TOP   money-SUBJ much-PRT
   'Sini has much money (Suni is rich).'

b. *Keu chaek-eun pyoji-ga   dukkeop-da.*
   the book-TOP cover-SUBJ thick-PRT
   'The book has a thick cover.'

c. *Suni-neun sinyong-i eops-da.*
   Suni-TOP   trust-SUBJ not.exist-PRT
   'Suni is untrustworthy.'

d. *Jeo namu-neun ip-i   kheu-da.*
   that tree-TOP   leaf-SUBJ big-PRT
   'That tree has big leaves.'

e. *Suni-neun nun-i   gop-da.*
   Suni-TOP   eye-SUBJ pretty-PRT
   'Suni has pretty eyes.'

f. *Kkoch-eun jangmi-ga yeppeu-da.*
   flower-TOP rose-SUBJ pretty-PRT
   'As for flowers, the rose is pretty.'

g. *Him-eun   Cheolsu-ga   se-da.*
   power-TOP Cheolsu-SUBJ strong-PRT
   'If we're talking about power, Cheolsu is strong.'

h. *Bihaenggi-neun 747-i   kheu-da.*
   aeroplane-TOP   747-SUBJ big-PRT
   'When it comes to aeroplanes, the 747 is big.'

4.8   The following data are from an Austronesian language Toba-Batak, spoken in Sumatra. For convenience they have been divided into two sets. The first set shows simple clauses. The second set shows coordinated sentences (with conjunction *jala* 'and') which involve a kind of gapping. Oddly (from an English speaker's point of view), the first clause is the one which undergoes gapping. That is, the first clause is missing an NP whose identity is "understood", as given in the translations. For your convenience, morpheme divisions have been shown. Prefix *mang-/man-* creates agent-oriented verbs, while prefix *di-* creates patient-oriented verbs. Analyze the data. Is it necessary to use the notion of subject in order to describe what is going on?

Data set A
a. *Mang-antuk si Ria si Torus.*
    'Torus hit Ria.'
b. *Man-jaha buku guru i.*
    'The teacher read a book.'
c. *Mate si Torus.*
    'Torus died.'
d. *Di-antuk si Torus si Ria.*
    'Ria got hit by Torus.'
e. *Laho guru i.*
    'The teacher went/left.'
f. *Mang-antuk si Torus si Ria.*
    'Ria hit Torus.'
g. *Di-jaha guru buku i.*
    'The book was read by a teacher.'

Data set B
h. *Laho jala di-antuk si Torus guru i.*
    'The teacher went and was hit by Torus.'
i. *Laho jala man-ipak guru si Ria.*
    'Ria went and kicked a teacher.'
j. *Mang-antuk si Torus jala mate si Ria.*
    'Ria hit Torus and [Ria] died.'
k. *Di-antuk si Torus jala mate si Ria.*
    'Ria was hit by Torus and [Ria] died.'
l. *Mang-antuk si Torus jala man-ipak guru si Ria.*
    'Ria hit Torus and kicked a teacher.'
m. *Mang-antuk guru jala di-sipak si Ria si Torus.*
    'Torus hit a teacher and was kicked by Ria.'
n. *Di-antuk si Torus jala di-sipak guru si Ria.*
    'Ria was hit by Torus and was kicked by a teacher.'
o. *Di-antuk si Ria jala man-ipak guru si Torus.*
    'Torus was hit by Ria and kicked a teacher.'

Chapter 5

5.1 Look at the following list of Japanese loan words and compare them with their English source words. Describe the different processes of phonological adaptation which occurred when the words were borrowed into Japanese.

Japanese	English source word
sararii	*salary*
marukusu	*Marx*
depaato	*department store*
waa-puro	*word processor*
han-suto	*hunger strike*
fooku	*fork*
supuun	*spoon*
sutoroberii	*strawberry*
kappu nuudoru	*cup noodle (instant noodles)*

5.2   Fig. E.1 shows the pitch shapes of six tones in Language G. For ease of reference they are labelled 1–6. Examine the diagram carefully and answer the questions below:

(i) Which of the Language G tones are register tones? (ii) Which are contour tones? If there are any difficult cases, explain the nature of the difficulty. (iii) What are appropriate descriptive labels for tone 5 and tone 6? (In difficult cases, try to think about the speakers and what they are likely to perceive, considering the set of tones as a whole.)

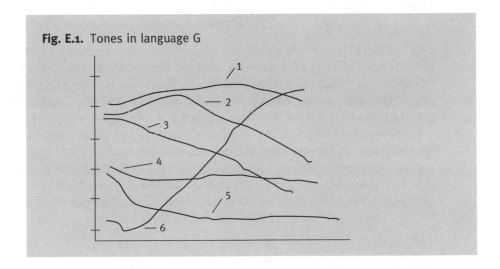

Fig. E.1. Tones in language G

5.3   Consider the following list of forms with their pitch shapes. Each form represents a different word in Language K. The meanings are not given, but you do not need to know them for the purposes of this exercise. A double number for a pitch shape, e.g. 55 or 21, indicates a longer tone. How many contrastive tones are there in this language?

Pitch shape	Examples	Pitch shape	Examples
55	[fa:], [fan]	24	[ma:], [fan]
5	[fat], [pit], [sik]	22	[ma:], [fan]
35	[pa:], [fan]	2	[fat], [pit], [sik]
33	[fa:], [fan], [fa:n], [fa:t]	21	[pha:], [fan]
3	[pit], [sik]		

5.4   From the following list of Lao words, describe the phonotactic structure of Lao syllables in as much detail as you can. Consonants are generally written in the same way as for Thai, i.e. *ph*, *th*, and *kh* each stand for /pʰ/, /tʰ/, and /kʰ/. Unlike as in Thai romanization, initial glottal stops are indicated as *ʔ*.

khaw⁴	'knee'	*phuam²*	"progressive" marker
khaaw²	'time, occasion'	*phiang²*	'only'
khiaw³	'chew'	*biip⁵*	'squeeze'
khiit⁵	'scrape'	*ʔaat⁵*	'might'
khaat⁵	'lack'	*ʔaa*	'aunty'
baang³	'some'	*paʔ²*	'abandon'
bang⁴	'bamboo tube'	*pap²*	'to fine, impose penalty'
bùang⁴	'side'	*ʔat²*	'close'
bùa⁴	'bilious, bored'	*saʔaat²*	'clean'
buang⁴	'spoon'	*padèèk⁵*	'jugged fish'
phua³	'husband'	*latthabaan⁴*	'government'
		lattathammanuun⁴	'constitution'

5.5   The following are examples of monosyllabic words in Language S. The transcription is phonemic. Vowels marked with an acute accent (′) are pronounced with creaky voice. (˜) indicates nasalization. A raised glottal stop, in front of a consonant, as in words like *ʔmɔ* 'to hug', indicates pre-glottalization. (i) What can you say about the phoneme inventory of Language S? Where there seem to be accidental gaps in the data, make plausible assumptions in the interests of clean generalizations. (ii) What can you say about the phonotactics of monosyllabic words? Consider initial consonants, final consonants, and vowel possibilities; include statements about relative frequency when they seem warranted. (iii) What language family is Language S most likely to belong to? Refer back to Chapter 2 if necessary.

pa	'father'	*pʰa*	'different'	*tʰa*	'hurry'
á	'I'	*cɛ́*	'cloth'	*kʰa*	'to block'
bau	'wash face'	*ma*	'eye'	*báu*	'field rice'
má	'we two'	*soi*	'to weave'	*na*	'to bud'
rɛm	'each'	*ɲa*	'grass'	*s̥õi*	'to sacrifice'
ká	'fish'	*tam*	'to wallow'	*kia*	'spirit'

tuo	'to bend over'	*kok*	'to carry'	*ŋám*	'heavy'
ɲḁ	'to lie down'	*tɛ*	'to sell'	*ka*	'to eat'
ŋa	'top edge'	*fa*	'to chip'	*lái̥*	'very'
kúan	'child'	*to*	'hot'	*la*	'to dip'
kat	'cabbage'	*taŋ*	'if'	*va*	'to want'
ciaŋ	'become'	*mán*	'night'	*suap*	'below'
ˀmɔ	'to hug'	*ˀdɔ́*	'small boat'	*ˀba*	'never'
ciak	'field'	*kán*	'chief'	*mḁ*	'know'
ˀna	'(particle)'	*tap*	'to bury'	*cam*	'down there'
ˀla	'papaya'	*ˀvɛ̃́*	'bowtrap arms'	*tak*	'bran'
pɔa	'grandfather'	*suan*	'also'	*dá*	'to continue'

5.6 Consider the following sets of related words in a dialect of Malaysian. They are given in a phonemic transcription. (i) What is the underlying form of each root? (ii) What rules are required to account for the attested forms?

Unsuffixed form		Suffixed form	
bukə	'open'	*kəbukaan*	'opening'
mura	'generous'	*kəmurahan*	'generosity'
baŋsə	'race, ethnicity'	*kəbaŋsaan*	'nationality'
ruma	'house'	*pərumahan*	'housing'
uba	'to change'	*kəubahan*	'change'
susa	'hard'	*kəsusahan*	'difficulty'
adə	'there is'	*kəadaan*	'situation'
katə	'say'	*pəkataan*	'word'
sukə	'to like'	*kəsukaan*	'enjoyment'
sala	'be wrong'	*kəsalahan*	'error, fault'

Chapter 6

6.1 Suppose that you have "inherited" the following set of graphs, with the meanings as shown. Note that sometimes a single graph can express two closely related meanings, e.g. 'bring' and 'take', or 'under' and 'down'.

↔ 'bring, take', ♦ 'come, go', ⤴ 'over, above', ⬂ 'under, down', ✱ 'put', ✔ 'stand', ④ 'four', ✚ 'again', ✍ 'write'

Using only these symbols, improvise ways to write the following English words: *defeat, comprehend, refer, humiliate, forego, undergo, right, rewrite, return, intimidate.* You can resort to any of the strategies discussed in the chapter, e.g. compounding, phonetic resemblance, semantic approximation. For example, you could decide to write *defeat* as ⤴♦, on the grounds that its meaning is very similar to that of the compound *overcome*.

6.2 The layout of an English keyboard is not motivated by any principles of phonology or script design, but it is a different story with the Korean

Fig. E.2. Korean keyboard

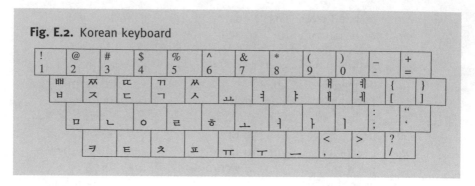

keyboard. Study the diagram, comparing it with the information in section 6.2.3 about Hangeul script. What can you say about the rationale for this layout? You will find that there are some symbols on the keyboard which are not mentioned in the chapter. These represent glide-plus-vowel combinations. You can ignore them for the purposes of this exercise. You needn't worry greatly about the vowels either. Concentrate on figuring out the layout of the consonants.

Chapter 7

7.1   Probably all languages make use of a miscellany of traditional sayings, clichés, and other fixed expressions, and English is no exception in this regard. Consider the following list. (i) Try to state the meaning of each expression (you will see that usually it takes many more words than the original expression). (ii) Where do each of these expressions come from? (iii) What can we deduce about the cultural history of the English-speaking speech community from facts like these? To do this exercise you will probably have to refer to a specialized reference work, such as a dictionary of clichés or fixed expressions.

a. *a dog in a manger*
b. *a rose by any other name*
c. *smoke and mirrors*
d. *the pot calling the kettle black*
e. *turn the other cheek*
f. *a bird in the hand is worth two in the bush*
g. *make hay while the sun shines*
h. *might as well be hung for a sheep as a lamb*
i. *wheels within wheels*
j. *gilding the lily*

7.2 Translating *pantuns* is no easy matter, and depending on the approach and intentions of the translator the results can vary widely. Below is a famous Malay *pantun* about the impermanence of love. Translation (a) by Sim (1987: 29) is more literal and does not attempt to mimic the rhyme scheme of the original. Translation (b) by Winstedt (1977: 183–4) tries to convey the meaning in a more direct way, but at the same time to reproduce the rhyme scheme. Discuss the pros and cons of these two different approaches. Do you have a preference?

> *Permata jatuh di dalam rumput,*
> *Jatuh di rumput bergilang-gilang*
> *Kasih umpana embun di hujung rumput*
> *Datang matahari nescaya hilang.*

a. A jewel falls into the grass,
   Falls into the grass glittering, gleaming,
 Love is like dew on the end of a blade
   Bound to melt in the heat of the day.

b. I lose a pearl, amid the grass,
   It keeps its hue, though low it lies
 I love a girl, but love will pass
   A pearl of dew that slowly dies.

7.3 In section 7.3.1, an example is given of how a company secretary might answer a phone enquiry about the whereabouts of the boss. Compare that with the following example of how a university lecturer might answer a similar call (from outside the university) about the whereabouts of a colleague. The answer would take the same form even if the colleague were a junior member of the faculty. (i) Identify the formal differences between this sentence and the one in section 7.1. (ii) Can you offer any explanation?

Mori sensei   wa gaishutsu shite   irasshai-mas-u.
Mori teacher TOP go.out   do:GER be:HON-POL-NONPAST
'Professor Mori has gone out.'

7.4 Do you think it makes sense to talk about a communicative style which is distinctly Australian (American, English, etc.—choose according to your home country)? What could qualify as characteristically or typically Australian (American, English, etc.) ways of speaking? If you have friends who have come to this country from East or Southeast Asian countries, ask them to relate their early impressions of ways of speaking here. If you yourself have come from an East or Southeast Asian country, share some of your impressions with native-born fellow students.

Solutions

Chapter 1

1.1 1: Japan. 2: South Korea (Republic of Korea). 3: China (People's Republic of China). 4: Myanmar (Burma). 5: Laos. 6: Vietnam. 7: Thailand. 8: Cambodia. 9: Philippines. 10: Malaysia. 11: Brunei. 12: Indonesia. 13: East Timor.

1.2 The Vietnamese data is from Nguyễn (1987: 58). Several typical features of mainland Southeast Asian languages can be seen in the examples. The main ones are the first three dot points. Students with a background in linguistics may have been able to spot the others too. • There is no sign of verbal inflection, i.e. morphological marking of distinctions in tense. The verbs *ra* 'go out' and *thích* 'likes' are not divisible into separate morphemes even though *ra* is used in a past tense context (as indicated by the expression *đêm qua* 'last night') and *thích* is used in a present tense context. • From the second part of sentence (a) (i.e. *anh thích giúp bạn* 'he likes (to) help friends') it looks like the constituent order is SVO. • There is no evidence of articles, i.e. words equivalent to English *the* or *a*. • There appears to be little or no morphological marking of grammatical relationships. For example, the verbs *giúp* 'help' and *đứng* 'stand' are used in complement function, but are not marked as such (whereas in English, the corresponding verbs would be introduced by the complementizer *to*). Similarly, the expression *bờ ao* [edge pond] 'on the edge of the pond' has a very simple structure compared with its English equivalent. • Possibly ellipsis may be normal in Vietnamese; in (b), the English translation has 'I' as subject, but there is no word corresponding to 'I' in the Vietnamese sentence.

1.3 The language is Ainu (Shibatani 1990). • Verbs appear in clause-final position. • The language has postpositions (*ta* 'in', *orun* 'to'). • Within a noun-phrase, adjectives and demonstratives precede nouns (as in *poro cise* 'big house', *pon pewrep* 'small bear', *tampe huci* 'this grandmother'). • Numerals follow nouns (as in *pewrep tup* 'bear two'). Two unusual features, in the typological context of East Asian languages, concern the verb forms. One is the presence of verb prefixes, and the other is that the prefixes appear to be inflectional in nature: they show the person and number of the subject, as in *ku-kore* (1SG-give) and *ci-hok* (1PL-buy) (*horari* 'live' appears without any explicit prefix, but it is quite likely that the 3SG prefix is ø). Even in Japanese and Korean, which have verbal inflection, the inflectional affixes are suffixes rather than prefixes. It is also unusual that there is no classifier in the expression *pewrep tup* 'bear two'.

1.4   Data and analysis of Tetum (Tetun Dili) are from Williams-van Klinken et al. (2002: 58, 59, 63ff., 84, 85).

(i) The question words in the data are *sé* 'who', *saida* 'what', and *nebe* 'where'. It seems that they do not normally "move" to the front of the sentence. The word order in questions is the same as in statements.

(ii) As for polar questions, they can be formed in several different ways, none of which involve any change in word order: simply by intonation; by addition of the particle *ka* 'or'; or by addition of *ka* 'or' plus a negative word such as *lae* 'not'.

1.5   The language is Zhuang (Luo 1993).

(i) The classifier constructions are *tua² maa⁴ hao¹ te* (animal horse white that) and *saam¹ tua² mu¹ te¹* (three animal pig that), where *tua²* is a classifier.

(ii) The measure constructions are *haa³ buŋ¹ hou⁴-hon¹* (five basket grain-seed) and *saam¹ som¹ maan¹ piaŋ¹* (three armspread cloth beautiful), where *buŋ³* 'basket' and *som³* 'armspread' function as measures.

(iii) Number—Classifier/Measure—Noun—Adjective—Demonstrative. Notice that from the data presented, the measure and the classifier are likely to be alternatives within the same slot.

1.6   I would like to thank Jaew Davies for her help with devising this problem.

(i) There are a number of relevant observations to be made. • To show respect when addressing someone, one uses the honorific *khun* either by itself or in combination with a role term or name. • In this same respectful mode, adult males use the pronoun *phǒm* to refer to themselves. • The teacher is always referred to in the third person, as 'teacher', rather than with a pronoun. • The little brother addresses his sister as *phîi* 'elder sibling' and refers to himself as *nǔu* (lit. 'mouse').

(ii) To address someone junior, one can use that person's name; to refer to a junior person (while speaking to that person), one uses *nǔu* (lit. 'mouse').

(iii) Use of the term *phîi* 'older sibling'. • A wife can use *phîi*, optionally in combination with a name, to address her husband. • Between a younger and older sibling, the pair use *phîi* 'older sibling' and *nŭu* for both address and self-reference.

(iv) There are a number of differences. • The description in section 1.8 gives the impression that *khun* is a pronoun, but it seems more likely to be a third person term. • The section doesn't mention the use of *phîi* (lit.'older sibling') from a wife to a husband. • Table 1.3 says that a child would address a teacher using a kin-term. • It also gives the impression that *chăn* 'I' and *kɛɛ* 'you' belong to different levels of usage, whereas in our passage they are used at the same level, between young children playing.

Chapter 2

2.1 (i) There are no tones and the vowel phonemes are fairly simple. In relation to consonants, it looks like voicing is significant (because there are contrasts between *p* and *b* and between *k* and *g*), but there is no evidence of aspiration being significant. From a phonotactic point of view, we can see that various consonants, including a stop and a fricative (*k*, *s*) can occur word-finally.

(ii) Looking now at the morphology, we can tell that the language has prefixes (e.g. compare: *muruk* 'be angry', *par-muruk* 'one who is angry'), suffixes (e.g. compare: *bereŋ* 'to look at', *bereŋ-i* 'to gaze at'), and infixes (e.g. compare: *las* 'hot' and *l-um-as* 'hotter').

(iii) All this is consistent with an Austronesian language. As a matter of fact, the language is Toba-Batak (Nababan 1981), spoken around Lake Toba on the island of Sumatra, Indonesia.

2.2 Lao, Cantonese, and Hmong data are from Enfield (p.c.), Matthews and Yip (1994), and Clark (1989), respectively. Lao is a member of the Tai-Kadai family. According to the chapter, adjectives and demonstratives in Tai-Kadai languages generally follow the nouns they modify. This generalization seems to hold for Lao: adjectives follow nouns in *khon² suung³* 'person tall' and *maa³ dam⁰* 'dog black', and the possessive phrase follows in *huan² (khòòng³) khòòj⁵* 'house (of) I'. Cantonese is a member of the Sinitic family. According to the chapter, in Sinitic languages nominal modifiers such as demonstratives, possessives, and adjectives usually precede the noun, as do classifiers. These generalizations all seem to hold for Cantonese. The expressions *dākyi gáujái* 'cute puppy' and *hāk gáu* 'black dog' both show adjectives preceding the noun. In *ngóh (ge) sailóu* 'my younger brother' and *ngóh ge hāk gáu* 'my black dog', the possessive elements *ngóh ge* 'my' precede the noun. Classifiers also precede, as shown in *jēung tói* 'CL table'.

The chapter also mentions that Sinitic languages have both prepositions and postpositions. The data showed a postpositional phrase *jēung tói hahbihn* 'CL table underneath'. Hmong is a member of the Hmong-Mien family. The patterns shown in the data are typical, i.e. possessors and classifiers preceding nouns, while adjectives follow.

2.3   The language family is Tibeto-Burman. The language is Hakha Lai, spoken in the Chin state of Burma (VanBik 2002: 102, 104, 112). The main indicators are as follows. • The word order is verb-final: SOV. Except in Tibeto-Burman languages, this is a relatively rare word order in mainland Southeast Asia. It is found in Japanese and Korean, but these are not minority languages. • There are verbal prefixes for person/number of subject and (sometimes) object, and nominal prefixes for possession. We can see that there is a verbal reflexive suffix and a nominal locative suffix. Most mainland Southeast Asia languages are rather sparse in their morphology, but this does not apply to Tibeto-Burman.

2.4   Language M is Acehnese (Durie 1985). The data has been slightly regularized.

(i) The affix has two allomorphs: a prefix *nu-* and an infix *-un-*, whose distribution is determined by the following three rules. RULE 1: Use prefix *nu-* with monosyllabic verbal roots beginning with a nasal (*n*, *ɲ*, *ŋ*), a glide (*y*) or liquid (*l*): items (a), (g), (h), (k), and (q). RULE 2: With disyllabic roots, insert infix *-un-* after the initial consonant: items (b), (c), (f), (j), (n), (p), (r). RULE 3: With monosyllabic roots other than those covered by Rule 1, first derive a disyllabic stem by reduplicating the initial consonant together with the vowel *u*, then insert infix *-un-* after the initial consonant: items (d), (e), (i), (m), (o), (s). A less elegant way of describing this is to say that there is a prefix *Cunu-*, where C is a copy of the root-initial consonant.

(ii) A notable feature of Language M is the large vowel inventory (four degrees of vowel height, plus diphthongs).

	front unrounded	*back/central unrounded*	*back rounded*
high	i(iə)	ɯ(ɯə)	u(uə)
high-mid	e	ɨ	o
low-mid	ε		ɔ(ɔə)
low		a	

Together with the presence of infixation, this kind of vowel inventory suggests a Mon-Khmer language. In fact, Acehnese is an Austronesian language of northern Sumatra, but there is evidence that the ancestral speakers once lived on the mainland, as Acehnese has many characteristics which are more Mon-Khmer in character than Austronesian.

Chapter 3

3.1 The loan words shown seem to be concentrated in the areas of: (a) military matters, e.g. 'artillery', 'map', and perhaps also 'radio', and (b) food, e.g. 'coffee', 'lettuce', 'soup', 'canned food'. The place of 'office' and 'bag' is not really clear, but both of them could fall under the heading of military matters. We can deduce that speakers of this language had contact with the French military, and with some aspects of the French lifestyle (specifically, the diet). Presumbly, this language must be situated in an area which was once under the control of France, such as present-day Vietnam or Laos. As a matter of fact, the language is Sedang (Smith 1979) and it is found in the central highlands of southern Vietnam. France was the colonial power for about 100 years, though French influence was attenuated due to the remoteness of Sedang territory. These loans probably entered the language mainly through French personnel at government and military outposts in the highlands.

3.2 The borrowing language is Tagalog and the donor language Hokkien (Yap 1980).

(i) /k^h/ → /k/. As for /c/ and /c^h/, they are reinterpreted as /s/ and /ts/, where /s/ occurs word-initially and /ts/ occurs medially.

(ii) There would appear to have been peaceful cultural contact, with the two linguistic communities living in close proximity to each other. They may have been engaged in trade, as evidenced by words referring to tools and medicine ('bamboo fishing raft', 'medicinal paper', 'frying instrument', 'goldsmith's chisel'). 'Gold bars' and 'gold earring' may be evidence of a goldsmith industry and/or of gifts exchanged between families. Other indications of cultural mixing are the food terms, as well as 'second elder sister'.

3.3 The Dehong Tai data and analysis is from Luo (1999).

(i) Parallel compounds: $kaan^6xɔŋ^1$ [work affair] 'work, affair, matter', $laat^5taap^3$ [speak.to answer] 'to answer', $tsɔɨ^6thɛm^1$ [to.help to.aid] 'to help, aid'.

(ii) head-modifier compounds: $kɨp^1mɨ^2$ [nail hand] 'fingernail', $kə^6waan^1$ [salt sweet] 'sugar', sop^3kat^5 [mouth capable] 'have a glib tongue', $kaaŋ^6wan^2$ [middle day] 'during the day, daytime', $po^3tsaɨ^6$ [happy heart] 'be happy', $tsaɨ^6yaau^2$ [heart long] 'to be broad-minded'.

(iii) elaborate expressions: $məŋ^2kaŋ^4taŋ^5loŋ^1$ [country wide mouth.of. river big] 'big place', $tso^6kɔn^3mɔn^3len^1$ [life before pass ancestor] 'ancestors', $laɔ^6la^1pha^1tsan^2$ [hill thick cliff steep] 'sheer precipice and overhanging rocks', $kaŋ^6tsai^6lai^2xo^2$ [centre heart inside throat] 'heart, innermost being'.

(iv) psycho-collocations: po^3tsai^6 [happy heart] 'be happy', $tsai^6yaau^2$ [heart long] 'to be broad-minded', $tsɔm^2tsai^6$ [put heart] 'to mind (doing), to take to heart'.

Some expressions belong in more than one category; e.g. some of the psycho-collocations have a head-modifier structure.

3.4 This problem is from Schiffman (n.d.), with data and analysis from Marivic Rigor. The Tagalog future tense is formed by partial reduplication. The first syllable of the non-future form is reduplicated to form the future (e.g. *la-la-kad* 'will walk', *bu-bu-kas* 'will open'). This applies even if the first syllable is a lone vowel, lacking any initial consonant (e.g. *u-u-po* 'will sit', *i-i-yak* 'will cry').

3.5 LaPolla (2000: 289–92) calls *-shì* a reflexive/middle morpheme. It can be used to mark true reflexives, i.e. when a person does something to him or herself, such as hitting oneself or cutting one's fingernails; but it can be also used for bodily actions which are inherently "self-affecting", such as smiling (this is the so-called 'middle' function). It can also be used to indicate that the subject is affected by an act on something else, as in the final pair of examples.

3.6 This problem is from Schiffman (n.d.), based on data from Refsing (1986).

(i) The Ainu derivational morpheme derives transitive verbs. Most of them are clearly causatives.
(ii) The allomorphs are: *-re*, *-e*, and *-te*.
(iii) The conditioning factor is the nature of the final sound of the base. Allomorph *-re* occurs following vowels, *-e* occurs after the consonant *r*, and *-te* occurs after other consonants.

3.7 This problem is from Schiffman (n.d.), based on data from Nacaskul (1978).

(i) Causative verbs in Khmer are formed by prefixation to the verb root. The causative prefix has a number of allomorphs (*p-*, *pʰ-*, *prə-*, *bɔŋ-*), which appear to be lexically conditioned. The final nasal of prefix *bɔŋ-* assimilates to the place of articulation of a following consonant (if there is one). That is, it is realized as dental *n* preceding dental *t* or *d*, and as palatal *ɲ* preceding palatal *c*.
(ii) There are a few sporadic changes to the vowel quality of the base, but these do not seem to be predictable on the basis of the data given.

3.8 This problem is modelled on data from Lao (Enfield p.c.), but it is presented in a simplified form. RULE 1: (for monosyllabic words) reduplicate placing the copied form after the original, but change the vowel in the copied form: back vowels become front vowels at equivalent height; front vowels become mid central, e.g. *tip tǝp*. RULE 2: (for disyllabic words and compounds) produce a modified reduplicated form by replacing the original vowel and final consonant (if any) of the second syllable with *-ɔɔk*, then place this before the base form.

3.9   Data and analysis of Hakha Lai is from VanBik (2002: 99–100). Set A are formed by aspiration (stops: *t*, *ts*, *k*) or devoicing (sonorants: *m*, *l*). Set B are formed by the addition of a final glottal stop (along with shortening of the vowel, if long). Set C is formed by the addition of suffix *-ʔter*, along with shortening of the vowel (if long) and deletion of a final stop consonant. Another way to analyze this formation would be to say that it takes B formation as a base, then adds *-tér*. (Note that in this language most verbs have two base forms, Form I and Form II. The data used in this problem show only Form I variants. A different analysis would be possible if both base forms were taken into account.)

3.10   Differences between Malay *sabar* and English *patient* include the fact that *sabar* is applicable to situations in which someone is angry or distressed, whereas *patient* is not; that is, in Malay one could urge someone to "be *sabar*" in such situations, whereas it wouldn't make sense in English to advise them to be *patient* (Goddard 2001*b*). The English concept is very much focused on the idea of waiting for something—of biding one's time without mental agitation. Though *sabar* can be used about these situations, it has a much broader range.

3.11   There are at least three differences between Japanese *omoiyari* and English *empathy* (Travis 1997). First, *empathy* is focused specifically on bad feelings— one cannot empathize with someone who is feeling good; for example, if someone announces that they have won a trip around the world, the response *I really empathize with you* is inappropriate, unless intended sarcastically. Second, the kind of understanding evident in *empathy* is not based on intuition, but on imagining oneself in the same situation as another person, "putting oneself in their shoes". Third, *empathy* does not imply that one actually does anything for that person on the basis of one's understanding, whereas *omoiyari* does.

Chapter 4

4.1   The measure constructions and unit counter constructions are as follows. The remainder are the true classifier constructions. Measure constructions: *dua helai kertas* 'two sheets of paper', *dua keping kertas* 'two sheets of stiff paper' *dua bakul beras* 'two baskets of rice', *dua potong roti* 'two slices of bread', *dua kilo beras* 'two kilos of rice', *dua sikat pisang* 'two hands of bananas', *dua helai kain* 'two pieces of cloth'. Unit counter constructions: *dua anggota keluarga* 'two members of the family', *dua ahli parti* 'two members of the party'.

The categorization achieved by the classifiers can be described as follows: *ekor*—birds, animals, fish; *helai*—things made of cloth; *keping*—stiff flat things; *buah*—big bulky thing; *biji*—small roundish things. Notice that *helai* can be used both as a shape-based measure and as a classifier. Though the data do not show this, the same goes for several other items.

4.2   The data and interpretation (slightly modified) are from Bisang (1993: 31–2). Hmong classifier *lub* appears to exhibit a radial polysemy structure, i.e. a network of overlapping and interconnected meaning categories. One way of describing it would be as follows: The central meaning is 'hollow objects'. Linked to this central meaning are two further categories: 'objects through which other things can pass' and 'round things'. Linked to this latter category are two further categories: 'things that go around (encircle) other things', and 'round or solid body parts'. Two additional categories which seem to be related to the idea of "containment" are 'vehicles' (possibly because people can be inside them) and 'places where people can live'.

4.3   This problem is from Jaisser (1987).

(i) Classifiers in Hmong are obligatory in NPs containing numerals and other quantifiers, including question words, as in examples (b), (c), (f), (h) and (k); in possessive NPs, as in examples (d), (g) and (j); in NPs with demonstratives, as in (e) and (i); and in definite NPs, in the sense of NPs whose English translation contains a definite article *the*, as in (a), (c), and (g). One can generalize by saying that Hmong classifiers are obligatory when an NP is specified or determinate.

(ii) On the other hand, classifiers are unacceptable in NPs which are non-referential, as in (l) and (m).

4.4   Language B is Bisu (Xu 1999), a Burmese-Yipho language spoken in southwestern China and northern Thailand. In view of the syllable structure and tones, Bisu seems to have been heavily influenced by the surrounding Sinitic languages, though it has retained the characteristic verb-final order of Tibeto-Burman languages. It appears that the marker ne^{55} is used to make generalizations, as in (a), (e), and (g), and to describe situations which hold over a long time, as in (b). The marker $pɤn^{33}ne^{55}$ is used to indicate actions which are in the process of happening, and which will not take much time.

4.5   The language is Colloquial Malay (cf. Koh 1990). Examples (b) and (c) are tight serializations, because in both cases the verbs occur juxtaposed, with no arguments or adjuncts intervening, and though the verbs identify distinguishable actions, they can be seen as together constituting a single event. Examples (a) and (d) look like classic quasi-adverbs (though they could conceivably be tight serializations), because they involve verbs of directed motion (*keluar* 'go out', *balik* 'go back') appearing to provide directional modification to the preceding verbs.

4.6   These Khmer serial verb constructions are all "verb-prepositions". In functional terms, *nɨw* acts like a locative preposition meaning 'at, in', *tɨw* acts like an allative preposition meaning 'towards (somewhere else)', and *mɔɔk* acts like an allative preposition meaning 'towards (here)'. In structural terms, they seem to combine with the following NP forming a unit analogous to a prepositional phrase. They cannot be serial adverbs, because they do not specify an absolute direction, orientation, etc. Could they be tight serializations? Against this is the fact that the NP objects of the main verbs all occur in their expected postverbal position, e.g. *yɔɔk qəywan nih* [take thing this], *tuul səmlaa* [head.carry stew]. In this data we never see two verbs simply juxtaposed with an NP or complement following both, as one would expect in a tight serialization. This doesn't mean that tight serialization does not occur in Khmer (it does), but it is not shown in this data.

4.7   Data and interpretation of Korean is from Park (1982). In examples (b), (d), and (e), the semantic relationships is part–whole: (the referent of) the subject is part of (the referent of) the topic—the cover is part of the book, the leaves are part of the tree, the eyes are part of Suni. In example (a), (the referent of) the subject is something which belongs to (the referent of) the topic, in the sense of ownership: the money belongs to Suni. In example (c), the subject refers to an abstract noun (i.e. trust) which is being considered as an attribute of Suni. In all these cases, the topic identifies a specific, concrete referent and the subject refers to a part, a possession or an attribute of this referent. Thus the "comment" part of the sentence can be seen as making a predication about the topic. In examples (f)–(h), the situation is different: the subject identifies something which is an instance or subtype of a category named by the topic. Thus in (f), a rose is an example of a flower, and in (h) a '747' is an instance of an aeroplane. In (g), the topic is an abstract one (power): Cheolsu is mentioned as someone who exemplifies a powerful person.

4.8   This problem has been adapted from one in Van Valin and LaPolla (1997: 310–11). It is based on Toba-Batak data from Schachter (1984) and Shugamoto (1984). Data set A shows some basic facts about simple clauses.

The verb comes first, i.e. this is a verb-initial language. Proper nouns like *Ria* and *Torus* occur with a preposed article *si*, while common nouns like *buku* 'book' and *guru* 'teacher' occur either alone, or with a postposed definite article *i* 'the'. The most interesting thing concerns the verbs. Intransitive verbs, e.g. *mate* 'die', *laho* 'went/left', don't have any prefix, but transitive verbs, e.g. *-antuk* 'hit', *-jaha* 'read', occur with one of two prefixes: *mang-/man-* or *di-*. Each prefix is associated with a different order of NPs. With *mang-/man-*, the order is: patient–agent. With *di-*, the order is: agent–patient.

Data set B shows sentences which consist of two clauses coordinated by *jala* 'and', but showing a peculiar kind of gapping. The first clause is incomplete, in the sense that it is missing an NP which is "understood". We can see this in its simplest form in (h) and (i), which have the intransitive verb *laho* 'went' in the first clause. There is no explicit NP in this clause, but its identity is supplied by the verb of the second clause. If this is a patient-oriented verb, with prefix *di-* as in (h), then the patient NP of the second clause fills the gap. If the second verb is an agent-oriented verb, with prefix *man-* as in (i), then the agent of the second clause fills the gap. If you don't follow, go back to the original sentences and reanalyze them. It can be a bit tricky to see on account of the word-order differences between Toba-Batak and English. Word-by-word translations of (h) and (i) would look like this. I will use the glosses PAT and AGT for the 'patient-oriented' and 'agent-oriented' prefixes, respectively.

(h) *Laho jala di-antuk   si   Torus   guru   i.*
   go   and PAT-hit   ART   Torus   teacher DEF.
   '—went and the teacher was hit by Torus.' (= 'The teacher went and was hit by Torus.')

(i) *Laho jala man-ipak   guru   si   Ria.*
   go   and AGT-kicked teacher ART Ria
   '—went and Ria kicked a teacher.' (= 'Ria went and kicked a teacher.')

Things get more complicated in the remaining examples. In (j) the first clause is *mang-antuk si Torus*, with an agent-oriented verb, but the translation tells us that Torus is the patient. In example (k) the first clause is *di-antuk si Torus*, with a patient-oriented verb, but this time the translation tells us that *si Torus* is the agent. It appears that agent-oriented verbs have the agent position gapped, while patient-oriented verbs have the patient position gapped. Either way, the identity of the gapped NPs is supplied by the second clause.

The remaining examples, (l)–(o), are still more complicated because they involve clauses which are both transitive. The first thing to observe is that the role of the missing NP still works according to the principle just mentioned. But how is its identity supplied from the second clause? Here is an interlinear gloss for (l). As you can see, the relevant NP from the second clause is the agent, i.e. Ria; and the second verb is itself agent-oriented, i.e. with prefix *man-*.

(l) *Mang-antuk si   Torus jala man-ipak guru   si   Ria.*
    AGT-hit   ART Torus and AGT-kick teacher ART Ria.
    '—hit Torus and Ria kicked a teacher.' (= 'Ria hit Torus and kicked a teacher.')

With (m), the interlinear gloss looks like this. In this case, the relevant NP from the second clause is the patient, i.e. Torus; and the second verb is itself patient-oriented, i.e. with prefix *di-*.

(m) *Mang-antuk guru   jala di-sipak si   Ria si   Torus.*
    AGT-hit   teacher and PAT-kick ART Ria ART Torus
    '—hit a teacher and Torus was kicked by Ria.' (= 'Torus hit a teacher and was kicked by Ria.')

So, although the role of the missing NP is determined by the orientation of the verb of the first clause, the identity of the NP in the second clause which is understood to fill that role is determined by the orientation of the verb in the second clause. To check that the same principles work for the final two examples, study the glosses below. They show that, yes, the role of the gapped NP is decided by the orientation of the first verb (patient-oriented in both cases); but the identity of the NP from the second clause which fills the gap is decided by the orientation of the second verb. Thus, in (n) Ria fills the gap, because *di-sipak* is a patient-oriented verb and *si* Ria is the patient of the second clause. In (o) Torus fills the gap because *man-ipak* is an agent-oriented verb and *si Torus* is the agent of the second clause.

(n) *Di-antuk   si   Torus jala di-sipak   guru   si   Ria.*
    PAT-hit   ART Torus and PAT-kick teacher ART Ria
    '—was hit by Torus and Ria was kicked by a teacher.' (= 'Ria was hit by Torus and was kicked by a teacher.')

(o) *Di-antuk   si   Ria jala   man-ipak   guru   si   Torus.*
    PAT-hit   ART Ria and AGT-kick   teacher ART Torus
    '—was hit by Ria and Torus kicked a teacher.' (= 'Torus was hit by Ria and kicked a teacher.')

Evidently, in Toba-Batak gapping works quite differently from English and Japanese. We have described the mechanics of it purely in terms of agents, patients, agent-oriented verbs, and patient-oriented verbs. It has not been necessary (as it is for English and Japanese) to say that gapping is "controlled" by the grammatical subject. On the basis of the current data, therefore, there is no evidence for a grammatical category of subject in Toba-Batak.

Chapter 5

5.1 Among the processes of phonological adaptation which occurred when the English words were borrowed into Japanese are the following:

(a) phonemic substitution, i.e. substitution of the nearest indigenous phoneme for one which has no direct counterpart, e.g. *sararii < salary*, where Japanese /r/ is substituted for English /l/; there are also various vowel substitutions necessary to adapt from English (which has over twenty vowels) to Japanese, which has only 5, though the nature of these substitutions is not always apparent because English spelling does not represent vowels in a very transparent manner;

(b) breakup of unacceptable consonant clusters, e.g. the /ks/ cluster in *Marx* becomes *kusu* in Japanese; the /sp/ cluster in *spoon* becomes *supu* in Japanese;

(c) elimination of word-final stops, which are not allowed in Japanese; e.g. *fooku < fork*; (d) truncation, often combined with other processes, e.g. *depaato < department store, waa-pro < word processor*.

5.2 This is a constructed example based on some of the tones found in Hmongic languages (cf. Edmondson 1992).

(i) The register (level) tones are 1 and 4. The slight fluctuations of level are unlikely to be significant compared to the big movements in the contour tones.

(ii) The contour (moving) tones are 2, 3, and 6. Tone 5 is a difficult case: it starts off at mid-level and falls very abruptly, so that it is level for most of its duration. It could be designated as either level or contour, as long as this peculiarity is noted.

(iii) If you regard tone 5 as a contour tone, it could be called either 'low-falling' or 'mid-falling'. If you regard it as a level tone, you could call it just 'low'. Tone 6 could be designated simply as 'rising', or as 'low-rising'.

5.3 This problem was devised by Nick Enfield. There are six contrastive tones in this data, which is from Cantonese: three register (level) tones and three contour (moving) tones. The register tones are High Level (55 or 5), Mid Level (33 or 3), and Low Level (22 or 2). Each has two allotones, long and short, depending on whether the vowel is long or short. Short vowels are found only in closed (checked) syllables, i.e. syllables ending in a consonant.

The contour tones are High Rising (35), Low Rising (24), and Low (or Low Falling) (21). They are found only in words with a long vowel, or a short vowel followed by a nasal consonant, presumably because a short vowel by itself (or followed by a stop) would not provide enough time for the change in tone to be articulated.

5.4 The question asks us to state the structure of Lao syllables in as much detail as we can. From the data provided, we can give the following formula as a first approximation: $C_1V_1(V_2)(C_2)$ + TONE. Given our expectations of mainland Southeast Asian phonotactics, we would expect heavy restrictions on the C_2 position. It looks like C_2 cannot be an aspirated stop, because *ph, th, kh* never appear in final position, though they are frequent in initial position. Quite likely, C_2 cannot be a voiced stop either, given that *b* is common in initial position but doesn't appear at all in final position. One could surmise that fricatives (and perhaps laterals) are unlikely to appear in final position, but the data doesn't give us much to go on (since *s* and *l* appear only once each).

As far as vowel combinations are concerned, it seems that (unless V_1 and V_2 are identical) there are heavy restrictions: the only attested combinations are *ia, ua,* and *ùa*. From this it seems that V_2 must be *a*, and V_1 is limited to *i, u,* or *ù*.

5.5 The language is Sedang (Smith 1979), a minority language of the central Vietnamese highlands.

(a) The inventory of consonant phonemes has four places of articulation—labial, dental, palatal, and velar—with voiceless stops and nasals in each position. There are aspirated voiceless stops /pʰ, tʰ, kʰ/, a pair of voiced stops /b, d/, and at least three fricatives /f, v, s/. Voiced front consonants /b, d, m, n, v/ have preglottalized counterparts. Nasals and the laterals have voiceless counterparts. These facts are indicative of a large phoneme inventory. So far as vowels are concerned, the data show six vowels: /i, ɛ, a, ɔ, o, u/. By far the most common is /a/. All the vowels except /i, o/ are attested in creaky voice, so the most economical assumption is that all vowels can occur with this voice quality. Creaky voice is less frequent than ordinary voice. Nasalization is infrequent—only two instances in the data.

(b) In initial position all the consonants can occur, but there are no clusters. In final position only /p, t, k, m, ŋ/ are attested, and most words lack final consonants. Various vowel-vowel combinations occur /ia, uo, ua, au, oi/, but most words have a simple vowel.

(c) In view of the consonant inventory and the presence of creaky voice, the most likely (and correct) family is Mon-Khmer.

5.6 The Malaysian data show two alternations between the final segment of the unsuffixed and suffixed forms: (i) final *ə* in an unsuffixed form corresponds to *a* in the suffixed form (e.g. *bukə* vs. *kə-buka-an*); (ii) a final *a* in an unsuffixed form corresponds to *ah* in the suffixed form (e.g. *mura* vs. *kəmurahan*). The easiest way to account for these facts is to posit underlying forms based on the suffixed forms (e.g. *buka* 'open', *murah* 'generous'), and to posit two ordered rules which modify the final segments when they occur word-finally. RULE 1: change word-final /a/ → /ə/ ("reduction to schwa"). RULE 2: delete word-final /h/. Assigning *h* to the root (rather than to the suffix) kills two birds with the one stone: it regularizes the form of the suffix, which now appears to be uniformly *-an*, and provides an environment to block the operation of the "reduction to schwa" rule. This analysis gives underlying forms as follows. As it happens, this analysis is the one implied by the official Malaysian othography.

Underlying form	Unsuffixed form		Suffixed form	
buka	*bukə*	'open'	*kəbukaan*	'opening'
murah	*mura*	'generous'	*kəmurahan*	'generosity'
baŋsa	*baŋsə*	'race, ethnicity'	*kəbaŋsaan*	'nationality'
rumah	*ruma*	'house'	*pərumahan*	'housing'
ubah	*uba*	'to change'	*kəubahan*	'change'
susah	*susa*	'hard'	*kəsusahan*	'difficulty'
ada	*adə*	'there is'	*kəadaan*	'situation'
kata	*katə*	'say'	*pəkataan*	'word'
suka	*sukə*	'to like'	*kəsukaan*	'enjoyment'
salah	*sala*	'be wrong'	*kəsalahan*	'error, fault'

Chapter 6

6.1   There are multiple "correct" solutions for this problem. Some possibilities are as follows:

comprehend ↘ ✔ (based on semantic resemblance to *understand*); *refer* ✚ ④ (*re-* as *again*, and second syllable has phonetic resemblance to *four*); *humiliate* ✱ ↘ (from *put down*) or ↔ ↘ (from *bring down*); *forego* ④ ♦, *undergo* ↘ ♦ (both on the rebus principle), *right* 🔊 (based on homophony), *rewrite*; ✚ 🔊, *return* ♦ ✚ or ↔ ✚ (semantic equivalence to *come again* or *bring again*); *intimidate*: ✔ ↗ (semantic equivalence to *stand over*).

6.2   First and foremost, the Hangeul keyboard has consonants to the left and vowels to the right (with glide-plus-vowel combinations also on the right). Some say that in itself this "CV" aspect of the layout makes it possible to type much faster in Korean than in English, because it allows for regular alternation of hand action. On the consonant side of the board, there is further logic to the layout. The bottom four keys are the aspirated stops (presented in the same order as in the classic diagram given in Fig. 6.3), i.e. ㅋ *kh*, ㅌ *th*, ㅊ *ch*, ㅍ *ph*. Then at the top, the first five keys give the simple letters ㅂ *b*, ㅈ *c*, ㄷ *d*, ㄱ *g* and ㅅ *s*, and using the same keys with SHIFT, one gets the "doubled" letter versions: ㅃ *pp*, ㅉ *cc*, ㄸ *tt*, ㄲ *kk*, and ㅆ *ss*. In the middle row (still on the left-hand side), there are the remaining consonants (except for the glide): ㅁ *m*, ㄴ *n*, ㅇ *ø/ŋ*, and ㅎ *h*.

The instructions said that you didn't have to worry about the vowels and glides, i.e. about the right-hand side of the keyboard. For your information, however, the simple vowels (ㅜ, ㅡ, ㅗ, ㅏ, ㅣ, ㅐ, ㅔ) generally occupy the central part of the vowel sector, with the glide-plus-vowel keys at the bottom and the top. By the way, many Koreans are unaware of the rationale for the keyboard.

Chapter 7

7.1   The point of this question is to help you see that English, like any language, has a great variety of fixed expressions. The origins and explanations are as follows (Ammer 1992):

(a) *a dog in a manger*. Meaning: a person who out of sheer meanness takes or keeps something wanted by someone else, even though it is useless to them. Origin: one of Aesop's Fables (a manger is a kind of box in a stable for horses or cattle to eat from).

(b) *a rose by any other name*. Meaning: superficial features, e.g. a name or family affiliation, do not change the real nature of a thing. Origin: Shakespeare's *Romeo and Juliet*.

(c) *smoke and mirrors*. Meaning: a clever set of tricks designed to bamboozle or confuse, to draw people's attention away from the real issues. Origin: a reference to magician's tricks.

(d) *the pot calling the kettle black*. Meaning: accusing someone of faults one has oneself. Origin: From the times when cooking was done over open hearths, when the smoke tended to blacken all of the cooking utensils.

(e) *turn the other cheek*. Meaning: to disregard an insult, attack, or provocation, to respond with non-violence. Origin: A saying of Jesus.

(f) *a bird in the hand is worth two in the bush*. Meaning: better to make use of what one already has than to go chasing after possibilities which might never be realized. Origin: An ancient Greek saying, quoted several times in Aesop's Fables.

(g) *make hay while the sun shines*. Meaning: make best use of favourable conditions while they last. Origin: A saying from sixteenth-century England. Making hay requires hot dry conditions to dry out the cut grass.

(h) *might as well be hung for a sheep as a lamb*. Meaning: if you are willing to risk severe punishment for doing something minor, then you may as well do something more serious. Origin: in seventeenth-century England, theft of either a lamb or a sheep was punishable by death.

(i) *wheels within wheels*. Meaning: complex motives or hidden agendas which interact with each other. Origin: Old Testament (Ezekiel).

(j) *gilding the lily*. Meaning: to try to improve something which is already valuable or special enough by adding excessive or ridiculous ornaments. Origin: Modified version of a saying in Shakespeare's *King John*.

Overall, this collection of sayings can be seen as reflecting: (i) an older, simpler rural lifestyle (*manger, pot and kettle, make hay, sheep for a lamb*), (ii) the influence of the Bible (*wheels within wheels, turn the other cheek*), and (iii) the influence of Shakespeare (*rose by any other name, gild the lily*) and Aesop's Fables.

7.3 Japanese honorific usage. The formal differences between this sentence and the earlier one are: • the use of an honorific title, *sensei* 'teacher', • the choice of an honouring or exalting form of the verb 'to be' *irasshai-*. The lack of these honorific features in the earlier sentence, from a company secretary about her boss, was explained as due to the fact that employees of a company regard themselves as belonging to a single in-group. One does not use honorifics about people from one's own in-group, even if they are higher in status or rank than oneself. It is also explained in section 7.3.1 however, that:

not all occupations consider themselves as belonging to in-groups, at least so far as honorific language is concerned. For instance, doctors who work at hospitals are full-time salaried employees, but they are not group-oriented. Similarly, though university professors regard their students as members of their in-group, they do not necessarily consider other staff at their universities as part of their group.

Evidently, lack of in-group identification explains why honorifics are used when a university lecturer speaks about one of his or her colleagues to a member of the public. We may assume that university lecturers enjoy high status and high respect in Japan. Without the in-group factor suppressing the use of honorifics, the difference in social status between a member of the general public and a lecturer (even a junior lecturer) calls for the use of the title *sensei* 'teacher' and selection of honouring verb forms.

Glossary of linguistic terms

Be aware that not all related words are listed individually; for example, *allomorph* and *mora* are listed, but *allomorphy* and *moraic* are not. Language family names are not listed.

accusative case or noun marker whose primary function is to indicate that a noun phrase is the direct object of a transitive verb. *See*: case; object.

actor a semantic role of a noun phrase: someone who does something, a "do-er". *See*: agent; undergoer.

adposition a cover term for prepositions and postpositions; they combine with a noun phrase to form a new phrase with the adposition as its head. *See*: head; preposition; postposition.

affix a bound morpheme which does not have a word-like meaning, but which functions to modify the meaning or the grammatical status of the word or stem it is attached to. There are several terms for specific types of affix. *See*: prefix; suffix; circumfix; infix.

affricate a term used in phonetics for a consonant whose articulation involves a complete oral closure (i.e. a stop) followed by a fricative-like release with audible friction noise; the only affricates in English are palato-alveolar *tʃ* and *dʒ*, as in *church* and *judge*, respectively; other affricates found in some East and Southeast Asian languages are dental *ts* and palatal *tç*.

affrication a phonological process in which a stop acquires a fricative-like release, and becomes an affricate; for example, Japanese /t/ becomes [ts] in certain environments.

agent a semantic role of a noun phrase: someone who does something or, more specifically, someone who does something *to* someone. *See*: actor; patient.

agglutinating a type of language in which complex words typically contain a sequence of easily identifiable morphemes, each with a single distinct meaning; Japanese is an agglutinating language.

agreement a grammatical process whereby one word changes its form (typically by taking an affix) so as to indicate a grammatical property of another word with which it has a particular grammatical relationship; for example, in English a present tense verb takes an affix -*s* if its subject is third person singular: we say that the verb "agrees" with its subject in person and number.

alienable possession ownership, i.e. a possessive relationship which can be controlled so that the "possessed" item can be transferred from one person to another, as in expressions like *my car* and *I have a car* (in contrast with inalienable possession, as with body parts and kin terms, e.g. *my head*, *my daughter*).

allo- a prefix used in linguistic terminology to refer to non-distinctive variants of a single distinctive unit, e.g. allophones of a phoneme, allomorphs of a morpheme.

allomorph one of a set of variants of a morpheme; the choice of which allomorph to use in a particular situation often depends on the phonological environment (phonological conditioning); for example, the English plural suffix is realized as -*s* after a voiceless stop but as -*z* after a voiced stop (compare: *cats* /kæts/, *pigs* /pɪgz/); alternatively, choice of allomorph may depend on the identity of the word (lexical conditioning); for example, English *child* and *ox* take the plural suffix -(*r*)*en* to form *children* and *oxen*.

allophone one of a set of non-distinctive variants of a phoneme; the choice of which allophone to use in a particular situation usually depends on the surrounding sounds (phonological conditioning); for example, in English, phoneme /p/ has an aspirated allophone [pʰ] at the beginning of words.

allotone one of a set of tonal variants of a toneme (tone); choice of which allotone to use usually depends on the shape of the syllable, on the nature of tones in the adjacent syllables, or on whether or not the syllable is at the end of a phrase.

alphabetic writing system a system of writing in which the letters stand for individual speech sounds (segments). English has an alphabetic writing system. *See*: logographic writing system; syllabic writing system.

anaphora in grammar, the situation when an expression which on its own does not identify any particular individual gets an interpretation in context by referring to the same person, thing, etc. as previously mentioned. e.g. *John caught a rabbit. He ate it*, where *he* refers to *John* and *it* refers to the *rabbit*. *See*: zero anaphora.

approximant in phonetics, a term for sounds produced when vocal organs come close to one another, but not so close as to produce the audible friction or hissing quality which would be the hallmark of fricative sounds; a cover term for *r*-sounds, *l*-sounds, *w*-sounds, and *y*-sounds.

archiphoneme in phonology, a hypothetical abstract phoneme which is unspecified for a particular phonemic feature; they are usually designated by a capital letter symbol. Many phonologists regard the archiphoneme as an outdated concept but it is still used in descriptive grammars.

argument a noun phrase which has a special grammatical link to a verb or other predicate. Predicates can differ in the number of arguments they take, in whether the arguments are obligatory or optional, and in the nature of the grammatical link.

For example, English *die* and *laugh* take one argument (a subject), but *kill* and *hate* take two arguments (a subject and a direct object).

article a small class of grammatical words, found in some languages which help identify what a noun refers to; English has two articles in the singular: the definite article *the*, and the indefinite article *a/an*. *See*: definite article; indefinite article.

articulation the movement of the speech organs involved in producing speech sounds; sounds can be classified according to their place of articulation (e.g. labial, dental, alveolar, palatal, velar) and manner of articulation (e.g. stop, nasal, fricative, lateral).

aspect a grammatical category concerned with the time structure of an event, as seen by the speaker; many different aspectual categories are found in various languages; some of the more common aspects depend on factors such as whether the event is seen as extended in time (durative) or as taking only a single moment (punctual), whether or not an event is being viewed in its totality (perfective vs. imperfective), or whether an event is being presented as routine (habitual).

aspiration a term in phonetics for an audible puff of air which can accompany the articulation of some speech sounds, especially voiceless stops. Aspiration is usually symbolized by a small raised [ʰ] following the main symbol; for example, [tʰ] represents an aspirated voiceless alveolar stop.

assimilation a term in phonetics which refers to the way in which one sound can influence the articulation of another, so that one sound becomes more like another.

auxiliary verb a verb used with a main verb to carry certain kinds of grammatical information such as aspect, mood and tense. For example, the English progressive construction uses a form of the verb *to be* as an auxiliary, e.g. *He is singing*.

breathy voice a term used in phonetics for a type of voicing (phonation); refers to the breathy, whispered effect produced by holding the vocal folds loosely together, so that the folds vibrate without closing as air from the lungs comes through.

calque a type of borrowing where a word or phrase is translated literally, morpheme by morpheme, from a foreign language.

case a grammatical category of nouns and pronouns which is determined by their grammatical relationship to other elements in the clause, especially the verb; cases can be associated with semantic roles (e.g. instrument, location) or with grammatical functions (e.g. subject, object); in inflecting languages, case is usually marked by affixes called case inflections. *See*: nominative; accusative; dative.

case marking a system of marking which indicates the case category of a noun phrase; sometimes a single case category can be marked by several different markers; or the same marker may be used for different categories.

causative a grammatical term used to describe a verb or verbal construction which depicts someone or something (the subject of the clause) *causing* some other event to take place; *kill* and *widen* are called causative verbs because they imply that the subject causes an event of 'dying' or 'becoming wider'; an example of a causative construction is the English *make*-causative, as in *She made him do it*.

circumfix an affix which has two parts, one of which occurs before and the other after the root morpheme; e.g. Malay *ke- -an*, as in *ke-baik-an* 'goodness' (from *baik* 'good').

classifier construction grammatical devices which 'categorize' the referent of a noun phrase in terms of certain semantic dimensions, such as shape, size, function, movability, animacy, or status. *See*: numeral classifier.

clitic a morpheme with an intermediate status between a word and an affix; they are grammatically and semantically word-like, but do not normally stand alone phonologically, instead attaching themselves to the nearest ordinary word.

closed class a grammatical word class whose membership is fixed or limited; e.g. prepositions or demonstratives. *See*: open class.

closed syllable a syllable which has a consonant or a consonant cluster in final position, as opposed to an open syllable which has a vowel in final position.

cognates words from related languages which are descended from a single original word in the ancestor language; French *père* and Spanish *padre* (both meaning 'father') are cognates because they both descended from a common ancestor word in Latin.

comitative a case or noun marker whose primary function is to indicate that the referent is doing something *with* another person.

comparative method a method used in historical linguistics to work out the vocabulary and grammar of an ancestor language by drawing inferences from the evidence that remains in several daughter languages.

complement a term used in grammar with two meanings: (i) a verbal phrase which fulfils the function of subject or object; e.g. in the sentence *I want to go to Vietnam* the phrase *to go to Vietnam* is functioning as the object of the verb *want*; (ii) a phrase which is required by a predicate in order for it to be grammatically complete, e.g. *fond* usually requires a prepositional phrase complement; one can't just **be fond*, one has to be *fond of something*.

complementary distribution when variants of linguistic units occur in mutually exclusive environments; allophones (i.e. non-distinctive variants of a phoneme) are often in complementary distribution. *See*: allo-.

compound word a word consisting of two or more morphemes, each of which can stand on its own, e.g. *bedroom*, *rainfall*, *underarm*.

consonant a category of speech sounds; those sounds produced with a significant obstruction to the flow of air through the vocal tract. Sounds which do not involve a significant obstruction to the airflow are called vowels.

constituent order the order in which the main constituents of a sentence (e.g. the subject, object, and verb, usually symbolized as S, O, and V, respectively) occur in a sentence; languages differ in their constituent order: e.g. English has SVO order, Korean has SOV.

contour tone in a tone language, a tone whose pitch varies as a significant part of its distinctive identity, e.g. falling, rising, rising then falling; a "moving tone". *See*: register tone.

copula a special verb, such as English 'to be' in its various forms (*is, am, was, were,* etc.), which links the two parts of an equational or attributive sentence, such as *George W. Bush is the president of the USA* or *Elephants are big*; some languages simply use juxtaposition for such sentences, with no copula.

creaky voice a kind of voicing (phonation), referring to the low-pitched, creaky effect produced by a very slow vibration of one part of the vocal folds, whilst the rest vibrates normally.

cultural key word a highly salient and deeply culture-laden word which acts as a focal point around which a whole cultural domain is organized; a word which designates a culturally important concept.

dative a case or noun marker whose primary function is to indicate that the referent is the recipient of an act of giving or saying; or to indicate the indirect object of the verb.

definite a term used in grammar to describe a noun phrase which is marked to indicate the speaker's assumption that the addressee will know the identity of the person or thing being spoken about; in English, definiteness (and indefiniteness) can be marked by words known as 'articles'. *See*: definite article; indefinite.

definite article a word, such as English *the*, whose function is to indicate definiteness. *See*: definite; indefinite article.

deictic a word whose referent changes depending on the context of use; e.g. *I, you, now, here, this.*

deixis the process or phenomenon whereby the referent of certain expressions depends on the context in which they are used; the term deixis comes from a Greek word meaning 'pointing'.

demonstrative a sub-class of determiners; words such as English *this* and *that* which are used to point out or indicate some specific person, thing or other referent.

dental a term in phonetics used to describe an articulation involving the teeth; for example, [d] and [ð] are dental sounds because they involve the blade of the tongue touching the upper teeth.

derivation (derivational) when a morphological process, e.g. affixation or reduplication, produces a new word; a derivational process may or may not involve a change of word class; for example, when *-ize* is added to the adjective *modern*, the new word *modernize* belongs to a different word class, i.e. verb; but when *un-* is added to *happy*, the word class does not change, because both are adjectives. *See also*: inflection.

diacritic a mark added to a symbol to alter its value; e.g. in the International Phonetic Alphabet, nasalization is indicated by adding [˜] above another phonetic symbol.

dialects regional or social varieties of a single language, each having some distinctive words and grammar, as well as a distinctive style of pronunciation (accent). Technically, dialects should be mutually intelligible. In the Chinese tradition, however, regional languages such as Cantonese and Hakka are referred to as dialects.

diglossia (diglossic) a term used in sociolinguistics to refer to a situation where two or more language varieties co-occur in a speech community each with its own range of social functions; in diglossic situations one can usually identify a high (H) variety and a low (L) variety; the L variety is learnt and used in the home and other informal settings, and has less prestige, while the H variety is learnt in school, is used in public, formal situations, in serious literature, etc., and has greater prestige.

direct object *See*: object.

dissimilation a term in phonetics which refers to a process whereby one sound becomes less similar to a nearby sound; the converse of assimilation.

distinctive feature in phonology, a term used to identify a feature of pronunciation which distinguishes one set of phonemes from another; e.g. voicing is a distinctive feature of English consonants.

disyllabic made up of two syllables.

ellipsis the omission of a word or words from a sentence, usually in cases where the listener can understand what is intended from the context. *See*: zero anaphora.

epenthetic describes a sound which has been inserted into a word in order to break up a sequence of sounds which would otherwise be difficult to pronounce.

equi-phrase a complement which lacks an overt subject but whose subject is understood to be the same as the subject of the main clause, e.g. *I want to go* (instead of *I want me to go*).

ethnocentrism culture bias; distorting another culture or language by imposing the categories of one's own culture or language upon it, instead of seeing it in its own terms.

expressive a word class, often found in mainland Southeast Asian languages, with distinctive phonetic characteristics linked to the expression of subtle differences in feeling, attitude, or experience; they often involve chiming or rhyming reduplication and tonal shifts; they can contain unusual sound combinations not found elsewhere in the lexicon.

featural script a hypothetical kind of writing system, in which symbols stand not for individual sounds but for lower-level features of pronunciation, such as whether a sound is a consonant or a vowel, whether it is voiced or voiceless, or its place of articulation. *See*: distinctive features.

final in traditional Chinese phonology, all of a syllable except for the initial consonant (*See*: initial), i.e. the vocalic nucleus and final consonant, if there is one; also called the rhyme.

formative a morphological unit which may or may not have an identifiable meaning or function; formative is a broader term than morpheme, which, strictly speaking, implies an identifiable meaning. For example, the element *-cern* in English words like *concern* and *discern* is a formative, but not a morpheme.

fricative a term used in phonetics to describe 'hissy' consonants whose articulation involves the airstream being forced through a constriction, producing a noisy turbulence. For example, [f] is a fricative because it is articulated by placing the upper teeth against the lower lip and forcing air through the gap.

fusional language a type of inflecting language in which the inflectional affixes typically indicate several different grammatical categories at the same time; e.g. in Latin the verb ending *-o* indicates present tense, indicative mood, and first person subject.

geminate cluster a sequence of two identical segments, especially consonants. Geminate consonants occur in English only at morpheme boundaries (e.g. *nighttime*, *bookcase*). Long vowels in some languages are sometimes analyzed as geminates, e.g. [o:] might be analyzed as /oo/.

gender a system in which the nouns of a language fall into two or more lexical classes, which are relevant to the grammatical workings of the language. German, for example, has three gender classes (called masculine, feminine, and neuter); the gender of a noun determines which article and which of various case and number allomorphs it takes (among other things). With nouns referring to people, the gender is usually predictable from the actual sex of the individual, but for other nouns it is either arbitrary or conditioned by the phonological shape of the word.

genetically related languages which are members of a single language family; i.e. languages which are all descended from a common ancestor language.

gerundive in grammar, a dependent verbal form which is neutral for tense, and, in some languages, has certain adjective-like properties, e.g. English *-ing* forms such as *laughing*.

glide in phonetics, a cover-term for *y*-sounds and *w*-sounds. *See*: semi-vowel.

glottal stop in phonetics, a stop sound produced by a sudden closure of the vocal folds in the glottis. *See*: stop.

glottalization a term in phonetics for a wide range of phenomena involving some kind of activity in the glottis. Strictly speaking, the term should refer to the use of a simultaneous glottal stop, but it is sometimes also used to refer to glottal constriction, creaky voice, or use of the glottalic airstream mechanism.

glottis the passage through the larynx (voicebox) which is opened, closed, constricted, etc. by the action of the vocal folds.

grapheme a minimal contrastive unit in the writing system of a language.

head in grammar, the main element of a grammatical construction; the element (usually obligatory) which gives a particular construction its individual character. For example, in a noun phrase like *those three fluffy kittens*, the head is the noun *kittens*. The other, subsidiary elements of the construction are called dependents; usually they are optional and can be seen as modifying or qualifying the head.

homonymy a situation in which different words (homonyms) happen accidentally to have the same form, either phonetically or graphically; e.g. *bank* the institution and *bank* as in *river bank; to, too,* and *two*. When the sameness of form is phonetic, the forms are called homophones; when the sameness of form is in writing, the forms are called homographs.

homorganic a term used in phonetics for sounds which are produced at the same place of articulation, such as [p], [b], and [m] which are all bilabials.

honorifics morphological or syntactic devices used to express levels of respect, either in relation to the social identities of the speaker and addressee, or in relation to a person or people being spoken about.

ideogram a graphic sign which is supposed to stand directly for an idea or concept, rather than for any particular word or sounds. Chinese characters are sometimes (misleadingly) described as ideograms.

imperative a special verb form or sentence type whose core function is to express forthright requests or commands, e.g. *Go away!*

inclusive/exclusive with reference to first-person plural pronouns, an inclusive pronoun implies that the addressee is included (i.e. *we* including *you*); exclusive implies that the addressee is excluded (i.e. *we* excluding *you*), e.g. Malay *kita* is 'we-inclusive', *kami* is 'we-exclusive'.

indefinite a term used in grammar to describe a noun phrase which is marked so as to indicate that the speaker is not assuming that the addressee will know the identity of the person or thing being spoken about; in English, indefiniteness (and its converse, definiteness) is marked by words known as 'articles'. *See*: indefinite article; definite.

indefinite article a word such as English *a* or *some*, whose function is indicate indefiniteness. *See*: indefinite.

indigenized a term used about a loan word, meaning that it has been adapted to conform to the phonological and/or grammatical patterns of the borrowing language.

indirect object a grammatical function of a noun phrase; typically associated with the semantic role of the recipient of a verb of giving, or the addressee of a verb of saying. *See*: object.

infix an affix which is inserted inside the root or stem; they are not found in European languages, but are common in some East and Southeast Asian languages.

inflection in grammar, a term used to refer to morphemes (typically affixes) which signal grammatical categories such as case, tense, and number. *See*: derivation.

information question (also called "wh-question") in grammar, a term used to describe questions which seek a particular kind of information, corresponding to questions formed in English with question words such as *what, who, which, when, why*, and *how*.

initial in phonology, the consonant or consonant clusters that are found prior to the first vowel in a syllable; traditional Chinese phonology tabulated all possible initials. *See*: final.

interrogative a special verb form or sentence type whose core function is to express questions.

intransitive refers to verbs such as English *smile*, which do not take direct objects: *She smiled.*

IPA International Phonetic Alphabet; a set of standard symbols for recording the pronunciation of words in different languages.

isolating language a type of language where the great majority of words are invariable in form, e.g. Mandarin Chinese, Vietnamese; in isolating languages, grammatical relationships are primarily shown by word order rather than by affixation. *See*: agglutinating; fusional language.

labial a term in phonetics to refer to a place of articulation involving one or both lips. There are two kinds: [f] is called labiodental because it involves the lower lip and the teeth, [p] is called bilabial because it involves both lips.

language family a group of languages which are genetically related; languages which have all developed from a common ancestor language.

larynx the voicebox, the hollow organ in the throat which houses the vocal folds.

lax a (problematic) term for sounds which are produced with less muscular effort and/or which are relatively short. *See also*: tense.

lexical conditioning when a variant form of a morpheme is determined by the identity of the word itself, so that it has to be learnt on a word-by-word basis, e.g. the English plural suffix *-ren*, as used with the word *child*.

lexical elaboration when a language has a large number of words or terms in a particular domain of meaning, so that speakers can easily make fine distinctions within this domain.

lexical stratum (pl. strata) a set of vocabulary items distinguished by certain phonological, morphological, semantic, and stylistic properties which set them apart from the rest of the lexicon; loan words often form lexical strata.

lexical tone *See*: tone.

lexicon all the words and bound morphemes of a language, along with information about their pronunciation, grammatical properties, and meanings; the internalized dictionary stored in the native speaker's memory.

lingua franca a language variety used for communication among people who do not otherwise share a common language.

linguistic area a geographical area in which languages from different families share many grammatical, phonological, and lexical characteristics due to long-standing language contact.

loan blend a loan word which has been borrowed with part of its original form retained, with only partial adaptation into the borrowing language, e.g. *restaurant* with a simulated French ending, /rɛstərɔ̃/.

loan translation *See*: calque.

loan word a word which has been borrowed from another language, often with phonological adaptation and some meaning change.

logographic writing system a writing system in which each symbol stands for a separate word or morpheme, as with Chinese character writing. *See*: alphabetic writing system; syllabic writing system.

manner of articulation terms in phonetics which describe various kinds of constriction in the vocal tract which take place in the production of consonant sounds; e.g. stop, fricative, lateral.

marker (marking) in grammar, any morpheme which signals grammatical information; e.g. English -*s* is a marker of plurality.

measure (i) in this book, a word which characterizes the form or quantity in which a substance occurs, e.g. a *drop* of water, a *cup* of water, a *litre* of water; measures are comparable in their grammar to true classifiers (*See*: classifier construction), but are found in all languages, (ii) some linguists use measure as a cover-term for measures, unit counters, and true classifiers.

metalanguage a language, or any set of terms, used to describe or interpret another language.

mimetic a term used in Japanese linguistics for a class of sound-symbolic words indicating subtle sensory or emotional aspects of an event.

minimal pair a pair of words which differ only in a single phoneme, e.g. English *cup* /kʌp/ and *cut* /kʌt/.

modality (modal) in grammar, a verbal category which includes meanings such as possibility, potentiality, ability, and necessity; modal verbs are auxiliary verbs which express this kind of meaning, e.g. English *can, should, must*.

mora a phonological unit found in some languages (e.g. Japanese) which is relevant to rhythm; in principle, sounds or sound sequences which consist of a single mora (pl. morae) take the same time to pronounce.

morpheme the minimal meaningful "bits" into which words can be divided.

morphology the branch of grammar which studies the structure of words.

morphophonemic relating to the interaction of morphology and phonology; refers to phonological factors which can affect the pronunciation of morphemes, or vice versa. For example, the English plural morpheme is pronounced as -*s*, -*z*, or -*əz* depending on the previous sound.

nasal alternation a term used in Austronesian linguistics to describe the situation in which an affix contains a nasal sound, sometimes symbolized as N, whose quality changes systematically depending on the adjacent sounds, sometimes appearing as *m*, sometimes as *n*, sometimes as *ŋ*, etc.

nasalization pronouncing a vowel while at the same time lowering the velum so that air passes out through the nose, thus imparting a distinctive timbre or voice quality to the sound. The IPA represents nasalization with a tilde, e.g. [ã] stands for a nasalized pronunciation of [a].

national language a language which has a special status as the main language of a country; usually the preeminent language in government and official uses; some countries recognize several official languages in addition to the national language.

native (indigenous) words words in a language which have descended from its own ancestor language, as opposed to those which have been borrowed from other languages.

neutral tone a term used to describe words in a tone language which do not have an inherent tone of their own, but which acquire a tonal pronunciation from adjacent words. *See*: tone.

nominal relating to nouns and/or to noun phrases; used by some linguists as a cover term for nouns and pronouns.

nominalizer a morpheme which turns words of other word classes into nouns.

nominative a case or noun marker whose primary function is to indicate that a noun phrase is the subject of a sentence. *See*: case; accusative.

non-finite verb form a form of the verb which is not inflected for any specific verbal category, such as tense or aspect.

noun phrase (NP) a word or group of words, with a noun or pronoun as its main element (*See*: head), which is capable of functioning as the subject or object of a sentence; a noun or pronoun together with any demonstratives, adjectives, etc. that go with it.

number a grammatical category, associated principally with nouns and pronouns, which indicates something about the number of referents of a noun phrase; e.g. singular, dual, plural. *See also*: pronoun.

numeral classifier a kind of classifier which is obligatory (in certain languages) in noun phrases containing numerals or other quantifying expressions. *See*: classifier construction.

object (direct object) a grammatical function of a noun phrase; it is associated with the semantic role of patient but it can also be borne by noun phrases which are not patients; e.g. in *The dog loves Max* and *She knew me*, the words *Max* and *me* are direct objects even though they are not patients; sometimes symbolized as O, as when the basic word order of a language is described as SOV, SVO, etc. *See*: patient; accusative; indirect object.

oblique argument an argument of a verb which does not have the grammatical function of subject, object, or indirect object; a noun phrase with a more peripheral relationship to the main verb.

obstruent a cover-term for stops, fricatives, and affricates, three classes of consonant sounds produced by creating a constriction in the airflow as it passes though the vocal tract. *See also*: sonorants.

open class a word class whose members are in principle unlimited in number, so that new items can be added freely; nouns and verbs are open classes. *See*: closed class.

open syllable a syllable which ends with a vowel, as opposed to a closed syllable, which ends with a consonant.

palatal a term used in phonetics to refer to a consonant produced by raising the middle of the tongue to the hard palate.

palatalization the process in which a non-palatal sound is replaced with a palatal or palato-alveolar variant, often under the influence of an adjacent high vowel.

particle a class of small morphologically invariable words which either have grammatical functions, e.g. indicating subject or topic, or which convey illocutionary or expressive meanings, e.g. marking a question or expressing surprise.

patient a semantic role of a noun phrase; the person or thing which is affected by the action of a transitive verb, e.g. in *The dog bit the child*, the noun phrase *the child* has the role of patient.

perfective a verbal category which presents an event in its totality and from the outside, as it were, without directing any attention to how it unfolds in time. *See*: aspect.

person a grammatical category associated with pronouns, based on whether a pronoun refers to or includes the speaker (first person, e.g. *I* and *we*), the addressee (second person, e.g. *you* singular and *you* plural), or someone else (third person, e.g. *he, she, it, they*).

phonation type the various different modes of vibration of the vocal folds, each of which imparts a different auditory quality; e.g. (ordinary) voicing, breathy voice, creaky voice, stiff voice.

phonemes the distinctive and contrastive units in the sound system of a particular language; words in any language can be segmented into sequences of phonemes. Languages differ in how many phonemes they have, and in the kinds of pronunciation differences that distinguish one from another. Changing any of the phonemes in a word will change the identity of the word, by turning it into another word or into a non-existent form; phonemes are often written in slanted brackets, e.g. /n/. *See*: allophone; minimal pair.

phonetic (P) in the Chinese writing system, that part of a compound character which gives an indication of the intended pronunciation.

phonetics the study of speech sounds, including how they are pronounced (articulatory phonetics) and the physical properties of the sound waves associated with them (acoustic phonetics). *See*: phonology.

phonographic writing system a writing system in which the individual symbols stand for sounds, either phonemes or syllables. *See*: logographic system.

phonological conditioning the selection of an variant form on the basis of the phonetic environment in which it occurs (i.e. the sounds nearby).

phonology the study of how speech sounds are organized and function in particular languages. *See*: phonemes; phonetics; phonotactics.

phonotactics the ways in which sounds can be combined to form syllables and words, according to the rules of a particular language.

pitch the impression of whether a word or syllable is pronounced "low" (low pitch) or "high" (high pitch) on a musical scale. Corresponds roughly to the fundamental frequency of the sound wave, which is determined by the rate of vibration of the vocal folds as the sound is being produced.

pitch-accent prominence of part of a word or phrase created by its being different in pitch (higher or lower) from its immediate surroundings.

place of articulation a term used in phonetics in relation to consonant sounds—the location in the vocal tract where the main constriction occurs; e.g. labial, dental, palatal, velar.

polar question in grammar, a question for which an appropriate response is one of two alternatives, e.g. *yes* or *no*, as opposed to open-ended "information questions"; also known as yes/no questions.

polysemy the situation in which a single word has several distinct but related meanings; e.g the English word *hot*. Polysemy differs from homonymy, which is the situation of two or more words which accidentally happen to have the same form (and so are unrelated in meaning).

postposition a function word that follows a noun phrase and combines with it to form a new phrase (a postpositional phrase); the postposition indicates the semantic role of the noun phrase, e.g. Japanese *ni* in *gakkoo ni* 'at school'; like a preposition except that prepositions precede the noun phrase. *See*: adposition; preposition.

prefix an affix which is added to the front of a root or stem, such as English *re-* or *in-*.

prenasalized (prenasalization) the articulation of a sound, most often a stop, with an initial brief period of airflow through the nasal cavity; in the IPA it is symbolized by means of a small raised letter before the main symbol, e.g. [^{m}b].

preposition a function word that precedes a noun phrase and combines with it to form a new phrase (a prepositional phrase); the preposition indicates the semantic role of the noun phrase, e.g. English *at* in the phrase *at school*. *See also*: adposition; postposition.

productive a process is productive if it can be used freely and repeatedly; e.g. the English plural *-s* is productive, but the plural *-(r)en* found in words like *children, oxen*, and *brethren* is not productive.

pronoun a class of words whose members refer to individuals by reference to their role in the speech act. For example, the word 'I' refers to the person who says it, 'you' refers to the person being spoken to, and 'he' or 'she' refers to someone other than speaker or addressee.

prototypical examples of a linguistic category which are more typical, more psychologically salient, and usually more frequent, than others; e.g. *sparrows* and *magpies* are prototypical birds, whereas *penguins* and *emus* are not.

radial polysemy a kind of polysemy in which there is a central or prototypical meaning with extensions in different directions; the extended meanings all share something with the central meaning, but need not share very much with one another. *See*: polysemy.

radical in Chinese linguistics, the meaning-based part of a compound character. *See*: signific.

reduplication a process by which a word, or part of a word, is repeated to form a new word; reduplication can be total, e.g. English *no-no*, or partial, e.g. Tagalog *lalakad* 'will walk' (*lakad* 'walk'). Other kinds of reduplication are rhyming reduplication, in which the consonants of the repeated element change, e.g. *silly-billy*, and chiming reduplication, in which the vowels of the repeated element change, e.g. *zig-zag*.

referent the real entity (person, thing, place, situation, etc.) referred to by a linguistic expression on a particular occasion.

reflexive in grammar, a term used for a word or marker whose primary function is to indicate that the subject or agent affects itself.

register (i) in phonetics, the voice quality brought about by a specific type of phonation, (ii) in sociolinguistics, a variety of language used for a specific purpose, as opposed to a social or regional dialect.

register tone in a tone language, a tone which has a constant pitch level, with no significant upward or downward movement; a level tone. *See*: contour tone.

retroflex a term used in phonetics to label sounds made with the tip of the tongue bent back in the direction of the hard palate. IPA symbols for retroflex sounds include [ʈ], [ɳ], and [ɭ].

roman letters the letters used in English and other Western European alphabets (so named because they were originally used by the Romans in writing Latin).

romanization a system for writing words in roman letters from a language which is usually written in another script, such as Chinese, Thai, Korean.

schwa an unstressed mid-central vowel, symbolized as [ə] in the IPA, produced with the tongue and lips in their rest positions; in English, schwa often replaces other vowel phonemes in unstressed syllables.

segment a term used in phonetics for an individual speech sound; although some syllables consist of only a single segment (e.g. a vowel), most syllables in any language have two or more segments.

segmental phonology a description of how segmental speech sounds are organized and function in a language; the phonology of a language excluding reference to tone, intonation, and other suprasegmental aspects.

semantic explication a description of the meaning of a word in the form of a paraphrase composed of simple, basic words.

semantic primes those words in any language whose meanings are so simple and clear that they cannot be defined or explained any further, e.g. 'someone', 'do', 'say', 'good', 'this', 'one'.

semantics the study of meaning in language.

semi-vowel in phonetics, a term for *y*-sounds and *w*-sounds, based on the fact that the shape of the oral cavity is relatively open when such sounds are produced; *y*-sounds approximate the high front vowel *i*, and *w*-sounds the high back vowel *u*, respectively. *See*: glide.

sentence-final particle in grammar, a small invariable word typically found at the end of an utterance, indicating the speech-function of the sentence and/or something about the speaker's attitude or feeling towards what is said.

serial verb construction a construction in which two or more verbs sharing the same subject occur together in one clause without any intervening conjunction.

sesquisyllabic literally, having one and a half syllables; a phonotactic structure which allows words with one full or major syllable and a second "reduced" or minor syllable, as in Khmer and Burmese.

signific (S) in the Chinese writing system, that part of a compound character which gives an indication of the intended meaning of the character. *See*: radical; phonetic.

sonorants a term used in phonetics for sounds produced with a relatively unconstricted flow of air through the vocal tract, and a vocal fold position such that spontaneous voicing is possible; a cover term for vowels, glides, liquids, nasals and laterals. *See*: obstruent.

specific (specificity) when a noun phrase is used with the intention to refer to a specific referent which the speaker has in mind; some languages explicitly mark noun phrases used in this way, while others, such as English, do not.

standard language in sociolinguistics, a term referring to a socially favoured variety of a language which is regarded as the norm of correct usage in the media, language teaching, and for other purposes. Standard languages are codified in dictionaries, school grammar books, and so on. They cut across regional differences, providing a unified means of communication. Historically, standard languages are usually based on the speech of the educated population of a cultural or political centre. Varieties which diverge from the accepted standard are called non-standard.

stative in grammar, a verb or adjective which depicts a state which does not vary or unfold over time; stative verbs such as *know* and *like* are incompatible with the English progressive aspect.

stiff voice a kind of phonation achieved by stiffening the muscle of the vocal folds. *See*: phonation type; creaky voice.

stop in phonetics, a speech sound produced by the speech organs coming into full contact, so that the flow of air through the vocal tract is stopped for a moment; e.g. sounds like *p, b, t, d, k, g*.

subject a grammatical function of a noun phrase; the noun phrase which is most important from a grammatical point of view; subject is usually associated with the agent (doer) of an action and/or with the topic of sentence (i.e. what the sentence is about). Most verbs in any language require a subject, though sometimes it is not necessary for it to be explicitly stated if it can be understood from context. *See*: object; nominative.

substrate in historical linguistics and language contact studies, a term used to refer to a language which has been replaced by a dominant language but which has nonetheless influenced the vocabulary or grammar of the dominant language in enduring ways.

suffix an affix which is added to the end of a stem, e.g. English *-ed* or *-ing* (as opposed to a prefix, which is added at the front of a stem).

suprasegmental a term used in phonetics to refer to aspects of the sound structure of words and phrases which manifest themselves across whole syllables, words, or phrases (as opposed to individual segments); lexical tone, stress, and intonation are examples of suprasegmentals.

syllabary a set of symbols used to write a language, where each symbol represents a different syllable of the spoken language, e.g. Japanese *hiragana* and *katakana*. *See*: alphabetic writing system.

syllabic writing system a writing system in which each symbol represents a different syllable.

syllable the smallest unit of sound structure which is normally pronounceable by itself; it usually contains a vowel (or a sequence of vowels) flanked by one or more consonants; the most common syllable types are CV and CVC. *See*: open syllable; closed syllable.

synonyms words with identical meanings. True or exact synonyms, i.e. words which can be substituted for each other in all contexts, are rare; most so-called synonyms are more accurately described as near-synonyms.

tense (i) in grammar, a grammatical category of verbs; its primary function is to indicate the relative time at which the event took place. For example, the primary function of a past tense category is to indicate that an event took place before the time of speaking; (ii) a term used by some phonologists to describe sounds which are articulated with relatively greater muscular tension, more extreme movements of the vocal organs, or greater duration. *See*: lax.

tone (lexical tone) the use of pitch shape as a distinctive feature of words, so that two words can consist of the same sequence of consonants and vowels and be distinguished from one another solely by contrasts in pitch and associated voice quality differences. In a tone language, such as Mandarin or Thai, pitch shape is an integral part of the lexical identity of words. *See*: pitch; contour tone; register tone.

tone sandhi in tone languages, a change in the tone which a word or syllable would have in isolation due to the influence of a neighbouring tone or to some aspect of syllable structure.

tonogenesis a process of phonological change by which tones are acquired by a language which formerly lacked them.

transitive verb a verb which takes a direct object.

typology the field of linguistics which attempts to find appropriate ways to classify the languages of the world into different types according to their structural characteristics.

undergoer a semantic role of a noun phrase which something happens to, or which someone or something does something to. *See*: actor.

underlying level an abstract representation (of a word or sentence) which does not necessarily correspond to the observable form, but which is postulated in order to explain facts about the observable form in an economical or logical way.

unit counter a word used in a noun phrase to single out one or more individuals from a collective or set; e.g. two *members* of the family, three *articles* of furniture. *See*: measure; classifier construction.

uvula the small pendulous fold of tissue attached to the back of the velum.

uvular a term used in phonetics to describe a consonant whose place of articulation is the uvular region.

velar a term used in phonetics to describe a consonant whose place of articulation is the velum; a consonant produced by the back of the tongue approaching or touching the roof of the mouth at the velum.

verb-preposition a word which is identical in form to a verb and which presumably originated as a verb, but which functions grammatically like a preposition, i.e. it combines with a following noun phrase to form a single phrase, and it can no longer take verbal marking or be negated like a verb.

vernacular the indigenous language or dialect of a speech community.

voice (system) a term used for a grammatical system which enables the arguments of a verb to appear in a variety of different grammatical functions; e.g. the English "passive" construction enables the argument which would normally be the object to appear instead as the subject: compare *The committee elected Max* (active voice) with *Max was elected by the committee* (passive voice); some languages, e.g. languages of the Philippines, have more elaborate voice systems than English.

voice quality a term sometimes used (loosely) to refer to phonation. *See*: phonation.

voicing (voiced, voiceless) a term used in phonetics to describe the effect produced by the vocal folds in the larynx vibrating while a sound is being produced; sounds produced while the vocal folds are vibrating are called voiced, and those produced with no such vibration are called voiceless or unvoiced.

vowels sounds produced with a relatively free flow of air through the vocal tract, i.e. without any real constriction being created by movement of the vocal organs. *See*: consonant.

wh-question *See*: information question.

word order the placing of words in a sequence according to the grammatical patterns of a particular language; the term can refer not only to the order of words in a phrase (e.g. to the relative order of adjective and noun in a noun phrase), but also to the order of the major constituents of a sentence, i.e. subject, object and verb—usually symbolized as S, O, and V, respectively.

yes/no question *See*: polar question.

zero anaphora in grammar, a term used to refer to situations in which no word is used to indicate an intended referent, on the understanding that the listener can work out from the context who or what is intended; English does not permit much zero anaphora, but it is common in many East and Southeast Asian languages.

References

ABDULLAH HASSAN and AINON MOHD (1995). *Peribahasa: Nilai-Nilai Murni KBSR*. Kuala Lumpur: Utusan Publications & Distributors Sdn. Bhd.

ADAMS, KAREN L. (1982). 'Systems of numeral classification in the Mon-Khmer, Nicobarese and Aslian subfamilies of Austroasiatic', Ph.D. thesis. Ann Arbor: University of Michigan.

AIKHENVALD, ALEXANDRA Y. (2000). *Classifiers: A Typology of Noun Categorization Devices*. Oxford: Oxford University Press.

ALLEN, CYNTHIA L. (1995). *Case Marking and Reanalysis: Grammatical Relations from Old to Early Modern English*. Oxford: Clarendon Press.

AMMER, CHRISTINE (1992). *The Methuen Dictionary of Clichés*. London: Methuen.

ASANO, YUKO (2003). 'A semantic analysis of epistemic modality in Japanese', Ph.D. thesis. Australian National University.

ASHER, R. E., and J. M. Y. SIMPSON (eds.) (1994). *The Encyclopedia of Language and Linguistics. 10 vols*. Oxford: Pergamon Press.

ASMAH HAJI OMAR (1975). *Essays on Malaysian Lingustics*. Kuala Lumpur: Dewan Bahasa dan Pustaka.

——(1983). *The Malay Peoples of Malaysia and their Languages*. Kuala Lumpur: Dewan Bahasa dan Pustaka.

AUSTIN, PETER K., and BERND NORTHOFER (2000). 'Speech levels in Sasak'. Paper presented at the Australian Linguistic Society Conference (ALS2k), July 2000. University of Melbourne.

BACHNIK, JANE M., and CHARLES J. QUINN, Jr. (eds.) (1994). *Situated Meaning*. Princeton, NJ: Princeton University Press.

BANKS, DAVID J. (1987). *From Class to Culture: Social Conscience in Malay Novels Since Independence*. New Haven, Conn.: Yale University Southeast Asia Studies.

BAUER, ROBERT S. (1988). 'Written Cantonese of Hong Kong', *Cahiers de Linguistique Asie Orientale* 17(2): 245–93.

——and PAUL K. BENEDICT (1997). *Modern Cantonese Phonology*. Berlin: Mouton de Gruyter.

BAUMAN, RICHARD, and JOEL SHERZER (1974). *Explorations in the Ethnography of Speaking*. Cambridge: Cambridge University Press.

BISANG, WALTER (1993). 'Classifiers, quantifiers and class nouns in Hmong', *Studies in Language* 17(1): 1–51.

BLUM, SUSAN D. (2002). 'Margins and centers: a decade of publishing on China's ethnic minorities', *Journal of Asian Studies* 61(4): 1287–1310.

BLUM-KULKA, SHOSHANA, JULIANE HOUSE, and GABRIELE KASPER (1989). 'Investigating cross-cultural pragmatics: an introductory overview', in S. Blum-Kulka, J. House, and G. Kasper (eds.), *Cross-Cultural Pragmatics: Requests and Apologies*. Norwood, NJ: Ablex, 1–34.

BOWDEN, JOHN (2001). *Taba: Description of a South Halmahera Language*. Canberra: Pacific Linguistics.

BROWN, C. C. (1989) [1951]. *Malay Sayings*, 2nd edn. Singapore: Graham Brash.

BURLING, ROBBINS (1965). *Hill Farms and Paddy Fields: Life in Mainland Southeast Asia*. Englewood Cliffs, NJ: Prentice-Hall.

CARPENTER, KATHIE (1987). 'How children learn to classify nouns in Thai', Ph.D. dissertation, Stanford University.

CHAFE, WALLACE L. (1976). 'Givenness, contrastiveness, definiteness, subjects, topics, and point of view', in C. N. Li (ed.), *Subject and Topic*. New York: Academic Press, 25–55.

CHAO, YUEN-REN (1968). *A Grammar of Spoken Chinese*. Berkeley: University of California Press.

CHAPPELL, HILARY (1991). 'Strategies for the assertion of obviousness and disagreement in Mandarin Chinese: a semantic study of the modal particle *me*', *Australian Journal of Linguistics* 11(1): 39–65.

——(2001). 'Language contact and areal diffusion in Sinitic languages: problems for typology and genetic affiliation', in A. Y. Aikhenvald and R. M. W. Dixon (eds.), *Areal Diffusion and Genetic Inheritance: Problems in Comparative Linguistics*. Oxford: Oxford University Press, 328–57.

CHEE, THAM SEONG (1993). 'Review of *The MBRAS Book of over 1,600 Malay Proverbs*, edited by Mubin Sheppard', *Journal of the Malaysian Branch of the Royal Asiatic Society* 66(1): 89–92.

CHEN, PING (1999). *Modern Chinese: History and Sociolinguistics*. Cambridge: Cambridge University Press.

——(2001). 'Functions of phonetic writing in Chinese', in Nancy Gottlieb and Ping Chen (eds.), *Language Planning and Language Policy: East Asian Perspectives*. Richmond, Surrey: Curzon, 75–94.

CHIANG, YEE (1973)[1938]. *Chinese Calligraphy. An Introduction to its Aesthetic and Technique*, 3rd edn. Cambridge, Mass.: Harvard University Press.

CLANCY, PATRICIA (1986). 'The acquisition of communicative style in Japanese', in B. B. Schieffelin and E. Ochs (eds.), *Language Socialization across Cultures*. Cambridge: Cambridge University Press, 213–50.

CLARK, MARYBETH. (1989). 'Hmong and areal South-east Asia', in David Bradley (ed.), *South-East Asian Syntax*. Canberra: Pacific Linguistics, 175–230.

CLYNE, MICHAEL. (1994). *Intercultural Communication at Work*. Cambridge: Cambridge University Press.

COMRIE, BERNARD (1976). *Aspect: An Introduction to the Study of Verbal Aspect and Related Problems*. Cambridge: Cambridge University Press.

——, STEPHEN MATTHEWS, and MARIA POLINSKY (eds.) (2003). *SBS Atlas of Languages*, rev. edn. Sydney: ABC Books.

COULMAS, FLORIAN (1992). 'Linguistic etiquette in Japanese society', in R. J. Watts, S. Ide, and K. Ehlich (eds.), *Politeness in Language*. Berlin: Mouton de Gruyter, 299–323.

CRYSTAL, DAVID (ed.) (1987). *The Cambridge Encyclopedia of Language*. Cambridge: Cambridge University Press.

DAILLIE, FRANÇOIS-RENÉ (1988). *Alam Pantun Melayu: Studies on the Malay Pantun*. Kuala Lumpur: Dewan Bahasa dan Pustaka.

DALE, PETER N. (1986). *The Myth of Japanese Uniqueness*. New York: St. Martin's Press.

DANVIVATHANA, NANTANA (1987). *The Thai Writing System*. Hamburg: Buske.

DEEPADUNG, SUJARITLAK (1997). 'Extension in the usage of the Thai classifier /tua/', in A. S. Abramson (ed.), *Southeast Asian Linguistic Studies in Honour of Vichin Panupong*. Bangkok: Chulalongkorn University Press, 49–56.

DEFRANCIS, JOHN (1984). *The Chinese Language: Fact and Fantasy*. Honolulu: University of Hawaii Press.

DELANCEY, SCOTT (1986). 'Toward a history of Tai classifier systems', in C. Craig (ed.), *Noun Classes and Categorization*. Amsterdam: Benjamins, 437–52.

——(1992). 'Sino-Tibetan Languages', in W. Bright (ed.), *International Encyclopedia of Linguistics*, vol iii. Oxford and New York: Oxford University Press, 445–9.

DE VOS, GEORGE A. (1985). 'Dimensions of the self in Japanese culture', in A. Marsella and F. Hsu (eds.), *Culture and Self: Asian and Western Perspectives*. London: Methuen, 141–84.

DIFFLOTH, GÉRARD (1992). 'Khmer', in W. Bright (ed.), *International Encyclopedia of Linguistics*, vol. i. Oxford and New York: Oxford University Press, 271–5.

——and NORMAN ZIDE (1992). 'Austro-Asiatic Languages', in W. Bright (ed.), *International Encyclopedia of Linguistics*, vol. ii. Oxford and New York: Oxford University Press, 137–42.

DILLER, ANTHONY (1988). 'Thai Syntax and "National Grammar"', *Language Sciences* 10(2): 273–312.

——(1992). 'Thai', in W. Bright (ed.), *International Encyclopedia of Linguistics*, vol iv. Oxford and New York: Oxford University Press, 149–56.

——(1996). 'Thai and Lao writing', in P. T. Daniels and W. Bright (eds.), *The World's Writing Systems*. New York: Oxford University Press, 457–66.

——and PREECHA JUNTANAMALAGA (1990). ' "Full Hearts" and empty pronominals in Thai', *Australian Journal of Linguistics* 10(2): 231–55.

DJAO, WEI (2003). *Being Chinese: Voices from the Diaspora*. Tucson: University of Arizona Press.

DOI, TAKEO (1971). *Amae no Koozoo [The Anatomy of Dependence]*. Tokyo: Koobundoo.

——(1973). *The Anatomy of Dependence*, trans. J. Bester. Tokyo: Kodansha International.

——(1974). '*Amae*: a key concept for understanding Japanese personality structure', in T. S. Lebra and W. P. Lebra (eds.), *Japanese Culture and Behavior*. Honolulu: University of Hawaii Press, 145–54.

DOWNING, PAMELA (1996). *Numeral Classifier Systems: The Case of Japanese*. Amsterdam: Benjamins.

DURIE, MARK (1985). *A Grammar of Acehnese*. Dordrecht: Foris.

——(1987). 'Grammatical relations in Acehnese', *Studies in Language* 11: 365–99.

EDMONDSON, JEROLD A. (1992). 'Pa-hng development and diversity', in Martha Ratliff and Eric Schiller (eds.), *Papers from the First Annual Meeting of the Southeast Asian Linguistics Society 1991*. Tempe: Arizona State University, 159–86.

EMENEAU, M. B. (1956). 'India as a linguistic area', *Language* 32(1): 3–16.

ENFIELD, N. J. (1994). 'Aspects of Lao syntax: theory, function and cognition', BA Hons. thesis, Australian National University.

——(2000*a*). 'Lao as a national language', in G. Evans (ed.), *Laos: Culture and Society*. Singapore: Silkworm Books, 258–90.

——(2000*b*). 'On the polyfunctionality of "Acquire" in mainland Southeast Asia: a case study in linguistic epidemiology', Ph.D. thesis, University of Melbourne.

——(2002). 'Cultural logic and syntactic productivity: associated posture constructions in Lao', in N. J. Enfield (ed.), *Ethnosyntax: Explorations in Grammar and Culture*. Oxford: Oxford University Press, 231–50.

——(2003). *Linguistic Epidemiology: Semantics and Grammar of Language Contact in Mainland Southeast Asia*. London: Routledge Curzon.

ERBAUGH, MARY S. (1986). 'Taking stock: the development of Chinese noun classifiers historically and in young children', in C. Craig (ed.), *Noun Classes and Categorization*. Amsterdam: Benjamins, 399–436.

ERRINGTON, J. JOSEPH (1998). *Shifting Languages: Interaction and Identity in Javanese Indonesia*. Cambridge: Cambridge University Press.

Ethnologue: Languages of the World, (2004). 14th edn. SIL International. URL http://www.ethnologue.com/

FAUCONNIER, HENRI (1990)[1931]. *The Soul of Malaya*, trans. Eric Sutton. Singapore: Oxford in Asia Paperbacks.

FOLEY, WILLIAM A., and ROBERT D. VAN VALIN (1984). *Functional Syntax and Universal Grammar*. Cambridge: Cambridge University Press.

GABRENYA, WILLIAM K. Jr., and KWANG-KUO HWANG (1996). 'Chinese social interaction: harmony and hierarchy on the good earth', in M. H. Bond (ed.), *The Handbook of Chinese Psychology*. Hong Kong: Oxford University Press, 309–21.

GODDARD, CLIFF (1996). 'The "social emotions" of Malay (Bahasa Melayu)', *Ethos* 24(3): 426–64.

——(1997). 'Cultural values and "cultural scripts" of Malay (Bahasa Melayu)', *Journal of Pragmatics* 27(2): 183–201.

——(1998). *Semantic Analysis: A Practical Introduction*. Oxford: Oxford University Press.

——(2000).' "Cultural scripts" and communicative style in Malay (Bahasa Melayu)', *Anthropological Linguistics* 42: 81–106.

——(2001*a*). '*Hati*: a key word in the Malay vocabulary of emotion', in J. Harkins and A. Wierzbicka (eds.), *Emotions in Crosslinguistic Perspective*. Berlin: Mouton de Gruyter, 167–95.

——(2001*b*). '*Sabar, ikhlas, setia*—patient, sincere, loyal? A contrastive semantic study of some "virtues" in Malay and English', *Journal of Pragmatics* 33: 653–81.

——and ANNA WIERZBICKA (eds.) (1994). *Semantic and Lexical Universals: Theory and Empirical Findings*. Amsterdam: Benjamins.

——— (1997). 'Discourse and culture', in Teun A. van Dijk (ed.), *Discourse as Social Interaction* (*Discourse Studies: A Multidisciplinary Introduction*, vol. ii). London: Sage, 231–57.

————(eds.) (2002). *Meaning and Universal Grammar: Theory and Empirical Findings*, vols i and ii. Amsterdam: Benjamins.

GOH, BEE CHEN (1996). *Negotiating with the Chinese*. Aldershot: Dartmouth.

GOTTLIEB, NANCY (2001). 'Language planning and policy in Japan', in Nancy Gottlieb and Ping Chen (eds.), *Language Planning and Language Policy: East Asian Perspectives*. Richmond, Surrey: Curzon, 21–48.

GRANT, ANTHONY and PAUL, SIDWELL (eds.). Forthcoming. *Chamic Studies: Further Progress*. Canberra: Pacific Linguistics.

GRIMES, CHARLES E. (ed.) (2000). *Spices from the East: Papers in the Languages of Eastern Indonesia*. Canberra: Pacific Linguistics.

GUMPERZ, JOHN J., and DELL H. HYMES (1972). *Directions in Sociolinguistics: The Ethnography of Communication*. Oxford: Basil Blackwell.

HAAS, MARY (1942). 'The use of numeral classifiers in Thai', *Language* 18: 201–5.

HAIMAN, JOHN (1998). 'Possible origins of infixation in Khmer', *Studies in Language* 22(3): 597–617.

HAJEK, JOHN (2000) 'Language planning and the sociolinguistic environment in East Timor: colonial practice and changing language ecologies', *Current Issues in Language Planning* 1: 400–14.

HANNAS, W. C. (1997). *Asia's Orthographic Dilemma*. Honolulu: University of Hawaii Press.

HEAH CARMEL LEE HSIA (1989). *The Influence of English on the Lexical Expansion of Bahasa Malaysia*. Kuala Lumpur: Dewan Bahasa dan Pustaka.

HEIDER, KARL G. (1991). *Landscapes of Emotion: Mapping Three Cultures of Emotion in Indonesia*. Cambridge: Cambridge University Press.

HEIMBACH, ERNEST E. (1969). *White Meo-English Dictionary*. Ithaca, NY: Department of Asian Studies, Cornell University.

HO, DAVID Y. F. (1996). 'Filial piety and its psychological consequences', in M. H. Bond (ed.), *The Handbook of Chinese Psychology*. Hong Kong: Oxford University Press, 155–65.

HO, JUDY (2002). *Narrative Writing in Australia and Chinese Schools*. Bern: Peter Lang.

HOGUE, CAVAN (2001). 'The spread of Anglo-Indian words into South-East Asia', in B. Moore (ed.), *Who's Centric Now: The Present State of Post-colonial Englishes*. Melbourne: Oxford University Press, 165–97.

HUDAK, THOMAS J. (1987). 'Thai', in B. Comric (ed.), *The Major Languages of East and South-East Asia*. London: Routledge, 29–47.

HUDDLESTON, RODNEY (1984). *Introduction to the Grammar of English*. Cambridge: Cambridge University Press.

HUFFMAN, FRANKLIN L., and IM PROUM (1978). *English–Khmer Dictionary*. New Haven, Conn.: Yale University Press.

IDE, S., M. HORI, A. KAWASAKI, S. IKUTA, and H. HAGA (1986). 'Sex differences and politeness in Japanese', *International Journal of the Sociology of Language* 58: 25–36.

INOUE, KYOKO (1979). 'Japanese: a story of language and people', in T. Shopen (ed.), *Languages and their Speakers*. Cambridge, Mass.: Winthrop, 241–99.

ITÔ, JUNKO, and R. ARMIN MESTER (1995). 'Japanese phonology', in J. A. Goldsmith (ed.), *The Handbook of Phonological Theory*. Cambridge, Mass.: Blackwell, 817–38.

JAISSER, ANNIE (1987). 'Hmong classifiers', *Linguistics of the Tibeto-Burman Area* 10(2): 169–77.

JAISSER, ANNIE (1990). 'DeLIVERing an Introduction to Psycho-collocations with SIAB in White Hmong', *Linguistics of the Tibeto-Burman Area* 13(1): 159–78.

JARKEY, NERIDA (1991). 'Serial verbs in White Hmong: a functional approach', Ph.D. thesis, University of Sydney.

KANG, SIN-HANG (1990). *Hwunmin Cengum Yenkwu [Research on the Hwunmin Cengum]*. Seoul: Seng-Kyunkwan University Press.

KARIM WAZIR JAHAN (1990). 'Prelude to madness: the language of emotion in courtship and early marriage', in W. J. Karim (ed.), *Emotions of Culture: A Malay Perspective*. Singapore: Oxford University Press, 21–63.

KARLGREN, BERNHARD (1950). *The Book of Odes: Chinese Text, Transcription and Translation*. Stockholm: Museum of Far Eastern Antiquities.

——(1962). *Sound and Symbol in Chinese*, rev. edn. Hong Kong: Hong Kong University Press.

KAVITSKAYA, DARYA (1997). 'Tense and aspect in Lai Chin', *Linguistics of the Tibeto-Burman Area* 20(2): 173–213.

KAYE, ALAN S. (1996). 'Adaptations of Arabic script', in P. T. Daniels and W. Bright (eds.), *The World's Writing Systems*. New York: Oxford University Press, 743–62.

KEELER, WARD (1984). *Javanese: A Cultural Approach*. Athens: Ohio University Centre for International Studies.

Kenkyusha's New Japanese–English Dictionary (1974), 4th edn., ed. Koh Masuda. Tokyo: Kenkyusha.

KESSLER, CLIVE S. (1992). 'Archaism and modernity: contemporary Malay political culture', in J. S. Kahn and F. L. K. Wah (eds.), *Fragmented Vision*. Sydney: ASAA with Allen & Unwin, 133–57.

KHANITTANAN, WILAIWAN (1988a). 'Some observations on expressing politeness in Thai', *Language Sciences* 10(2): 353–62.

——(1988b). 'Thai written discourse: a change toward a more autonomous style?', in Cholticha Bamroongraks *et al.* (eds.), *The International Symposium on Language and Linguistics* (Faculty of Liberal Arts, Thammasat University, 1988). Bangkok: Thammasat University, 120–8.

KIM, NAM-KIL (1987). 'Korean', in B. Comrie (ed.), *The Major Languages of East and South-East Asia*. London: Routledge, 153–70.

——(1992). 'Korean', in W. Bright (ed.) *International Encyclopedia of Linguistics*, vol. ii. New York and Oxford: Oxford University Press, 282–6.

KING, AMBROSE YEO-CHI (1991). '*Kuan-hsi* and network building: a sociological interpretation', in Tu Wei-ming (ed.), *The Living Tree: The Changing Meaning of Being Chinese Today*. Stanford, Calif.: Stanford University Press, 107–67.

KING, ROSS (1996). 'Korean writing', in P. T. Daniels and W. Bright (eds.), *The World's Writing Systems*. New York: Oxford University Press, 218–27.

KLAMER, MARIAN (1998). *A Grammar of Kambera*. Berlin: Mouton de Gruyter.

——(2000). 'Typical features of Austronesian Languages in C/E Indonesia', Ninth International Conference on Austronesian Languages, Australian National University, Canberra, 2000.

KOH, ANN SWEESUN (1990). 'Topics in colloquial Malay', Ph.D. thesis, University of Melbourne.

KOJIMA, SETSUKO, and GENE A. CRANE (1987). *A Dictionary of Japanese Culture*. Singapore: Chopmen.

KUMMER, MANFRED (1992). 'Politeness in Thai', in R. J. Watts, S. Ide, and K. Ehlich (eds.), *Politeness in Language: Studies in its History, Theory and Practice*. Berlin: Mouton de Gruyter, 325–36.

KUNO, S. (1973). *The Structure of the Japanese Language*. Cambridge, Mass.: MIT Press.

KWOK, HELEN (1984). *Sentence Particles in Cantonese*. Hong Kong: Centre of Asian Studies, University of Hong Kong.

LADEFOGED, PETER, and IAN MADDIESON (1996). *The Sounds of the World's Languages*. Oxford: Blackwell.

LAKOFF, GEORGE (1987). *Women, Fire and Dangerous Things: What Categories Reveal about the Mind*. Chicago: Chicago University Press.

LAPOLLA, RANDY (1993). 'Arguments against "subject" and "direct object" as viable concepts in Chinese', *Bulletin of the Institute of History and Philology* 63(4): 759–813.

——(1995). 'Pragmatic relations and word order in Chinese', in P. Downing and M. Noonan (eds.), *Word Order in Discourse*. Amsterdam: Benjamins, 297–329.

——(2000). 'Valency-changing derivations in Dulong/Rawang', in R. M. W. Dixon and A. Y. Aikhenvald (eds.), *Changing Valency: Case Studies in Transitivity*. Cambridge: Cambridge University Press, 282–311.

LAT (1980). *With a Little Bit of Lat*. Kuala Lumpur: Berita.

LAU CHUN-FAT (1999). '"Gender" in the Hakka dialect: suffixes with gender in more than 40 nouns', *Journal of Chinese Linguistics* 27(2): 124–31.

LEBRA, TAKIE SUGIYAMA (1976). *Japanese Patterns of Behavior*. Honolulu: University of Hawaii Press.

LEE, HANSOL H. B. (1989). *Korean Grammar*. New York: Oxford University Press.

LEE, HO-YOUNG (1996). *Korean Phonetics*. Seoul: Thaehaksa.

LEE, IKSOP, and S. ROBERT RAMSEY (2000). *The Korean Language*. Buffalo: State University of New York Press.

LI, CHARLES N. (1992). 'Chinese', in W. Bright (ed.), *International Encyclopedia of Linguistics*, vol i. Oxford and New York: Oxford University Press, 257–62.

——(1996). 'A cryptic language with a minimal grammar: the Confucian analects of Late Archaic Chinese', in E. Weigand and F. Hundsnurscher (eds.), *Lexical Structures and Language Use*. Tübingen: Niemeyer, 54–118.

——and SANDRA A. THOMPSON (1981). *Mandarin Chinese: A Functional Reference Grammar*. Los Angeles: University of California Press.

LIN, YU-TANG (1935). *My Country and My People*. New York: John Day.

LOVEDAY, LEO (1996). *Language Contact in Japan: A Socio-linguistic History*. Oxford: Oxford University Press.

LUKE, KANG KWONG (1990). *Utterance Particles in Cantonese Conversation*. Amsterdam: Benjamins.

LUO, YONGXIAN (1993). 'Some auxiliary verbs in Zhuang', Paper presented at the 26th International Conference on Sino-Tibetan Languages and Linguistics, Oct. 1993, Osaka, Japan.

——(1999) *A Dictionary of Dehong, Southwest China*. Canberra: Pacific Linguistics.

MANASTER-RAMER, ALEXIS (1992). 'What's a topic in the Philippines?', in M. Ratcliff and E. Schiller (eds.), *Papers from the First Annual Meeting of the Southeast Asian Linguistics Society 1991*. Tempe: Arizona State University, 271–91.

Matisoff, James A. (1973). *The Grammar of Lahu*. Berkeley: University of California Press.

——(1986*a*). 'The languages and dialects of Tibeto-Burman: an alphabetic/genetic listing, with some prefatory remarks on ethnonymic and glossonymic complications', in J. McCoy and T. Light (eds.), *Contributions to Sino-Tibetan Studies, Presented to Nicholas C. Bodman*. Leiden: Brill, 3–75.

——(1986*b*). 'Hearts and minds in Southeast Asian languages and English: an essay in the comparative lexical semantics of psycho-collocations', *Cahiers de Linguistique Asie Orientale* 15(1): 5–57.

——(1991*a*). 'Areal and universal dimensions of grammatization in Lahu', in E. C. Traugott and B. Heine (eds.), *Approaches to Grammaticalization*. Amsterdam: Benjamins, 383–453.

——(1991*b*). 'Sino-Tibetan linguistics: present state and prospects', *Annual Review of Anthropology* 20: 269–504.

——(1991*c*). 'Endangered languages of mainland Southeast Asia', in R. H. Robins and E. M. Uhlenbeck (eds.), *Endangered Languages*. Oxford: Berg, 189–228.

——(1992). 'Southeast Asian languages', in W. Bright (ed.), *International Encyclopedia of Linguistics.* vol iv. Oxford and New York: Oxford University Press, 44–8.

——(2003). 'Aslian: Mon Khmer of the Malay Peninsula', *Mon Khmer Studies* 33: 1–58.

Matsumoto, Yoshiko (1993*a*). 'Japanese numeral classifiers: a study of semantic categories and lexical organization', *Linguistics* 31(4): 667–713.

——(1993*b*). 'Linguistic politeness and cultural style: observations from Japanese', in P. Clancy (ed.), *Japanese/Korean Linguistics*, vol ii. Stanford, Calif.: Stanford University, 55–67.

Matsushita, D. (1977) [1930]. *Hyōjun Nihon Kōgo-hō* [Standard Colloquial Grammar of Japanese]. Tokyo: Benseisha.

Matthews, Stephen (2003). 'South and Southeast Asia', in Bernard Comrie, Stephen Matthews, and Maria Polinsky (eds.), *SBS Atlas of Languages*, rev. edn. Sydney: ABC Books, 56–71.

——and Patrizia Pacioni (1997). 'Specificity and genericity in Cantonese and Mandarin', in X. Liejiong (ed.), *The Referential Properties of Chinese Noun Phrases*. Paris: Ecole des Hautes Etudes en Sciences Sociales, 45–58.

——and Virginia Yip (1994). *Cantonese: A Comprehensive Grammar*. London: Routledge.

Maynard, Senko K. (1997). *Japanese Communication: Language and Thought in Context*. Honolulu: University of Hawaii Press.

Miller, R. A. (1967). *The Japanese Language*. Chicago: University of Chicago Press.

Milliken, Stuart, Zhang Guang-Ping, Zhang Xue-Yi, Li Zhi-Qiu, and Lü Ying (1997). 'Resolving the paradox of Tianjin tone sandhi', in J. Wang and N. Smith (eds.), *Studies in Chinese Phonology*. Berlin: Mouton de Gruyter, 53–79.

Milner, Anthony C. (1982). *Kerajaan: Malay Political Culture on the Eve of Colonial Rule*. Tucson: University of Arizona Press.

——(1995). *The Invention of Politics in Colonial Malaya*. Cambridge: Cambridge University Press.

Muhammad Haji Salleh (1991). *The Mind of the Malay Author*. Kuala Lumpur: Dewan Bahasa dan Pustaka.

NABABAN, P. W. J. (1981). *A Grammar of Toba-Batak*. Canberra: Pacific Linguistics.

NACASKUL, K. (1978). 'The syllabic and morphological structure of Cambodian words', *Mon-Khmer Studies* 7: 183–200.

NAKANE, C. (1970). *Japanese Society*. London: Weidenfeld & Nicolson.

NAKATSUGAWA, KYOOKO (1992). 'Japanese cultural values reflected in education guidelines', unpublished MS, Canberra: Australian National University.

NATIONAL ACADEMY OF THE KOREAN LANGUAGE (2000). *The Revised Romanisation of Korean*. Seoul: Ministry of Culture and Tourism.

NGUYỄN, ĐÌNH-HOÀ (1987). 'Vietnamese', in B. Comrie (ed.), *The Major Languages of East and South-East Asia*. London: Routledge, 49–68.

——(1996). 'Vietnamese verbs', *Mon-Khmer Studies* 25: 141–59.

——(1997). *Vietnamese*. Amsterdam: Benjamins.

NORMAN, JERRY (1988). *Chinese*. Cambridge: Cambridge University Press.

OEY, ERIC M. (1990). ' "Psycho-collocations" in Malay: a Southeast Asian areal feature', *Linguistics of the Tibeto-Burman Area* 13(1): 141–58.

OKELL, J. W. A. (1994). 'Burmese', in R. E. Asher and J. M. Y. Simpson (eds.), *The Encyclopedia of Language and Linguistics*, vol. i. Oxford: Pergamon Press, 433–6.

PARK, BYUNG-SOO (1982). 'The double subject construction revisited', in Linguistic Society of Korea (ed.), *Linguistics in the Morning Calm*. Seoul: Hanshin, 645–57.

PICKLE, LINDA S. (2001). 'Written and spoken Chinese: expression of culture and heritage', in Howard Giskin and Bettye S. Walsh (eds.), *An Introduction to Chinese Culture through the Family*. New York: State University of New York Press, 9–40.

POLINSKY, MARIA, and GEOFFREY SMITH (2003). 'Pacific', in Bernard Comrie, Stephen Matthews, and Maria Polinsky (eds.), *SBS Atlas of Languages*, rev. edn. Sydney: ABC Books, 90–107.

PRENTICE, D. J. (1987). 'Malay (Indonesian and Malaysian)', in B. Comrie (ed.), *The Major Languages of East and South-East Asia*. London: Routledge, 185–207.

QU LEI LEI (2002). *The Simple Art of Chinese Calligraphy*. New York: Watson Guptill.

QUAKENBUSH, J. STEPHEN (1998). ' "Other" Philippine languages in the third millennium', *Philippine Journal of Linguistics* 29(1/2): 1–22.

RAMSEY, S. ROBERT (1987). *The Languages of China*. Princeton, NJ: Princeton University Press.

REFSING, K. (1986). *The Ainu Language*. Aarhus: Aarhus University Press.

ROBSON, STUART (1992). *Javanese Grammar for Students*. Melbourne: Centre of Southeast Asian Studies, Monash University.

SAMPSON, GEOFFREY (1985). *Writing Systems*. London: Hutchinson.

SARDESAI, D. R. (1997). *Southeast Asia: Past and Present*, 4th edn. Boulder, Colo. Westview Press.

SASEE, HANS-JÜRGEN (1987). 'The thetic categorical distinction revisited', *Linguistics* 25: 511–80.

SCHACHTER, PAUL (1976). 'The subject in Philippine languages: topic, actor, actor-topic, or none of the above?', in C. N. Li (ed.), *Subject and Topic*. New York: Academic Press, 492–518.

——(1984). 'Semantic-role-based syntax in Toba Batak', in P. Schachter (ed.), *Studies in the Structure of Toba Batak*. Los Angeles, Calif.: UCLA Department of Linguistics, 122–49.

——(1987). 'Tagalog', in B. Comrie (ed.), *The Major Languages of East and South-East Asia*. London: Routledge, 208–30.

SCHIFFMAN, HAROLD F. (n.d) 'Workbook for Asian 401: Introduction to Asian Linguistics', unpublished, University of Seattle.

——(1994). 'Diglossia, linguistic culture and language policy in Southeast Asia', in K. L. Adams and T. J. Hudak (eds.), *Papers from the Second Annual Meeting of the Southeast Asian Linguistics Society*, 1992. Tempe: Arizona State University, 297–307.

SHEPPARD, MUBIN (ed.). (1992). *The MBRAS Book of over 1,600 Malay Proverbs*. Kuala Lumpur: Council of the Malaysian Branch of the Royal Asiatic Society.

SHIBATANI, MASAYOSHI (1990). *The Languages of Japan*. Cambridge: Cambridge University Press.

SHUGAMOTO, NOBUKO (1984). 'Reflexives in Toba Batak', in P. Schachter (ed.), *Studies in the Structure of Toba Batak*. Los Angeles, Calif.: UCLA Department of Linguistics, 150–71.

SIDWELL, PAUL JAMES (2000). *Proto South Bahnaric: A Reconstruction of a Mon-Khmer Language of Indo-China*. Canberra: Pacific Linguistics.

SIEGEL, JAMES T. (1986). *Solo in the New City: Language and Hierarchy in an Indonesian City*. Princeton, NJ: Princeton University Press.

SIM, KATHERINE (1987). *More than a Pantun: Understanding Malay Verse*. Singapore: Times Books International.

SINGH, CHUNGKHAM YASHAWANTA (1999). 'Tense and aspect in Kuki-Chin', *Linguistics of the Tibeto-Burman Area* 22(2): 149–67.

SMALLEY, WILLIAM A. (1994). *Linguistic Diversity and National Unity: Language Ecology in Thailand*. Chicago: University of Chicago Press.

SMITH, JANET S. (1996). 'Japanese writing', in P. T. Daniels and W. Bright (eds.), *The World's Writing Systems*. New York: Oxford University Press, 209–17.

SMITH, KENNETH D. (1979). *Sedang Grammar*. Canberra: Pacific Linguistics.

SNEDDON, JAMES NEIL (1996). *Indonesian Reference Grammar*. Sydney: Allen & Unwin.

——(2003). *The Indonesian Language: Its History and Role in Modern Society*. Sydney: UNSW Press.

SPANOS, GEORGE (1977). 'A textual, conversational, and theoretical analysis of the Mandarin particle *le*', Ph.D. dissertation, University of Arizona.

STEVENS, JOHN (1996). 'Asian calligraphy', in P. T. Daniels and W. Bright (eds.), *The World's Writing Systems*. New York: Oxford University Press, 244–51.

STRECKER, DAVID (1987). 'The Hmong-Mien languages', *Linguistics of the Tibeto-Burman Area* 10(2): 1–11.

STUART-FOX, MARTIN (1997). *A History of Laos*. Cambridge: Cambridge University Press.

SUZUKI, TAKEO (1978). *Japanese and the Japanese: Words in Culture*, trans. Akira Miura. Tokyo: Kodansha International.

SWIFT, M. G. (1965). *Malay Peasant Society in Jelebu*. London: Athlone Press.

THOMAS, DAVID (ed.) (1998). *Chamic Studies*. Canberra: Pacific Linguistics.

THOMPSON, LAURENCE C. (1987) [1965]. *A Vietnamese Reference Grammar* (Mon-Khmer Studies 13 and 14). Honolulu: University of Hawaii Press.

TRAVIS, CATHERINE (1992). 'How to be kind and considerate in Japanese', BA Hons. thesis, Australian National University.

——(1997). 'Omoiyari as a core Japanese value: Japanese-style empathy?', in A. Athanasiadou and E. Tabakowska (eds.), *Speaking of Emotions: Conceptualization and Expression*. Berlin: Mouton de Gruyter, 55–82.

TSUJIMURA, NATSUKO (1996). *An Introduction to Japanese Linguistics*. Cambridge, Mass.: Blackwell.

UNITED NATIONS POPULATION DIVISION (2003). *World Population Prospects: The 2002 Revision*. http://www.un.org/esa/population/publications/wpp2002annextables.PDF/

VAN VALIN, ROBERT D., Jr., and RANDY J. LAPOLLA (1997). *Syntax: Structure, Meaning and Function*. Cambridge: Cambridge University Press.

VANBIK, KENNETH (1998). 'Lai psycho-collocation', *Linguistics of the Tibeto-Burman Area* 21(1): 201–32.

—— (2002). 'Three types of causative constructions in Hakha Lai', *Linguistics of the Tibeto-Burman Area* 25(2): 99–122.

VOS, F. (1964). 'Papers on Korean studies', in J. K. Yamagiwa (ed.), *Papers of the CIC Far Eastern Language Institute, the University of Michigan*. Ann Arbor, Mich.: Committee on Far Eastern Language Instruction of the Committee of Institutional Cooperation.

VREELAND, N., G. B. DANA, G. B. HURWITZ, P. JUST, P. W. MOELLER, and R. S. SHINN (1977). *Area Handbook for Malaysia*, 3rd edn. Glen Rock, NJ: Microfilming Corporation of America.

WANG, JIALING, and NORVAL SMITH (eds.) (1997). *Studies in Chinese Phonology*. Berlin: Mouton de Gruyter.

WATKINS, JUSTIN (2001).'Illustrations of the IPA Burmese', *Journal of the International Phonetics Association* 31(2): 291–5.

—— (2002). *The Phonetics of Wa*. Canberra: Pacific Linguistics.

WHEATLEY, JULIAN K. (1987). 'Burmese', in B. Comrie (ed.) *The Major Languages of East and South-East Asia*. London: Routledge, 106–26.

WIERZBICKA, ANNA (1992). *Semantics, Culture, and Cognition: Universal Human Concepts in Culture-specific Configurations*. New York: Oxford University Press.

—— (1994a). ' "Cultural scripts": a semantic aproach to cultural analysis and cross-cultural communication', in L. Bouton and Y. Kachru (eds.), *Pragmatics and Language Learning*. Urbana: Division of English as an International Language, University of Illinois.

—— (1994b). ' "Cultural scripts": a new approach to the study of cross-cultural communication', in M. Pütz (ed.), *Language Contact Language Conflict*. Amsterdam: Benjamins, 69–87.

—— (1994c). 'Emotion, language, and "cultural scripts" ', in S. Kitayama and H. R. Markus (eds.), *Emotion and Culture: Empirical Studies of Mutual Influence*. Washington, DC: American Psychological Association, 130–98.

—— (1996). *Semantics: Primes and Universals*. New York: Oxford University Press.

—— (1997). *Understanding Cultures through their Key Words*. Oxford: Oxford University Press.

—— (2003) [1991]. *Cross-cultural Pragmatics: The Semantics of Human Interaction*, 2nd edn. Berlin: Mouton de Gruyter.

WILLIAMS-VAN KLINKEN, CATHERINA LUMIEN, JOHN HAJEK, and RACHEL NORDLINGER (2002). *Tetun Dili: A Grammar of an East Timorese Language*. Canberra: Pacific Linguistics.

WILSON, PETER J. (1967). *A Malay Village and Malaysia*. New Haven, Conn.: Hraf Press.

Winstedt, Richard (1977) [1969]. *A History of Classical Malay Literature*. Kuala Lumpur: Oxford University Press.

Wolff, John, Dede Oetomo, and D. Fietkiewicz (1986). *Spoken Indonesian*. Ithaca, NY: Cornell University Press.

Xu Ju (1998). 'Comprehending word meanings in Chinese', in K. Parry (ed.) *Culture, Literacy and Learning English: Voices from the Chinese Classroom*. Portsmouth, NH: Boynton/Cook, 70–3.

Xu Shixuan (1999). 'Aspect and tense in the Busi language', *Linguistics of the Tibeto-Burman Area* 22(2): 183–97.

Yap, Gloria Chan (1980). *Hokkien Chinese Borrowing in Tagalog*. Canberra: Australian National University.

Ye, Zhengdao (2001). 'An inquiry into "sadness" in Chinese', in J. Harkins and A. Wierzbicka (eds), *Emotions in Crosslinguistic Perspective*. Berlin: Mouton de Gruyter, 359–404.

——(2002). 'Different modes of describing emotions in Chinese: bodily change, sensations, and bodily images', *Pragmatics and Cognition* 10(1/2): 304–40.

——(in press). 'Why the "inscrutable" Chinese face? Emotion and facial expressions in Chinese', in C. Goddard (ed.), *Ethnopragmatics: Understanding Discourse in Cultural Context*. Berlin: Mouton de Gruyter.

Yip, Moira (1990). *The Tonal Phonology of Chinese*. New York: Garland.

——(1995). 'Tone in East Asian languages', in J. A. Goldsmith (ed.), *Handbook of Phonological Theory*. Cambridge, Mass.: Blackwell, 476–94.

Index

The following items appear in bold font – **b** for boxes; **f** for figures; **m** for maps; **t** for tables. Where more than one table appears on the same page, they have been numbered **(a)** and **(b)**. *Italics* are used for linguistic forms.